AF690639

Changing the Dynamics and Impact of Innovation Management

A Systems Approach and the ISO Standard

Series on Technology Management

Series Editor: Joe Tidd (*University of Sussex, UK*) ISSN 0219-9823

The Technology Management Series is dedicated to the advancement of academic research and management practice in the field of technology and innovation management. The series features titles which adopt an interdisciplinary, multifunctional approach to the management of technology and innovation, and includes work which seeks to integrate the management of technological, market and organisational innovation. All titles are based on original empirical research, and includes research monographs and multiauthor edited works. The focus throughout is on the management of technology and innovation at the level of the organisation or firm, rather than on the analysis of sectoral trends or national policy.

Published

Vol. 40 *Changing the Dynamics and Impact of Innovation Management: A Systems Approach and the ISO Standard*
edited by Joanne Hyland (rInnovation Group, USA, International Society for Professional Innovation Management (ISPIM), UK & Standards Council of Canada (SCC), Canada), Magnus Karlsson (KTH Royal Institute of Technology, Sweden, Research Institutes of Sweden (RISE), Sweden & Swedish Institute for Standards (SIS), Sweden), Ingrid Kihlander (Research Institutes of Sweden (RISE), Sweden & KTH Royal Institute of Technology, Sweden), John Bessant (University of Exeter, UK), Mats Magnusson (KTH Royal Institute of Technology, Sweden) & Jimmi Kristiansen (Aalborg University Business School, Denmark, rInnovation Group, Europe & Danish Standards Foundation, Denmark)

Vol. 39 *Corporate Underground: Bootleg Innovation and Constructive Deviance*
edited by Peter Augsdorfer (Technical University Ingolstadt, Germany)

Vol. 38 *Artificial Intelligence and Innovation Management*
edited by Stoyan Tanev (Carleton University, Canada) & Helena Blackbright (Mälardalen University, Sweden)

Vol. 37 *Managing Knowledge, Absorptive Capacity and Innovation*
edited by Joe Tidd (University of Sussex, UK)

Vol. 36 *Digital Disruptive Innovation*
edited by Joe Tidd (University of Sussex, UK)

Vol. 35 *Developing Holistic Strategic Management in the Advanced ICT Era*
by Mitsuru Kodama (Nihon University, Japan)

More information on this series can also be found at http://www.worldscientific.com/series/stm

(Continued at the end of the book)

SERIES ON TECHNOLOGY MANAGEMENT – VOL. 40

Changing the Dynamics and Impact of Innovation Management

A Systems Approach and the ISO Standard

Editors

Joanne Hyland
rInnovation Group, USA, International Society for Professional Innovation Management (ISPIM), UK & Standards Council of Canada (SCC), Canada

Magnus Karlsson
KTH Royal Institute of Technology, Sweden, Research Institutes of Sweden (RISE), Sweden & Swedish Institute for Standards (SIS), Sweden

Ingrid Kihlander
Research Institutes of Sweden (RISE), Sweden & KTH Royal Institute of Technology, Sweden

John Bessant
University of Exeter, UK

Mats Magnusson
KTH Royal Institute of Technology, Sweden

Jimmi Kristiansen
Aalborg University Business School, Denmark, rInnovation Group, Europe & Danish Standards Foundation, Denmark

ispim CONNECTING INNOVATION PROFESSIONALS

World Scientific

Published by

World Scientific Publishing Europe Ltd.
57 Shelton Street, Covent Garden, London WC2H 9HE
Head office: 5 Toh Tuck Link, Singapore 596224
USA office: 27 Warren Street, Suite 401-402, Hackensack, NJ 07601

Library of Congress Cataloging-in-Publication Data
Names: Hyland, Joanne, 1960– editor.
Title: Changing the dynamics and impact of innovation management : a systems approach and the ISO standard / editors, Joanne Hyland, rInnovation Group, USA, International Society for Professional Innovation Management (ISPIM), UK & Standards Council of Canada (SCC), Canada and [5 others]
Description: USA : World Scientific, [2023] | Series: Series on technology management, 02199823 ; Vol. 40 | Includes bibliographical references and index.
Identifiers: LCCN 2022005797 | ISBN 9781800612099 (hardcover) | ISBN 9781800612105 (ebook) | ISBN 9781800612112 (ebook other)
Subjects: LCSH: Technological innovations--Management. | Information technology--Management. | Organizational change.
Classification: LCC HD45 .C4473 2023 | DDC 658.5/14--dc23/eng/20220207
LC record available at https://lccn.loc.gov/2022005797

British Library Cataloguing-in-Publication Data
A catalogue record for this book is available from the British Library.

Copyright © 2023 by World Scientific Publishing Europe Ltd.

All rights reserved. This book, or parts thereof, may not be reproduced in any form or by any means, electronic or mechanical, including photocopying, recording or any information storage and retrieval system now known or to be invented, without written permission from the Publisher.

For photocopying of material in this volume, please pay a copying fee through the Copyright Clearance Center, Inc., 222 Rosewood Drive, Danvers, MA 01923, USA. In this case permission to photocopy is not required from the publisher.

For any available supplementary material, please visit
https://www.worldscientific.com/worldscibooks/10.1142/Q0356#t=suppl

Desk Editors: Jayanthi Muthuswamy/Adam Binnie/Shi Ying Koe

Typeset by Stallion Press
Email: enquiries@stallionpress.com

© 2023 World Scientific Publishing Europe Ltd.
https://doi.org/10.1142/9781800612105_fmatter

Foreword

The role of innovation as a growth engine has long been established. If innovation was still to demonstrate its aptitude to assist in solving grand challenges and laying the foundations for more resilient and sustainable organisations and societies, the context of the COVID-19 pandemic provides a testimony of its invaluable contribution. Be it for the spectacularly fast development of multiple vaccines and treatments, which was made possible thanks to decades of prior, yet potentially unrelated research, or the recombination and repurposing of technologies and products to deliver oxygen to human beings suffering from respiratory distress.

The common understanding and popular imagery of innovation is a novelty, taking the form of a new or improved product, resulting from the adoption and use of a technological invention. As research on innovation progressed and matured, other forms of innovation came under scrutiny, with the delineation of innovation as an outcome (e.g., a new or improved product, service, etc.) and as a process (i.e., the act of innovating). A plethora of concepts and paradigms, such as digital, open, collaborative, frugal, green, democratic, ethical, free, responsible innovation, have subsequently emerged, and the view that innovation is a socially constructed phenomenon has been forged.

But despite its undeniable strengths, affordances and great promise, innovation — as the act of innovating — remains a source of polarised perspectives. Concerns have been voiced on the feasibility and desirability for innovation to be managed — can and should it be managed, and if so, how? How can the innovation process be made more effective, efficient, predictable, and replicable?

The managerial and scholarly literature abounds with management frameworks, toolkits and toolboxes, playbooks and other, at times, proprietary artefacts that are exactly intended to meet this purpose — improve, accelerate and replicate the innovation process and increase its success rate. This myriad of resources have contributed to shaping the field of innovation management, and to grow its body of knowledge. Few though have convincingly passed the test of time.

Taking the stance that innovation not only needs to be managed, but more importantly that it requires a systems, systemic and systematic approach, *Changing the Dynamics and Impact of Innovation Management: A Systems Approach and the ISO Standard* is a significant step towards addressing the lacuna created by the lack of a comprehensive and holistic approach to innovation management, based on a commonly agreed terminology.

The wealth of expertise and experience of the editorial team consisting of Hyland, Karlsson, Kihlander, Bessant, Magnusson and Kristiansen, has been instrumental in sharpening our understanding of the rationales for a systems approach to innovation, and in laying out guiding principles and foundations of a holistic approach to innovation, which fosters its embeddedness in an organisation's ethos.

This volume demystifies the perceived oxymoron that standards and standardised approaches stifle innovation. Through a selection of 16 cases across public and private sector organisations globally, from diverse industries and contexts, the authors astutely contrast patterns on the antecedents, contingencies and impacts of adopting, fully or partially, the de jure ISO 56002 standard or underlying principles of a management system for innovation.

With a gifted ability to articulate complex ideas and provide actionable insights for innovation researchers, practitioners and educators alike, Hyland and colleagues compel us to ponder on how to grow the science of innovation, how to increase its professionalisation and how to master its practice to raise it to the next level.

Anne-Laure Mention
Professor of Innovation, Director of the Global Business Innovation Enabling Capability Platform, RMIT University

© 2023 World Scientific Publishing Europe Ltd.
https://doi.org/10.1142/9781800612105_fmatter

About the Editors

Joanne Hyland is President of the rInnovation Group and an accomplished innovation strategist and implementation expert. She is co-author, of *Pivot: How Top Entrepreneurs Adapt and Change Course to Find Ultimate Success* and author of *What's Next — Strategic Innovation.* She represents Canada as an ISO/TC 279 expert for the Innovation Management System and the forthcoming Managing Ideas and Opportunities Guidance Standards. Joanne is a member of International Society for Professional Innovation Management (ISPIM) Board. The rInnovation Group advises executives in diverse, complex organisations seeking to transform their organisations through innovation. Clients have included BASF, Bekaert, Bosch, Clariant, Danfoss, Evonik, Grundfos, HP, LEO Pharma, Moen, NOVA Chemicals, Novozymes, Shell, Tetra Pak, US Air Force, Vestas and Westinghouse. She is a faculty member in corporate innovation executive education programmes at the Danish Technical University (DTU) and Danish Business Institute and previously at Babson College, MIT, RPI, Stanford University and TATA Management Training Centre. Joanne was formerly Vice President and Founder of Nortel Networks' internal venturing programme that led to the creation of 12 business start-ups, one of which reached a billion-dollar exit. Email: joanne.hyland@rinnovation-group.com.

Magnus Karlsson is an Adjunct Professor in innovation management at KTH Royal Institute of Technology in Stockholm and project manager of innovation management system at RISE Research Institutes of Sweden. He is national expert and chairman of the Swedish committee on innovation management at SIS Swedish Institute for Standards and ISO/TC 279 expert. Magnus is a partner at Amplify and an advisor to multinational organisations in innovation management, research fellow at Institute for Management of Innovation and Technology (IMIT), and former director of new business development & innovation at Ericsson. Areas of expertise include innovation management in large organisations, innovation management systems (IMS), innovation capabilities in teams and innovation policy. Magnus served as Science & Technology Counsellor at the Embassy of Sweden in Washington D.C. and had a similar assignment in Tokyo, Japan. Magnus is a founding member and chairman of the Association for Innovation Management Professionals in Sweden (Innovationsledarna). He has degrees in International Relations (B.S.Sc.), Applied Physics (M.Sc.) and Technology and Social Change (Ph.D.). Email: magnus.karlsson@ri.se.

Ingrid Kihlander is a Researcher at RISE Research Institutes of Sweden and at KTH Royal Institute of Technology, in Stockholm, Sweden. She holds a Ph.D. in Machine Design from KTH and defended a Ph.D. thesis focusing decision-making in early phases of product development. Kihlander also holds a M.Sc. in Mechanical Engineering from KTH and has over 10 years of experience from the automotive industry working with change management as well as product development. Previously, she was the Director of PIEp Product Engineering Innovation Program, a research and change programme for increasing innovation capabilities, involving researchers, teachers and students from five Swedish universities. Kihlander is a research fellow at IMIT Institute for Management of Innovation and

Technology. Her research interests are different aspects of innovation management for private and public organisations. Further, Kihlander serves as a national expert in the Swedish committee SIS/TK 532 on innovation management at SIS Swedish Institute for Standards, mirroring ISO/TC 279. Email: ingrid.kihlander@ri.se.

John Bessant, originally a Chemical Engineer, has been active in the field of research and consultancy in technology and innovation management for over 40 years. He holds degrees in Chemical Engineering and also Psychology and a Doctorate in Innovation Studies. He is currently Emeritus Professor of Innovation and Entrepreneurship at the University of Exeter and has visiting appointments at the universities of Stavanger, Norway and Erlangen-Nuremburg, Germany. In 2003, he was elected a Fellow of the British Academy of Management. He has acted as advisor to various national governments and international bodies including the United Nations, the World Bank and the Organisation for Economic Co-operation and Development (OECD). He is the author of 30 books and many articles on the topic and has lectured and consulted widely around the world. Clients have included Toyota, Novo-Nordisk, Hella, Lego, Morgan Stanley, Coloplast, Corus, Danfoss, GSK, Grundfos, Hewlett-Packard and Kumba Resources. Email: johnrbessant@googlemail.com.

Mats Magnusson is Professor of Product Innovation Engineering at KTH Royal Institute of Technology in Stockholm and Permanent Visiting Professor at LUISS School of Business and Management in Rome. He holds a Ph.D. in Innovation Engineering and Management, an M.Sc. in Industrial Engineering and Management from Chalmers University of Technology, and a B.A. in Japanese from the University of Gothenburg. He has previously been Director of the Institute for Management of Innovation and Technology in

Sweden, and Visiting Professor at LUISS Guido Carli University, the University of Bologna and Aalborg University. He is the elected chairman of the Continuous Innovation Network, an international research network in the field of innovation management and senior advisor to the *Creativity and Innovation Management* journal. His research, teaching and consultancy activities cover topics in the fields of innovation management, product development, R&D management and strategic management, with published articles in *Journal of Product Innovation Management, R&D Management*, etc. Email: matsmag@kth.se.

Jimmi Normann Kristiansen is Associate Professor of Innovation Management at Aalborg University Business School as well as Senior Consultant at rInnovation Group. He has served as a national expert (Denmark) for the ISO/TC 279 on Innovation Management. Jimmi is a published author in the academic literature and his research and management interests include radical innovation, new product development and strategic management in large, international firms. He has been in management consulting for several years, where he has also solved complex problems in different industries. Jimmi holds a Ph.D. and Elite M.Sc. degree in Economics and Business Administration with specialisation in Innovation Management from Aalborg University. His Ph.D. thesis focused on large, international firms and developing a competency in radical innovation. Email: jimmi@business.aau.dk.

© 2023 World Scientific Publishing Europe Ltd.
https://doi.org/10.1142/9781800612105_fmatter

About the Contributors

Jean-François Barrand, Head of Innovation Faculty, AirBusiness Academy, France. Email: jean-francois.barrand@airbus.com.

Markus Søbstad Bensnes is a Senior Innovation Manager at Norconsult, Norway. Email: markus.sobstad.bensnes@norconsult.com.

Jin Chen is a Professor of Innovation Management at the School of Economics and Management, and the Director of the Research Center of Technological Innovation, Tsinghua University, Beijing, China. Email: chenjin@sem.tsinghua.edu.cn.

Leopoldo Colombo, Chemical Engineer, Senior Consultant in Conformity Assessment and Management Systems, Director Quara Group, Argentina. Email: lcolombo@quaragroup.com.

Alice de Casanove, Ph.D., ERPI Lab Member at Lorrain University and Culture Evolution, Intrapreneurship Director, Airbus, USA. Emails: alice.decasanove@airbus.com; alice.de-bigault-de-casanove@univ-lorraine.fr.

Marie Denward is a Senior Research Officer at the Sustainable Development Department, Swedish Environmental Protection Agency, Sweden. Email: marie.denward@swedishepa.se.

Richard Duncombe, Executive Director of Impact Studio at Oregon State University, USA. Email: rich.duncombe@oregonstate.edu.

Edward Feser, Provost and Executive Vice President, at Oregon State University, USA. Email: ed.feser@oregonstate.edu.

Åse Lundh Gravenius is an Innovation Manager/Innovation Lawyer at the Center for Innovation at Karolinska University Hospital, Sweden. Email: ase.lundh-gravenius@regionstockholm.se.

Rongyu Guo is a Ph.D. Student of Innovation Management at the School of Economics and Management, and the Research Center of Technological Innovation, Tsinghua University, Beijing, China. Email: gry19@mails.tsinghua.edu.cn.

Catrin Gustavsson, Executive Vice President Innovation, Södra Innovation, Sweden. Email: catrin.gustavsson@sodra.com.

Oskar Jonsson is an Innovation Officer at the Sustainable Development Department, Swedish Environmental Protection Agency, Sweden. Email. Email: oskar.jonsson@naturvardsverket.se.

Law Zhi Xiong is the Innovation Futurist at Alpha Catalyst Consulting, Malaysia. Email: zxlaw@alphacatalyst.com.

Roger Lundegård is a Management Consultant at Implement Consulting Group, Sweden. Email: rolu@implement.se.

Yannick Marin, Bizlab Tech Lead, Airbus, France. Email: yannick.marin@airbus.com.

Susanne Nilsson is an Innovation Management Researcher at KTH Royal Institute of Technology and an Associate of KTH Global Development Hub, Sweden. Email: suni@kth.se.

Hiro Nishiguchi is the CEO of Japan Innovation Network and Professor at Sophia University, Japan. Email: n-nishiguchi@ji-network.org.

Dan Oscarson, Product Process Development Manager, Södra Innovation, Sweden. Email: dan.oscarson@sodra.com.

Azim Pawanchik is the Innovation Strategist at Alpha Catalyst Consulting, Malaysia. Email: azim@alphacatalyst.com.

Marina Pérez Zelaschi, Industrial Engineering, Career Director and Professor, Universidad Nacional de San Martin, and Former Innovation Manager at INTI, Argentina. Email: pzmarine@gmail.com.

Mike Pickett was formerly the Vice President of Global Strategy Development at Moen Incorporated, USA, and is now retired. Email: mgpickfence@gmail.com.

Elodie Ponchel, Advanced Consultant Engineer, Altran, France. Email: elodieponchel@hotmail.com.

Syakiratul Ezwana Shahrul Niza is the Innovation Polymath at Alpha Catalyst Consulting, Malaysia. Email: syakira@alphacatalyst.com.

Suraya Sulaiman is the Innovation Provocateur at Alpha Catalyst Consulting, Malaysia. Email: suraya@alphacatalyst.com.

In memory of Dr. Vasell. **Jesper Vasell** held the position as Director of KTH Global Development Hub at KTH Royal Institute of Technology, Sweden.

Zhaohui Wang is an Undergraduate Student at the School of Management and Economics, Beijing Institute of Technology, Beijing, China. Email: wangzhaohui@bit.edu.cn.

Anders Wikström, Ph.D., Innovation & Design, Senior Researcher RISE Research Institutes of Sweden, and Affiliated Researcher, Mälardalen University, Sweden. Email: anders.wikstrom@mdu.se.

Daniel Witthaut, MBA is former Head of Innovation Strategy, Portfolio and Processes at Evonik Operations GmbH, Germany. Email: dwi@cefic.be.

Ximing Yin is an Assistant Professor and Associate Researcher of Innovation Management at the School of Management and Economics, Beijing Institute of Technology, Beijing, China. Email: yinximing@bit.edu.cn.

© 2023 World Scientific Publishing Europe Ltd.
https://doi.org/10.1142/9781800612105_fmatter

Contents

Foreword		v
About the Editors		vii
About the Contributors		xi
Part I	**Perspectives**	**1**
Chapter 1	Introduction *Ingrid Kihlander, Joanne Hyland and Magnus Karlsson*	3
Chapter 2	The Standard for Innovation Management *Joanne Hyland and Magnus Karlsson*	9
Chapter 3	Academic Perspectives on the Systems Approach to Innovation Management *Mats Magnusson, Jimmi Normann Kristiansen and John Bessant*	21
Part II	**Implementing an Innovation Management System: Case Studies from Around the World**	**35**
Chapter 4	Introduction to Case Studies *Ingrid Kihlander and Joanne Hyland*	37

Chapter 5 Airbus: Foster Innovation Culture in Practice within a Large International Corporation — Case of Airbus Defence and Space Division 45
Alice de Casanove, Elodie Ponchel, Jean-François Barrand and Yannick Marin

Chapter 6 China International Marine Containers Group: Cultivating World-Class Champions — A Systems Approach 65
Ximing Yin, Zhaohui Wang, Rongyu Guo and Jin Chen

Chapter 7 Evonik Industries AG: Capability Building for Strategic Innovation in the Innovation Management System 85
Jimmi Normann Kristiansen and Daniel Witthaut

Chapter 8 Humanitarian Innovation Fund: Managing Innovation in Humanitarian Aid 103
John Bessant

Chapter 9 Instituto Nacional de Tecnologìa Industrial: Innovation Management System Implementation at INTI — Argentina 121
Marina Pérez Zelaschi and Leopoldo Colombo

Chapter 10 Kanthal: Building Bridges for Increased Innovation Capability 139
Anders Wikström

Chapter 11 Karolinska University Hospital: Implementing an Innovation Management System at a University Hospital Providing Highly Specialised Care 157
Ingrid Kihlander and Åse Lundh Gravenius

Chapter 12 KTH Global Development Hub: Developing an Innovation Management System for Global Sustainable Development 177
Jesper Vasell and Susanne Nilsson

Chapter 13 Midea Group: The Systems Approach to Becoming a Global Leader in Household Appliance Sector 197
Jin Chen, Rongyu Guo, Ximing Yin and Zhaohui Wang

Chapter 14 Moen Incorporated: Initiating and Sustaining Transformational Growth Through a Systems Approach 217
Joanne Hyland and Mike Pickett

Chapter 15 Naturvårdsverket, Swedish Environmental Protection Agency: Innovation Capability in a Government Agency — Key Drivers in a Systemic Innovation Platform 237
Marie Denward, Oskar Jonsson and Roger Lundegård

Chapter 16 Norconsult AS: Management by Definition — The Role of Terminology and Shared Understandings in Implementing an Innovation Management System 259
Markus Søbstad Bensnes

Chapter 17 Oki Electric Industry Company: Implementation of Yume Pro, an Innovation Management System 273
Ingrid Kihlander, Mats Magnusson and Hiro Nishiguchi

Chapter 18 Oregon State University: Impact Studio — Advancing a University's Institutional Innovation Capability 289
Richard Duncombe and Edward Feser

Chapter 19 Sime Darby Plantation: A Top-Down Approach to Innovation Management in a State-Owned, Globally Integrated Plantation Company 313
Suraya Sulaiman, Azim Pawanchik, Law Zhi Xiong and Syakiratul Ezwana Shahrul Niza

Chapter 20 Södra Skogsägarna: The Sustainable Innovator 331
Catrin Gustavsson, Dan Oscarson and Magnus Karlsson

Part III Reflections 345

Chapter 21 Common Themes and Success Factors 347
Joanne Hyland, Magnus Karlsson and Jimmi Normann Kristiansen

Chapter 22 Conclusions and Path Forward 371
Joanne Hyland, Magnus Karlsson, John Bessant, Ingrid Kihlander, Jimmi Normann Kristiansen and Mats Magnusson

Index 389

Part I

Perspectives

© 2023 World Scientific Publishing Europe Ltd.
https://doi.org/10.1142/9781800612105_0001

Chapter 1

Introduction

Ingrid Kihlander, Joanne Hyland and Magnus Karlsson

Abstract

This chapter covers the purpose of this book, describes its structure and asks for a call to action for changing the impact and dynamics of innovation management. The urgent need for innovation in our organisations and societies is well recognised, yet why are we not making more progress in the field? The book's purpose is to help those within and outside the innovation management community understand the why, what, and how of managing innovation activities and the benefits of a systems approach for greater impact. The book has three parts. Part I provides background about the international standard ISO 56002 for innovation management system guidance (ISO, 2019) and the development of innovation management research, with the aim for better integration of theory and practice via the common framework of the standard. Part II is the core of the book, featuring 16 case studies about how diverse organisations built their innovation capabilities. In Part III, the editorial team looks across the cases to capture common themes, prerequisites for success and insights about the relevance of the standard for the innovation management community and the future of the field of innovation management. Most importantly, the book is a call to action for the innovation management community and others to move beyond making the case for why we need innovation. It is now time to be clearer on what it is and how to make it work through a systems approach.

1.1. Changing the Impact and Dynamics of Innovation Management

Many of us believe that the innovation management discipline and profession is at a tipping point. We all understand the urgent need for innovation in our organisations and societies, yet we have often asked ourselves why we are not making more progress in the field. How can we use our knowledge and experiences better to strengthen innovation capabilities and to create greater impact again and again? We now have the opportunity to change the impact and dynamics of innovation management by taking a systems approach.

The purpose of this book is to help those within and outside the innovation management community to understand the why, what and how of managing innovation activities and the benefits of a systems approach.

We have made significant progress in making the case about "the why" of innovation in terms of its importance and relevance. Innovation is often one of an organisation's top strategic priorities, which brings us to "the what" part of the equation. Despite the high demand for it to be on agendas, what it is and what it can offer to organisations and society is still unclear for many. Finally, and perhaps the most daunting challenge of all, is "the how" part. Organisations repeatedly confirm that they are not satisfied with their innovation performance.

We argue that it is, firstly, because a common and credible approach is missing to learn how to do this well. Secondly, a systems perspective is missing that can demonstrate how different innovation enablers are connected to each other. Of course, there are a myriad of approaches that address selected elements, but they are mostly at the process level. In addition, many of them are proprietary making it difficult to bring together a complete picture to understand the prerequisites for success. Finally, we argue that these challenges can be addressed by using an innovation management system (IMS) to build awareness and guide capability building.

While this book covers the why of innovation, its greatest value is in offering a wealth of perspectives about how organisations clarified what innovation meant for them and how they went about building the capabilities needed to improve their innovation outcomes using an IMS as the framework. Therefore, at the core of this book, we focus on defining what innovation is within the context of different organisations and reflecting upon how they developed and evolved their innovation management capabilities. This is possible through the 16 case studies featured in this book. The cases are used to capture insights that can be valuable for other organisations interested in embarking on an IMS journey, as well as for researchers, educators, standard developers, professional associations and policymakers.

The timing for this book is related to the International Organization for Standardization (ISO) publication of the international standard "ISO 56002:2019 Innovation management system — Guidance" (ISO, 2019). There are an increasing number of examples, but still quite few, from different parts of the world where this framework has been explicitly deployed. This brings a timely possibility to strengthen the sharing of innovation management knowledge and experiences using a systems approach. It would have been difficult to do without the IMS standard in place. Now that we have it, this book is the first collection of case studies providing diverse perspectives on how the ISO 56002 standard can be applied.

1.2. Structure of the Book

There are three parts in this book.

In Part I, Chapter 2 provides background for how the IMS standard was developed. It describes the framework for building a common language and approach for innovation, including descriptions for the eight innovation management principles (published in ISO, 2020) and the seven key IMS elements (published in ISO, 2019). Chapter 3 provides background about the development of innovation management research over the decades and how the standard can act as a catalyst for better integration of theory and practice in innovation management from a systems perspective.

Part II is the core of the book. Chapter 4 provides an overview and support for navigating among the case studies. Chapters 5–20 feature the 16 case studies in alphabetical order sharing insights about how they built their innovation capabilities through a systems approach. The case studies provide descriptions and reflections from a diverse set of contexts and situations, which provides rich and unique perspectives for accumulated learning.

In Part III, the editorial team reflects in Chapter 21 about common themes from the cases, how the standard was used, prerequisites for success, and practical guidance it can offer for a successful IMS journey. In Chapter 22, we look across the cases and the emerging themes to offer insights about the standard and its implications for the innovation management community and the future of the field of innovation management.

1.3. Call to Action

Most importantly, this book is intended to be a call to action. The ISO standard for IMS provides an excellent platform for designing systemic change and becoming more systematic in our approaches to innovation.

It is worth noting that the guidance standard is not advocating for one approach that fits all situations. Organisations can use the standard in different ways. In the case studies, some followed the standard to implement a full IMS, while others focused on certain elements. Some organisations used a systems approach prior to the release of the standard and others used the standard as a lens for a retrospective analysis. Regardless of the standard's use, organisations have been able to move from *ad hoc* or process driven activities to a systems orientation, create a common language to collaborate, clarify their innovation ambitions, and start their journeys via a bottom-up, top-down or combination of both approaches.

The call to action depends on an engaged innovation management community of practitioners rallying around the benefits of the systems approach, of academic educators teaching about open, connected innovation models that go beyond internally focused ones, and of researchers studying the interdependencies of the system elements and how to adapt these elements in different organisational contexts. For standard developers, a key issue is to ensure that a core IMS can handle the variations and complexities of different organisations and types of innovations. For professional associations, it is about continuing to build the identity of the profession and supporting professionals to strengthen the innovation management discipline in organisations. For policymakers, it starts with understanding where the standard could have policy relevance and broadening the range of innovation policy instruments available to policymakers.

Finally, it is about imagining a future where in 10 years innovation management is a well-recognised discipline and profession, with systemic and systematic approaches that accelerate learning to realise value more quickly for a better world.

In the end, it is about the brilliance of people and organisations with the right mindsets to make this call to action become a reality. The challenge is not about why we need innovation anymore, it is being clear on what it is and how to make it work — again and again. This is our motivation for this book.

Before moving on to Chapter 2, we would like to take this opportunity to thank all those who have contributed to this book and recognise our sponsors for lighting the path, especially, the International Society for Professional Innovation Management (ISPIM), the International Organization for Standardization (ISO), and the International Collaboration Platform for Innovation Management System (ICP4IMS), supported by Vinnova, the Swedish Innovation Agency.

References

ISO (2019). *ISO 56002:2019 Innovation management — Innovation management system — Guidance.* International Organization for Standardization.

ISO (2020). *ISO 56000:2020 Innovation management — Fundamentals and vocabulary.* International Organization for Standardization.

UN (2021). *Sustainable Development Goals.* United Nations, https://sdgs.un.org/goals.

© 2023 World Scientific Publishing Europe Ltd.
https://doi.org/10.1142/9781800612105_0002

Chapter 2

The Standard for Innovation Management

Joanne Hyland and Magnus Karlsson

Abstract

This chapter provides background for how the innovation management system standard was developed, including its link with other international standards work. It also makes the case for why a standard is important for innovation management and outlines what a management system is. Innovation management fundamentals are covered in terms of definitions and different types of innovation. Descriptions for the eight innovation management principles (International Organization for Standardisation, ISO 56000) and seven key innovation management system (IMS) elements (ISO 56002) are provided. Finally, the benefits, challenges and call to action related to the use of a guidance standard are highlighted.

2.1. Background

2.1.1. *The development of the standard*

Innovation management is today an emerging profession, similar to how quality management and project management evolved in the past. In the case of both, ISO 9001 and ISO 21500 guidance standards, respectively, were fundamental to professionalising the disciplines, including establishing a common language and body of knowledge (ISO, 2012, 2015). To enable innovation management to take its rightful place as a well-recognised, legitimised profession, a management system standard would be an important vehicle.

The development of the innovation management system guidance standard started at the European level in 2008. The ISO level work was initiated in 2013, building on that work. Over 50 countries were involved in drafting the standard, supported by their respective committees representing national positions and many other experts. The first main publication, ISO 56002:2019 Innovation management system — Guidance, was released in July 2019 (ISO, 2019). This was the first step in providing guidance for how to implement an innovation management system. A certifiable standard, outlining minimum requirements to be fulfilled by an organisation, is under development (ISO 56001). It will include knowledge gained from validation of the guidance standard.

2.1.2. *Why a standard for innovation management?*

The discipline of innovation management is facing challenges:

- We have over 100 years of innovation management and related research from economics (Schumpeter, 1911, 1942), engineering, marketing, etc. that has given us good knowledge of the factors supporting innovation success. Still, there has been limited adoption of practices in most organisations. With this slow progress, there is a need for guidance.
- There are many proposed frameworks by consultants and professors. Organisations are confused by the plethora of methods, tools and processes. Many are seeking a framework and common language to integrate and build upon an extensive body of knowledge for practical guidance that will lead to success. The market has demonstrated that a management system standard has boosted value and impact for the quality and environment fields.
- Management fads come and go. There is a need for a more stable generic foundation based on insights from innovation management research that is long-lasting and provides the basis for developing the discipline and profession (Tidd and Bessant, 2018).
- Organisations ask themselves if they have the right innovation capabilities and how they can be improved, but there has been no common framework to compare against.

To address these challenges, the objectives of the ISO innovation management system guidance standard are to provide the following:

- Practical guidance that is compatible with other management systems to increase organisational understanding and value without prescribing specific actions or tools. Guiding principles are fundamental to enable implementation flexibility.
- A common language and framework based on consensus among an international community of experts and practitioners to integrate a diverse body of knowledge.
- A durable foundation for innovation management that is applicable for most sectors, organisation types and sizes, etc. to implement dynamic and adaptable innovation capabilities.

2.1.3. *What is a management system?*

We know from research and practice that managing innovation activities can be particularly challenging in established organisations. This is especially true for radical or breakthrough innovations that challenge the current ways of working, business models or organisational culture (Leifer *et al.*, 2000). Transformation and change are often an uphill battle.

We also know that innovation activities can be managed by creating the right conditions, removing barriers and engaging people in the organisation. The ability of an organisation to innovate is dependent on several interconnected factors, such as leadership, resources, culture, structures, processes and so forth. Therefore, a systems approach is necessary for managing innovation activities to link together the related parts (Karlsson and Magnusson, 2019).

An innovation management system provides a systemic and systematic approach for any organisation to address its innovation challenges. It creates a common language, establishes a credible and shared framework, and enhances the importance of innovation management activities.

The structure of the guidance standard for innovation management system (ISO 56002) covers seven key high-level elements. These elements are the same for all management system standards. By adopting a common format, organisations can benefit from the integration of different management systems for more effective and efficient operations across functional areas. In comparison, quality management standards have resulted in fewer product defects, more loyal customers, increased regulatory compliance, precision and accuracy in laboratory testing, safety in construction, etc.

2.1.4. *Innovation intent, opportunities and value equation*

An innovation management system includes an innovation strategy comprising a core strategy and an innovation intent. An emergent innovation or strategic intent sets direction for an uncertain future and is about a vision of what could be possible over the longer-term. A core strategy sets direction based on what is probable, following the most optimal path through a shorter-term strategic planning process.

Whether the strategic lens is about a core strategy or an innovation intent, there is always an intent to innovate. The difference will be the level of uncertainty an organisation is able to take on within its capacity to innovate. However, the drivers of value within any type of innovation management system remain the same. They are about how to create, capture and realise value.

2.2. Innovation Management Fundamentals

2.2.1. *The ISO definition of innovation*

A shared understanding of what innovation means is critical for building an effective innovation management system. ISO provides a broad definition with a focus on novelty and value.

Innovation is defined as a "new or changed entity, realising or redistributing value" (ISO, 2020). Value is not limited to financial value but can be any kind of value, such as an experience, well-being or social value. Furthermore, anything can be innovated according to the definition. The innovation entity can be, for example, a product, service, process, model, method, etc., ranging from incremental to radical.

According to the definition, innovation is an outcome rather than a process or activity. The broad nature of this definition often requires the use of one or more attributes in order to be more specific, for example, process innovation, incremental innovation, radical business model innovation or social innovation.

The definition of innovation is a cornerstone of the ISO 56000-family of standards and was published in "ISO 56000:2020 Innovation management — Fundamentals and vocabulary" (ISO, 2020). It was developed in collaboration with the terminology group of ISO 9000 in 2014 and in liaison with the development of the updated definition of innovation in the OECD Oslo Manual that was published in 2018.

2.2.2. *Different types of innovation*

ISO 56000 also includes definitions for different types of innovation along a continuum associated with the degree of change. Radical or breakthrough innovation is at one end of the continuum, characterised by a high degree of change, and incremental innovation is at the other end, with a low degree of change. While disruptive innovations also lead to change, they are initially about displacing directly or indirectly established offerings and occur outside the organisation through market forces. Regardless of the origins of change, any organisation's aim is to bring about change and realise value through product, service, process, business model, social, organisational, technological and other forms of innovation.

2.2.3. *Other key definitions*

Per the definitions in ISO 56000, a management system is a "set of interrelated or interacting elements of an *organisation* to establish *strategies, policies, objectives,* and *processes* to achieve those objectives." A management system can be about one discipline or several, such as, innovation management, environmental management or quality management.

A process is a "set of interrelated or interacting activities that use inputs to deliver an intended result... An innovation process consists of several innovation activities, such as, identification of opportunities, creation and validation of concepts, and development and deployment of solutions."

Therefore, the purpose of an innovation management system is to provide the framework in which to innovate and deliver value through a set of interacting innovation activities.

2.3. Innovation Management Principles

In addition to definitions, innovation management principles, published in ISO 56000, were developed to capture the essence of effective management of innovation activities. There are eight principles that can be used as an introduction to understanding the innovation management system or as a tool for assessing the innovation management capabilities of an organisation (see Figure 2.1).

- **Realisation of value:** Value, financial or non-financial, is realised from the deployment, adoption and impact of new or changed solutions for interested parties.
- **Future-focused leaders:** Leaders at all levels, driven by curiosity and courage, challenge the status quo by building an inspiring vision and purpose and by continuously engaging people to achieve those aims.
- **Strategic direction:** The direction for innovation activities is based on aligned and shared objectives and a relevant ambition level, supported by the necessary people and other resources.
- **Culture:** Shared values, beliefs and behaviours, supporting openness to change, risk-taking and collaboration, enable the coexistence of creativity and effective execution.

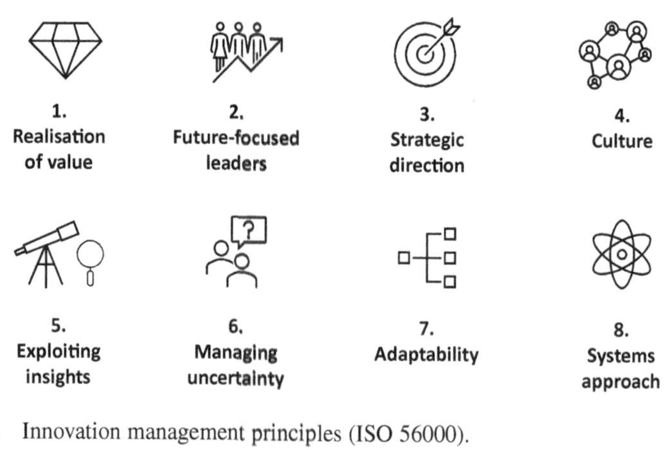

Fig. 2.1. Innovation management principles (ISO 56000).

Source: Inspired design from ISO 56000 principles (ISO, 2020).

- **Exploiting insights:** A diverse range of internal and external sources are used to systematically build insightful knowledge to exploit stated and unstated needs.
- **Managing uncertainty:** Uncertainties and risks are evaluated, leveraged and then managed, by learning from systematic experimentation and iterative processes within a portfolio of opportunities.
- **Adaptability:** Changes in the context of the organisation are addressed by timely adaptation of structures, processes, competences and value realisation models to maximise innovation capabilities.
- **Systems approach:** Innovation management is based on a systems approach with interrelated and interacting elements and regular performance evaluation and improvements of the system.

2.4. Elements of the Innovation Management System

The innovation management system, published in ISO 56002, comprises seven key high-level elements. Each of these corresponds with one heading in the document. The input to the system is the intent to innovate, and the output is the realisation of value (see Figure 2.2).

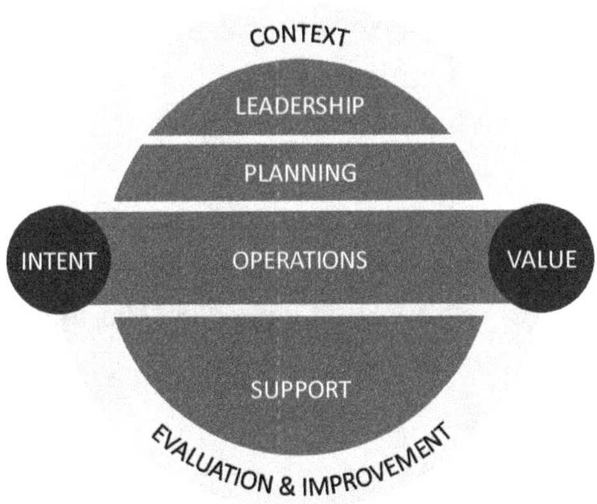

Fig. 2.2. Main headings of the description of the innovation management system (ISO 56002).

Source: Adapted from ISO 56002 (ISO, 2019).

- **Context:** The organisation should track external and internal issues and trends, e.g., user preferences, technology developments and internal capabilities, to identify opportunities and challenges that can trigger innovation activities and leverage organisational resources.
- **Leadership:** Based on the understanding of the context, top management should demonstrate leadership and commitment by establishing an innovation vision, strategy and policy, including the necessary roles and responsibilities.
- **Planning:** Innovation objectives, organisational structures and innovation portfolios should be established based on the direction set by top management and the identified opportunities and risks.
- **Support:** The support necessary for innovation activities should be put in place, e.g., people with the right competences, financial and other resources, tools and methods, communication and awareness creating activities, as well as approaches for intellectual property management.
- **Operations:** Innovation initiatives or projects should be established in line with the strategies and objectives. Innovation processes should be configured according to the types of innovations to be achieved: identify opportunities, create and validate concepts, and finally develop and deploy solutions.
- **Evaluation:** The performance of the innovation management system as a whole should regularly be evaluated to identify strengths and gaps.
- **Improvement:** Based on the evaluation, the system should be improved by addressing the most critical gaps with regards to the understanding of the context, leadership, planning, support and operations.

The guiding framework is based on the eight innovation management principles and is applicable for all types of organisations, regardless of type, sector or size. An organisation can select the most relevant parts of the system to be implemented, depending on its specific situation.

2.5. Concluding Remarks

2.5.1. *Benefits*

There are many potential benefits associated with the use of a guidance standard. A few examples most relevant to the cases within this book are as follows:

- A shared understanding within and outside an organisation can be created through a common language.
- A framework helps an organisation to develop its innovation strategy, understand its capacity to innovate, engage interested parties, improve its reputation and increase the value of the organisation.
- A systematic and systemic approach provides a mechanism for maturing innovation capabilities over time, transforming the culture, navigating uncertainty, managing a portfolio of investment options, and attracting partners and funding.
- A standard provides organisational legitimacy with customers, government entities and other interested parties.
- Ultimately, a standard provides for the realisation of financial and non-financial value by:
  - Delivering upon growth, organisational renewal and sustainability objectives,
  - Increasing revenues, profitability and competitiveness, and
  - Achieving critical mission and societal goals.

2.5.2. *Challenges*

There are also challenges related to the use of the standard within an organisational context. Questions within innovation management circles are as follows:

- Is the discipline too immature for a management system standard, comparable to a quality or environmental one, or is it long overdue to use standards to help organisations reach the next level of innovation performance?
- Is a standard for innovation management an oxymoron?
- Can we even build a systematic and systemic approach?

2.5.3. *Call to action*

We can no longer hide behind arguments that innovation is all about serendipity or we do not know enough about how to create the right conditions for innovation success!

It has been at least 20 years since the front end of innovation was considered "fuzzy" (Koen *et al.*, 2001). It is uncertain and chaotic, yet we now understand how to navigate this uncertainty via a systematic approach. This is supported by the start of the European standard work in 2008. In addition, the findings from the breakthrough innovation research programme at Rensselaer Polytechnic Institute (RPI), also published in 2008, led to seminal insights in the development of the innovation management system guidance standard (O'Connor *et al.*, 2008). Ultimately, the ISO 56002 standard draws upon the vast body of knowledge to codify what was "fuzzy" through an innovation management system.

The standard (ISO 56002) provides guidance through principles and allows for implementation flexibility based on sectoral diversity, organisation size, profit, social purpose, etc. It is not based on current popular approaches or skewed to any organisation. Many references were considered from research and practice. In fact, within the ISO community, the focus is on generic approaches, not proprietary practices. Further, as a guidance standard, it is not about certifying compliance via a minimum set of requirements an organisation needs to measure up against. It is intended to be a framework to move forward with a common language and approach. It is about enabling an innovation management profession to unfold.

As a final discussion point, the distinction between innovation processes and an innovation management system is an important one. The standard is about the system, with processes as parts of its elements. Due to the importance of linking the management system with an innovation strategy, the success of the system requires the top-down support of leadership, set within the right organisational context. On the other hand, innovation is the result of many individuals' contributions and any process needs to be bottom-up and top-down for its very success. Further, it is important to view the system as the enabler to building a capability for innovation work. It is only with a focus on capability building that a legitimised innovation management profession can proliferate. Processes alone will not get us there!

In Chapter 3, perspectives on the development of innovation management research and practice are provided, within the context of a systems approach.

References

ISO (2012). *ISO 21500:2012 Guidance on project management*. International Organization for Standardization.

ISO (2015). *ISO 9001:2015 Quality management systems — Requirements*. International Organization for Standardization.

ISO (2019). *ISO 56002:2019 Innovation management — Innovation management system — Guidance*. International Organization for Standardization.

ISO (2020). *ISO 56000:2020 Innovation management — Fundamentals and vocabulary*. International Organization for Standardization.

Karlsson, M. and Magnusson, M. (2019). The systems approach to innovation management. In Chen, J., Brem, A., Viardot, E. and Wong, P. K. (eds.), *The Routledge Companion to Innovation Management*. Routledge, London.

Koen, P., Ajamian., G., Burkart, R., Clamen, A., Davidson, J., D'Amore, R., Elkins, C., Herald, K., Incorvia, M., Johnson, A., Karol, R., Seibert, R., Slavejkov, A. and Wagner, K. (2001). Providing clarity and a common language to the "Fuzzy Front End". *Research-Technology Management*, *44*(2), 46–55.

Leifer, R., McDermott, C., O'Connor, G., Peters, L., Rice, M. and Veryzer, R. (2000). *Radical Innovation: How Mature Companies can Outsmart Upstarts*. Boston, MA: Harvard Business School Press.

O'Connor, G. C., Leifer, R., Paulson, A. S. and Peters, L. S. (2008). *Grabbing Lightning: Building a Capability for Breakthrough Innovation*. San Francisco, CA: Wiley & Sons.

Schumpeter, J. A. (1934). *The Theory of Economic Development*. Harvard University Press, Cambridge, MA.

Schumpeter, J. A. (1942). *Capitalism, Socialism, and Democracy*. Harper & Brothers, New York.

Tidd, J. and Bessant, J. (2018). Innovation management challenges: From fads to fundamentals. *International Journal of Innovation Management*, 22(5), 1840007-1–13.

© 2023 World Scientific Publishing Europe Ltd.
https://doi.org/10.1142/9781800612105_0003

Chapter 3

Academic Perspectives on the Systems Approach to Innovation Management

Mats Magnusson, Jimmi Normann Kristiansen and John Bessant

Abstract

In this chapter, we provide a background view and insight into the development of innovation management research, in particular, and discuss the outlook an application of an innovation management system may have, both for organisations and research. The chapter explains how innovation management research is well-developed, but often done so for a single phenomenon; and rarely analysed in research from a systems perspective. This can make the coupling between research and practice difficult (or at least misunderstood) because innovation practice happens in a system. The ISO 56002 brings about an opportunity to systematically discuss innovation research from a systems perspective and can act as a catalyst for better integration of theory and practice in innovation management.

3.1. Background

Innovation management has for several decades been an intensely researched field of investigation, resulting in a substantial wealth of knowledge. Despite this, many organisations are not satisfied with their innovation performance (Anthony *et al.*, 2019). Renewal and growth are not perceived to be substantial enough and rarely deliver the radical change that so frequently is sought after. This does not mean that innovation management practice has not evolved over time. This has been an area characterised by continuous improvement and significant change. Some of these changes should arguably be referred to as fashionable trends or fads that have had limited effects and have not been sustained. Other new ways of working and tools for innovation management have, however, gradually turned into broadly diffused, well-established practices that offer great value to organisations and their customers and users.

In most of the above cases where change, or new ways of understanding and developing innovations, are injected into the organisation, these often involve a single phenomenon that is dealt with in an isolated sense (e.g., open innovation, business model innovation, and agile methods and tools), where most works are consolidated or "recapped" in conceptual literature reviews (see, e.g., de Medeiros *et al.*, 2014; Schneider and Spieth, 2013; West and Bogers, 2014). As in other research disciplines, innovation management research offers a myriad of specific contributions into the innovation management discipline. This provides a natural development and accumulation of scientific knowledge within any field and is in no way particular to the innovation management domain.

Nevertheless, it can be argued that no single contribution would have a significant enough impact to drastically change the innovation performance of firms. If companies want to excel in innovation, it is not sufficient that new processes are introduced. New processes, methods, and tools have to be complemented with appropriate leadership, governance, metrics, culture, etc. (Slater *et al.*, 2014). For example, implementing new processes and methods for managing radical innovation, which is normally characterised by higher uncertainty (O'Connor and Rice, 2013), is unlikely to be successful in an existing governance model with focus on, e.g., early-stage calculable performance metrics, such as net present value (NPV), for portfolio valuation (Kristiansen and Ritala, 2016). This implies that changes and improvements for innovation management in organisations, in analogy, would have to be reflected throughout a wide range of their management practices. This suggests that management practices need to be adapted also to the type of innovation that the organisation desires to address. To do so successfully, a management system that allows for different types of innovation should be designed and implemented.

To meet this challenge, this book addresses the topic of complementarity and integration between multiple dimensions of innovation management research to provide a holistic and systemic view of innovation. In order to be successful, organisations need to see innovation management from multiple perspectives, and to recognise that the system only works effectively when all its constituent elements are aligned. Although some critical voices can be heard regarding the use of standards in the fields of innovation and innovation practices, the "ISO 56002:2019 Innovation management system — Guidance (ISO, 2019)" offers valuable support for the design and implementation of systematic and systemic innovation management practices. This chapter addresses the benefits and potential drawbacks of a systems perspective on innovation management and some key implications of such a perspective for both innovation management research and practice.

3.2. Development of Innovation Management Research and Practice

Early studies of innovation primarily focused on the diffusion or adoption of innovation (see, e.g., Rogers, 1962), investigating factors influencing how new technologies and/or products were put to use. These seminal studies have, among other things, informed us about customer and user behaviours in terms of, for instance, well-known patterns of innovation diffusion over time, addressing customer categories with different preferences and needs. Parallel strands are found in the Hindsight studies of the sources of innovation, revealing how scientific knowledge flows and creates value for businesses and society at large (Kreilkamp, 1971), and in the SAPPHO studies of success factors in innovation (Rothwell *et al.*, 1974). The latter highlighted the importance of understanding user needs, strong marketing efforts, the use of technology and scientific advice from external sources, and the seniority and authority of individuals in charge of innovation.

The insights from these studies on how companies create innovations has thereafter been further developed, addressing a wide range of aspects such as organisational structures (Burns and Stalker, 1961), innovation processes (Cooper, 1990), innovation culture and climate (Amabile, 1998; Amabile *et al.*, 1996), front-end innovation (Koen *et al.*, 2001), business model innovation (Chesbrough and Rosenbloom, 2002; Teece, 2010), open and collaborative innovation (Chesbrough, 2004) and innovation measurement and control (Adams *et al.*, 2006; Cordero, 1990; Richtnér *et al.*, 2017). Much attention has been paid to the operational level of innovation processes, arguably influenced by numerous studies of new product development (e.g., Cooper, 1990; Cooper and Edgett, 2007). Looking back at these developments, it can easily be concluded that the innovation management field has indeed flourished over the past decades, with accelerating growth in contributions coming in the new millennium (Salam *et al.*, 2020).

With the above in mind, it can hardly be questioned that the accumulated wealth of knowledge about innovation management is substantial. It is therefore quite surprising that innovation practices rarely reflect this abundance of insights. This apparent knowing–doing gap can to some extent be explained by the continuous change of the phenomenon at hand, as innovation without doubt has changed drastically over the decades in terms of both its content and its execution. Another contributing factor is arguably that there is an increasing divide between innovation research and innovation practice, resulting in large parts of the performed innovation management research focusing more on fulfilling internal academic requirements on scientific rigour than on producing practically useful and usable knowledge. A key effect of this is the apparent lack of more systemic approaches in innovation management research as such approaches require more phenomenon-based type of studies (von Krogh *et al.*, 2012), making use of diverse theories in an eclectic way, in order to capture the complexity and multi-dimensionality of the issue at hand.

Although the list of specific innovation management topics today is extensive, a salient characteristic of this extant theory on innovation management is that scientific articles tend to address only one or a few of its aspects. As a consequence, many organisations aiming to improve their innovation performance try to do so by using only one or a few innovation tools, methods and approaches, depending on what is in fashion at the moment. Although Van de Ven (1986) underlined the systemic nature of innovation management, the described tendency towards reductionism is increasingly accentuated. This development may indeed make sense from a traditional academic perspective where focus is on continuous refinement of previously gained knowledge, with a strong emphasis on scientific rigour, reflected in the use of well-established and validated research methods. Furthermore, practitioners may perceive the use of specific tools and methods as focused and prefer relying on only a select few vehicles for innovation as it is far less complex. However, as for most other things, this belief in a silver bullet is in the end normally deluding.

Summarising the above we can conclude that today we know very much about innovation management. Nevertheless, there is the aforementioned issue that many organisations struggle to achieve the innovation performance they are striving for. Innovation management theory is not always put to practical use, and when it is deployed, this may too often take place in a piecemeal fashion. There are some notable exceptions to this trend, in particular methods and tools that address the understanding of challenges at hand more than proposing specific solutions. One such example is design thinking (see, e.g., Dorst, 2011), which offers a fundamental approach for understanding and clarifying customer and innovation needs, and in that way can be used as an integrating framework for innovation efforts. Altogether, the need for more comprehensive ways of handling innovation calls for a revision of our approaches to both innovation research and innovation practice. In particular, we see a strong need for an increasingly systemic view of innovation management, allowing for the development of more holistic approaches to innovation management.

3.3. Towards an Understanding of Innovation Management as a Comprehensive System

A more pronounced focus on innovation management systems holds great promise to reduce or resolve a number of frequently observed issues in innovation management. One important change is to make innovation an organisational capability, and thereby make it a valuable asset that is durable over time, moving away from an exaggerated reliance on single outstanding individual initiatives and efforts. Another important change is to not consider innovation simply as an event or a campaign taking place intermittently, but consistently and systematically make it part of everyday activities, thereby creating continuity and avoiding boom-and-bust innovation, where many innovations are discontinued because of rapid changes to priorities and related resource reallocations. Finally, a systemic approach to innovation holds great promise to reduce innovation failures as weak links in the development from insights and ideas to implementation in terms of new products, services and processes can be avoided. Moreover, with a more systemic and systematic approach innovation activities can be handled in a more strategic way and can be given adequate organisational support (Karlsson and Magnusson, 2019).

3.4. Benefits of a Systems Approach to Innovation Management

As the research within the field of innovation management continues to expand, it becomes increasingly complex to coordinate and understand the role of both new technology and concepts to align with the organisation. It can in this regard be argued that knowledge *richness*, in itself, only becomes truly valuable when it can be contextualised and used in interplay with other areas of related knowledge. For instance, if we make breakthrough discoveries of new, efficient processes and methods within innovation management, we need to understand how these new methods and processes interact with the existing practices of the organisation. For instance, if a company has a certain way of conducting steering committees' evaluation in terms of asking for milestones, risk mitigation plans, etc. for projects, how will, e.g., a "radical," highly uncertain project be evaluated in such a meeting, where it is more about asking the right questions to learn? This could basically imply that new input, also on the surface appreciated and wanted by the organisation, does not comply or fit with other aspects of innovation management in the organisation, and as a consequence does not generate desired results.

Concurrently, managers need to understand that the innovation activities performed in their organisations are only truly fruitful when encompassed and aligned with the way innovation is governed and managed (e.g., organise meetings, rewards, budget, measures). This is also exemplified through the adoption of many adaptations of phase gates (Cooper, 1990) in organisations managing for innovation. Proven very valuable over the years for new product development processes, many organisations have an adaptation of processes based on phase gates in the heart of their innovation activities. This leads to a certain way of working and thinking, and can give issues with higher uncertainty, iterative opportunities in companies that may not fit with the existing divisions or opportunity pipeline in the organisation. However, even adapted phase gates might not go far enough to handle the different mindsets required to navigate uncertainty where the focus is on a portfolio options mindset to look for possibilities rather than solving a particular problem.

In a similar vein, failure to reflect about use of Open Innovation techniques may be misleading as different firms have different needs in terms of external knowledge input, and their possibilities to buy and sell Intellectual Property Rights also may differ substantially. Another tension that can be seen in many organisations is the increasing ambition to measure and control innovation. Whereas this often is beneficial in terms of ensuring that innovation activities are indeed prioritised and that related investments are ensured, this can also lead to questionable actions if the chosen Key Performance Indicators for innovation are not properly derived from specific innovation objectives and strategies but merely copy what other organisations use. This further accentuates an important point that processes, tools, methods and governance must be aligned in the innovation management system for innovation opportunities with different characteristics.

3.4.1. *Explicit systems approach*

As mentioned above, an explicit systems approach to innovation management in both research and practice holds a potential to amend some frequently observed problems. More specifically, such an approach offers possibilities to overcome issues by increasing the alignment of strategy, organisation and processes/methods/tools and thereby improve, (1) comprehensiveness, (2) continuity, (3) consistency, (4) coordination, and (5) collaboration of innovation activities.

As mentioned above, innovation is often a complex activity. One example is the challenge of combining science-push with market-pull (Scouder, 1991) and thus requiring in-depth understanding of technologies as well as capturing of customer and user needs, and connecting these different areas of expertise (Mangelsdorf and Posner, 2017). Moreover, the chosen approach to innovation should be comprehensive enough to encompass both strategic and operational aspects, in order to make sure that these are compatible and mutually supporting.

Continuity of innovation stands out as another important feature, as this reduces the risk that investments in innovation are lost due to rapid changes in priorities. Urgent actions in many cases tend to have precedence over other important ones that do not have immediate effects but may be very valuable in the longer term. Shifting resources from long-term innovation to activities with a more direct effect is thus often seen in innovation portfolios. This prioritisation is in some cases understandable, but its potential negative impact on value creation should not be neglected. Using a deliberate innovation portfolio, such as, the Innovation Ambition Matrix (Nagji and Tuff, 2012) increases the possibilities that innovations targeting improvements of core offerings, development of adjacent innovations and transformational innovation initiatives are all handled in a balanced way.

That the different parts of an organisation's innovation management system are consistent with each other is reflected in them supporting the same objectives. If an organisation, for example, has a strategy that aims to generate more radical innovations, it is necessary that the organisation accepts uncertainty in the selection of projects for its innovation portfolio, but also that there is acceptance for experimentation and failure in their execution (Gallo, 2017; Giaccone and Magnusson, 2021). If different inter-related parts of the innovation system are not aligned, the possibilities for achieving the desired outcome will most likely be limited, as the "weakest link of the chain" will limit the probabilities to succeed.

Taking a systems approach on innovation also implies that substantial efforts will be needed in terms of coordination and collaboration. Including and aligning different stakeholders inside and outside organisations require the use of suitable coordination and integration mechanisms, which at times are costly, especially when the innovations have high levels of uncertainty and include many interdependent activities.

The ISO 56002 guidance standard offers additional support in this work by providing a holistic framework covering the essential elements of an innovation management system, improving communication and learning about innovation management, and offering a common framework for academic research, which enables more comparable and cumulative innovation management research. However, proposing a standard for innovation management systems has not always been easy, and has frequently met with resistance.

3.5. Standardising for Innovation

According to the Cambridge Dictionary (Cambridge University Press), standardisation is "the process of making things of the same type all have the same basic features." This definition underlines one of the main issues concerning standardisation in relation to innovation. It is here important to emphasise that ISO 56002 refers to standardisation of innovation management systems, and not standardisation of innovations as outputs. Innovation, broadly defined as something novel and valuable, should, of course, not be standardised as that would be against the basic idea of novelty. However, the process (and broader system) used to generate innovation can arguably benefit greatly from standardisation, based on insights from both scientific knowledge and proven experience.

Experiences from the use of ISO standards in the field of quality management offer an indication of the potential gains from improving the understanding and communication of key concepts, methods and systems, which in turn has facilitated the accumulation of new and validated knowledge, and in the end simplified the improvement of practices. Even though there is a fundamental difference between quality management, basically striving for the reduction of variation, and innovation management, aiming to generate desired variation (Reinertsen, 2009), the means to support these different aims could still be very similar. A clear indication of this can be gained from scientific practice, where fundamental research methods display a striking permanency and similarity, despite the very strict requirement to generate novel results. Although science is not governed by explicit standards, the norms guiding this type of work are extremely strong and could in many cases arguably be seen as *de-facto* standards.

One contributing factor to the reluctance to embrace a standard for innovation management systems is arguably a misunderstanding that the standard aims to standardise output instead of enablers. In the specific case of innovation, this confusion is not at all new, but has been dealt with in earlier research. It is widely acknowledged in existing research that "innovation" can be referred to both as a process and as an outcome (Crossan and

Apaydin, 2010). As a process, we can refer to innovation (*ex-ante*), meaning before an innovation is successfully commercialised/implemented (Dahlin and Behrens, 2005). This would pertain to any input and/or throughput activity related to innovations, before these have been successfully implemented in organisations (e.g., as a process innovation) or commercialised in the market (e.g., as a product innovation). As an outcome (*ex-post*), we can refer to either the introduction of a new product or service, a new technology, entering a new market, or the introduction of a new business model. The market or the organisation test would likewise, over time, define the order of magnitude (incremental — radical) of the innovation.

The lines defining the innovation process (*ex-ante*) and innovation (*ex-post*) are blurred. There may in fact be multiple iterations of a product launch, and similarly it may thus be hard to determine exactly when an innovation is implemented/commercialised (Crossan and Apaydin, 2010). Nevertheless, by making a clear distinction between innovation as an output and innovation management as a process, it is hopefully easier to accept the idea of standardisation. In the case of ISO 56002, the standard clearly refers to the process and its supporting system, and not their resulting output.

With such a clear distinction, the expressed reluctance towards standardisation of innovation management systems appears less relevant, although we should be aware that it to some extent may limit innovation of an organisational nature, if defined, and used in an overly detailed and prescriptive way. This is, of course, an important area to investigate empirically as the diffusion and use of ISO 56002 accelerate and its effects can be studied at a larger scale. Our perception is however that the benefits of the standard have substantial advantages for both innovation management research and practice, which definitely outweigh potential negative effects. More specifically, we see that the ISO standard can improve innovation practice by facilitating and supporting the development of more systemic management systems for innovation, thereby avoiding missing or weak links that previously have stopped or stifled innovation initiatives (see, e.g., Karlsson and Magnusson, 2019; Mangelsdorf and Posner, 2017).

Moreover, a more systematic approach to innovation management opens up new opportunities to measure and analyse the true efforts and effects that go into innovation. This also makes it easier to evaluate this at management and board levels, which in the end hopefully leads to increased attention to innovation and better decision-making and resource allocations. In a longer perspective, the standard can also offer improved communication through shared language and improved learning from increased transferability of practices, making it easier to exploit the existing wealth of knowledge on innovation management and avoiding innovation methods and tools with little or no proven value.

The shared terminology and overall framework presented in ISO 56002 also open up a number of possible benefits for research. In particular, this development may lead to a shared language and understanding also among researchers, as well as possibilities to aggregate and compare data from different organisations. This will, in the end, lead to better insights about what individual factors, as well as combinations of factors, really support innovation, and will hopefully also allow us to understand contingencies moderating these relationships in a much better way than before. A first step towards this understanding of different designs and uses of innovation management systems is found in the numerous case studies presented in this book.

References

Adams, R., Bessant, J. and Phelps, R. (2006). Innovation management measurement: A review. *International Journal of Management Reviews*, *8*(1), 21–47.

Amabile, T. M., Conti, R., Coon, H., Lazenby, J. and Herron, M. (1996). Assessing the work environment for creativity. *The Academy of Management Journal*, *39*(5), 1154–1184.

Amabile, T. M. (1998). How to kill creativity. *Harvard Business Review*, *Sept–Oct*, 77–87.

Anthony, S. D., Cobban, P., Nair, R. and Painchaud, N. (2019). Breaking down the barriers to innovation. *Harvard Business Review*, Nov–Dec, 93–101.

Burns, T. and Stalker, G. M. (1961). *Management of Innovation.* London: Tavistock Publications.

Cambridge University Press (n.d.). Standardisation. In *Cambridge Dictionary*. Retrieved October 1, 2021.

Chesbrough, H. (2004). Managing open innovation. *Research Technology Management*, *47*(1), 23–26.

Chesbrough, H. and Rosenbloom, R. (2002). The role of the business model in capturing value from innovation: Evidence from Xerox Corporation's technology spin-off companies. *Industrial and Corporate Change*, *5*(4), 1143–1180.

Cooper, R. G. (1990). Stage-gate systems: A new tool for managing new products. *Business Horizons*, *33*, 44 –56.

Cooper, R. G. and Edgett, S. J. (2007). *Generating Breakthrough New Product Ideas: Feeding the Innovation Funnel*. Product Development Institute.

Cordero, R. (1990). The measurement of innovation performance in the firm: An overview. *Research Policy*, *19*, 185–192.

Crossan, M. M. and Apaydin, M. (2010). A multi-dimensional framework of organizational innovation: A systematic review of the literature. *Journal of Management Studies*, *47*(6), 1154–1191.

Dahlin, K. B. and Behrens, D. M. (2005) When is an invention really radical? Defining and measuring technological radicalness. *Research Policy*, *34*(5), 717–737.

de Medeiros, J. F, Ribeiro, J. L. D. and Cortimiglia, M. N. (2014) Success factors for environmentally sustainable product innovation: A systematic literature review. *Journal of Cleaner Production*, *65*, 76–86.

Dingsøyr, T., Nerur, S., Balijepally, V. and Moe, N. B. (2012). A decade of agile methodologies: Towards explaining agile software development. *Journal of Systems and Software*, *85*, 1213–1221.

Dorst, K. (2011). The core of 'design thinking' and its application. *Design Studies*, *32*(6), 521–532.

Furr, N. and Dyer, J. (2014). *The Innovator's Method: Bringing the Lean Startup into Your Organization*. Boston: Harvard Business Review Press.

Gallo, A. (2017). A refresher on discovery-driven planning. *Harvard Business Review*, *February*.

Giaccone, S. C. and Magnusson, M. (2021). Unveiling the role of risk-taking in innovation: Antecedents and effects. *R&D Management, 52*(1), 93–107.

ISO (2019). *ISO 56002:2019 Innovation management — Innovation management system — Guidance*. International Organization for Standardization.

Karlsson, M. and Magnusson, M. (2019). The systems approach to innovation management. In Chen, J., Brem, A., Viardot, E. and Wong, P. K. (eds.), *The Routledge Companion to Innovation Management.* Routledge, London.

Koen, P., Ajamian, G., Burkart, R., Clamen, A., Davidson, J., D'Amore, R., Elkins, C., Herald, K., Incorvia, M., Johnson, A., Karol, R., Seibert, R., Slavejkov, A. and Wagner, K. (2001). Providing clarity and a common language to the "Fuzzy Front End". *Research-Technology Management*, *44*(2), 46–55.

Kreilkamp, K. (1971). Hindsight and the real world of science policy. *Science Studies*, *1*(1), 43–66.

Kristiansen, J. and Ritala, P. (2016). Measuring radical innovation project success: Typical metrics don't work. *Journal of Business Strategy*, *39*(4), 34–41.

Mangelsdorf, M. E. and Posner, B. (2017). 12 Essential innovation insights. *MIT Sloan Management Review*, *59*(1), 28–36.

Nagji, B. and Tuff, G. (2012). Managing your innovation portfolio. *Harvard Business Review, May*.

O'Connor, G. C. and Rice, M. P. (2013). A comprehensive model of uncertainty associated with radical innovation. *Journal of Product Innovation Management*, *30*(1), 2–18.

Reinertsen, D. (2009). *The Principles of Product Development Flow*. Celeritas Publishing, Redondo Beach, CA.

Richtnér, A., Brattström, A., Frishammar, J., Björk, J. and Magnusson, M. (2017). Creating better innovation measurement practices. *MIT Sloan Management Review*, *59*(1), 5–53.

Ries, E. (2011). *The Lean Startup: How Constant Innovation Creates Radically Successful Businesses*. Penguin Group, London.

Rogers, E. (1962). *Diffusion of of Innovations*, 1st edn. New York: Free Press of Glencoe.

Rothwell, R., Freeman, C., Horsley, A., Jervis, V. T. P., Robertson, A. B. and Townsend, J. (1974) SAPPHO updated — Project SAPPHO phase II. *Research Policy*, *3*, 258–291.

Salam, S., Senin, A. A., Sheeraz, M. I. and Zainab, S. S. (2020) Innovation management: A bibliometic analysis. *Journal of Public Value and Administrative Insight*, *3*(4), 169–182.

Schneider, S. and Spieth, P. (2013). Business model innovation: Towards an integrated future research agenda. *International Journal of Innovation Management*, *17*(1), 1–34.

Scouder, W. E. (1991). Improving productivity through technology push. *Research Technology Management*, *32*(2), 19–31.

Slater, S. F., Mohr, J. J. and Sengupta, S. (2014). Radical product innovation capability: Literature review, synthesis, and illustrative research propositions. *Journal of Product Innovation Management*, *31*(3), 552–566.

Teece, D. J. (2010). Business models, business strategy and innovation. *Long Range Planning 43*(2–3), 172–94.

Van de Ven, A. H. (1986). Central problems in the management of innovation. *Management Science*, *32*(5), 590–607.

von Krogh, G., Rossi-Lamastra, C. and Haefliger, S. (2012). Phenomenon-based research in management and organisation science: When is it rigorous and does it matter? *Long Range Planning, 45*(4), 277–298.

West, J. and Bogers, M. (2014). Leveraging external sources of innovation: A review of research on open innovation. *Journal of Product Innovation Management*, *31*(4), 814–831.

Part II

Implementing an Innovation Management System: Case Studies from Around the World

© 2023 World Scientific Publishing Europe Ltd.
https://doi.org/10.1142/9781800612105_0004

Chapter 4

Introduction to Case Studies

Ingrid Kihlander and Joanne Hyland

Abstract

Part II includes 16 case studies that all share insights addressing innovation capabilities from a systems perspective. The case studies provide descriptions and reflections from a diverse set of contexts and situations. The breadth of cases has enabled a display of several learnings related to how management systems for innovation may be designed and implemented. This introduction to Part II has the purpose to provide support for navigating among the case studies.

4.1. Selection of Cases and Guidance for Writing the Case Studies

The purpose of the book is to gather knowledge and experiences related to the design and implementation of innovation management systems (IMSs) within the context of an organisation. Therefore, the case studies are based on experiences and reflections from the authors' perspectives. The objectives for case selection were to have diverse representation, by geography, type of organisation, explicit or implicit use of the ISO 56002 standard, etc., to be able to compare and reflect upon important insights. Since this is a *selection* of cases, the list of cases is certainly not fully representative. However, the cases have been selected as thoughtfully as possible, bringing in relevant and up-to-date reflections to showcase different perspectives related to IMSs.

For the case studies, the author teams received guidance regarding both focus of content and structure for their chapters. These instructions had the purpose to align the chapters sufficiently for comparison among the cases and, thereby, increase the possibilities for aggregated learning. Each case was encouraged to consider case context, challenges, drivers for change, actions taken and reflections related to taking a more systemic and systematic approach to innovation management, and reflections forward.

As further direction, the content of the ISO 56002 IMS standard was provided as a guiding framework (ISO, 2019). Key elements of the standard were used as a foundation and formed a common approach that authors used when developing their case studies. This common approach provided guidance for how the international standard could be interpreted and used, and what issues might surface in each context. Some cases explicitly used the ISO standard, others implicitly followed it via a systems approach, and others used it as a lens to reflect on their innovation capabilities and to, retrospectively, reinforce and validate what they had already implemented.

4.2. Diversity of Cases

While the diversity of the cases offers unique perspectives, there can also be value in organising the cases for ease of reference. Therefore, we present some guidance for navigating among the cases based on geography, type of organisation, and in relation to ISO 56002. For a more complete overview of the cases, see Table 4.1.

4.2.1. *Geography*

All cases share an international perspective, such as operations in several parts of the world, a global customer base, international collaboration initiatives, societal development objectives, environmental challenges,

Table 4.1. Cases by author, geography, organisation type, and in relation to ISO 56002.

Ch.	Case Name	Authors	Geography	Type of Organisation	Relation to ISO 56002
5	Airbus, Defence and Space Division (Airbus)	de Casanove, Ponchel, Barrand and Martin	France	Public sector aerospace company	Used ISO 56002 explicitly for implementing selected innovation capabilities
6	China International Marine Containers Group (CIMC)	Yin, Wang, Guo and Chen	China	Private sector supplier of logistics and energy equipment	Used a systems approach prior to the release of ISO 56002
7	Evonik Industries AG, (Evonik)	Kristiansen and Witthaut	Germany	Private sector speciality chemicals company. Internal incubator focusing on sustainability topics	Used a systems approach prior to the release of ISO 56002
8	Humanitarian Innovation Fund (HIF)	Bessant	United Kingdom	Public and private sector programme for innovation in the humanitarian system	Used ISO 56002 to reinforce and validate steps already taken
9	Instituto Nacional de Tecnologìa Industrial (INTI)	Pérez Zelaschi and Colombo	Argentina	Technical institute operating in the national industrial ecosystem	Used ISO 56002 explicitly for implementing an IMS

(*Continued*)

Table 4.1. *(Continued)*

Ch.	Case Name	Authors	Geography	Type of Organisation	Relation to ISO 56002
10	Kanthal	Wikström	Sweden	Private sector industrial products and services company	Used ISO 56002 to reflect on innovation capabilities
11	Karolinska University Hospital (Karolinska)	Kihlander and Lundh Gravenius	Sweden	Public university hospital	Used ISO 56002 explicitly for implementing an IMS
12	KTH Global Development Hub (KTH GDH)	Vasell and Nilsson	Sweden (Kenya, Tanzania, Rwanda and Botswana)	Collaboration among universities on new education models for sustainable development	Used ISO 56002 to reflect on innovation capabilities
13	Midea Group (Midea)	Chen, Guo, Yin and Wang	China	Private sector consumer products company	Used a systems approach prior to the release of ISO 56002
14	Moen Incorporated (Moen)	Hyland and Pickett	United States	Private sector consumer products company	Used a systems approach prior to the release of ISO 56002
15	Naturvårdsverket, Swedish Environmental Protection Agency (Naturvårdsverket)	Denward, Jonsson and Lundegård	Sweden	Public sector national authority	Used ISO 56002 to reflect on innovation capabilities

16	Norconsult AS (Norconsult)	Søbstad Bensnes	Norway	Private and public sector consulting engineering company	Used ISO 56002 explicitly for implementing selected innovation capabilities
17	Oki Electric Industry Company (OKI)	Kihlander, Magnusson and Nishiguchi	Japan	Private sector information and technology company	Used ISO 56002 explicitly for implementing an IMS
18	Oregon State University Oregon State (Oregon State)	Duncombe and Feser	United States	International public research university	Used ISO 56002 to reinforce and validate steps already taken
19	Sime Darby Plantation (SDP)	Sulaiman, Pawanchik, Law and Niza	Malaysia	Private sector, state-owned plantation company	Used ISO 56002 to reinforce and validate steps already taken
20	Södra Skogsägarna (Södra)	Gustavsson, Oscarson and Karlsson	Sweden	Private sector forestry group, member owned	Used ISO 56002 explicitly for implementing selected innovation capabilities

global research, and knowledge development activities, etc. The simplest way to introduce these cases is by region and home country as follows:

- *Asia*: China — China International Marine Containers Group (CIMC) and Midea Group (Midea); Japan — Oki Electric Industry Company (OKI); and Malaysia — Sime Darby Plantation (SDP).
- *Americas*: Argentina — Instituto Nacional de Tecnologìa Industrial (INTI) and the United States — Moen Incorporated (Moen) and Oregon State University (Oregon State).
- *Europe*: France — Airbus, Defence and Space Division (Airbus); Germany — Evonik Industries AG (Evonik); Norway — Norconsult AS (Norconsult); Sweden — Kanthal, Karolinska University Hospital (Karolinska), KTH Global Development Hub (KTH GDH), Swedish Environmental Protection Agency (Naturvårdsverket), Södra Skogsägarna (Södra); and United Kingdom — Humanitarian Innovation Fund (HIF).

4.2.2. *Type of organisation*

To organise the case studies according to the type of organisation is relatively complex due to the diversity of the cases. Organisations span multiple sectors in consumer products, communications, energy, speciality chemicals, forestry, education, healthcare, industrial development, government, aerospace, consulting, humanitarian aid, etc. In addition, they represent both private and public sectors and operate for profit and non-profit purposes.

4.2.3. *Relation to ISO 56002*

Six cases were selected based on the knowledge that the ISO 56002 standard was explicitly being used, either in implementing a complete innovation IMS or with a focus on selected elements. Four cases were selected due to their use of other models that addressed a systems approach to innovation management prior to the release of the standard. Finally, six cases were selected due to their focus on systematically building innovation capabilities either through explicit reflection of the standard or as a retrospective lens.

4.3. Overview of Case Studies

In Table 4.1, an overview of the cases that follow in Part II is provided. The case studies are presented in alphabetical order based on the case name/organisation.

Reference

ISO (2019). *ISO 56002:2019 Innovation management — Innovation management system — Guidance*. International Organization for Standardization.

© 2023 World Scientific Publishing Europe Ltd.
https://doi.org/10.1142/9781800612105_0005

Chapter 5

Airbus: Foster Innovation Culture in Practice within a Large International Corporation — Case of Airbus Defence and Space Division

Alice de Casanove, Elodie Ponchel, Jean-François Barrand and Yannick Marin

Abstract

In 2019, ISO published a standard on innovation management system, ISO 56002:2019. The technical committee ISO TC 279 is chaired by one of the authors who was, during the development of ISO 56002:2019, also leading the innovation culture in a Defence and Space division of Airbus, the largest aeronautics and space company in Europe. The authors of this chapter have actively driven a culture shift in their organisation in animating company networks, upskilling employees, adapting the workspace and proposing new tools. After the presentation of the changes of the business challenges and their impacts on innovation strategy, the authors explain how the innovation culture has to evolve and how it has been implemented in relationships with the other divisions in the group, with different innovation strategies. This chapter focuses on the change of company culture to answer the needs to shift from a techno push culture to a customer-centric culture. It concludes in showing how company culture enables the innovation journey of an organisation based on a subset of the recommended innovation management system from ISO 56002:2019.

5.1. Introduction

In this chapter, we present the innovation culture shift within a private company called Airbus Defence and Space, which is a Division of Airbus. We present the impact of the business context on the innovation strategy and how culture change can drive a successful innovation journey. This change happened while standards on innovation management were under development in ISO TC 279. Of course, Airbus Defence and Space's innovation management journey started way before the development of the innovation management standards. In this chapter, we will also present the Airbus approach regarding innovation and how a cross-divisional coordination has been established regarding innovation management.

We do not intend to explain how ISO 56002:2019 has been deployed in Airbus Defence and Space. Our goal is rather to show that innovation culture is fundamental to launch an innovation dynamic within an organisation and that it is not mandatory to have a complete innovation system deployed to start the innovation journey of an organisation.

In Section 5.2, we present the business context (as shown in Clause 4 of ISO 56002:2019). Sections 5.3 and 5.4 of this chapter will address how the innovation strategy (the focus of Clause 5.1.3 of ISO 56002:2019) is defined and its influence on the corporate innovation culture (Clause 4.4.2 of ISO 56002:2019). Section 5.5 focuses on how to foster culture through the training for the innovation projects leaders and the tools for innovation management practitioners.

5.2. Introduction to Airbus Defence and Space

The collective experiences shared in this chapter come from the implementation of some elements of an innovation management system within Airbus Defence and Space company. The systemic approach for innovation started in 2014 when three divisions, Astrium (Space activities), Cassidian (Defence activities) and Airbus military aircraft, merged into a new company called Airbus Defence and Space, based in four core countries: France, Germany, Spain and the UK, along with a global presence especially in Asia, Middle East and North America.

5.2.1. *Business context*

Space area of the business

Airbus Defence and Space builds satellites for mobile communications, fixed services and direct broadcast missions for television, radio and the Internet, as well as a variety of other related applications. Its activities range from system design, satellite manufacturing, launch and stationing, to total control on the ground and telecommunications networks. Supplier to the world's largest operators, Space Systems has built more than 100 geostationary telecommunication satellites as a prime contractor. The Eurostar series satellites have accumulated more than 500 years of service without in-orbit failure and hold the world record for longevity. More than 40 geostationary communications satellites built by Airbus Defence and Space are currently in operational service. Space Systems also designs earth observation and scientific satellites.

Defence area of the business

The Military Aircraft branch deals mainly with the in-flight part (Airbus A400M Atlas, Eurofighter Typhoon, Airbus A330 MRTT, UAVs) but also with all management in the air (air services, maintenance, repairs, avionics systems, intelligence and reconnaissance, light transport, etc.). The Communication, Intelligence, and Security branch deals with activities for satellite and terrestrial communication systems, intelligence and security solutions. It also manages border security, Terrestrial Trunked Radio and secure telecommunications solutions (TETRAPOL), switches, control and management centres. This branch has developed the shareable national transmission infrastructure and the software for the Population Alert and Information System.

5.2.2. *Innovation in the defence and space industry*

Airbus Defence and Space is doing business in two sectors where innovation and techno push approach have been the rule during the past decades.

Techno push approach, supported by governmental policies

As mentioned by a report from the French agency for defence (DGA, 2022), innovating is vital for the Defence sector. Vital in the literal sense for the militaries, who must stay "one step ahead" to make a difference in theatres of operation. Vital in the economic sense to enable companies to win new markets and compete globally. Innovation also means knowing how to speed up the passage from idea to product by taking risks to develop new technical and scientific solutions. Ministries of Defence in European countries rely on a strong ecosystem of industrialists to perform research activities as well as to develop innovative solutions.

The European Space Agency (ESA) is the third-largest space agency in the world after NASA and the Chinese National Space Administration by its budget (€6.68 billion in 2020). The activities of the Agency cover the whole civil space field: astrophysics, exploration of the Solar System, fundamental physics; study and observation of the Earth by specialised satellites; development of launchers; manned flights through its participation in the International Space Station; satellite navigation with the Galileo programme; space telecommunications for which the Agency finances the development of new concepts; and research in the field of space technologies.

The ESA entrusts, after selection and following a call for tenders, the Research and Development (R&D) of spacecraft to the industrialists of the member countries by applying the principle of "geographical return": The Agency's expenses in each country are in proportion to their contributions.

Space and Defence activities are strongly supported by the public orders, nevertheless, during the past years, these budget lines have been strongly challenged.

Challenges of the reduction of the public budgets

In a climate of increasing fiscal tension, most European countries have slowed down considerably their defence spending since 2008. European countries are redeploying spending to meet their financial commitments. The European Defence Industry has undergone a major transformation over the last 15 years, moving from a strictly national industry to the formation of groups with a European dimension. The various mergers, acquisitions and privatisations at the end of the 1990s have accelerated the effect of trivialisation of this industry. Firms are more subject to competitive pressures. The reduction of military budgets and the institutional reforms undertaken by the States and the European Union favours the opening up of national markets, and initially accentuates competition.

The ESA budget is decided regularly by Council meetings at the ministerial level. In 2014, Europe committed to an overall budget for its launchers of eight billion Euros over 10 years, half of which will go to the development of Ariane 6 and the construction of a launch pad at the Kourou site in French Guiana. The other half will be divided between Ariane 5 adaptations and financial support for launches. In this annual €800 million programme, France remains the leading contributor, accounting for half of the total.

Innovation DNA at the heart of the core values of Airbus

Innovation has always been part of the DNA of Airbus as a company and also part of the employee mindset. From systems to structure, architecture to flight physics, manufacturing to procurement, every single employee is part of this mechanism that drives innovations as new long-term programmes get developed. It is not difficult to picture this when we look at Airbus products like the Concorde, A320, A330, A380 and A350 (see Figure 5.1 for a historical overview).

From 2010, following the completion of the Airbus family with the newly born A350-1000, customised roads needed to be taken to keep on pushing innovation beyond the boundaries, with a need to "balance incremental progress with true disruption" as stated by Tom Enders, Airbus CEO at that time. While legacy aircrafts aimed to achieve their targets in terms of ramp up and cost, a Research and Technology (R&T) team has been created to support technology improvement. On this first road, the

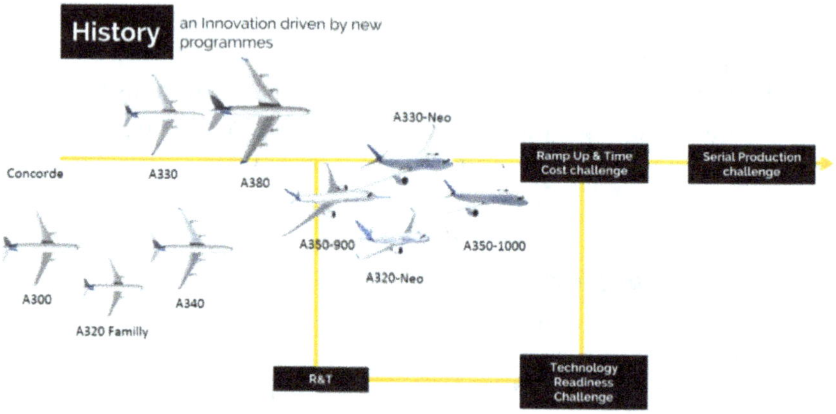

Fig. 5.1. History of Airbus commercial aircraft family developments.
Source: Airbus internal.

objectives are to keep increasing the maturity of the aircraft, while extending the performance and reducing the cost of production, without disrupting the existing business. Ultimately, this road focuses on ensuring the profitability of the company.

A second road was also created to identify ways to disrupt the company in the core business in a safe manner. A first innovation unit was then created and called "Innovation Cell" sparking innovation in an organisation and supported by methodologies creating a new context to support innovators across the company.

5.3. Development of the Innovation Management System at Airbus Defence and Space

In 2014, Airbus Defence and Space faced many challenges: how to create a company culture with entities having strong and different cultures and how to produce sustainable and breakthrough innovation. The challenge was to do better with less and to speed up the time to market. We present in the subsections below the influence of the strategy shift on the culture of the company.

5.3.1. *The relationship between innovation strategy and innovation culture in a large corporation*

The key idea in strategy is to use the past and anticipate the future to make strategic decisions today. This makes it possible to generate different possibilities for the future to anticipate possible strategic options for managing the challenges and possible risks that will arise. All this, therefore, contributes to building the capacity to think in the long term to provide proactive responses to current changes. These global challenges are macroeconomic and geostrategic forces that are shaping our deep and global future. They are called megatrends. For example, the PwC report (PwC, 2020) presents these megatrends: Shift in Global Economic Power, Demographic Change, Rapid Urbanisation, Rise of Technology and Climate Change/Resource Scarcity.

5.3.2. *How different innovation approaches impact culture*

Once the strategy is set, there are different approaches to define the innovation strategy as follows: Technology Driver, Market Reader and Need Seeker strategies.

In technology-oriented companies, technical novelty is generated by R&T, most of the time in collaboration with external research laboratories. This technical novelty is valued in patents and knowledge. New products or services with technical uncertainties are developed by the Research and Development (R&D) department, which is funded by customers' orders. In other words, R&T is supported by large corporation funds to generate knowledge, and R&D is transforming this knowledge into new products and services when the market has been identified.

We can model the role of R&T, R&D and innovation with the following triangle from our research and experience (Figure 5.2).

With money, a large corporation creates knowledge through R&T. From a given piece of knowledge (developed internally or externally), the R&D function can transform it into technology. The innovation team transforms the technology bricks into revenues.

Technology is one of the entries considered by the innovation team, other elements, such as customers' needs and market context, also influence

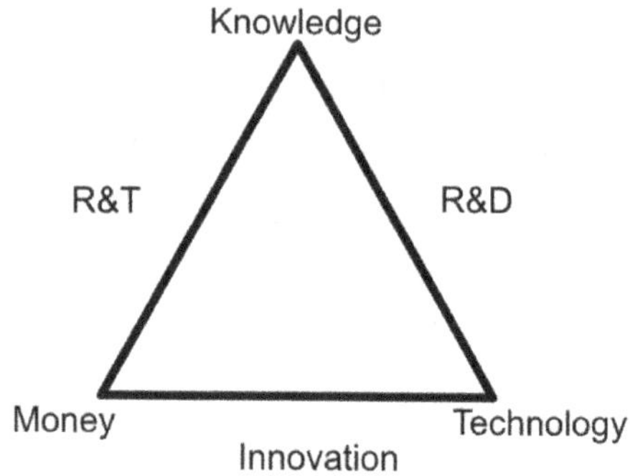

Fig. 5.2. R&T, R&D, innovation interrelated triangle.
Source: Our research (de Casanove, 2020).

the innovative activities. The three different approaches to and typologies of innovation strategies are fundamental to these entries and provide significantly different answers in how to address strategy objectives.

Technology Driver strategy

The *Technology Driver strategy* consists of developing products with high technological added value. The innovation process relies on intensive R&T and R&D to bring as many new technologies and inventions as possible to market and thus lead to successful innovations and products. As it is mainly based on R&D activity, this strategy is conducive to radical innovation.

Some patents subsequently become innovations when they reach the market: to do so, they must result in a product that is marketed, distributed to users, or adopted in social practice. The success of innovation will depend on how it responds to market needs. Then the role of the innovation department is to transform new products and services into commercial success.

Market Reader strategy

The *Market Reader strategy* is symmetrical to the previous one. It consists of creating value through incremental innovation and product customisation. This strategy is based on listening closely to the demands and needs expressed by customers, orienting R&D according to these demands, and leads to successful innovations. This strategy is relevant for incremental innovation, but it is likely to block radical innovation. This phenomenon is known as the "innovator's dilemma" by Christensen (1997): when the innovation process is user-centric, companies tend to miss disruptive innovation opportunities.

These organisations are regularly asked to become hyper agile in the twinkling of an eye. Then they must challenge everything, to break down all the silos that have been put in place between the different parts of their organisation (finance, marketing, IT, etc.).

Need Seeker strategy

The *Need Seeker strategy* is positioned on the market side, like the Market Reader strategy. However, it is not based on listening to the needs and demands as expressed by customers. It consists in anticipating future needs and future uses, aiming to be the first to produce a product that meets these as yet unstated needs.

By legacy, Airbus Defence and Space inherited a technology driver approach. With the reduction of the public budgets and the growing global competition, it has been mandatory to adopt a Need Seeker approach. With this innovative approach, it becomes easier to embed the future customers in the innovation journey and meet their expectations with the best ratio of features versus cost. Further, having regular interactions with customers eases the decisions and then accelerates the design and development process of the innovation.

5.4. Basics Elements of Innovation Culture

Deploying an innovation strategy requires the support and engagement of all the employees (not only the engineering or design office but support functions have also a fundamental role to play in this journey). Generally, these intangible ways of working and mindset are called cultural evolution. More precisely, cultural innovation of an organisation is the set of behaviours, routines and symbols related to innovation in the organisation.

5.4.1. *Routines and rituals to reinforce the values*

Rituals are excellent ways to animate collaborative innovation. They stimulate the collective intelligence and creativity of our employees. For example, we organise events, such as, workshops and internal challenges, to encourage co-development to break silos, create co-design habits and increase networking. These rituals are particularly suitable for any type of function or multifunctional team in the organisation.

Another type of ritual that helps to make innovation visible: the presentation of innovative projects to the executives. These types of events stimulate the teams and make innovation more visible to the leaders. Top management must be involved to ensure the success of a participative innovation process. Why bother inventing and proposing ideas if one has the impression that the leaders do not feel concerned, or if one does not expect any recognition?

5.4.2. *Places to encourage creativity and collaboration*

Located on the Toulouse site, the PlayLab is a creative space that is equipped with both simulation and 3D imaging facilities, as well as a 3D printer for rapid prototyping, this space is open to all company employees. It highlights innovation in small-to-medium enterprise (SME) and start-up business models, products and services as sources of inspiration. This creative space is close to the company cafeteria: every employee knows the space and its name. The prototypes made in this space are also presented to all the employees. It is a radical change in terms of the perception of prototyping. If you have to prototype, it means that you don't know. That's why most of the time they were made over the weekend in the garages of the employees who wanted to test an idea. In having prototypes in a corporate showcase, we change this paradigm. The engineer is no longer the one who does not know, but becomes the one who tests to know.

Other sites in Airbus Defence and Space host such an innovation lab: In Ottobrunn, X-works offer skill and space to build a minimum viable product and test them with the market. In London, the innovation hub reinforces our collaboration with local start-ups. In Madrid, the dock allows making a community of employees vibrant around digital transformation, agile methods. One of its members demonstrates well the pioneering mindset:

> *"We, Dockers — Stand for Airbus values — Help & respect each other — Look for value, beyond siglum, over borders — Promote what is transversal, multifunctional, common & coordinated — Re-use (algorithms, plastic bottles, architectures, good ideas...) — Commit to eco-responsibility — Have fun innovating — Are allowed to have crazy behaviours, sometimes."*

5.4.3. *Share the culture to encourage feedback and collaboration*

To spread this culture and mindset, the network is key. Internally, we have developed a network of catalysts who in each function can support the innovation journey. These catalysts are regularly invited to networking events where they are asked to develop the cross-fertilisation activities and break the silos.

They also need to be upskilled as they are the representatives of the innovation within each function, branch and the business of the organisation. Training is also a motivation to keep the catalysts engaged in their mission. Rarely is it a full-time mission. Most of the time, it is in addition to their regular mission.

5.4.4. *Airbus innovation from culture to value*

In innovation unit after innovation unit, Airbus employees and organisations have built an ecosystem answering the complexity of the products and organisations generated by this wonderful group. The different transformations that are also visible outside of Airbus can be described in three main phases: Pioneering, Collaboration and Value.

- *The Pioneering Phase (2010–2015)* is the first stage where charismatic leaders needed to impose a vision to create a new standard enabling innovation in a large corporation. Several units were created internally covering several dimensions from:
    - "*Corporate Innovation*" to guide employees with key methodologies and identify innovation representatives at all levels of the organisations called innovation managers and catalysts.

- "*Emerging Technologies and Concepts*" supports technology development at a high rate enabled by Incubation, Sprint and Acceleration phases fused by prototyping capabilities.
- "*Bizlab*" to create a unique link between the inside and the outside, giving access to our unique platforms and products.

- *The Collaboration Phase (Starting 2015)* is the second stage of the rocket. Indeed, while those transversal entities were created and progressing in their understanding of innovation development, only few and informal exchanges were performed between them. Energies were consumed to set and install good practices among those teams so there was only a small amount of time left to contribute to supporting a collective approach. The momentum really started to build up when newcomers were brought to this game. With this phase, the main point was to picture what was the strength and weakness of each team to support the innovators, which are and will become the fuel of the innovation machine.
    - The "*Innovation Ecosystem*" (Ref. Figure 5.3) is one graphical representation of how collaboration and how innovation units (*more than 71 of them before the COVID-19 crisis*) could fit together and serve the company and employees willing to create an impact.
    - The setting of the "*Innovation Federation*" has also been a big step in furthering the collaboration, encouraging exchanges between the different entities and clarifying innovation perimeters. The objective is to create a common and official ground where portfolio, progresses and actions are shared for the Airbus company.
- *The Value Phase (Starting 2018)* is clearly the biggest step and most sensitive one. Providing innovation services (methods, guidelines, acculturations, incubations, accelerations) are important, but can stay forever the biggest achievement of an innovation as an organisation. Indeed, Innovation needs to be transparent with its costs and values that it generates. Valuation of the return on investment needs to be computed in a clear and transparent way agreed by all parties to create a consensus and protect the organisations that are created, especially in crisis time. This task is almost impossible to achieve if a company masters only a piece of the development phase as Incubation and Acceleration are only the beginning of the journey for the innovation

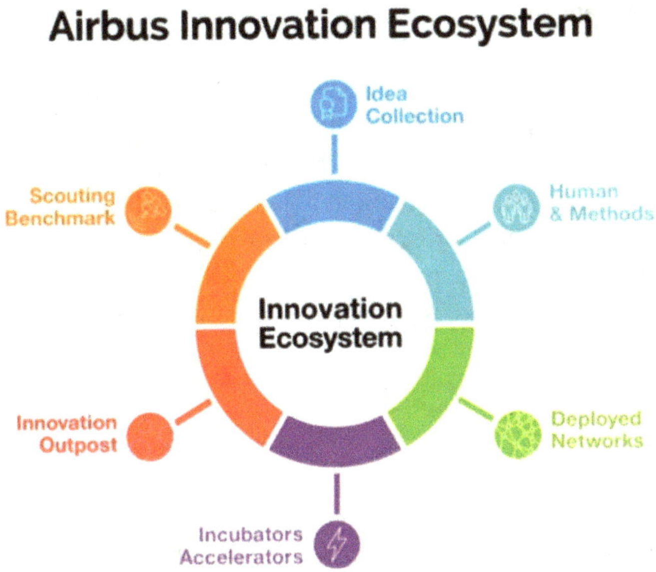

Fig. 5.3. Top view of the Airbus Innovation Ecosystem.
Source: Airbus internal.

fellows. The addition of Implementation and Scaling stages become more often needed to make sure that the Innovation Organisation remains accountable for the benefits that are sparked with its support.

These three different phases could also be complemented with a fourth dimension that could be called *Consolidation* or *Fusion phase* to identify the synergies among those innovation organisations and build more robust framing, implementation and scale dimensions enabling bigger impact and stronger values and return of investment. A top view of the Airbus Innovation Ecosystem is presented in Figure 5.3.

5.5. Foster Culture by Employees Upskilling

In large, corporate organisations that are not digital natives, such as Airbus, developing a strong culture of innovation with a view to accelerate the development of new technologies represents a great transformation challenge.

To support this transformation, we developed a network of catalysts with representatives from all functions. Their mission is to disseminate the innovation culture and mindset built around values such as customer-centricity, failing fast, collective intelligence and collaborative ways of working. With presence across the organisation, they support each function on their innovation journey.

The catalysts network is animated as a community of practice with regular networking events designed to foster open innovation, and break silos across the organisation. We also developed a clear learning path to equip them with the right methods, tools and practices.

5.5.1. *The key competencies (considering the strategy and the culture)*

Our learning strategy is inspired by the methods and tools emerging from the start-up world. Design Thinking, Lean Start-up, Business Modelling, System Thinking and Agile Development are revolutionising the way intrapreneurs successfully create, refine and bring new ideas to market. They help engineers, designers and developers' lower uncertainties and risk through cheap and rapid experimentation, placing the user at the heart of their innovation. At Airbus, we developed a comprehensive learning path to equip our innovators with competencies ranging from technical know-how on the methods to developing the mindset and behaviours required to boost innovation.

Our learning path shows these intrapreneurs how to apply the methods used by the most successful start-ups, in a more traditional organisational context. We provide a step-by-step approach in a context that is ever-changing, unpredictable and often messy. We answer questions such as: How do we know whether we are addressing a real need? Is this idea worth pursuing? Have we found the right solution? What is the best business model for this new offering? We focus on the how: How to engage the right users? How to test, validate and commercialise ideas?

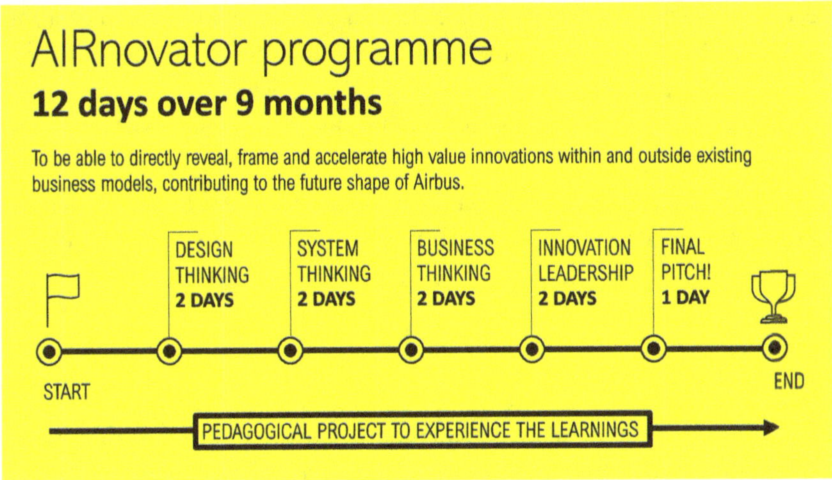

Fig. 5.4. Overview of the Airnovator programme.
Source: Airbus internal.

Our Airnovator programme comprises four modules of 2 to 3 days of training each, taking place over 4 to 6 months. The modules include Design Thinking, Business Modelling, System Thinking and Innovation Leadership (see Figure 5.4 for a programme overview).

Design thinking

Design thinking is the famous method introduced by the California-based designer firm IDEO. It aims at designing innovations based on the needs of the users. It encourages innovators to focus on the people they are creating for, which leads to better products, services and internal processes. Adopting a user-centric approach to design remained a challenge for aeronautical engineers that were mostly driven by technical excellence and feasibility. It helps to move the prototype from the employee garage to the corporate showcase.

Business thinking

Business thinking intends to revisit the business model and its impact on the business case. Our module is designed to develop catalyst's ability to create strategies for delivering value to and capturing value from customers. Once they have nailed the solution to an important problem for a particular group of customers, they are ready to test and validate the other critical components of a business model to build an effective, data-driven go-to-market strategy.

We have built the training on the application of the famous Business Model Canvas (developed by Alex Osterwalder and Yves Pigneur) on the participants' real projects, hence, encouraging learning by doing.

Systems thinking

Systems thinking aims at understanding the impact of innovation on an ecosystem and also the issues of the innovation project within its system (Airbus, corporate stakeholders management).

With this competence, our employees can apply systems thinking to identify, model and assess the interdependencies between the entities involved in a problem or value creation opportunity. It provides them with the means to assess the value chain through the phases of innovation (conception, elaboration and implementation).

Innovation leadership or intrapreneurship

> *If this industry wants to avoid its own 'Kodak Moment,' we must balance incremental progress ... lower risk, solid and steady performance, which is obviously good for profits and shareholder value — we must balance that with true disruption,* Airbus Group CEO Tom Enders, 2015.

Many creative ideas remain hidden in the depth of organisations because of the level of uncertainties surrounding them. They are risky. And most individuals in our large corporation are programmed to avoid risks.

Trainees experiment in this course the process to successfully create, refine and bring new ideas to the market lowering uncertainty and risks through cheap and rapid experimentation. They learn to identify and deploy the most appropriate innovation methods, techniques, tools and support according to the specific nature of an innovation opportunity, and innovation lifecycle phase. They develop an ability to engage their ecosystem with effective change management tools and techniques.

5.5.2. *Identify the target population to be trained*

As innovation is not only the development of new products and services but also organisational or societal impact, all functions deal with innovation (including finance, human resources, procurement…). The first advantage to identify competencies for innovation management is to map all the employees dealing with innovation in all the functions.

As managing practices are different from a "regular" project (Leifer *et al.*, 2000), we developed training to help our employees understand the differences. In an innovation project, the team identifies all the uncertainties and defines approaches to reduce these uncertainties, whereas, in a regular project, the milestones are known as well as the deliverables.

For this population working on the innovation projects, the Airnovator was helpful to develop the relevant reflex learning and ability to manage the uncertainties and understand the right to fail as a badge of honour to build new knowledge.

These teams are generally supported by internal coaches. These coaches unblock the situation, they develop the networking of the project team, and they help to make the project visible within the organisation. We realised that these coaches had different approaches, depending on their background. A coach with a sales background will be focused on the market whereas a coach with a technical background will encourage more prototyping. As we needed a baseline for the coaching approach, and the number of coaches cannot justify the creation of specific training, we decided to train them through the tools used to manage the innovation project.

5.5.3. *Design a learning solution for the innovation coaches with a set of cards*

The ISO standard allowed us to have a framework to organise training. We also based our thinking on the ISO standard to create project monitoring supports. This allowed us to train the project leaders. This population is supported by a team of innovation coaches. With the ISO standard, we ensure common methodology used by the innovation coaches.

Concretely, a set of cards has been produced in the form of recommendations and checklists to support innovative projects throughout their development. To define each step, we used the four last steps presented in Clause 8 of the ISO 56002:2019. We did not consider Phase 8.3.2, as it is too early to assign a coach for the project. The four steps are as follows:

(1) Formulation phase (8.3.3),
(2) Feasibility phase (8.3.4),
(3) Development phase (8.3.5),
(4) Launch phase (8.3.6).

We use also the matrix approach of the French standard FDX 50-271:2013 to define the innovation management domains:

(1) Marketing and Sales,
(2) Technology,
(3) Legal, Normative, Financial, and
(4) Project Management.

Based on these two dimensions, we created a matrix of 16 cells and developed one-page explanations for each cell covering the needed inputs, job to be done, the stakeholders, the expected outcome and some recommendations of tools (see Figure 5.5). All the actions to be performed are under a checklist form.

The coach has in hand a simple and useful tool to move forward on a project: only four checklists per phase. While using the cards, the coach learns the main aspects of innovation management. From a company perspective, it helps to ensure that all the projects are coached with a common baseline.

5.5.4. *From the learning solution to the portfolio management*

This structure is also helpful to the creation of a one-pager describing the status of each project. As the innovation coaches are familiar with the structure, the one-pager is easy to be filled out. Initially, we created this

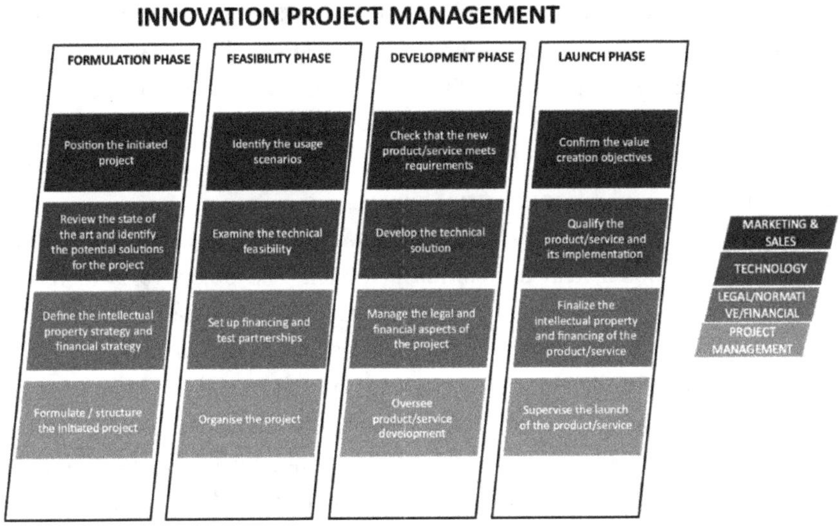

Fig. 5.5. Diagram for monitoring an innovation project.
Source: AFNOR FDX 50-271, AFNOR.

one-pager to make it easier to match skills for supporting projects with the already-trained network.

In a few months, we saw it helps to obtain an overview of the project maturity for the top management as well as the project team. So, once we have created this structure for our projects, we decided to keep the same framework to create an innovation portfolio management tool. This tool is used by the innovation steering committee to manage portfolio evolution with a constantly up-to-date overview of the portfolio.

5.6. Conclusion

In this chapter, we presented some elements of the innovation management systems implemented in Airbus Defence and Space. We showed the different factors impacting the innovation strategy of today's large corporation. During the creation of Airbus Defence and Space, employees needed a new perspective to become engaged through a strong company culture. Further, we analysed the different aspects of an innovation culture and made a deep dive in the training aspect. We saw how to structure the innovation curriculum to answer the challenges from the innovation strategy. Developing a strong innovation culture takes the burden of corporate processes off employees and moves them from administering a business to venturing into an entrepreneurial business.

We have also seen how the innovation culture has moved from a centralised, corporate model to a decentralised model. The objective is to move towards an ecosystem, where a federated model identifies and animates or brings to life the most relevant epics or stories. These experiences then provide the direction for the innovation steering committee and others to manage the innovation portfolio using the filter of consolidated priorities across the federation. As part of this journey from the Pioneering to Fusion phase, the ISO 56002:2019 Standard development work helped guide and reinforce the need for a systematic approach to building innovation capabilities.

References

AFNOR (2013). *AFNOR FDX 50-271 Management of Innovation — Guidelines for Implementing an Innovation Management Approach.*

Christensen, C. (1997). *The Innovator's Dilemma: When New Technologies cause Great Firms to Fail.* Boston, MA: Harvard Business School Press.

de Casanove, A. (2020). Stimuler les relations d'innovation ouverte entre les grandes entreprises et les startups. Application à l'écosystème français (In English: Fostering open innovation relationships between large corporations and startups. Implementation in the French ecosystem), Doctoral Thesis, University of Lorraine, http://www.theses.fr/2020LORR0268.

DGA (2022). Agence de l'innovation de défence, Direction general de l'armement, https://www.defense.gouv.fr/aid/mieux-nous-connaitre/documentation-laid.

ISO (2019). *ISO 56002:2019 Innovation management — Innovation management system — Guidance.* International Organization for Standardization.

Leifer, R., McDermott, C., O'Connor, G., Peters, L., Rice, M. and Veryzer, R. (2000). *Radical Innovation: How Mature Companies can Outsmart Upstarts.* Boston, MA: Harvard Business School Press.

PwC (2020). Megatrends, PwC, https://www.pwc.co.uk/issues/megatrends.html.

© 2023 World Scientific Publishing Europe Ltd.
https://doi.org/10.1142/9781800612105_0006

Chapter 6

China International Marine Containers Group: Cultivating World-Class Champions — A Systems Approach

Ximing Yin, Zhaohui Wang, Rongyu Guo* and Jin Chen

Abstract

CIMC is a group of "Hidden Champions," famed for its series of champion products from containers, vehicles to offshore segments and so on. The company's effective and efficient development is driven by its innovation dynamics and Leanovation system, which is a typical case of an innovation management system in line with ISO 56002. CIMC's innovation dynamics are coupled with the context and conditions of the evolution of the innovation management system, which could be divided into two main stages. The first stage is driven by external stimulation and market-central strategy. The second stage is driven by internal and resource-based strategy. Furthermore, we proposed a Leanovation framework that presents the remaining components and key factors for the system's implementation. It consists of a commanding World-Class Champion Strategy, front and back ends of CIMC operational structure, coordinated by the coaching leadership that ensures the coherence and alignment between soft and hard factors. With the context element of globalisation, combined with more practical market strategies, so-called "glocalisation" is emphasised considering the trend of deglobalisation, and the more "VUCA (volatility, uncertainty, complexity, ambiguity)" world after the pandemic.

*Corresponding author.

6.1. Introduction

China International Marine Containers (Group) Ltd. (CIMC) is a world-leading supplier of logistics and energy equipment, headquartered in Shenzhen of China. As a diversified multinational industrial group that shoulders the mission of global serving, CIMC has over 300 member enterprises and four listed companies in Asia, North America, Europe, Australia and others. The company's extensive customers and sales networks cover more than 100 countries and regions. In 2019, 50,000 excellent staff delivered ￥85.8 billion in sales revenue and ￥1.54 billion net profit.

However, CIMC's development path has not been all smooth sailing. "The childhood memory for industrial manufactory industry is 'path dependence,'" Ya Yu, the former vice president of CIMC said. Path dependence means "the future development of an economic system is affected by the path it has traced out in the past" (Page, 2006), similar to the concept of inertia in Physics. Douglass C. North, the Nobel Prize winner, succeeded in using the theory to illustrate the research of the economic system. For a successful company, dependence is a fortune but also a barrier. How to deal with the potential disadvantage of path dependence and leap towards the new innovation peaks becomes a key issue for those companies that have succeeded in the past. For a prolonged period of time, the employees of CIMC were trapped in the "Container Manufacture Mode." Managers even regarded research investment and service as costs. The R&D expenditure only took less than 1% of CIMC's revenue, which was much lower than the average level compared with other manufacturing companies around the world (Zheng, 2012). Thanks to the innovation management system improvement in line with the innovation system approach by ISO 56002 (ISO, 2019), this situation has changed and CIMC has started cultivating groups of world-class championship products.

How did CIMC become the hidden champion at the end of the last century in China? In which way did the company grow up from a company famed for container manufacturing to a group with a series of championship products?

6.2. Hidden Champion and Leanovation

Hidden champions are relatively small but highly successful companies that are concealed behind a curtain of inconspicuousness, invisibility and sometimes secrecy (Simon, 2009). A company must meet three criteria to be considered a hidden champion: (1) be number one, two or three in the global market, or number one on the company's continent, determined by market share, (2) have a revenue below $5 billion, and (3) have a low level of public awareness. Regarding CIMC, its scale has exceeded the upper limit of the turnover of a generally hidden champion. However, the business units of CIMC are relatively independent and possess typical characteristics of hidden champions, which made it a "Hidden Champion Group." What's more, considering input and output, the innovation efficiency of the hidden champion is 25 times that of large enterprises. Only a few innovations are major technological breakthroughs, which generally take 10–15 years on average. Most innovation by hidden champions is the improvement and perfection of existing technology. The progress of every innovation seems to be minimal, but the gathering of sand into a tower has led to the achievement of the top products and services of the hidden champion.

CIMC's success as a hidden champion drew lessons from a series of foreign companies, among which the Lean Management method followed by Japanese companies played an irreplaceable role. The Lean philosophy has proven to be an important way to boost a firm's innovation capability, by first, "doing the right thing," and then "doing it right," and finally "doing it better" all the time (Sehested and Sonnenberg, 2010). Lean Innovation Management (named Leanovation) is an application of these principles and practices to the innovation management system (Solaimani *et al.*, 2019). For example, Toyota, the pioneer of Lean philosophy, has been one of the most consistent innovators alongside Apple, Google and Microsoft with the Lean Innovation mode (Ringel, Taylor, and Zablit, 2015).

Academically, the complementary relationship between lean and innovation is broadly recognised, and Solaimani *et al.* (2019) synthesised a holistic framework on Leanovation which was regarded as a more

Fig. 6.1. Leanovation Framework.

Source: Solaimani, Talab and van der Rhee (2019).

efficient and effective "system" instead of being limited to the "scattered" or "siloed" segments (Figure 6.1). The framework consists of five dimensions, where each dimension requires a set of multi-layered ambidextrous capabilities, mutually supporting and reinforcing one another. The Leanovation framework has also been empirically studied by Solaimani (Solaimani, Talab and van der Rhee, 2019), and provides us with a good tool to review CIMC's innovation management system.

6.3. CIMC's Innovation Journey and Dynamics

Reviewing the origination context and conditions of CIMC's innovation power in the past 40 years is helpful to understand its innovation management system today. CIMC's innovation dynamics, coupled with the dynamics of the innovation context and conditions as well as CIMC's response, can be divided into three main stages (see Figure 6.2). In the

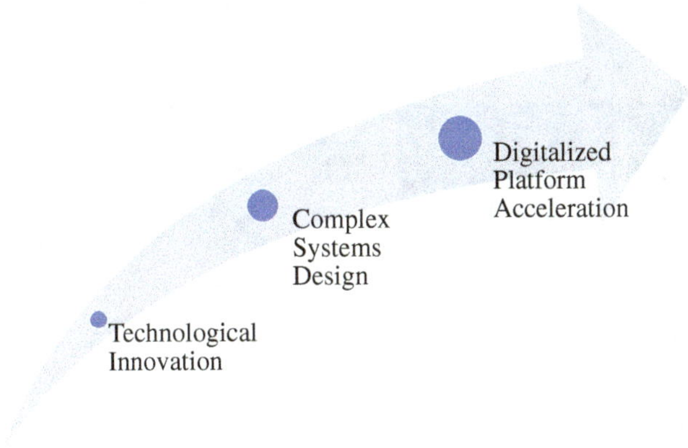

Fig. 6.2. CIMC's journey of innovation.

first stage, CIMC mainly focuses on technological innovation. It successfully changed the container industry and even influenced the whole manufacturing industry at the beginning of the 20th century in China. The second stage of innovation was reflected in the creation of complex systems driven by informatisation. A series of management information systems (MIS) and advanced ideas like "Lean ONE Mode" were developed. CIMC's "World Champion" strategy has been carried out consistently during the innovation dynamics, and the lean innovation system has been continually improved. Today, CIMC is trying to create a digitalised platform to accelerate its innovation speed.

What is the dynamic of CIMC's innovation? One simple way to classify the innovation driving force is to see whether it is external or internal. The debate between resource-based strategy and market-central strategy has lasted for a long time (Simon, 2009). The resource-based theory believes that a company's strategy should be based on its internal resources, that is, driven by its resources. While the market centre scholars believe that it is necessary to always pay attention to and make strategic decisions based on the opportunities brought by the market. According to a series of studies made by Simon, hidden champions commonly have a more comprehensive and synthetic mode of innovation strategy than large-scale companies. For CIMC, in the early period, the external stimulation and market-central strategy pushed CIMC to produce several

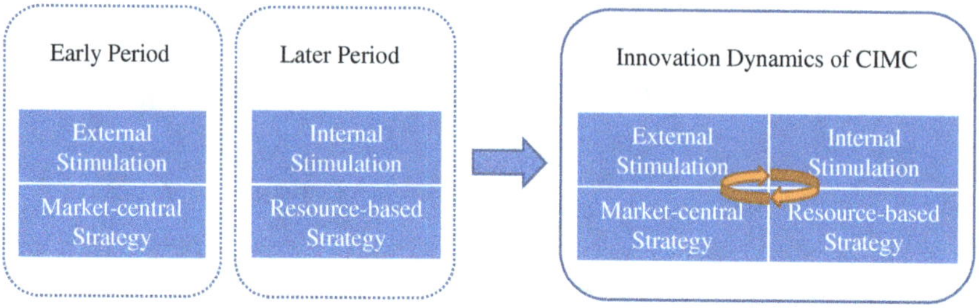

Fig. 6.3. Innovation dynamics of CIMC.

championship products with a relatively lower technological threshold. After that, internal stimulation and resource-based strategy played a role and different types of power constituted the innovation engine of CIMC, which contributed to today's championship products group. The engine also facilitated the company's transition from cost-saving innovation to technology-leading innovation mode, from individual wisdom to the strategic development system for technology (see Figure 6.3). Although it is difficult to find an exact point in time that indicates the beginning of the transformation, as the result of facing the global financial crises in 2008 and the decrease of demographic dividends, CIMC began focusing more on indigenous innovation.

6.3.1. *External stimulation and market-central strategy*

As one of the earliest Chinese-foreign equity joint ventures, CIMC, founded in 1980, was a direct beneficiary of the reform and opening-up policy. The partnership with other stakeholders was the first step for CIMC's innovation development. At the beginning of China's reform and opening-up since 1978, Chinese firms commonly lacked in knowledge and experience in company operation. As a foreign shareholder of CIMC, Bao Long firm brought a series of modern business management tools to CIMC, such as inventory management and just-in-time delivery methods. In 1987, China's COSCO shipping corporation altered CIMC's equity structure and brought the company back to the container industry again. Later, COSCO supported CIMC again when the company was in the process of reducing costs by ordering a fixed number of containers even with a higher price. The company's growth was also promoted with direct engagement with foreign customers. The meeting with Mitsubishi in 1987 gave Mr. Mai Boliang, the CEO of CIMC, an opportunity to access the Lean Production Method. Since then, numerous managers of CIMC had been dispatched to Japanese companies to learn the method, setting up the foundation of CIMC's business philosophy later. During this process, by processing products designed by foreign companies, CIMC learned many advanced technologies. For example, CIMC learned about the boarding bridge technology during the cooperation with Mitsubishi, which then became its second championship production.

At the end of the last century, the invisible barrier caused by the discrimination towards the Chinese manufacturing industry made CIMC's business negotiation difficult. However, it was national pride that drove leaders of CIMC to make more efforts towards "Making the Chinese manufacturing industry great" and successfully refreshed the world's impression of Chinese enterprises. As the senior purchasing managers of Schiphol Airport in the Netherlands said: "a good product speaks for itself."

6.3.2. *Internal stimulation and resource-central strategy*

The scale effect accelerated CIMC's innovation speed. After a long-term investment in the development of special containers, the patent of CIMC had become an important chip when it came to the negotiation with Clive-Smith Cowley, who owned the DOMINO technique, which was widely used in the production of folding containers. "Transfer it to us, or we develop it by ourselves and own your market" reflects the CIMC's resource advantage and confidence at that time. In this stage, CIMC entered a series of industries through mergers and acquisitions. For example, the acquisition of Yantai Raffles marks that CIMC has officially entered the marine oil and gas development equipment field. In March 2009, C&C Trucks Co., Ltd. was registered and established with the joint investment of CIMC Vehicle Group, marking that the CIMC heavy truck project had officially entered the substantive start stage.

Meanwhile, after learning Midea's right allocation system and Hewlett-Packard's "101" system, CIMC's top management team published a series of reports and introduced the advanced management experience into CIMC's innovation system. On January 18, 2008, the "CIMC Lean ONE Mode" was officially proposed at CIMC's annual meeting, with the purpose of applying a world-class management mode to support a world-class group. CIMC ONE (Optimisation Never Ending) means relentless and everlasting improvement, adherence to the PDCA management philosophy and the idea of all staff's participation besides consisting of many management sub-systems, evaluation criteria, ideologies, methodologies and pioneers. After 4 years of explorations, CIMC ONE took its basic shape and featured unique glamour, which reliably facilitated CIMC to fulfil its goal of becoming a "world-class player."

6.4. CIMC's Leanovation System

An overview of the CIMC's Leanovation System is presented in Figure 6.4.

6.4.1. *World-class champion strategy*

Top management commitment, clear innovation vision and strategy are the upfront factors of successful practice of innovation management

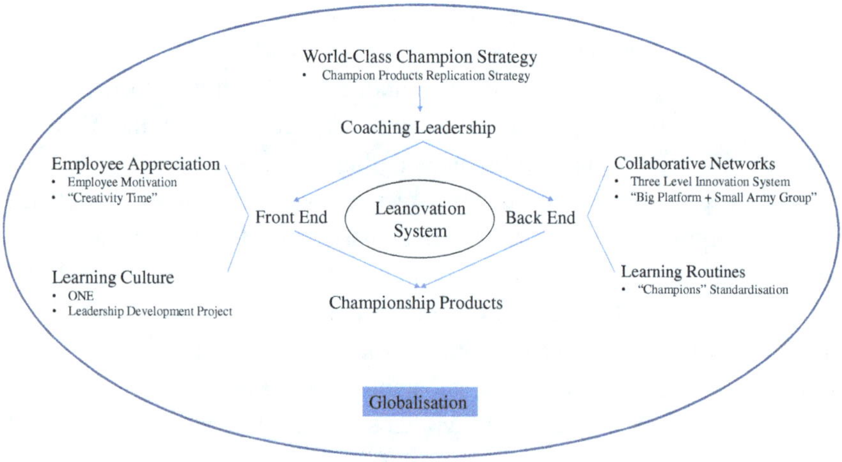

Fig. 6.4. CIMC's Leanovation system.

system approach. In 1996, CIMC became the largest company producing containers in terms of its scale. However, Mr. Mai thought there was still a significant gap between his company and those from Japan and Korea considering the product's quality. He believes that a World-Class Champion company means owning and leading the development direction of the industry globally, and a corporate level strategy is necessary for CIMC's road towards becoming a World-Class Champion company.

There are two pillars that support the hidden champions strategy, that of centralisation and depth, and leadership in the global market. Both pillars are related to the market: one involves the content and the other involves space. Both are based on customer orientation, the pursuit of excellence, innovation and competitive advantage (Simon, 2009). If these can be implemented smoothly, then the goals of growth and market leadership pursued by the company can also be achieved. To build the two pillars, CIMC has never stopped improving the innovation process. Since the first 20-foot dry cargo container was launched in Shenzhen and then its output ranked the first in the world in 1996, 11 production bases have been set up with an annual capacity of 2 million TEUs. Besides that, CIMC's container business also involves reefer, special containers and modular building aspects, etc. (Figure 6.5), where the company owns the

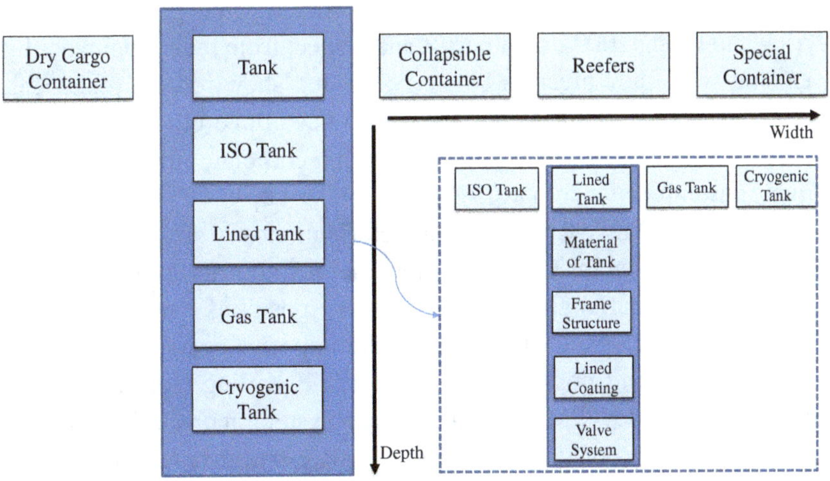

Fig. 6.5. The width and depth of CIMC's container R&D.

obvious advantages in terms of the market and technology. In 2002, CIMC started the diversification strategy. In the continuously growing industries like special vehicles and cold chains, CIMC still keeps this strategy: to become the number one in the foreseeable future and have the industry discourse power. The industries CIMC has chosen have not been usually huge, but where CIMC has the capability to become the champion. This is a very handy "Champion Product Replication" strategy: just ensure the industry itself continues, then the company can keep its long-term vitality.

6.4.2. *Coaching leadership*

Talent is the first resource for innovation development. After years of rapid development, CIMC was confronted with a series of challenges such as industry upgrades, business expansion and management mode upgrades. As a result, a large number of leading talents were required to be nurtured to realise the goal of becoming a world-class enterprise, so as to drive future business transformation, organisation transformation and management transformation of CIMC (Zheng, 2012).

Lean innovation scholars have a shared view of Lean coaches as supportive, respectful and inspiring role models in nurturing talents and innovative teams (Adler, 1993; Boehm, 2012; Takeuchi, 2009). Lean coaches usually have a long-term vision and near-unattainable goals (Lindeke, Wyrick and Chen, 2009), obtain trust and respect from their employees by practising what they preach (Adler, 1993), and show respect (Takeuchi, 2009). Besides these, CIMC's leaders also have three other characteristics: (1) a high degree of identification with a corporate mission. Similar to many entrepreneurs around 1990, the initial group of CIMC leaders had a shared vision, "Make Chinese manufacturing industry great." This belief was a special power for Chinese entrepreneurs, motivating them to work hard due to the national sentiment, (2) key positions carried out over a long term. Mr. Mai himself and the top managers remained in the decision-making positions for a long time starting from their early years, which made CIMC's management system more coherent, and (3) recognizing the position and value of female executives. Simon (2009) found it interesting that women usually took an important role in the hidden champion companies. We can also find this phenomenon in the growth of CIMC. For example, the effort of Lian Zhou enabled CIMC leaders to recognise what a world-class enterprise's human resource management system looks like. Xiaokui Liu, who had been pregnant at the beginning of the project, led CIMC into the modular building market of Australia. The strength of female leaders manifests in their performance in many ways, such as better emotional expression, greater patience in difficult negotiations.

6.4.3. *Collaborative networks and organisational structure of innovation*

An important way to achieve the hidden champion status is to merge with other leading companies in Europe and the United States (Simon, 2009). However, post-investment management and integration are even more difficult for any company. The method followed by CIMC to settle this problem is to make every single subsidiary company become the champion. In the "Building Champion Product" project kick-off meeting in 2018, CIMC put forward the "Big Platform + Small Army Group" plan. As shown in Figure 6.6, a three-level R&D system was developed under this method. This decentralised organisational structure and independent business departments strengthen the relationship between CIMC and customers. Additionally, the scale effect and resource advantage make it easier to reach the advanced technology as a whole group. "The cooperation among

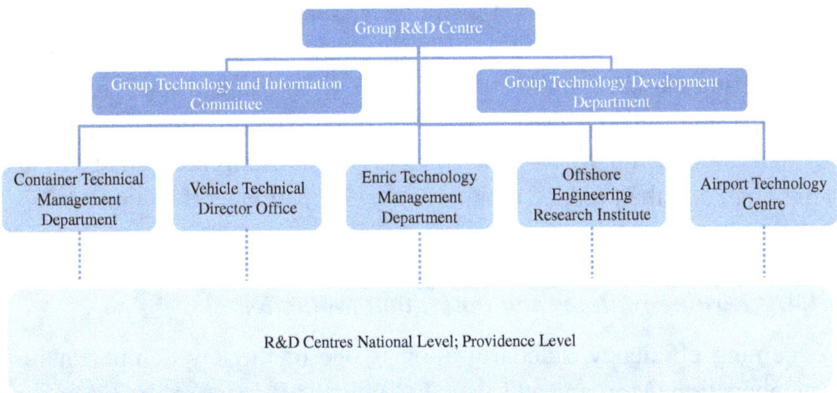

Fig. 6.6. Organisational structure of CIMC's three-level R&D System.

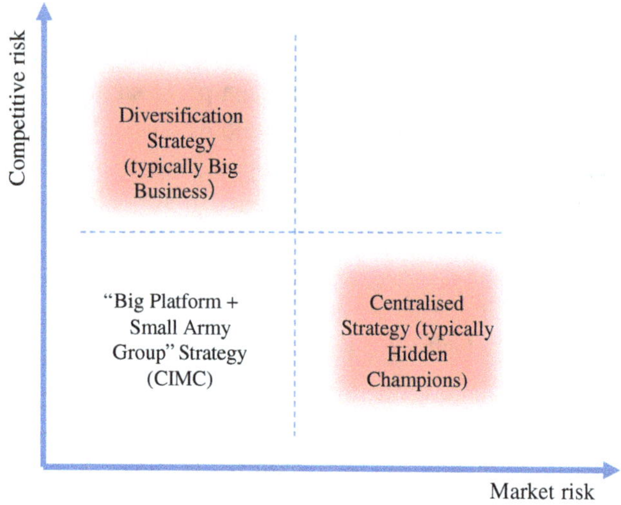

Fig. 6.7. Competitive risk versus market risk.

different modules would not be forced for unification just because of the group's organisational structure, it should respect the market rules," said a manager of CIMC.

The risk for a company can be classified according to its sources, that of market and competitors. For a typically hidden champion, the danger of "putting all eggs in one basket" is obvious. A company with such a high market share as the hidden champion will inevitably fall into a huge dilemma when its core market encounters catastrophic changes. In comparison, a big company with a diversification strategy has more choices encountering market changes, while its risk from competitors is relatively higher (Simon, 2009). CIMC's "Big Platform + Small Army Group" strategy makes the company own the flexibility and resource advantage at the same time, and then reduce the market or competitive risk (Figure 6.7).

6.4.4. *Learning routines and innovation evaluation*

Concerning efficiency, standardisation is one of the key components of lean innovation (Morgan and Liker, 2020). It can help to free up resources,

Table 6.1. World champion products criterion.

<table>
<tr><th colspan="4">Acceptance Requirement</th></tr>
<tr><td colspan="4">Ranked among the top three in the global market, or the largest in the continent of the mainstream market.
Annual product sales ≥300 million.
The product is in the mature stage of the industry.</td></tr>
<tr><th>First-Level Index</th><th>Second-Level Index</th><th>Weight</th><th>Third-Level Index</th></tr>
<tr><td>Financial Dimension</td><td>Revenue
Gross profit rate</td><td>15%
25%</td><td>Annual sales
Annual gross profit rate</td></tr>
<tr><td>Brand Influence</td><td>Market Share</td><td>25%</td><td>Annual product market share
International ranking of annual product market share
Proportion of sales in mainstream regions</td></tr>
<tr><td>Technical Dimension</td><td>Technical advantage and outcomes</td><td>25%</td><td>Product core technology
Patents and achievements in the past 3 years (relevance, importance and technology source)</td></tr>
<tr><td>Corporate Management</td><td>Proportion of R&D expenditure
Project management</td><td>5%
5%</td><td>R&D expenditure as a percentage of sales proportion
Enterprise-management level evaluation or certification</td></tr>
<tr><td>Evaluation Results</td><td colspan="3">Level A (85 ≤ X ≤ 100)
Level B (75 ≤ X < 85)
Level C (85 ≤ X < 75)</td></tr>
</table>

which in turn are to be re-invested in creativity-demanding, non-repetitive, difficult to standardise activities (Sewing *et al.*, 2008). As shown in Table 6.1, CIMC has developed a complete criterion to evaluate world champion products, which has become an important reference for the champion products cultivation plan published by the Chinese government.

On August 27, 2009, CIMC launched the Executives Reserve Talent Management Committee. The criteria of the CIMC leadership and development plan were discussed and passed at the first meeting. The Group launched "Plan A" to foster business unit leaders and "Plans B & C" to cultivate business managers and functional managers, and the "internal coach plan" for the immediate supervisor for Plans A, B and C. The three plans, "sailing plan" and new manager training camp were integrated systemically to form an "intermediate leadership development plan" covering management at all levels.

6.4.5. *Employee appreciation and innovation process*

Mr. Mai doesn't worry about the turnover of new employees. "It is good for young people to look at the outside world. The employees who come back later can be more committed," he said. This reflects the confidence in CIMC's employee appreciation culture.

Dickson *et al.* (2009) define the people system as "designed to provide the tools for people to continually improve their work and add value to the product or service they are producing." To implement lean innovation on a long-term basis, employees have to be involved even if measures are reasonable (Schuh, 2006). Learning from the Toyota Production System (TPS), CIMC focused heavily on its human capital with the fundamental premise that employees are not just viewed as pairs of hands but as knowledge workers who accumulate *chie* — the wisdom of experience — on the company's front lines" (Takeuchi, 2009). On the one hand, the vision to become a market leader is motivating for employees. Like other hidden champions, CIMC usually uses some traditional values to motivate employees, such as hard work, careful selection, etc. "Joint business" was the core human resource principle of CIMC, which emphasises the connection between individual success and the development of the company. This idea appears to be the prioritisation of team interests over individual interests. On the other hand, CIMC put forward "Creativity time" (Creativity "*Gong Fu*" in Chinese, which refers to the skill that results from hard work and the cultivation of character) to encourage employees to challenge the status quo, even by voicing contrarian opinions if necessary. What's more, the company has also designed a reward mechanism for different types and levels of innovation. For example, the motivations for the development of champion products (Table 6.2).

Table 6.2. Champion products reward.

Champion Products Reward	
Bonus Incentive	Segmented bonus; performance incentive (10~30%), etc.
Honourary Incentive	Certificate issued by president; CIMC Champion Product Case Collection, etc.
Promotion Incentive	Professional Technical Level; Leadership Development Qualification, etc.

6.4.6. *Learning culture*

In 2005, the direct and indirect benefits contributed by the advice from the production line reached around 40 million dollars. Someone said that "CIMC has earned all the money they should earn by taking control of the cost and manufacturing process," it seemed that there has been no space left for CIMC to make progress. However, with the introduction of Optimisation Never Ending (ONE) system, described in what follows, nowadays the employees of CIMC can still deliver over 80,000 proposals every year. The improvement of CIMC seems endless. It should be noted that not limited to incremental innovation, CIMC's continuous improvement mindset can also enable firms to unlock radical innovation by a more effective reconfiguration and reallocation of existing resources (Bicen and Johnson, 2015).

Continuous improvement mindset is emphasised a lot in CIMC, which refers to a careless inner urge to strive for perfection, ingrained at an individual level. When you go to General Electric, you must talk about 6-sigma; when you go to United Technologies, you will talk about ACE (Achieving Competitive Excellence); when you go to Toyota, you will talk about Toyota Production System (TPS). "When people come to CIMC, what can we talk about?" To inspire the initiative of employees and build a characteristic learning atmosphere for CIMC, Fapei Wu, the vice president of CIMC, developed a platform where people could work independently to get paid, called "ONE mode." He thought, in the context of Chinese culture, people were more willing to become managers rather than being regulated as common employees. The ONE model allowed almost every employee to become a "change agent" and have a sense of "problem ownership," be willing to take responsibility and act autonomously. What's more, as Evans and Wolf (2005) figured out, lean innovation does not rely so much on traditional monetary "carrots" and control "sticks" to encourage engagement. CIMC also holds activities like the "Technology Festival" to inspire creativity. To make the process continuable in the long run, CIMC has developed a complete succession training system as well, including a series of workshops that aim to cultivate employee leadership.

6.4.7. *Glocalisation and global competence*

"Global cooperation, local wisdom" is the slogan for CIMC's glocalisation strategy and the experience of CIMC's global competence. For most hidden champions, globalisation does not develop gradually with time but manifests itself in the early stages of the company's development (Simon, 2009). As China's first batch of Sino-foreign joint ventures, CIMC had positioned its market in the world since its establishment. Its process of globalisation involves two stages (Liu and Yang, 2019). The first stage was from 1982 to 2002, named "Made in China, sells globally" The main product was containers, 80% of which were sold abroad. The second stage was from 2004 to 2018, named "Global mergers and acquisitions, global operations, local wisdom." At this stage, its products have expanded to the fields of vehicles, energy, chemicals and airports, among which 40% of CIMC's products are manufactured overseas.

Glocalisation means that the standardisation versus the adaptation, and the homogenisation versus the tailoring, of companies' business activities are optimised to achieve harmony and balance (Svensson, 2001). It is exactly the strategy of CIMC to establish its leadership position around the world. For example, in the case of the merger and acquisition of Ziegler, a German fire rescue equipment company with a history of more than 120 years, CIMC only appointed one manager, Mr. Luan, to implement related business. With the support of CIMC's platform, resources and proper coordination of corporate culture, a new model was developed, that of "German R&D, global sales, and distributed manufacturing units (Germany, Croatia, China's Sichuan, Shenyang and Shanghai)." Ziegler had turned losses into profits in the first year and achieved an annual growth of 30% in sales and profits within 5 years, with an average of 20 patents annually, and a 50% increase in production efficiency.

6.5. Challenges and Prospect of CIMC Innovation Management

The export value of most countries is positively correlated with the number of large companies. Only Germany and China are exceptions, where the share of export value is much higher than that of countries with similar numbers of large companies. The development of the national manufacturing industry should be attributed to great enterprises like CIMC. For the last several decades, the company has maintained a high level of creativity and produced a series of Champion Products with the Lean Innovation method and "World-Class Champion" strategy. The success of CIMC's innovation is the consequence of continuous improvement and the pursuit of details, rather than the disruptive breakthrough, which could be leveraged into other firms' practice around the world to foster innovation and build up their own competitive advantage, or the so-called "World-Class Champion Enterprise that Can Be Copied" (Zheng, 2012).

However, CIMC also faces many challenges today regarding its long-term sustainable innovation development. The first one is the possibility and tendency of deglobalisation. So far, our discussions and reviews are based on a peaceful development environment, the same as other companies' innovation environments. The prospect for the development of globalisation that we describe is an optimistic picture, while it should be noted that the major premise for the picture is that trade can flow freely without hindrance (Simon, 2009). Voices against globalisation have risen significantly in the past few years, especially since the China–US started a new "trade war" in 2018 and the global pandemic caused by COVID-19. Populism lurking in protectionism is most dangerous and politicians tend to use it to please voters. The COVID-19 pandemic made it even worse for the sustainability of the global value chain and the free market. These elements will certainly cause serious damage to worldwide hidden champions, of course including CIMC.

The second challenge comes from the national market. Former Australian Prime Minister Paul Keating once gave an instructive interpretation of the relationship between population growth and the process of globalisation: For more than two centuries, Western countries' productivity has severed the traditional relationship between population and GDP. Globalisation made productivity more even. Therefore, countries with population advantages will benefit more from globalisation, and the world will become more just and fair as a result (Buchsteine, 2012). During the past decades, China was definitely one of the biggest winners in the process of globalisation. However, in the foreseeable future, China's demographic dividend is disappearing. According to the population forecast of the United Nations, from 2010 to 2050, China's population will experience the smallest change, almost the same as it is now (Li *et al.*, 2009), and China is entering into the stage of an ageing economy. Under this condition, the original advantage from the cheap labour force will transfer to other countries and the domestic demand will also be limited in a certain perspective. What's more, the impact of the COVID-19 pandemic, the uncertainty caused by environmental issues, human rights problems, and so on, frequently remind us that we are in a more and more "VUCA" (volatility, uncertainty, complexity, ambiguity) world (Bennett and Lemoine, 2014). In the future, the cultivation of organisational resilience will be more and more critical for a large-scale company's survival and sustainable innovation development, such as CIMC (Kantur and Iseri-Say, 2012). This would be an emerging and important topic for not only CIMC but also all the firms who want to leap forward in the post-COVID-19 pandemic world.

Acknowledgements

The authors would like to thank the interviewees from CIMC, the editors and the anonymous referees of this book for their constructive comments and feedbacks. The authors acknowledge the support from the National Science Foundation of China (Project No. 72104027) and National Postdoctoral Science Foundation of China (Project No. 2021M690388).

References

Adler, P. S. (1993). Time-and-motion regained. *Harvard Business Review*, *71*(1), 97–108.

Bennett, N. and Lemoine, G. J. (2014). What a difference a word makes: Understanding threats to performance in a VUCA world. *Business Horizons*, *57*(3), 311–317.

Bicen, P. and Johnson, W. H. (2015). Radical innovation with limited resources in high-turbulent markets: The role of lean innovation capability. *Creativity Innovation Management*, *24*(2), 278–299.

Boehm, E. (2012). Improving efficiency and effectiveness in an automotive R&D organization. *Research-Technology Management*, *55*(2), 18–25.

Buchsteine, V. J. (2012). *Australiens Helmut Schmidt*. Frankfurter Allgemeine Zeitung.

Dickson, E. W., Anguelov, Z., Vetterick, D., Eller, A. and Singh, S. (2009). Use of lean in the emergency department: A case series of 4 hospitals. *Annals of Emergency Medicine*, *54*(4), 504–510.

Evans, P. and Wolf, B. (2005). Collaboration rules. *IEEE Engineering Management Review*, *33*(4), 50–57.

ISO (2019). *ISO 56002:2019 Innovation management — Innovation management system — Guidance standard*. International Organization for Standardization.

Kantur, D. and Iseri-Say, A. (2012). Organizational resilience: A conceptual integrative framework. *Journal of Management Organization*, *18*(6), 762–773.

Li, Q., Reuser, M., Kraus, C. and Alho, J. (2009). Ageing of a giant: A stochastic population forecast for China, 2006–2060. *Journal of Population Research*, *26*(1), 21–50.

Lindeke, R. R., Wyrick, D. A. and Chen, H. (2009). Creating change and driving innovation in highly automated and lean organizations: The Temporal Think Tank™(T3™). *Robotics Computer-Integrated Manufacturing*, *25*(6), 879–887.

Liu, C. and Yang, Y. (2019). Eight key elements to build a world champion product group. *Tsinghua Business Review*, (4).

Morgan, J. and Liker, J. K. (2020). *The Toyota Product Development System: Integrating People, Process, And Technology*. CRC Press, New York.

Page, S. E. (2006). Path dependence. *Quarterly Journal of Political Science*, *1*(1), 87–115.

Ringel, M., Taylor, A. and Zablit, H. (2015). The most innovative companies 2015, https://media-publications.bcg.com/MIC/BCG-Most-Innovative-Companies-2015-Nov-2015.pdf.

Schuh, G. (2006). *Change Management-Prozesse strategiekonform gestalten*. Springer, Berlin, Heidelberg.

Sehested, C. and Sonnenberg, H. (2010). *Lean Innovation: A Fast Path from Knowledge to Value*. Springer Science & Business Media, Heidelberg.

Sewing, A., Winchester, T., Carnell, P., Hampton, D. and Keighley, W. (2008). Helping science to succeed: Improving processes in R&D. *Drug Discovery Today*, *13*(5–6), 227–233.

Simon, H. (2009). *Hidden Champions of the Twenty-First Century: The Success Strategies of Unknown World Market Leaders*. Springer Science & Business Media, New York.

Solaimani, S., Talab, A. H. and van der Rhee, B. (2019). An integrative view on Lean innovation management. *Journal of Business Research*, *105*, 109–120.

Solaimani, S., van der Veen, J., Sobek II, D. K., Gulyaz, E. and Venugopal, V. (2019). On the application of Lean principles and practices to innovation management. *The TQM Journal*, *31*(6), 1064–1092.

Svensson, G. (2001). "Glocalization" of business activities: A "glocal strategy" approach. *Management Decision*, *39*(1), 6–18.

Takeuchi, H. (2009). The contradictions that drive Toyota s success. *Strategic direction*, *25*(1).

Zheng, X. (2012). *A World-Class Champion Enterprise that Can Be Copied*. China Machine Press, Beijing.

© 2023 World Scientific Publishing Europe Ltd.
https://doi.org/10.1142/9781800612105_0007

Chapter 7

Evonik Industries AG: Capability Building for Strategic Innovation in the Innovation Management System

Jimmi Normann Kristiansen and Daniel Witthaut

Abstract

This chapter describes and analyses the journey of the development of an innovation management system at Evonik Industries, one of the world's leading companies in speciality chemicals. Evonik started a pilot for enhancing their innovation management system in 2013, focusing on the core area of augmenting the strategic innovation capability of the company. Through a series of intensive workshops and work with innovation opportunities carried out from September 2017 through February 2020, Evonik identified several specific, idiosyncratic areas related to business model option experimentation, business vision, stakeholder management and iterative learning from opportunities that were distinct from the incremental innovation project management. The case similarly aided understanding of how existing metrics and project evaluation systems within Evonik benefited from adjustments to secure a better fit with strategic innovation in the company. The case reveals and raises the question whether the innovation management system standard touches upon "one innovation management system" or comprises two subsystems, each optimised for incremental and strategic innovation, respectively.

7.1. Background

Headquartered in Essen, Germany, Evonik is one of the world leaders in speciality chemicals. The company is active in more than 100 countries around the world and generated sales of €12.2 billion and an operating profit (adjusted EBITDA) of €1.91 billion in 2020. Evonik has more than 33,000 employees. With innovation as a centrepiece, around 80% of Evonik's sales come from leading positions in different markets (Evonik, 2020a, 2020b). The expenditure on R&D is roughly €428 million (3.3%) (Evonik, 2020c). To focus innovation activities and ensure significant additional growth through innovation, in 2016 Evonik had introduced six growth fields with the aim of generating more than €1 billion in additional sales by 2025. The growth fields are:

- Sustainable Nutrition: "Establishing additional products and services for sustainable nutrition of livestock and people."
- Healthcare Solutions: "Developing new materials for implants, as components of cell culture media, and for custom-tailored, innovative drug formulations."
- Advanced Food Ingredients: "Creating a portfolio of health-enhancing substances and nutritional supplements as a contribution to healthy nutrition."
- Membranes: "Extending SEPURAN technology for efficient gas separation to further applications."
- Cosmetic Solutions: "Developing further products based on natural sources for cosmetics and sensorially optimised formulations for skin care products."
- Additive Manufacturing: "Developing products and technologies for additive manufacturing"

(Evonik, 2020d).

The growth fields are related to different operating segments (some growth fields have opportunities that go across segments) within:

- Nutrition & Care (primarily consumer goods, animal nutrition and healthcare).
- Smart Materials (high-performance materials for environment-friendly and energy-efficient systems such as paints, coatings, automotive, adhesives, construction and more).
- Speciality Additives (e.g., cross-linkers and additives for oil, coatings, polyurethanes and more)

(Evonik, 2020e).

In addition to the segments, Evonik has a strategic innovation unit, referred to as "Creavis," with the aim of incubating new businesses. With approximately 140 employees, Creavis is a catalyst working as the "front-end" of strategic innovation (also denounced adjacent, evolutionary, transformational), representing the above six growth fields in Evonik and developing future growth fields.

7.2. A Management System for Strategic Innovation

The focal point of this case is to highlight the development of a strategic innovation (also called radical, breakthrough, transformational, cf. Kristiansen, 2014) capability in the Evonik innovation management system.

Based on a pilot project done in Evonik in 2013, followed up by a series of workshops and discussions on strategic innovation, a group of external researchers, specialists and consultants started a comprehensive training and implementation programme on strategic innovation at Evonik in September 2017. The motivation for starting this programme was to support the journey of Evonik becoming even more efficient at managing strategic innovation opportunities in the organisation (Workshop 1, 2017). Working closely with corporate innovation at Evonik, the group followed a total of 11 strategic innovation opportunities[1] in the period from September 2017 to February 2020.

The onset of this case development was before the finalisation of the Innovation Management System document (ISO 56002: 2019 Innovation management — Innovation management system — Guidance). Hence, it was not part of the narrative that Evonik should "follow the standard," yet with the same intention to enhance the capability for strategic innovation within Evonik. As the work carried out at Evonik was in connection with the principles of the standard, the standard elements can thus be reflected

[1] The term opportunities in this respect both covers front-end as well as mature opportunities. This is done for ease of readability as "opportunities" have progressed over the course of the programme to become "projects" at a later stage.

on retrospectively with reference to the ISO 56002:2019 (ISO, 2019), and its ongoing elements.

For this chapter, the focal elements of the case relate to:

- How Evonik has worked with managing uncertainty (ISO 56002:2019 0.3.3).
- The Innovation Strategy and Structure in Evonik to enable strategic innovation management within the system (ISO 56002:2019 5.1.4; 6.3).
- The Strategic Innovation Process in Evonik (ISO 56002:2019 8.3).
- Performance Evaluation of Opportunities (ISO 56002:2019 9).

The aim of the case study is to discuss how Evonik Industries has improved its capability of strategic innovation in relation to the above parts of the innovation management system. In this respect, key learnings and challenges emerging as part of the case work will be discussed. Other points from the innovation management system standard will also be included where relevant yet related to the above four points for consistency.

7.2.1. *Brief on the methodology*

The present case has been developed through engaged scholarship (Van de Ven, 2007). The core emphasis is on summary case studies (Van de Ven, 2007), with samples concerning the following:

- Direct interaction with 11 strategic innovation opportunities in Evonik.
- Interaction with innovation leadership to discuss uncertainty management, process and evaluation.

As part of the above, the group held 12 two-day workshops spanning across different stages of the strategic innovation funnel (early-stage, mid-stage, development-stage, also called Discovery, Incubation and Acceleration, cf. O'Connor *et al.*, 2008, Leifer *et al.*, 2000). The opportunities moreover had different degrees of readiness across types of technical-, market-, resource- and organisation uncertainties.[2] The workshops were coupled with a total of 105 sessions with the respective innovation teams managing the 11 opportunities (mostly ranging between 1 hour for online sessions to 3–4 hour onsite sessions). Opportunities 1–6 were followed in between September 2017–September 2018, and opportunities 7–11 approximately from January 2019–February 2020. This allowed the team of researchers to get extensive insight into the process and strategic capability building within Evonik. Dialogue between the group and senior management (mainly SVP level) was held throughout the period to report on programme progress as well as address resource and organisation uncertainties.

7.3. Development of an Innovation Management System in Evonik

Based on the work that began with the external experts back in 2013, the comprehensive strategic innovation programme began in September 2017, when the first kick-off workshop was held. Most of the opportunities selected (opportunities 1; 3–6) were either in early- or mid-stage of development (Discovery or early Incubation). In this workshop, the focus was to discuss how to manage uncertainty (ISO 56002:2019 0.3.3, p. viii) and enhance the capability for managing the strategic innovation process (ISO 56002:2019 8.3, pp. 18–21).

As per the call to action from Evonik, it became clear that the process for incremental innovation was well-developed within the organisation (Workshop 1, 2017). Simultaneously, the onset revealed that the call to action set by Evonik — to further build the capability for strategic innovation management — was well justified. Just like other organisations, Evonik had refined over the years an effective internal system for managing the incremental innovation process, as well as the risks associated with incremental innovation management (Workshop 1, 2017). From discussions in several workshops, it became evident that the management system

---

[2]Evonik uses "Business Readiness Levels," inspired by the NASA technology readiness levels, to gauge progression of their opportunities.

for uncertainty-driven, strategic innovation had to be rethought. The challenges for the teams and the organisation were described as follows:

(1) How do we more effectively manage uncertainty in strategic innovation opportunities that are in our portfolio? (Workshop 1, 2017; cf. ISO 56002:2019 0.3.3).
(2) How should the process for strategic innovation management be different from managing incremental innovation? (Workshop 1, 2017; cf. ISO 56002:2019 8.3).
(3) How do we deal with performance evaluations and budget approvals for strategic innovation opportunities — where a major key performance indicator (KPI) currently is net present value? (Workshop 1, 2017; cf. ISO 56002:2019 9).
(4) How can we manage strategic innovation in the current structure of the organisation? (Workshop 1, 2017; cf. ISO 5002:2019 5.1.4; 6.3).

The four questions posed above turned out to be centrepieces for the enhancement of a strategic innovation capability in the Evonik Innovation Management System. As per the ISO 56002:2019, it is clear that the elements in the system are interlinked and should be aligned. An apparent example is if organisations are able to very effectively manage uncertainty in a bottom-up manner, with a well-defined process for strategic innovation (cf. Questions 1–2; ISO 56002:2019 0.3.3; ISO 56002:2019 8.3), yet at the same time have detrimental KPIs and organisational structures for strategic innovation (cf. Questions 3–4; cf. ISO 56002:2019 9; ISO 5002:2019 5.1.4; 6.3), progression will be thwarted (see also, Smith and Tushman, 2005; de Visser *et al.*, 2010; Braganza and Ward, 2001).

7.4. Implementation of the System Elements

Four questions will be discussed in two related groups. Questions 1 and 2 primarily concern the operations of "managing innovation" and how that level is structured within the organisation. Specifically, Section 7.4.1 will cover the first two questions related to uncertainty and process management.

Questions 3 and 4 primarily concern the "governance" of innovation in the innovation management system and will be discussed collectively.

Hence, Section 7.4.2 will cover topics related to key performance indicators (KPIs) as well as structural topics related to strategic innovation.

7.4.1. *Managing uncertain opportunities in a strategic innovation process*

In considering how to systematically address uncertainty in select strategic innovation opportunities in Evonik — it quickly became clear that established processes for incremental innovation were insufficient (based on participant feedback, cf. Workshop 1, 2017; interviews September 2017–February 2018). From the first workshop held with the participants in September 2017, to the second workshop held in December 2017 — 33 sessions were held with team members of opportunities 1; 3–6. Based on these discussions, the research group was looking to identify the most important topics for further discussion. Using thematic coding (Miles, Huberman and Saldaña, 2014) on extended summaries of each of the 33 sessions in between, we identified the topics that were mostly covered as part of the sessions. These topics are covered in Table 7.1 whereby:

- $N = 187$ equated to the number of times the theme was identified in the 33 sessions.
- Percent used as a proxy for how important the elements were.

The following will focus on the topics highlighted in bold.

In relation to the business model discussion for opportunities, extant, popular tools such as the Business Model Canvas (Osterwalder and Pigneur, 2013) required levels of details that many of the opportunities did not have yet. This suggested that tools in the organisation needed adaptation to fit with uncertain, strategic innovation opportunities (see also ISO 56002:2019, 7.6, p. 15). The teams worked with an options and uncertainty lens when identifying business model options based on technical, market, resource, and organisation considerations. Concurrently, the tools and methods used for different types of innovation (incremental and strategic) needed to be fitted to the context.

Another important aspect relates to the vision of the business each of opportunities should deliver in the future. Several teams were used to

Table 7.1. Topics covered in the 33 sessions between workshops 1 and 2.*

Theme (Ranked Based on # of Mentions)	Percent (N = 187)
Business Model Options	**18%**
Business Vision	**16%**
Stakeholder Management	**11%**
Iterative Learning	**11%**
Partnering	9%
Learning Prototype	7%
Resource Availability (Internal)	5%
Other: Including opportunity pacing, regulatory and IP, coaching roles, project termination procedures, organisational setup…	23%
	100%

Notes: *These have been coded based on executive summaries of the sessions. Topics are expressions of the frequency of which they came up in the dialogue with people working on strategic innovation opportunities in Evonik. It is used as a simple proxy for their relevance. Own composition based on executive summaries from 33 sessions between September 24, 2017–December 4, 2017. Topics turned out to be important throughout the 2.5-year training programme.

working systematically with incremental innovation, in which elements such as planning horizons and milestones were important (ISO 56002:2019, 6.2.2, p. 9). In their work with strategic innovation, it became apparent to many of the teams that: (a) it was extremely difficult to set traditional project milestones (in terms of delivery) and (b) the project milestones would change over time. This can be particularly attributed to a core difference in managing goals (causation) versus means (effectuation) (Sarasvathy, 2008). Along with the research group, the teams discussed the need for a "bigger plan" with strategic innovation. In essence, this implied a vision for where the opportunities wanted to build a business in the future, and identifying steppingstones for how smaller elements, or single applications, within the project could lay the groundwork for the future.

The stakeholder management element referred to how the project teams would have a conversation about strategic innovation with senior stakeholders. As for many other companies having a systematic approach to innovation, there were portfolio- and strategy meetings overseeing and reviewing the progression of opportunities. In this respect, opportunity leads needed to navigate in their innovation management system by communicating the value of their opportunities, without necessarily having a project net present value, expected commercial value, or other metric, often used by portfolio managers (Kristiansen and Ritala, 2018). In this perspective, understanding how to manage different stakeholders in the organisation and building support for strategic innovation opportunities within the innovation management system were a struggle and a core point of interest to the opportunity managers. This pertains particularly to the importance, and variance, of communication relevant to the innovation management system when dealing with different types of innovation (ISO 56002:2019, 7.4, p. 14).

The final point highlighted in the dialogue were related to teams working on iterative Learning Plans, rather than milestone plans as part of their work with strategic innovation (see e.g., ISO 56002:2019, 0.3.3, p. viii). For internal work purposes, the teams had actively produced learning sprints, which directed their learning in shorter cycles, rather than setting longer milestone plans. This entailed a learning-driven versus solution-driven approach that was more commonplace for incremental innovation projects. It highlighted a significantly different way of working with opportunities than from established projects. The Learning Plan tool was designed for identifying and reducing uncertainty (Rice, O'Connor and Pierantozzi, 2008), and turned out to be a core element in the work with strategic innovation opportunities in Evonik.

Barriers and challenges for implementation of uncertainty management and strategic innovation processes

Throughout the work with Evonik, it has become apparent that having a one-size-fits-all approach to the innovation management process is inexpedient. Reflecting on the innovation management system standard (ISO 56002:2019), a key learning from the Evonik case is thus that the process, methodology and tools relevant for strategic innovation differ from that of incremental innovation.

With many large corporations building on their past successes, they have become increasingly adept at operational excellence and development (i.e., continuous improvement and incremental innovation) with processes, tools, methodologies very suitable for efficiently developing improved product and/or service offerings for the market. For strategic innovation, a lot of the activities mimic those of entrepreneurship (Lassen, Gertsen and Riis, 2006). Managing core business and entrepreneurial activities simultaneously inherently lead to organisational challenges.

This should not be attributed to the failings of managers and stakeholders who are very qualified and successful in the right roles. Rather, building success in an ongoing operational excellence and development environment, and in a more entrepreneurial, corporate innovation one, are two different worlds (Kristiansen, 2018). In following Evonik's enhancement of their strategic innovation capability, the notion of having the right organisational structure to handle exploration and experimentation, on the one hand, and development, deployment and efficiency, on the the other, were of high relevance to the evolution of its innovation management system (see ISO: 56002, 6.2.2). This will be further elaborated in the next section.

7.4.2. *Organisational structure and performance evaluations*

For strategic innovation, Evonik has supported their activities through the operating segments as well as within their strategic innovation unit, Creavis. In parallel to developing a process for managing uncertain, strategic innovation opportunities within Evonik, there was also a discussion of governance for strategic innovation. In this respect, governance implied the organisational structure as well as how performance evaluations of opportunities should be handled for strategic innovation.

While a governance model was set in the context of Creavis, Evonik still needed to elaborate and discuss governance of strategic innovation within segments — where the structure was primarily geared for incremental innovation. Similarly to insights in previous research (Slater, Mohr and Sengupta, 2014), senior leadership had a key impact on elements that affected the strategic innovation capability of the organisation (e.g., the structure and performance metrics). At the beginning of the strategic innovation programme, Evonik wanted to determine how the organisation could change elements of setting up a better structure for strategic innovation (e.g., surroundings, meetings, reporting structure that would enable the strategic innovation process) as well as suggest key performance or achievement indicators that would be suitable for evaluations of strategic innovation opportunities. In this respect, it was — and still is — a balancing act of how tightly coupled strategic innovation opportunities should be with the core organisation (O'Connor *et al.*, 2008).

For implementation of structure, the segments had a great deal of influence on how they wanted to set it up. This also implied that some segments had more significant changes in terms of reporting, resource fluidity, meeting structures, etc. than others. A major explanatory factor for this was that many of the segments sponsored the opportunities, and they accentuated that they knew which models were best for their own opportunities. While this line of argumentation makes good sense from a segment perspective, it simultaneously holds challenges for the innovation management system as a whole. It implies that structures for strategic innovation in Evonik would vary from segment to segment, among which Evonik is aware that cross-segment opportunities would require careful alignment.

A new set of metrics suitable for strategic innovation was also discussed. This included a set of forward-looking, process-oriented indicators due to the uncertain nature of strategic innovation. The group discussed how Evonik could measure progression across different dimensions of uncertainty (technical-, market-, resource- and organisation) (O'Connor and Rice, 2013) while simultaneously monitoring resource spend on the opportunities. The metrics have been gradually implemented at the discretion of the segment leadership in Evonik.

Revelations in the strategic innovation management journey

The work Evonik has undertaken with enhancing its strategic (transformational) innovation capability has led to a significant revelation of key areas important for strategic innovation success:

- It was clear that the innovation management system for incremental innovation was working very well. Evonik has custom-tailored phase-gated processes that enables them to meet customer needs with great success.

- Initially, the methodology, tools and mindset from phase-gated initiatives were applied for strategic innovation. Evonik realised that this showed a lack of efficiency for strategic innovation, which was why Evonik implemented DIA (Discovery, Incubation and Acceleration) for handling strategic innovation.
- The case revealed that it was important to accentuate, and actively work with, higher degrees of uncertainty. Acknowledging this in the organisation was a big step for managing innovation.
- This paved the way for the acknowledgement from business leadership that strategic innovations should be managed in a different way; a good basis for the uncertainty management dialogue within Evonik.

Going forward, Evonik has developed the foundation for more efficiently managing strategic innovation.

With reference to the ISO Innovation Management System standard, it was discussed how an innovation management system can gradually be implemented and which elements would be most important to focus on first.

How do we continuously optimise and align the role of Creavis, the strategic innovation unit, to meet industry and organisational needs? There are still strategic innovation activities taking place in other parts of Evonik than Creavis, and a core question is how to simultaneously ring-fence activities that make sense in segments, while focusing on bundling activities with Creavis.

This gives food for thought for the innovation management system standard. Will corporations implement an "entire" innovation management system or rather subsystems (e.g., one for incremental innovation and one for strategic innovation) that are interrelated? How do we set up organisational boundaries (i.e., where is strategic and where is incremental innovation handled in the organisation) in the innovation management system going forward, and should we?

Without a doubt, Evonik has come a long way in the transformational innovation journey (Wojciechowski *et al.*, 2019), and it will be exciting to see and also discuss how the innovation management system standard is rolled out in organisations in the future.

7.5. Achievements of the Innovation Management System

From the initial assessment of Evonik's innovation management system, which took place in 2016, and the group's observations in the period between September 2017 and February 2020, and additional workshops in November/December 2020, the comments on the achievements of a strategic innovation capability development in the Evonik innovation management system are as follows:

- Direct training and coaching of 40+ people in managing strategic innovation opportunities.
- Important discussions about the language of innovation at Evonik, clearly distinguishing incremental from strategic innovation in terms of methodologies needed (Kuesthardt, 2019).
- Multiple opportunities applying suitable strategic innovation methodologies in the innovation management system (Kuesthardt, 2019).
- Implementation of metrics suitable for strategic innovation in select areas of Evonik.
- Increased senior leadership involvement at Creavis — the strategic innovation hub at Evonik (Evonik workshop, December 2020).

Continuing the transformation journey to build a better capability for strategic innovation in Evonik, stakeholders as well as senior leadership are aware that there are still elements to be developed going forward. These will be discussed in the following.

7.6. Overall Reflections and Way Forward

Building a dual set of capabilities for incremental and strategic innovation management within the same innovation management system is difficult. It raises questions as to whether it is one management system or two subsystems that are interlinked. Additionally, it needs to be further revealed whether the innovation management systems for incremental and strategic innovation are diametrically opposed to be considered as one system. While the ISO 56002:2019 standard identifies relevant elements to be considered when building an innovation management system, there are significant differences in what is needed for incremental and strategic (radical) innovation within the system. Paradoxically, a well-built strong innovation management system for incremental innovation may hinder the development of strategic innovation capability development within that same system (due to a potential misuse of processes, tools, etc.). This was indicated by the case from the need to apply distinct tools and processes for strategic innovation, as well as rethinking evaluation techniques and budgeting approval processes for strategic innovation. Moreover, this is also indicated through the development and enhancement of Creavis, allowing arms-length between strategic innovation initiatives where needed, until ready to be gauged in the core organisation. This also builds on a classical discussion of ambidexterity, and implications hereof (March, 1991). In this respect, it becomes critical that top management is aware that the methodology, tools, structure, processes and metrics for strategic innovation are fittingly developed. Conclusively, organisations wishing to implement the innovation management system standard — guidance (ISO 56002:2019) — should be vigilant as to how that system is tailored to work both with exploration and exploitation of innovation (March, 1991).

7.7. Summary

This case study discusses the development of a strategic innovation capability within the innovation management system of Evonik Industries, a global leader in speciality chemicals. This case has been written to highlight the importance of building an innovation management system that is able to simultaneously host incremental and strategic (radical) innovation activities.

It shows that the structure, metrics, processes in the organisation for managing uncertain, strategic innovation are different from the same elements for incremental innovation.

The key elements addressed in the case relate to (Table 7.2).

Evonik has addressed these questions through a dedicated and active journey since the early pilot in 2013, an understanding of elements within the innovation management system in 2016, through a training programme on strategic innovation from September 2017 — December 2020. This case covers that journey on the above four elements and discusses overall reflections and key learnings for innovation management system implementation in organisations.

Table 7.2. Questions with case learnings.

Question	Answer
How do we more effectively manage uncertainty in strategic innovation opportunities that are in our portfolio? (ISO 56002:2019 0.3.3)	In the Evonik case, it was shown that it required a dual yet complementary approach for incremental and strategic innovation, respectively
How should the process for strategic innovation management be different from managing incremental innovation? (ISO 56002:2019 8.3)	Evonik adopted and developed a new mindset, processes and tools within Discovery, Incubation and Acceleration for strategic innovation
How do we deal with performance evaluations and budget approvals for strategic innovation opportunities — where a major KPI now is net present value? (ISO 56002:2019 9)	Evonik is gradually adjusting more process-oriented metrics focusing on value creation first, then value capture and monetisation over the longer term for strategic innovation
How can we manage strategic innovation in the current structure of the organisation? (ISO 5002:2019 5.1.4; 6.3)	It requires a separate, yet interlinked structure, methods, tools and processes with Creavis as the main strategic innovation unit for implementation

Acknowledgements

We acknowledge the hard and dedicated efforts of all people taking part in the Evonik transformational innovation journey.

For this chapter, a special thanks goes out to Joanne Hyland, for additional details and feedback in developing the chapter.

References

Braganza, A. and Ward, J. (2001). Implementing strategic innovation: Supporting people over the design and implementation boundary. *Strategic Change*, *10*(2), 103–113.

de Visser, M., de Weerd-Nederhof, P., Faems, D., Song, M., van Looy, B. and Visscher, K. (2010). Structural ambidexterity in NPD processes: A firm-level assessment of the impact of differentiated structures on innovation performance. *Technovation*, *30*(5–6), 291–299.

Evonik (2015). *Evonik to Invest over €4 Billion in Research and Development,* https://corporate.evonik.cn/en/media/news/evonik-to-invest-over-4-billion-in-research-and-development-104256.html.

Evonik (2020a). *Company Portrait — Evonik at a Glance*, https://corporate.evonik.com/en/media/evonik-at-a-glance-618.html.

Evonik (2020b). *Evonik — Leading Beyond Chemistry*, https://corporate.evonik.com/en/company.

Evonik (2020c). *Invest in the Future — Facts & Figures*, https://corporate.evonik.com/en/company/research-development/facts-and-figures-112841.html.

Evonik (2020d). *Setting Course for the Future — Growth Fields*, https://corporate.evonik.com/en/company/research-development/growth-fields-112835.html.

Evonik (2020e). *Speciality Chemicals — Operative Segments*, https://central-south-america.evonik.com/en/company/evonik-industries/profile.

ISO (2019). *ISO 56002:2019 Innovation management — Innovation management system — Guidance.* International Organization for Standardization.

Kristiansen, J. N. (2014). *Managing Radical Innovation Projects: Understanding Competency Building in a Complex Discipline*. Aalborg University Press, Aalborg, 2014, p. 271.

Kristiansen, J. N. (2018). *Top Management Mental Models and Radical Innovation*. Presented at The ISPIM Innovation Conference — Innovation, The Name of The Game, Stockholm, Sweden, 17–20 June 2018.

Kristiansen, J. N. and Ritala, P. (2018). Measuring radical innovation project success: Typical metrics don't work. *Journal of Business Strategy*, *39*(4), 34–41.

Kuesthardt, U. (2019). *Strive to be "Leading in Innovation." Morgan Stanley Innovation Call*, https://corporate.evonik.com/Downloads/Corporate/IR/190715%20MS%20Innovation%20Call.pdf.

Lassen, A. H., Gertsen, F. and Riis, J. O. (2006). The Nexus of Corporate Entrepreneurship and Radical Innovation. *Creativity and Innovation Management*, *15*(4), 359–372

Leifer, R., McDermott, C. M., O'Connor, G. C., Peters, L. S., Rice, M. and Veryzer, R. W. (2000). *Radical Innovation: How Mature Companies can Outsmart Upstarts*. Boston, MA: Harvard Business School Press.

March, J. G. (1991). Exploration and exploitation in organizational learning. *Organization Science*, *2*(1), 71–87.

Miles, M. B., Huberman, M. and Saldaña, J. (2014). *Qualitative Data Analysis: A Methods Sourcebook* (3rd edn.). Thousand Oaks, CA: Sage Publications.

O'Connor, G. C. and Rice, M. P. (2013). A comprehensive model of uncertainty associated with radical innovation. *Journal of Product Innovation Management*, *30*(1), 2–18.

O'Connor, G. C., Leifer, R., Paulson, A. S. and Peters, L. S. (2008). *Grabbing Lightning: Building a Capability for Breakthrough Innovation*. San Francisco, CA: Wiley & Sons.

Osterwalder, A. and Pigneur, Y. (2013). *Business Model Generation*. Hoboken, NJ: Wiley.

Rice, M. P., O'Connor, G. C. and Pierantozzi, R. (2008). Implementing a learning plan to counter project uncertainty. *MIT Sloan Management Review*, *49*(2), 54–62.

Sarasvathy, S. D. (2008). *Effectuation: Elements of Entrepreneurial Expertise*. Northampton: Edward Elgar.

Slater, S. F., Mohr, J. J. and Sengupta, S. (2014). Radical product innovation capability: Literature review, synthesis, and illustrative research propositions. *Journal of Product Innovation Management*, *31*(3), 552–566.

Smith, W. K. and Tushman, M. L. (2005). Managing strategic contradictions: A top management model for managing innovation streams. *Organization Science*, *16*(5), 522–536.

Van de Ven, A. H. (2007). Designing process studies. In Van de Ven, A. H. (ed.), *Engaged Scholarship: A Guide for Organizational and Social Research*. Oxford University Press, Oxford.

Wojciechowski, A., Becker, B., Kirchner, M. and Kreidler, B. (2019). Implementation of sustainability in innovation management: The Idea to People, Planet And Profit (I2P3®) Process. *Journal of Business Chemistry*, 2019(1) — *Practitioner's Section*, 26–40.

Workshop 1 (2017). (Based on notes from workshop).

© 2023 World Scientific Publishing Europe Ltd.
https://doi.org/10.1142/9781800612105_0008

Chapter 8

Humanitarian Innovation Fund: Managing Innovation in Humanitarian Aid

John Bessant

Abstract

The humanitarian sector is characterised by an extreme innovation challenge. Under disaster conditions there is an urgent need for problem solving and normal solution pathways may be blocked off; much depends on finding new ways to deal with the crisis. Yet, although innovation has been a core feature of the sector it is only recently that thinking has moved towards how it might be managed more systematically and in particular how learning about good practice might be exchanged across the sector. This case study explores the context for humanitarian innovation (HI) and looks at the emergence of a system level model for managing it in systematic fashion. Based on the experiences of humanitarian innovation, this reinforces that taking a more systemic and systematic approach would pay dividends in terms of more effective innovation processes. It highlights the specific issues in this context and the value of generic frameworks which might enable cross-sector learning around good innovation management practices. Finally, the discussion suggests that there are promising signs that a more strategic approach is being taken, informed by a well-developed understanding of innovation.

8.1. Introduction

A powerful metaphor often used in the context of innovation is that it relates to survival, but in the context of humanitarian aid it takes on a very literal meaning. Crises, whether natural or man-made, require rapid problem solving, if agencies and aid workers are to avoid the huge negative impacts of such disasters. For this reason, the issue of "innovation management" is one of central importance in the sector. How can the humanitarian sector best organise to enable innovation and what are the roles for key actors — donors, agencies and most importantly "users"? This chapter summarises the nature of the challenge and reviews experience so far in humanitarian innovation (HI). In particular, it looks at the growing interest in taking a more systemic and systematic approach to managing innovation.

8.1.1. *Origins of HI*

The idea of HI is not new. Back in 1867, Henry Dunant proposed the idea of a supportive infrastructure, asking "*...would it not be possible, in time of peace and quiet, to form relief societies for the purpose of having care given to the wounded in wartime by zealous, devoted and thoroughly qualified volunteers?*"

His idea led to the founding of the International Federation of Red Cross and Red Crescent Societies and through agencies like these, the humanitarian sector has developed. It is important however, to recognise that there is a blurred line between "HI" (primarily targeted at acute disaster-related contexts) and the broader "development" agenda where concern is for long-term improvement of living standards.

8.1.2. *The nature of HI today*

HI is typically underpinned by a sense of urgency: "*...nearly 150 million people were affected by a combination of natural disasters, wars and conflicts in 2013, and the number of people needing assistance as a result has more than doubled over the last decade.*" (UNOCHA, 2015). However, according to Obrecht and Warner "*many emergencies are also protracted and complex with more social and political barriers to access humanitarian assistance combined with an increasing range of needs*" (Obrecht and Warner, 2016). As the nature of emergencies changes, so the underlying "business models" for humanitarian action may also be challenged bringing about changes in HI accordingly (Ramalingam, Scriven, and Foley, 2010).

Within the sector, HI is usually discussed in the context of five major challenges: food supply; nutrition; WASH (water, sanitation and hygiene); shelter and healthcare. Examples of HI range widely under these categories — from badges that clearly identify humanitarian volunteers in battle to satellite imagery for crisis management; from cash-based programming to the invention of Plumpy'Nut peanut paste to treat malnourished children (Obrecht and Warner, 2016).

8.1.3. *Growing interest in HI*

Until recently HI activity took place in a responsive mode, often on an *ad hoc* basis; the focus was on the innovations themselves rather than looking for an underlying process that could be mobilised to generate a steady stream of solutions and enable learning between projects (Betts and Bloom, 2014). As such, only a small number of organisations had invested in innovation capacity (for example, Oxfam and Médecins Sans Frontières (MSF) and water, sanitation and hygiene (WASH) or medicine or UNICEF's technology-focused innovation teams).

A key turning point was a study carried out in 2009 by ALNAP (the Action Learning Network for Accountability and Performance in the humanitarian sector), which developed an HI definition and framework, drawing on a series of case studies and building on relevant literature (Ramalingam, Scriven, and Foley, 2010). This triggered a growing interest and led to a variety of policy actions. For example, the UK Department for International Development (DFID) funded £3 million for exploration in HI practices and the UN Office for the Coordination of Humanitarian Affairs (OCHA) began to focus on innovation as a core workstream (Betts and Bloom, 2014).

In the UK the Humanitarian Innovation Fund (HIF) was established in 2010, initially to provide early stage "venture capital" to promote innovation projects but also for capacity building around innovation management. Its role has expanded in recent years with more emphasis on the challenges of moving innovations to scale as well as funding promising pilots. Between 2010 and 2016 the HIF granted over £6M to fund 68 projects (Lauday, Foley, and Poulson, 2017).

Although the sector is becoming more innovation focused, paying attention to the phenomenon, the interest has still been mainly on the innovations themselves rather than the process whereby they are organised and managed. For example, the 2016 United Nations World Humanitarian Summit identified "Innovation" as one of the four key themes, thus funding increased substantially: through traditional channels with bilateral donors and through novel mechanisms within agencies as organisational innovation funds and labs. But these initiatives and funds are focused on the development of the products or services themselves and not on the process of managing the development and delivery of these innovations.

Increasing policy interest in HI has triggered a corresponding increase in research on the topic; a systematic literature review of the relevant journals in the field, carried out by Ramalingam *et al.* (2015), identified that innovation is now cited extensively in the two leading journals dealing with humanitarian aid [*Disaster* and *Journal of Humanitarian Assistance*]. However, once again the coverage is primarily concerned with the innovations themselves; the term "innovation management" is entirely excluded. There are a few exceptions; some journals (for example, the *Journal of Humanitarian Logistics and Supply Chain Management*) offer coverage of operations and process innovation and some of these touch upon how innovation takes place.

8.1.4. *Focus on innovation management*

As suggested above, although HI has always taken place there has been little formal attention paid to how it might be organised and managed until comparatively recently. The 2009 ALNAP study attempted a definition and offered a suggested framework for HI, drawing on a series of case studies as illustrations and building on relevant literature (Ramalingam, Scriven, and Foley, 2010). That study closed with a framework for HI and an outline process model to help guide funding and review.

Part of the problem is in the nature of HI — by its nature it is crisis-driven. There is an apparent paradox in trying to take a systematic routines-based approach (as might be the case in the commercial world) when the challenges are unexpected, and uncertainty is high. Nonetheless, there has been some progress in the past 5 years towards a process orientation and within that to exploring how well innovation might be managed and how it could benefit from good practices elsewhere.

Some of this sharpening of the focus has come around highlighting key areas or practice; an example is the Humanitarian Emergency Response Review of the UK Government's aid efforts. HI research involves multiple themes — for example, the University of Oxford's Humanitarian Innovation Project (OxHIP) highlights the need for more bottom-up, user-driven innovation, especially among refugee groups. MSF takes a sectoral perspective in their review of medical innovations.

Other indicators of this expansion of interest have been the proliferation of job titles like "Innovation Manager" and "Chief Innovation Officer" and the establishment of a number of R&D centres and innovation labs. Some reviews of aid provision have taken an innovation strategy approach, looking at the potential of innovation to improve practices. For example, the HIF commissioned a review of the gaps in emergency water and sanitation that would be the focus of targeted innovation management processes and The Shelter Centre has convened similar research in emergency shelter.

There have also been stand-alone case studies of specific innovation processes. Most have been developed by the institutions already mentioned here: ALNAP have produced an extensive range of case studies by way of follow-up to the original report and there are a number of HIF project reports and several OxHIP reviews. And there are a few examples where reflective practitioners have attempted to explore their innovation journey, looking at innovation management processes as a key focus in explaining their success or failure.

Overall, innovation practices appear to be slowly evolving, for example, the growing use of design-led approaches in public, social and development innovation is now diffusing into the humanitarian sector. An example is the UK Amplify project, conducted with support from IDEO (DFID, 2014). There is also a growing number of training programmes aimed at capacity building, feeding back lessons about innovation management and embedding these into tools and techniques that can be applied. For example, NESTA (UK National Endowment for Science, Technology and the Arts) offers an extensive set of resources and a "DIY" kit for social entrepreneurs, the content of which is relevant for the humanitarian aid context (NESTA, 2014). Elrha has an "Innovation Management Guide" which offers a development programme for innovation skills supported by relevant cases from the sector and offering a wide range of tools adapted for use in this context (Humanitarian Innovation Guide, 2017). And the Global System for Mobile Communications Association (GSMA) is one of a number of umbrella organisations doing similar work based around innovation which utilises the powerful platform offered by mobile phones.

8.2. Thinking About Innovation Management from a Systemic and Systematic Perspective

Decades of "mainstream" innovation research has highlighted that innovation is a process and not an event, comprising structures, procedures and policies (Tidd and Bessant, 2020). The development of the core model underpinning the ISO Innovation Management standard has drawn extensively on this "body of knowledge" and there is, not surprisingly, considerable convergence as to what research and practice tell us supports an effective approach to innovation management and which skills and capabilities will be useful in this context (ISO, 2019).

While the HI sector has not been a formal part of this process, its journey towards more effective innovation management has brought it to a similar destination with the growing recognition of the value of taking a systemic and systematic approach. The HIF Guide mentioned above is a good example of the distilling of experience and approaches from within the sector to inform such a model.

The approach is normative; as the Guide states in its introduction, the purpose is to use a process model which helps act "*...as a map that will help you to identify where you are on your innovation journey, what milestones you need to reach, and what tools or approaches you can use to navigate the different stages...*"

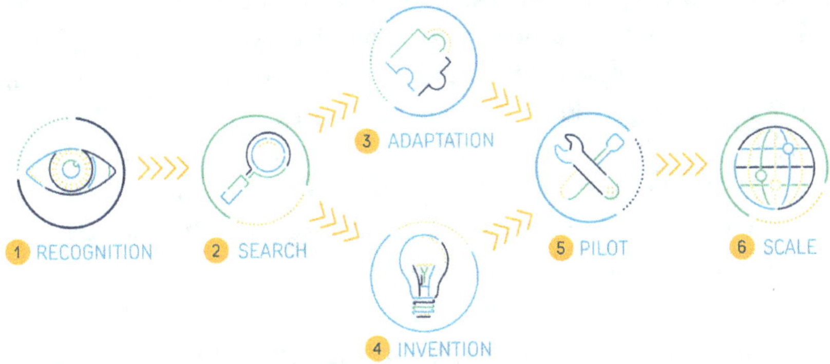

Fig. 8.1. Innovation process model for the humanitarian sector.
Source: Humanitarian Innovation Guide, Elrha (2017).

Their research and extensive review of experience from within and outside the sector leads to a model which they *think is right for innovation in the humanitarian sector*. It is reproduced in Figure 8.1.

- **Recognition** — Recognition of a specific problem or opportunity. This stage involves identifying a problem or opportunity to respond to, collecting and assessing readily available knowledge on the issue and context, diagnosing root causes, and properly framing the challenge.
- **Search** — Search for existing solutions to the problem. This stage involves looking for solutions that might already exist in the context, in the wider humanitarian sector and in other sectors or industries.
- **Adaptation** — Adaptation of a solution from elsewhere that requires significant rethinking of certain elements. This stage involves identifying the changes that are required to adapt an existing solution to a new context.
- **Invention** — Invention of a solution through the generation of new ideas. This stage involves working with users and primary beneficiaries (whether crisis-affected populations or humanitarian workers) to design a solution and develop a prototype.

- **Pilot** — Testing a potential solution to learn whether and how it works in a complex real-world environment. This stage consists of three workstreams: implementing your innovation, developing learning and evidence, and providing support and logistics.
- **Scale** — Scaling the impact of an innovation to better match the size of the social problem it seeks to address. This stage involves building in the complexity required for a sustainable innovation and distilling this complexity to make it replicable.

8.3. Experience with Innovation in the HI Sector

One example of the way in which the sector is shifting in its thinking can be seen in the retrospective study of cases carried out by ALNAP (Obrecht and Warner, 2016). Taking a sample of 24 projects funded by HIF between 2010 and 2016, this research looked at key factors associated with success or failure, mapped on to the process model originally offered by HIF. As the title of the report suggests, successful innovation was "more than just luck."

HIF provides various grants which span various steps in the innovation process, so to ensure coverage of the whole process over time cases were selected from among completed, large grants. This narrowed the sample to 24 projects of which four were used as pilots to test the research instrument. The remaining 20 projects were reduced to 11 detailed cases. Selection of these was based on three factors:

- Achieving a 75/25 split between HIF grants with diffusion funds, or who were applying for diffusion funds and non-diffusion grants. This enabled a contrast between successfully adopted innovations and those that were not.
- Building a balanced cohort of information, communication and technology (ICT)-focused innovations and non-technology-dependent innovations. This enabled the researchers to isolate any challenges that were technology specific.
- Covering a wide range of positions along an innovation spectrum, in terms of degree of novelty (incremental/radical) and across many

different types (product, process, service, business model, etc.) (Francis and Bessant, 2005).

Each case was mapped against the framework model of the innovation process (recognition, ideation, development, implementation and diffusion) originally proposed in the ALNAP report (Ramalingam, Scriven and Foley, 2010). Interviews were carried out with key individuals responsible, with end-users and other stakeholders. Table 8.1 gives outline details of these case studies.

Table 8.1. Case studies of humanitarian innovation.

Title	Innovation Type	Organisation	Description
Listening to Haitians	Product innovation	Haiti Red Cross & IFRC	An interactive communication platform using SMS and Interactive Voice Response (IVR) technology
Words of relief	Process innovation	Translators without Borders	Offers local language translation services to non-governmental organisations, UN agencies and other actors during humanitarian response
Emergency wheelchairs	Product innovation	Motivation	A wheelchair and training package for use in emergency response contexts
Improving water quality	Product innovation	Université Laval	A water treatment system that increases the supply of water in an emergency, at a significantly reduced cost
Open aerial map	Product/ process innovation	OpenStreetMap Team (HOT))	Creates and provides maps to support humanitarian organisations in their response to conflict or natural disasters

(*Continued*)

Table 8.1. (*Continued*)

Title	Innovation Type	Organisation	Description
Improving menstrual hygiene management	Product innovation	International Federation of the Red Cross	Menstrual hygiene management (MHM) kits that are culturally appropriate and effective relief items for emergencies, complemented by improvement and scale-up of training and participatory hygiene promotion tools related to MHM
Urban DRR in Gaza	Process innovation	Catholic Relief Services	An approach to disaster risk reduction (DRR) for complex humanitarian emergencies that occur in urban, conflict-prone areas with non-state actors
SMS feedback in Somalia	Process innovation	Danish Refugee Council	A mobile phone-based feedback mechanism that helps enhance two-way communication and accountability in contexts of remote management
The Humanitarian Genome Project	Product innovation	University of Groningen	An open source application allowing humanitarian workers to quickly access the results and findings of relevant evaluation reports
Community-based Management of Acute Malnutrition	Product innovation	Save the Children UK	The Community-based Management of Acute Malnutrition (CMAM) Report is a technology-based product innovation designed to facilitate more reliable reporting of data

Table 8.1. (*Continued*)

Title	Innovation Type	Organisation	Description
Vulnerability Analysis & Maps (mVAM)	Product innovation	World Food Programme	A programme that integrates mobile technology, including SMS, Interactive Voice Response (IVR) and live calls, into established food security monitoring systems
Bio-rights	Process innovation	Wetlands International & CARE Netherlands	A financial incentive mechanism that unites community- and ecosystem-based Disaster Risk Reduction measures
Humanitarian eXchange Language	Process innovation	UN Office for the Coordination of Humanitarian Affairs (OCHA)	A data standard designed to help the sharing and consolidation of data to improve coordination across agencies responding in a humanitarian crisis
Linking communities to mine action	Process innovation	Danish Demining Group	A two-way communication web portal and parallel SMS service to improve information provision and exchange about mines and other explosive remnants of war between affected communities and the humanitarian actors
Speed evidence	Product innovation	World vision	A platform that will enable a continuous near real-time feedback loop between affected communities and responders after a disaster, with the aim of increasing the situational awareness of both

Source: Active Learning Network for Accountability and Performance (ALNAP).

8.3.1. *Influences on success — Learning from the cases*

Taking the process approach and focusing on key stages within it helped identify a number of key issues. For example, the "recognition" stage is often taken as a given since HI is essentially about responding to urgent need signals. But the risk is that the system quickly jumps from perception of the problem to either applying existing solutions (adaptation) or generating new ones within a bounded frame.

In particular, the HI sector is often rather insular in operation with solutions being sought from within a narrow and bounded search space. The potential for "recombinant" innovation (Bessant and Trifilova, 2017) and for drawing on a wider suite of technologies from other sectors is significant but unrealised. The research identifies the challenge around in fostering appropriate relationships and creating a space and a capability to allow HI actors to gain experiences from outside of the HI field. The value of approaches like those seen in the Open Street Mapping (OSM), TWB or Field Ready cases lies in their ability to take models already proven outside the sector (3D printing as a platform, mobilising an open-source community around design, translation or mapping) and adapt them.

A second challenge relates to engaging end-users in the early stages of the innovation (in ideation or design). Here, the principal difficulty "*lies in incorporating end-user preferences without overburdening them with repeated and prolonged focus groups and interviews, or raising their expectations for a potential prototype*" (Obrecht and Warner, 2016). They found the problem was compounded by the difficulty of accessing user needs from a population which may have been traumatised by recent events and may lack skills and language with which to articulate their needs in coherent fashion. The value of the "*Words of Relief*" project lay in part in helping to address this gap, but it would appear to remain a significant problem for HI.

Another area at the "front-end" of innovation relates to this dominance of need pull; as the researchers point out "*the balance is skewed with relatively little 'knowledge push' type activity such as R&D, horizon scanning or other 'search and discovery' activities*" (Obrecht and Warner, 2016). There are also barriers to entry for external ideas and experience; "*low investment in partnership and a resistance to outsiders seen to be unfamiliar with humanitarian contexts*" (Obrecht and Warner, 2016).

Communication between different stakeholders is another important theme in innovation and, in these cases, it was clear that there is considerable potential value in the prior experience held by field workers, but this is often poorly connected to the front-end of innovation. When their insights are clearly communicated, they can help develop rapid and novel solutions. "*Translators without borders*" (TWB) is a case in point, the concept emerging out of the frustration and difficulties experienced first-hand in communicating and acquiring information because of local language barriers. User innovation — in this case coming from frustrations among the front-line experienced personnel — led to prototyping and later effective solutions.

Although there is scope for adopting practices used outside the HI sector to support innovation, there is also a need to adapt and contextualise. In particular, the strong emphasis placed on lean and agile approaches that require fast failure and early test/learn cycles may not be appropriate in contexts where the "market" consists of vulnerable people. Emergency settings do not lend themselves to an approach where prototypes may not work, and it is difficult to pilot any new products; under crisis conditions there is a strong bias towards staying with "tried and tested" solutions.

By definition, innovation involves a degree of risk-taking: it is a process where outcomes are highly uncertain, and many factors outside the control of the innovating team can affect success. Innovation processes in humanitarian action need an appropriate relationship to risk, one that maximises the potential benefits of risk-taking while minimising the potential costs to the project and protecting against any losses or harm to pilot participants. In practice, this concentrates attention on finding "safe spaces"; for experimentation (for example, in some of the "Innovation Labs" being set up by key agencies).

Surprisingly, given the strong ethical concerns about risk to vulnerable users the level of risk anticipation in many HI projects was low. Innovating teams that did not undertake strong risk assessments often faced delays and setbacks that could have been mitigated through a better approach to risk early on. But having formal risk assessments and monitoring practices in place was less important than maintaining a responsive and open attitude towards identifying new risks and responding to them when appropriate. It seemed more important that innovation processes were agile enough to respond to risks as they arose.

In several case studies, some of the most significant hurdles faced by innovating teams lay within their own organisations, particularly with senior leadership. As part of the wider research for the study ALNAP sought out input from grantees with track records of repeated innovation to understand what they had done to encourage innovation in their organisation. Some cited the non-hierarchical nature of their organisation as key to enabling innovative ideas to take root and bloom into full innovations. As an illustration of this, DRC hosts an annual innovations platform where staff at all levels can pitch ideas for improvement to gain core funding.

8.4. Discussion

The experience of HI suggests that taking a more systemic and systematic approach would pay dividends in terms of more effective innovation processes. There are signs that the kind of good practice model contained within the ISO standard is being adopted and diffused across the HI community, not least through extensive training programmes and suitably adapted enabling toolkits. At the same time, there is growing interest in working at the wider — ecosystem — level to understand what elements might be necessary to create a supporting and healthy environment within which innovation can flourish (Ramalingam *et al.*, 2015).

The ALNAP study reported above supports the view that such an approach could be of value, but it also highlights several areas where the nature of the sectoral context means that considerable adaptation is needed. Taking a more systematic approach to innovation management and using "best practices" should not be seen as a simple "plug and play" exercise; instead, the tools and techniques of managing innovation need adapting and configuring to suit the very specific world of HI.

For example, the concept of moving innovation to scale is significantly complicated in public goods markets such as HI; there may be several layers of stakeholders, some with funding autonomy, some with decision-making authority and some as target end-users. Finding an approach which resolves the potential conflicts of interest and strategy among these groups is a significant issue. Or again, the need to bring in external expertise means that building effective partnerships takes on a high degree of importance; but ensuring effective collaboration between players with different values and purposes is not always simple.

One of the valuable contributions of an international standard is that it makes explicit many of the "good practice" themes which any organisation ought to reflect upon. In this sense the ISO 56002 framework highlights areas where the HI sector has made good progress — not least (see the preceding discussion) in establishing a visible reproducible process and reinforcing its widespread use through extensive capacity-building efforts. There is clearly good progress being made towards one of the ISO goals, which is establishing a common language with which to talk about and work with innovation.

At the same time there are challenges not least in the way in which senior management responsibility for innovation is aligned with operational practices. The growth in interest in innovation across the humanitarian community means that most strategy documents refer to its importance; however, the degree to which top management support and commitment along the lines suggested in the ISO standard as good practice is actually present is variable. The sector is still somewhat "oligopolistic" in that a few large organisations dominate activities and the tendency for those organisations to adopt a "safe" approach is understandable.

By its nature the HI system needs to be careful — it is deploying donated money and resources and it is trying to meet the needs of very vulnerable people. Not surprisingly it becomes skilled at innovations which involve "doing what we do but better" but has less capability in handling radical high risk activity.

The paradox is that it needs the radical ideas to move the frontier — and so needs to learn alternative ways of handling that kind of innovation. But setting up a team or licensing individuals to explore and push the frontiers, challenge taboos, and work outside the box of the organisation, sets up an inevitable tension. Sooner or later those people are going to come back with something which by its nature will challenge — and is likely to trigger the corporate immune system. This acts in homeostatic fashion, with the best intentions at heart of preserving it from harmful changes — but its unfortunate side-effect is to stop radical innovation in its tracks.

It's a difficult balancing act, allowing enough freedom to permit novel ideas to emerge and become promising pilots without committing the organisation to high risk activity. At some point there is also the need to move beyond prototypes and deploy innovation at scale — but this can take a long time in a conservative system like HI. An example is the case of cash programming, a radical change in the business model associated with providing food assistance. The original entrepreneurial experiments took place back in the mid-1980s, but it took a further two decades before this powerful approach became accepted and legitimate as a mainstream model (Ramalingam *et al.*, 2015).

There are promising signs that a more strategic approach is being taken, informed by a well-developed understanding of innovation. For example, the HI Fund in allocating its funding resources for innovation projects has made conscious use of strategic frameworks (the 4Ps approach) to ensure that projects are not just focused on product innovations but also explore business model, process and other changes (Francis and Bessant, 2006). In similar fashion it uses portfolio approaches to ensure a good balance between high risk/high reward and "safer" low risk projects. And its fund is available not simply for front-end and start-up support but particularly in addressing the significant question of how to move innovation diffusion to scale.

One area of strength in the sector is the key role that evidence has always played in guiding project and programme development. Monitoring and evaluation are cornerstones of effective humanitarian aid and there are encouraging signs that this approach is being used systematically to strengthen the approach being taken to innovation management. Reports like the "more than just luck" study by ALNAP suggest that the sector is well-positioned to embed a culture of continuous improvement around its innovation management practices.

References

Bessant, J. and Trifilova, A. (2017). Developing absorptive capacity for recombinant innovation. *Business Process Management Journal*, *23*(6), 1094–1107, https://doi.org/10.1108/BPMJ-10-2016-0215.

Bessant, J., Rush, H. and Trifilova, A. (2012). Jumping the tracks: Crisis-driven social innovation and the development of novel trajectories. *Die Unternehmung — Swiss Journal of Business Research and Practice*, *66*(3), 221–242.

Betts, A. and Bloom, L. (2014). *Humanitarian Innovation: The State of the Art*. Oxford Humanitarian Innovation Project.

DFID (2014). *Amplify and the Collaborative Challenge Fund*, https://www.ideo.org/programs/amplify.

Francis, D. and Bessant, J. (2005). Targeting innovation and implications for capability development. *Technovation*, *25*(3), 171–183.

Francis, D. and Bessant, J. (2006). Targetting innovation and implications for capability development. In Mayle, D. (ed.), *Managing Innovation and Change*. Sage Publications.

Humanitarian Innovation Guide (2017). *Humanitarian Innovation Fund*, https://higuide.elrha.org/about/.

ISO (2019). *ISO 56002:2019 Innovation management — Innovation management system — Guidance*. International Organization for Standardization.

Lauday, A., Foley, C. and Poulson, C. (2017). *The Humanitarian Innovation Fund External Evaluation*. Triple Line, https://www.elrha.org/wp-content/uploads/2017/09/HIF-Evaluation-submitted.pdf.

NESTA (2014). *Making it Big*. NESTA.

Obrecht, A. and Warner, A. (2016). *More than just Luck. Innovation in Humanitarian Action*. Humanitarian Innovation Fund/ALNAP.

Ramalingam, B., Scriven, K. and Foley, C. (2010). *Innovations in International Humanitarian Action*. ALNAP.

Ramalingam, B., Rush, H., Bessant, J., Marshall, N., Gray, W., Hoffman, K., Gray, I., Bayley, S. and Warren, K. (2015). *Strengthening the Humanitarian Innovation Ecosystem*. University of Brighton/DFID.

Tidd, J. and Bessant, J. (2020). *Managing Innovation* (7th edn.). John Wiley and Sons.

UNOCHA (2015). *World Humanitarian Data and Trends 2014*. United Nations Office for Humanitarian Aid.

© 2023 World Scientific Publishing Europe Ltd.
https://doi.org/10.1142/9781800612105_0009

Chapter 9

Instituto Nacional de Tecnologìa Industrial: Innovation Management System Implementation at INTI — Argentina

Marina Pérez Zelaschi and Leopoldo Colombo

Abstract

This chapter provides an overview of the process carried out at the Instituto Nacional de Tecnologìa Industrial — INTI — in order to implement an Innovation Management System (IMS) in a public R&D Institute. Implementing an IMS aligned with ISO 56002 was aimed to reinforce the role INTI plays to promote innovation through the industrial network of Argentina. The authors explain how the process was deployed and why the work was done in two tracks simultaneously: one addressing awareness and training, for managers and technical staff, and another track addressing the deployment of the strategic components of the IMS by top management. Three elements are highlighted and explained in detail showing the important role they played in the IMS implementation and how they were addressed, namely the innovation process itself, collaboration awareness, and project portfolio balance. The certification of INTI's IMS under the Argentinean standard IRAM 50501:2016, in October 2019, positioned INTI as a pioneer in the innovation management field, it being the first public organisation in Argentina with a certified IMS.

9.1. Background and Introduction

This chapter is devoted to providing an overview of the process carried out at INTI in order to implement an IMS in a public R&D Institute.

Argentina, most commonly known for the Pope, meat and football, also holds certain titles such as being one of select countries recognised for its satellite industry, hosting a world-class nuclear industry for peaceful uses, a strong seed genetics industry and having a National Institute of Industrial Technology — INTI — which has become the dean of this type of institutions in Latin America.

INTI was founded in 1957 as a decentralised public institution under the Ministry of Industry and Commerce to provide technological assistance to the country. A distinctive characteristic of INTI is its close relationship with Argentina's industrial ecosystem.

INTI supports Argentine industry by providing a wide variety of services through its R&D and Regional Centres network. These services include tests and analysis, calibrations, technological assistance, R+D+i, professional training, products, processes and people certification, as well as serving as the country's Metrological authority. Every Centre performs these activities, to different degrees, according to the needs and requirements of its industrial sector.

Today, INTI has over 3,000 employees working in 25 R&D Centres devoted to specific industrial sectors (textiles, constructions, plastics, rubber, meat, dairy products, micro nanomaterials, chemicals and pharmaceuticals, etc.) and 24 Regional Centres, located one in each province, with multisectoral focus according to the local needs. More than 60% of the staff hold a career degree.

INTI pioneered the implementation of management systems back in the 1990s when its labs were the first in Argentina to achieve ISO 17025 accreditation (ISO, 2017), as they did with ISO 9001 (ISO, 2015) a few years after. The purpose of obtaining those accreditations/certifications was not only to show the solidity of its laboratory services and the excellent management of its Centres, but also to show industry the way forward. INTI was recognised with the National Quality Award of Excellence for the public sector in 1999.

Considering that background and the strategic commitment to promote innovation through the industrial network of the entire country, by focusing on SMEs, it became clear that there was a need for a strategic decision to establish an Innovation Management System (IMS) according to the guidelines included in ISO 56002 (ISO, 2019a) and the requirements of IRAM 50501 (IRAM, 2016).

The challenge was evident and entailed a significant undertaking, especially considering that the public sector in Latin American countries is affected by greater political volatility than in developed nations. Presently, the world is becoming more and more familiar with the challenges of living in a VUCA (volatility, uncertainty, complexity and ambiguity) environment; in Argentina in the last 40 years, we have been living in VUCAx2 or VUCAx3. Inflation has been greater than 25% per year over the last 10 years, there have been 5 years of heavy recession and the dollar exchange rate moved from 3 pesos in 2005 to 150 in 2020. Committing to a long-term project in such a scenario is extremely challenging and in INTI it was only possible due to the strong determination of the Board of Directors as well as the unwavering commitment of the implementation team.

Under the joint leadership of in-house representatives as well as external consultants, the project started in December 2017 and ended in August 2020. The ISO 56002 standard was taken as a model, even though it was under development. The national standard IRAM 50501, which is also aligned with CEN 16555-1:2013, was chosen as the certification standard.

9.2. Description of Innovation Components in a System Perspective

INTI's IMS was designed taking into consideration the elements of "IRAM 50501:2016 Innovation Management System — Requirements standard" (IRAM, 2016), which is strongly based on European experiences with CEN 16555-1:2013 (CEN, 2013) and elements of "ISO 56002:2019 Innovation management system — Guidance" (ISO, 2019a), which represents the state of the art in innovation management at the time the implementation process was deployed.

Other elements were also taken from the National Award for Quality in Innovation Management (leadership, strategy) (FPNC, 2021) and the Uruguayan Model for Innovation Management — MUGI (recognition of people, diversity, leadership) (Blasina *et al.*, 2012). In addition, the Guide to good practices in management of technology transfer and intellectual property in institutions and agencies of the National System of Science, Technology and Innovation was employed (MINCYT, 2013).

The IMS in INTI uses the Spanish acronym SGInn (Sistema de Gestion de la Innovation) and can be depicted in a graphic as follows (Figure 9.1).

The resemblance between SGInn and the graphic figure in ISO 56002 is due to the active participation of Argentina (i.e., the authors of this chapter) in the development of that standard.

The main challenge for the IMS was to clearly define the steps in the ideation process (create concepts), stressing divergent thinking for creating new ideas and concepts, taking into account that INTI is an R&D organisation that uses extensively the scientific method (AENOR, 2006). In addition, when INTI acts as a technical advisor, it has to arrive efficiently at one, and only one, answer.

The vision for innovation at INTI was redefined in a participative way, starting bottom-up by first collecting and synthesising the view of technical managers and project leaders. In a second step, top management and the Board of Directors set the definition of innovation at INTI and the institutional vision and strategy for innovation.

The vision was deployed at three tiers: the vision of INTI as a referral organisation (how we would like to be recognised by society); the vision regarding its own innovation processes with a focus on upcoming

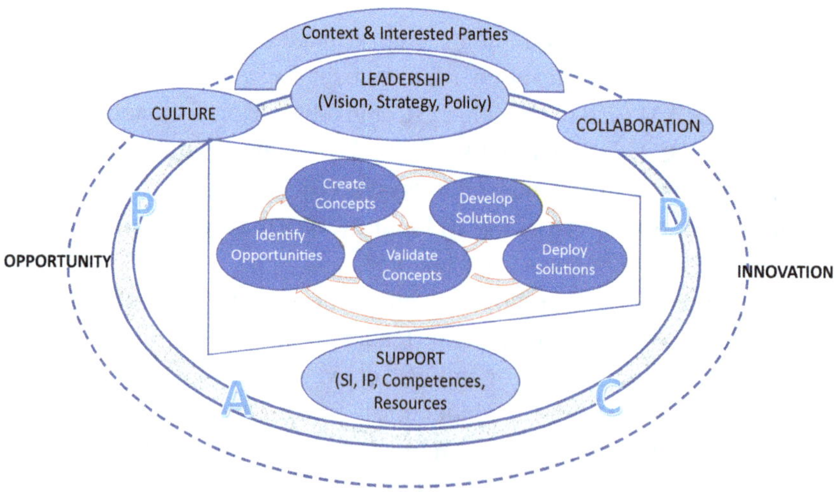

Fig. 9.1. INTI — SGInn — IMS process map.

technological trends and the vision for the people working in innovation, creativity, collaboration and professional growth.

The IMS implementation was carried out with the understanding that it had to be integrated with other management systems (MSs) already existing at INTI, such as ISO 9001 and ISO 17025. Nevertheless, some differences should be pointed out: Culture and collaboration, for instance, are two processes that deserve special consideration in an IMS but do not have a role in the other MSs.

Regarding support processes, the focus was on two vital areas for an Institute such as INTI: Strategic Intelligence (SI) and Intellectual property (IP). In both cases the system approach was to set a network within the Institute supported by a central area that provided the tools and/or platforms of knowledge and pivots or "pillars" in each R&D or Regional Centre. These platforms are capable of understanding the context of the IMS and its market and thus are able to develop the "key words" for using the SI and IP tools.

Excessive focus on "Documented Procedures" or "Manuals" was avoided in order to reduce the always present criticisms such as: "Too much paperwork," "Too bureaucratic," "Innovation is not managed through paperwork," "Innovation is not ISO 9001!!," and so on. However, it was agreed that documented information was needed and would have to be developed. After analysing various alternatives, the option selected was to develop a handbook that would condense the best practices to manage Innovation and be designed in a didactic way, covering all aspects related to the IMS. This ensured tools and methods were readily available and also reinforced awareness.

9.3. How Were These Components of the System Implemented?

No matter how great the talent or efforts, some things just take time.
You can't produce a baby in one month by getting nine women pregnant.

Warren Buffet

In early 2012, a training programme to enhance creativity capabilities within the Centres was developed by the R&D Department, in order to promote innovation. It was an approach focused on improving the technical staff's competencies in creativity, design thinking and mentoring (Hamel, 2006).

At the same time, there was as a national strategy to develop specific industrial sectors (renewable energy equipment, dairy industry, natural fibres, industrial nanotechnology, pharmaceutical and medical equipment, etc). INTI, along with the other public Science and Technology organisations, was strongly encouraged to compete for R&D project funding, in partnership with private companies. Having set this strategy, most INTI's R&D Centres enhanced their capabilities in identifying opportunities and planning innovative projects by working with the most successful companies.

With the advancement of best practices for a global IMS, in December 2017, with the support of a local consulting company and an external expert from Spain, a gap analysis was carried out to understand the challenges to face when implementing an IMS. The result of that exercise revealed that 25% of the IMS elements were already in place; the challenge would lie in the development of the remaining 75%.

With the results of the gap analysis in its hands, the conviction that INTI should foster innovation in industry and the desire that INTI itself should become more innovative, the Board of Directors took the strategic decision to implement an IMS.

The R&D manager (later R&D & Innovation manager) was appointed as Project Leader. External assistance was also requested from a leading local consulting company.

Historically, the influence of the R&D Centre's Technical Directors was key in achieving and maintaining technical excellence. Therefore, the strategy proposed by the R&D Department and approved by INTI's Board was to encourage all areas to perform innovation activities to participate in the IMS project. Participation was encouraged yet not mandatory. No Centre was forced to deploy the IMS if its Technical Director considered the project as not appropriate or beneficial for the Centre.

Considering the background of the different Centres regarding innovation, its critical mass and competence for innovation, a goal was set to get the commitment of 25 Centres to take part in the IMS implementation.

To start the project, it was decided to work in two tracks, simultaneously: one addressing *awareness and training*, for managers and technical staff, and another track to deploy the *strategic components* of the IMS with upper management.

The link between both groups was provided by the Technical Directors of the Centres that took part in both activities.

9.3.1. *Awareness and training*

From the beginning it was clear that *time was needed* to raise awareness and commitment and for INTI to manage its innovation activities using best practices, as well as for that idea to mature and flourish.

The *awareness programme* reached almost 20% of INTI's technical and managerial staff with special consideration for the diversity of technical specialities, age and gender. The programme was designed to provide the best understanding of the benefits of an IMS, to focus on the strengths and weaknesses when implementing the system and also to encourage a collective reflection on the reasons why INTI should innovate.

The *training programme* was delivered over 8 months with eight workshops (four editions of each workshop and 25 participants per edition) covering the following topics:

- Innovation management systems: elements and structure,
- Creativity,
- Innovation processes,
- Intellectual property,
- Strategic intelligence,
- Risk management,
- Context analysis and interested parties' needs and expectations, and
- Portfolio management.

Each workshop was designed to last from 8 to 16 hours and was conducted by local and international experts.

9.3.2. *Strategic components*

In parallel to the awareness and training programmes, several workshops were carried out with top management to enable discussion of the importance of INTI as an innovative organisation, and how to develop an innovation culture, within INTI and at the same time developing the *Innovation Vision* and the *Innovation Strategy*.

These two activities entailed a large investment in resources, especially time and considerable logistical effort. However, undoubtedly it helped to build a solid foundation and support for the IMS project at all levels of INTI and across the country. This solidly built commitment proved to be critical in the survival of the project when, a few months after and in the middle of the process, a political crisis exploded.

9.3.3. *Stakeholders and their interests*

Although the awareness and the training programmes were considered the right things to be done and at the right time, their deployment had to face some reluctance towards the project. This is totally understandable in senior employees, who have gone through so many political changes over the last years. They had seen so many "flavour of the month" projects that it is not easy to open new initiatives.

As mentioned before, INTI is a public organisation; which means that the top management (President and Board of Directors) changes every 4 years (or even less) and sometimes their interest is frequently related to very noticeable short-term goals. By contrast, the Technical Directors are professional staff with more than 20 years in INTI on average, acknowledged by their technical competence; the pursuit of technological excellence and reliability are their main aims. Likewise, Unions are quite strong in INTI and an organisation-wide project, like this one, should not be regarded as an initiative to change the contractual conditions of the work force. The IMS implementation would not be possible if those interests were not taken into account.

Each element of a system is key for the overall success. However, sometimes due to cultural, historical or strategic reasons some elements stand out over others. In retrospect, three elements deserve to be mentioned:

- *Innovation process*: Due to the wide and deep insights that led to agreements upon a common flow of activities.

- *Collaboration awareness*: As a better enabler to traditional collaboration.
- *Project portfolio*: Because of the deeper understanding of a balanced portfolio in the planning process instead of a collection of R&D initiatives.

More details are provided on the role these three elements played in the IMS implementation and how they were addressed below.

Innovation process

One of the most enriching tasks in the implementation process was generating a clear definition of each of the phases of the innovation process, the core of an IMS.

The first step was to ensure that everybody understood the differences between working in an R&D project and an innovation project. The OECD Oslo Manual (2005) and the Frascati Manual (2015) helped us in that endeavour.

After ensuring everyone was on the same page, the innovation process phases were introduced. Innovation is a nonlinear process and, although there is an apparent logical path between the phases, uncertainty itself and the discoveries or failures in each phase may force a return to previous stages. Knowing this, the leading team decided to carry out three workshops aimed to get consensus on a common visualisation of the activities that exist between opportunity identification and value generation. In those workshops, focus was aimed to describe inputs and outputs of each phase, the tools, methods and competencies required, the most frequent activities carried out and a set of indicators for each phase. Reflecting on every single element helped to ensure teams were on the same page.

The exercises allowed us to verify that even though different technical teams had different views, there were many points in common. The nonlinear process was clearly understood by all teams, as well as the convergent/divergent sequence of each phase.

An interesting point was that the ideation phase (concept creation) was very poorly described by all teams, mixing up the idea phase

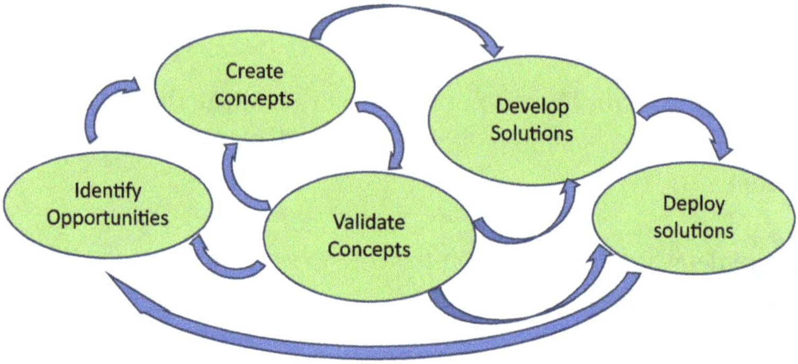

Fig. 9.2. INTI — Innovation process — phases.

(identifying opportunities and creating concepts) with the validation of concepts selected and the development of solutions: there was a clear "gap" in understanding the concept creation as a process itself made up by defined steps: understanding the need/opportunity — idea generation — selection and development — conceptualising — selling the idea.

The output of this series of workshops was a model quite similar to the figure included in ISO 56002, see Figure 9.2.

Reaching consensus on this image was a huge step forward in the implementation process. There was agreement on inputs/outputs of each phase, most frequent activities performed in each of them, and the resources, competencies and indicators for each phase (Michanek and Breiler, 2013).

After the awareness campaign, there was a common agreement on what innovation management meant and why a formal process should be used to manage it. Another great step was to ensure that INTI had a common image of the different phases of the innovation processes and how they interacted with each other. Mission accomplished!

Collaboration awareness

Individually, we are one drop. Together, we are an ocean.

Ryunosuke Satoro

The word "collaborate" comes from the Latin "colaborare," meaning "working together"; as a long-standing R&D institution, collaboration is in INTI's DNA.

However, during the day-to-day operation collaboration flows naturally, and usually goes unnoticed. The implementation of the IMS provided clarity by defining different levels of collaboration, considering the level of commitment with the execution and the attainable results regarding IP as well as in terms of the collaboration process itself.

Initial focus pointed to the need to clearly understand why to collaborate and the advantages that can be derived from partnership.

In managing collaboration (ISO, 2019b), the first step is to find the right partner and so a comprehensive search for possible partners was conducted with first a long list and then a short list. Benefits were kept in mind and included learning opportunities, increased motivation in a technical team, branding or reputation, sharing facilities, collaboration willingness, leverage for new opportunities, operative cost reductions, access to financial resources, and impact on future growth. This approach, while explicit in the IMS, became one of those "eureka" moments bringing a broader scope of searching for possible partners.

The second step was to check the strategic alignment with partners to verify if interests, shared vision, long-term commitment and risk analysis could be easily aligned with partners. After reaching this point, framework agreements were developed.

And last but not least, the settings for interaction were cleared up. This considered roles, governance, confidentiality and IP issues. In addition, working teams, plans and milestones, funding, resources and ending strategy were addressed.

Once again, the IMS proved to be useful in clarifying the steps and all the variables / dimensions that needed to be considered. It has to be said that INTI has the collaboration gene embedded in its DNA. Since solutions often required a multidisciplinary approach, collaboration among the 25 industry sector centres located in the Buenos Aires campus grew naturally.

Innovation portfolio

One of the tools for managing an IMS is the innovation portfolio. In INTI's case it proved to be one of the most powerful tools to align so many different projects and initiatives from R&D Centres.

As an R&D organisation, strategic and operational planning is based on projects. The variables for projects' characterisation have been implemented for decades, with revisions and adjustments over the last 30 years.

Some were adopted by the IMS, such as:

- Degree of collaboration (between Centres within INTI, with other national institutions, and international partnerships).
- Origin funding sources (in-house, competitive projects, private contract).
- Type of demand (internal, suggested by client or requested by client).

New variables were set in place with the IMS implementation:

- *Core/incremental/transformational* according to the innovation ambition matrix (disruptiveness versus market maturity).

The first task was to bring definitions into practical terms. Workshops were organised to cross-examine different ongoing projects to understand what a variable actually meant.

In those workshops, when analysing the portfolios of over 120 innovation projects an interesting question arouse: Could this project be considered as "core" for INTI? Is it also "core" from the client's perspective? As INTI provides innovation services to companies, some projects may be characterised internally by INTI staff as core, due to already existing competencies and knowledge. But the same projects, as seen from the client's point of view, may be considered incremental or more disruptive for the company than it is for INTI. This difference was another issue to be considered.

When aligning the portfolio to the innovation strategy, it appeared clear that INTI's mission was to develop some projects, with challenging goals, facing new opportunities in newly developed technologies. These are necessary to acquire and deploy internally the capabilities and competencies needed for the future and to show the path forward to industrial companies.

9.4. Achievements of the Innovation System

It always seems impossible until it's done.

Nelson Mandela

The IMS was set in place and was certified under the Argentinean standard "IRAM 50501:2016 Innovation management System-Requirements." The audit was conducted during June–August 2019 (phase 1 and phase 2) and the certification was granted in October 2019.

This certification puts INTI in a pioneering role, it being the *first public organisation with a certified IMS* and the second entity in Argentina (after an SME closely related to INTI).

Some of the strengths reported by the Certification Body's audit team are:

- The elaborated structure of the IMS stands out because it takes into account the adequate fulfilment of all the requirements of the standard and, on the other hand, allows a high degree of flexibility compatible with the characteristics of the organisation.
- The methodology used to develop the vision, policy, and general guidelines of the IMS is considered a strength, giving participation to the personnel involved in the system, which gives a high level of commitment and very good promotion of the culture of innovation.
- The emphasis placed on determining the necessary competencies of the people who develop and work in the innovation process stands out, with emphasis on attitudinal aspects.
- The amount and diversity of knowledge available to the organisation to tackle innovative projects is remarkable.
- The level of commitment to the IMS observed in the people involved in its activities is considered a strength.
- The use in a transversal way of the services of the Technical Department of Industrial Design in the innovation activities developed by the other Sections of the Department of Knowledge Areas is considered a strength for the IMS.

Last, but not least, after major changes in INTI top management in December 2019, the IMS is working well (COVID-19 aside). There were no major changes in the IMS, nor in procedures nor in managing staff.

INTI IMS will be extended to other provinces and research areas.

9.4.1. *Summary of findings regarding the most relevant issues in the IMS implementation*

In previous pages, three highlighted components in the IMS were described, pointing to the challenges and most significant outcomes.

Taking a cross-sectional analysis, parts or elements of these three components were already part of INTI's culture. The systemic approach was a major contribution and provided a common and enriched view on process definitions and also enhanced awareness of managing collaboration and project portfolios.

In order to give a complementary perception, the Implementation Team Leaders developed a Perception Thermometer, showing their feelings about some variables of the implementation processes such as:

- The reluctancy of technical staff and managers before implementation (1: maximum reluctance; 10: minimum reluctance);
- The previous knowledge within the organisation, thus showing the novelty of the component (1: minimum not knowledge at all; 10: maximum knowledge);
- The easiness to deploy the implementation, (1: very hard, 10: very easy); and
- The overall satisfaction from participants' feedback (1: very unsatisfied, 10: very satisfied).

Figures 9.3–9.5 show the perception thermometer regarding the innovation process (Figure 9.3), collaboration (Figure 9.4) and innovation portfolio (Figure 9.5).

9.5. Overall Reflections and Way Forward

Leading an IMS requires more energy than leading other MSs; extra energy is needed to deal with uncertainty and risk, failure and disappointment, empowering people and instilling enthusiasm, on a daily basis. Innovation leaders must be supportive, creative and employee focused, very much like leaders required in pandemic times!

Onboarding and training strategies for innovation must be continuous, keeping diversity as a main driver: diversity in technical skills to foster the

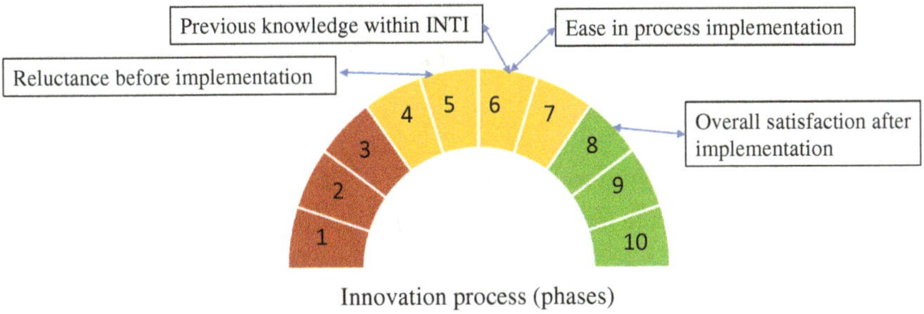

Fig. 9.3. Perception thermometer: Innovation process.

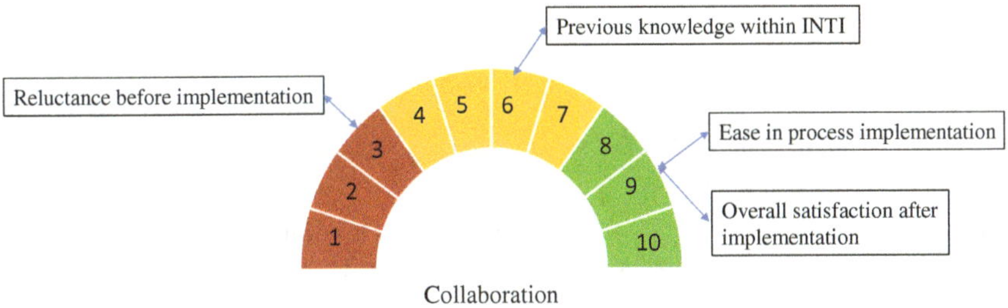

Fig. 9.4. Perception thermometer: Collaboration.

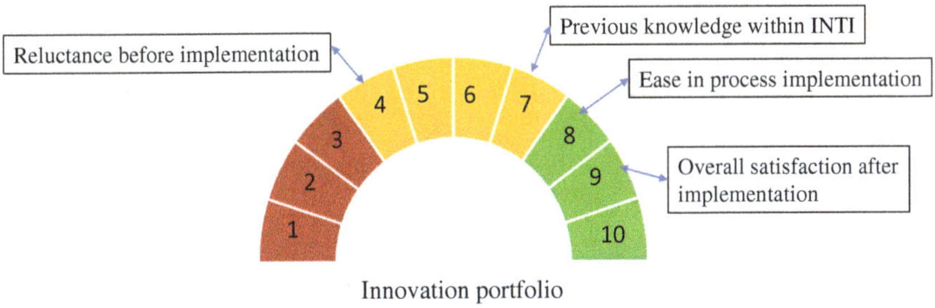

Fig. 9.5. Perception thermometer: Innovation portfolio.

Source: Implementation team leaders.

"tech combination"; diversity in ages and degrees of expertise, to encourage new approaches to old problems; and, gender diversity to enrich context analysis and opportunity detection.

Developing a culture that encourages creativity and empowers "out of the box" thinking may be distressful in an "operational culture." Management, at any level, must always be aware to keep both in balance.

When the IMS has been designed collaboratively, managed in a transparent way, focused on lessons learned and encourages people to think of new possibilities, it will survive even in harsh or politically changing environments.

INTI's IMS is proving to be in good shape, after political changes that lead to top management replacement, the decision of new authorities is not only to maintain the IMS certification but also to expand the scope adding more technical fields and geographical regions, as stated in the "Strategic Plan INTI 2025."

References

AENOR (2006). *UNE166002:2006 — R&D&I Management: R&D&I Management System Requirements*. Spanish Association for Standardization and Certification, Madrid, Spain.

Blasina, G., López Migues, V., Almansa, M., De Guida, M., Cristobal, S, Sorondo, Á., González, A. and Miles, J. (2012). *Modelo Uruguayo de Gestión de Innovacion — MUGI*. Editorial Laboratorio Tecnológico del Uruguay (LATU).

CEN (2013). *CEN/TS 16555-1 Innovation Management — Innovation Management System*. European Committee for Standardization.

FPNC (2021). *Modelo de Excelencia Para la Gestión de la Innovación República Argentina*. Sector Privado, Edición 2021, Fundación Premio Nacional a la Calidad.

Hamel, G. (2006). The why, what, and how of management innovation. *Harvard Business Review*, February.

IRAM (2016). *Norma IRAM 50501 Gestión de la innovación. Sistema de gestión de la innovación. Requisitos*. Instituto Argentino de Normalización y Certificación — IRAM.

ISO (2015). *ISO 9001:2015 Quality management systems — Requirements*. International Organization for Standardization.

ISO (2017). *ISO/IEC 17025:2017 General requirements for the competence of testing and calibration laboratories*. International Organization for Standardization.

ISO (2019a). *ISO 56002:2019 Innovation management — Innovation management system — Guidance*. International Organization for Standardization.

ISO (2019b) ISO 56003:2019 *Innovation management — Tools and methods for innovation partnerships — Guidance*. International Organization for Standardization.

Michanek, J. and Breiler, A. (2013). *The Idea Agent: The Handbook on Creative Processes*. Routledge, New York.

MINCYT (2013). *Guía de Buenas Prácticas en gestión de la Transf de Tecnología y de la Propiedad Intelectual en Instituciones y Organismos del Sistema Nacional de Ciencia*. Tecnología e Innovación, Ministerio de Ciencia, Tecnología e Innovación Productiva.

OECD/Eurostat (2005). *Guidelines for Collecting and Interpreting Innovation Data — The Oslo Manual* (3rd edn.). Paris: OECD.

OECD (2015). *Frascati Manual 2015: Guidelines for Collecting and Reporting Data on Research and Experimental Development*. The Measurement of Scientific, Technological and Innovation Activities. Paris: OECD Publishing.

© 2023 World Scientific Publishing Europe Ltd.
https://doi.org/10.1142/9781800612105_0010

Chapter 10

Kanthal: Building Bridges for Increased Innovation Capability

Anders Wikström

Abstract

This chapter describes and analyses the development of an Innovation Management System (IMS) at Kanthal — a world-leading brand for products and services in industrial heating technology and resistance materials, based in Sweden. The journey began with late-night thoughts and discussions by the coffee maker on leveraging the organisation's potential regarding innovation capability. There was a feeling that an improvement could be made. In 2017, Process Industrial IT and Automation (PiiA), part of Sweden's Strategic Innovation Program, launched a research project to understand the innovation capability within the Swedish process industry. Kanthal joined, and the journey started with the implementation of a programme for increased innovation capability. The assessment revealed a focus on incremental innovation, barriers in the climate for innovation, and an inability to take advantage of the expertise and competencies available in the organisation. While this journey started before releasing the ISO 56002 innovation management standard, these insights align well with this standard.

10.1. Introduction to Kanthal

Kanthal has been driven by innovation since the very beginning of its now 90-year journey. Since it all started in 1931, a lot of water has passed by the old factory building in Hallstahammar in Sweden. The legacy of innovation from Kanthal is profound. The company is world-leading in high temperature and resistance materials.

10.1.1. *Company origins*

Hans von Kantzow is the man behind the discovery and the innovation. He graduated from the Royal Academy of Technology, Stockholm, in 1910. Due to the recession, he decided to leave Sweden for Great Britain and, after that, went to Austria, working as a researcher at Europe's largest ironworks: Witkowitz. After a melting accident in 1916, Hans discovered unique characteristics in the combination of iron and aluminium. The discovery remained a thought in young Hans's head when he returned to Sweden and worked at Bultfabriks AB (the largest industry in Hallstahammar, manufacturing fasteners, i.e., hardware devices for joining objects). This thought became more defined while Hans was on a business trip to the US, where he saw the production of nickel-chromium thread for kitchen supplies. Combining this new knowledge, and his former insight into the iron-aluminium characteristics, formed an idea about using this new alloy as electric resistance material.

When he returned to Sweden, Hans von Kantzow presented his idea to the board of Bultfabriks AB. To make a considerable investment in these challenging times was not an option, but he did receive access to testing facilities and engineers, who he paid out of his own pocket. As a result, a long testing period began, where the team experimented with different melts to make test rods and measure their resistance. The team tested adding chromium, nickel, cobalt, wolfram and other metals. Finally, they chose an iron-aluminium-chromic combination, with aluminium providing both electric and fire resistance. The critical point in this process is to balance the amount of aluminium: too much of it makes the alloy frangible or brittle. In 1931, with the success of these experiments, Kantzow started Kanthal. The industrial journey had begun!

10.1.2. *From invention to innovation*

The industrial excellence of Kanthal — which ultimately defined their competitiveness — was based on two things: the capability to (1) find the perfect balance between the components of the materials, and (2) respond to the demand for precision. However, as we all know, making an invention is not making an innovation. Intellectual Property Rights (IPR) became essential, as did the ability to find source materials throughout Europe in wartime. However, even the war itself became an enabler for Kanthal since nickel (traditionally used in resistance materials) became expensive and even banned in some countries. Instead, Kanthal used iron, which was much cheaper. That being said, the timing might have been the most crucial factor for making the invention an innovation by global measures.

10.1.3. *Maintaining a leadership position*

Today, Kanthal is a world-leading brand for products and services in industrial heating technology and resistance materials. With growing competition from new markets and an increased interest in materials related to electrification, the ability to remain a front-runner has its challenges. In addition to competitive forces, Kanthal has a strong tradition of developing new applications based on its core competence and infrastructure. This has led to an increasing number of their products becoming the leading ones in the market. Expectations are high to maintain the product portfolio and further develop it in a rapidly changing market.

10.1.4. *Long-term innovation investment*

Within the field of new materials and new applications for existing materials, the transformation of the automotive industry and the electrification of transportation create new opportunities for companies. This is especially true for those with both broad and deep knowledge of heating and resistance materials. There is a window of opportunity about to open, and the ones ready for it will capture market share early to develop these new applications. Also, the transition towards zero-emission production of heat-intensive industries (e.g., steel and mining) opens up new opportunities within the field of industrial heating technology and resistance materials.

To use Kanthal's deep knowledge and broad competence within these future areas, Kanthal needs to make a long-term investment in innovation.

This requires new products and services to be developed alongside both incremental and radical process improvements for implementation and industrialisation. A systematic and systemic approach to innovation is needed on a strategic level in the organisation.

10.1.5. *Preconditions for innovation*

As most organisations sooner or later realise, an implemented Innovation Management System (IMS) is not a quick fix. However, since Kanthal has its legacy in innovation, there are vital elements in place already. Within Kanthal, employees within the Research and Development (R&D) department (including the R&D manager and a newly employed senior R&D engineer) started exploring the way innovation was organised to understand what the drivers could be for improving Kanthal's innovation capability.

In 2018, a programme for increased preconditions for innovation was initiated. Here, a research project assessed both the climate and system for innovation. One crucial part of the programme was to evaluate the innovation climate. Building on Ekvall (1996), an instrument with new methods for capturing and analysing data had been developed within the research project. The assessment ensured that preconditions on the individual, team and organisational levels were identified, analysed and understood.

The activities in the programme included:

- Innovation climate assessment, one performed in 2018 and one in 2019.
- Workshop on the result from innovation climate assessment.
- Workshop on enablers and disablers for increased innovation capability.
- Workshop on measurements for increased innovation capability.

The activities were intertwined with conversations and discussions among a few people in the R&D department to (1) further develop knowledge and understanding of ways forward in developing the right preconditions for innovation, and (2) implementing a more systematic approach to innovation in the organisational structure. It was complemented in 2020 by seven interviews with people at different levels and functions within Kanthal.

10.2. Description of Innovation Elements from a Systems Perspective

The story of Hans von Kantzow does not only reveal that innovation stems from people with insights, it also demonstrates the joint efforts of a team working together with a clear mission, experimenting, and going through learning cycles to adjust and fine-tune the solution. An innovative organisation must focus on developing preconditions to fuel employee creativity. In addition, it must direct and support that power through processes, strategies and policies to make innovation possible in an organisation. Organisations that continuously prove to be innovative involve the entire organisation in their innovation efforts.

10.2.1. *Embedding innovation in an organisation*

Five areas were probed to understand the innovation elements from a systems perspective at Kanthal: *context*, *leadership*, *processes*, *support* and *system*. The results were further explored through the lens of *strategy* (Mintzberger *et al.*, 1987), *tactics* (Tidd and Bessant, 2009) and *people* (Ekvall, 1996; Amabile *et al.*, 1996) to enable embedding innovation in the entire organisation at an individual level. These three areas intersect with new fields of importance on an individual level: *clarity*, *control* and *self-confidence*. Further, the system assessment was combined with the innovation climate assessment to understand the preconditions for innovation at Kanthal. All six elements are essential for embedding innovation in an organisation (see Figure 10.1).

The relationship of the intersection points are as follows:

- Strategy and tactics set the level of *clarity* in the innovative work.
- Tactics and people set the level of *control* regarding the skills and capabilities.

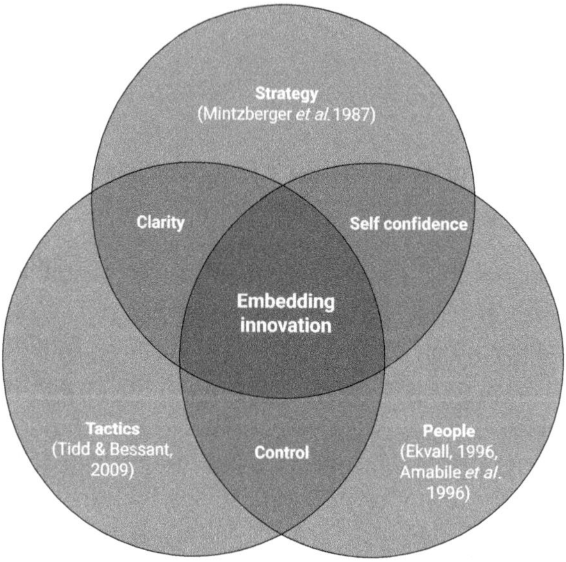

Fig. 10.1. Embedding innovation in an organisation.
Source: Wikström (2020).

- Strategy and people set the level of *self-confidence* regarding how individuals perceive they can contribute to the overall innovation strategy.

10.2.2. *Recommendations for increased innovation capability at Kanthal*

Strategy, tactics and people are the cornerstones to understand and set the right preconditions for success. A suitable climate for innovation is critical for increased innovation capability.

Strategy

On a strategic level, Kanthal worked primarily with short-term, result-oriented improvement work. This is, of course, important, but the innovation potential was perceived to be more substantial than that. The strategy, routines and processes required to increase innovation capability have to be designed so that preconditions for innovation will benefit both the short-term, continuous improvement work and the long-term, explorative innovation work. The strategy must ensure that people reach efficiency in everyday work and, at the same time, take advantage of their creativity. New metrics need to be developed on a system level to complement the current more short-term, result-oriented ones, with long-term innovation and learning metrics. There is also a need for a clear and communicated strategic direction of the initiatives for innovation.

Tactics

With a focus on short-term incremental innovation, there was a need to develop long-term innovativeness, creativity, transparency and structure linked to innovation. One important part was to ensure cross-functional teamwork, another was to communicate the process of how value is created. In its first phase, trend analysis and business intelligence needed to be systematised to develop new insights and identify opportunities for innovation. In changing processes, structures and control, the risks are that the preconditions for innovation decline and creativity decreases, it becomes one of the challenges leadership needs to address. Leaders also need to ensure that knowledge and skills for using methods and tools are in place for continuous learning and implementation. There are ways to design innovation processes to create, and take advantage of, learning in the entire organisation and at the same time support implementation.

People

The current structure primarily focuses on exploiting *what is* versus the exploration of *what might be*. Therefore, the process of seeking out new opportunities needs to be enhanced. Extended processes, with e.g., design-inspired methods and tools, can stimulate creativity and increase exploration. Design methodology also encourages learning and experimentation that increases playfulness, challenge and psychological safety. A strategy is needed for leadership and team development to increase process output and value and enable a suitable climate for innovation. Kanthal needs to develop ambidexterity, where leadership focuses on two things in parallel: delivering in the short term and encouraging curiosity to explore opportunities for long-term prosperity.

10.2.3. *Understanding intersection points — Clarity, self-confidence and control*

Understandably, the essential parts of the model in Figure 10.1 are also about understanding what happens at the intersection points of clarity, control and self-confidence. For Kanthal, these aspects affect attaining the clarity of what to do, creating control of how to do it and increasing the self-confidence of the people who are doing it.

Clarity

Clarity can be increased by expressing the organisation's direction and "why you do what you do, the way you do!" For innovation work, clarity was required regarding what to do (direction and goals) and how to do it (the process of creating value).

Self-confidence

For exploration to be fruitful, a well-defined direction of where to innovate is required. Closely linked to this is that employees need to have the freedom to act, be brave and be more challenged (preferably at the team level) to increase trust.

Control

One way to achieve control was to create a clear connection between what is to be done tactically (the innovation process) and the employees' abilities and opportunities to carry out these tasks. This may include the knowledge and support for the different tools and methods used to achieve ambition and create value.

10.3. Elements of Interest in This Case

Kanthal's system for innovation (through the ISO 56002) incorporates many of the elements defined in the standard. But whether or not these elements are linked systemically is not apparent. As outlined in the IMS standard, committed leadership (5.1) and a clear innovation strategy (5.1.4) are essential to set the right preconditions for success. Leadership commitment is present, and leader's competence development is continuously ongoing at Kanthal. This has been most prominent in the past years, specifically for innovation behaviours and to enable the right climate for innovation. The improved innovation strategy enables an IMS to unfold with a long-term commitment. These elements above are prerequisites for success, however, there are three additional elements, *culture* (4.4.2), *competence* (7.2) and *"identify opportunities"* (8.3.2), that are most significant in this case.

10.3.1. *Culture*

As stated in the ISO 56002 Clause 0.3.1 (2019), *the effective implementation of the innovation management system relies on … a culture supporting innovation activities.* It is imperative to understand the organisational preconditions for innovation. As mentioned earlier, an initial assessment of the 10 dimensions of an innovation climate (Ekvall, 1996), complemented by three other dimensions (*support from colleagues, common mental models* and *creative autonomy*), was made in 2018, with a follow-up in 2019. This uncovered two overall important aspects regarding the climate for innovation. Firstly, from 2018 to 2019, the innovation climate increased on all dimensions measured. Secondly, the result revealed preconditions for incremental innovation, whereby converging activities and cooperation, focused on consensus building and collective reflection, were dominant.

In detail, the results indicated a low challenge level that did not leverage the high competence among employees, a lack of freedom that might hinder new initiatives, and low psychological safety due to conflicts and risk aversion, which created obstacles for cooperation and new initiatives.

10.3.2. *Competence*

As part of Clause 7, Support in the ISO 56002, competence is essential for organisational knowledge concerning direction and goals of innovation initiatives. It is also important regarding what abilities and skills are needed, on the individual level, to achieve these goals, i.e., being able to fully utilise tools and methods to accomplish the goal. Kanthal employees are experts within a narrow scope of knowledge, and the ability to challenge and continuously develop individual competencies are traditionally a management task. When they found the challenge level was below expected, they initiated a discussion on how to increase knowledge development. One initiative developed from this discussion was letting employees set up knowledge development targets in dialogue with their manager. Also, in the R&D department, new Key Performance Indicators (KPIs) were discussed, mainly conversational KPIs building on Brattström *et al.* (2018).

10.3.3. *Identify opportunities*

There is a need to identify and define opportunities where the organisation, from a resource and competence perspective, could develop innovations. Signals from the market and new learnings within the organisation need to be captured systematically. This means that several information streams need to be gathered to define where the high-value opportunities are, and then prioritise these. At Kanthal, this was a potential bottleneck for new initiatives. Looking at the culture element, we can see that the low levels of "freedom" and "challenge" also hinder new insights from the market to reach the correct phase of the innovation process. Managing information and culture is needed in ways that bridge new insights, with the right competence.

10.4. Building Bridges

Traditionally, the system elements at Kanthal have not been linked. However, several bridges between elements were identified in the innovation process. These include:

- Developing and deploying solutions.
- Collaborating with external partners for new knowledge.
- Co-creation of new solutions and the application development centre serving both the R&D and the sales department.

In addition, there was a need to strengthen (or even build some new) bridges. However, using the term "building bridges" might be puzzling since the term refers to improving relationships between different groups of people. But, in looking at innovation as originating from people, all systemic interrelationships between elements of a system result from interactions among people.

Identifying the need for new bridges was made possible by understanding both the preconditions for innovation and the structure and interrelationship of the elements. It is, therefore, not surprising that the relationship between the elements is not apparent for all employees. As a matter of fact, how they interact is a mystery for most of them. But they do relate and interact; the following is a visualisation of this interaction (Figure 10.2).

As shown in Figure 10.2, the three elements are linked through specific enablers, dependent on preconditions, such as, psychological safety and idea management. However, the existence of these enablers depends on the innovation climate and other elements of the system.

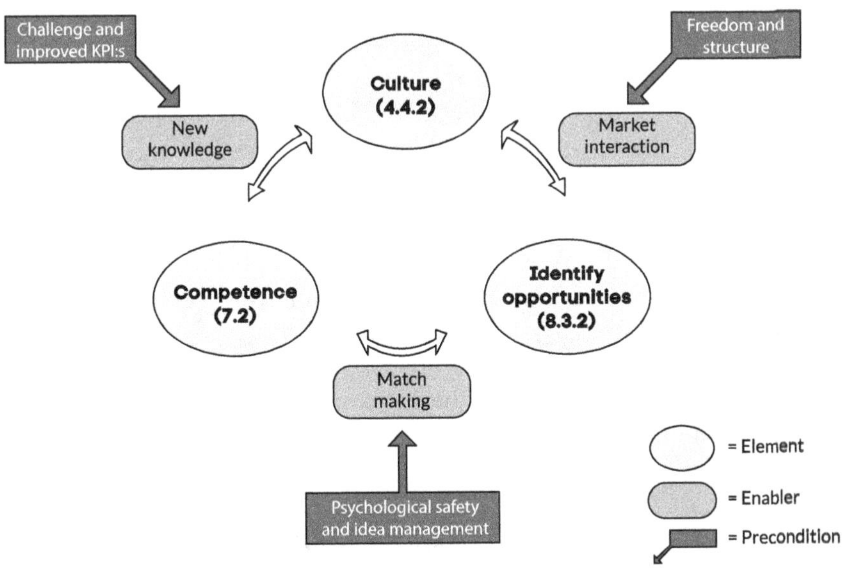

Fig. 10.2. The relation between culture, competence and identify opportunities.

10.4.1. *How were these elements of the system implemented?*

There are several layers of implementation regarding the bridges between elements at Kanthal. Firstly, building bridges is an ongoing process, and bridges need to be maintained. Secondly, there are several enablers for the bridges to work, and these have been identified and addressed accordingly:

- Capture new insights through market interaction with clear roles in the organisation.
- Create new knowledge through increased expectations on individual and team levels.
- Match knowledge and insights through an idea management system.

To simplify the creation of new ideas, in an organisation like Kanthal, the generation of ideas occurs in the interaction between knowledge and needs. But to leverage this and become even more innovative, new knowledge is needed, along with the increased understanding of needs. Due to this, new initiatives have been undertaken to:

- Connect direction/scope of innovation with new knowledge development: The R&D department initiated and implemented new KPIs focusing on knowledge development and increased expectations on the individual and team levels.
- Address the possible bottleneck: An idea management system was implemented to match needs/ideas with competence and gather all needs in one place.
- Resource sharing and common understanding on the path forward: An innovation board was established with representatives from different parts of the organisation to secure matchmaking between support, needs and competence.

As visualised in Figure 10.2, the initiatives above go together to build bridges among innovation system elements at Kanthal.

10.4.2. *What were the barriers to bridge-building?*

Addressing barriers has been identified as critical for building the bridges between elements. One is breaking habits of doing things in one way and changing these habits by adopting new routines and procedures. For example, a new habit is to capture insights and identify new opportunities for input into the idea management system and not through the old habits of established relationships with R&D employees — or directly to the application development centre. This barrier needs both time and psychological safety. Time is vital for changing habits, and psychological safety is required, if people are to feel free to share new insights into the internal open space of the idea management system.

10.4.3. *Innovation timing and communication*

In looking back to how Hans von Kantzow created the idea that was the starting point for Kanthal, there are many similarities. From the combination of knowledge and insights to the experimentation of different balances between materials, Hans himself employed engineers equivalent to the application development centre at Kanthal today. However, there is a crucial point still missing in Figure 10.2. How do we plan for and take advantage of the timing? Of course, this is a question everyone asks. In this case, the timing lies in exploring new opportunities and ensuring a continuous stream of market needs to generate insights.

Also, and not surprisingly, an initiative that reinforces both understanding and interest is to communicate about the value of innovation and how the organisation defines, delivers and creates this value. An internal podcast was created in 2020 to respond to the lack of meetings in different settings due to COVID-19 and to communicate innovation within Kanthal efficiently and comprehensively. The podcast has put innovation back at the heart of the conversation during coffee breaks at Kanthal.

10.5. Achievements of the Innovation Management System

10.5.1. *Innovation climate*

Between 2018 and 2019, there was an increased level in all dimensions of the innovation climate through leadership efforts by demonstrating a clear interest and undertaking several initiatives. This was possible via new knowledge development through the assessment and analysis.

10.5.2. *Innovation board*

An increased understanding of the interacting elements, described in Section 4.1, has decreased the barriers between different parts of the organisation. People were able to relate through a common structure by being involved in the various activities in the system elements and creating the bridges between them. One aspect that helped in this is the "Innovation Board," where representatives from several different parts of the organisation gather to discuss questions related to managing innovation. This has led to increased transparency regarding resources and competencies, but also with understanding needs and challenges.

10.5.3. *KPIs*

The new and improved KPIs of the R&D department, which make knowledge development matter, will take time for these achievements to be fully understood and realised. Nonetheless, this greater focus on capturing insights and creating new business opportunities will increase the performance of the innovation process. Also, these KPIs add acceptance for spending time on new areas, methods and techniques that bring new knowledge to the organisation.

10.5.4. *Implications*

Engaging all employees in an organisation to capture ideas puts the demand and responsibility on all leaders in the organisation, specifically on the "Innovation Board." Learning how to request ideas, what questions to ask and answer as an idea provider, and how to aim the power of the organisation in one specific direction is essential. Kanthal is still exploring this.

Also, looking at the enablers of the system described in Figure 10.2, they rely heavily on the culture element and specifically on the climate for innovation. Without psychological safety, the systems perspective of innovation will encounter problems. Even if the climate dimensions are in place, there needs to be a structure to capture and disseminate market needs and insights and match these with new or existing knowledge via an idea management system. In addition, knowledge development is required to discover new opportunities and manage market timing for these opportunities.

A challenge is also at the top management level of the organisation. It needs to understand that a narrow focus on short-term profit will affect long-term prosperity. Returning to Hans von Kantzow and his exploration and experimentation in the premises: he was allowed to use facilities he could not afford and spent his own money on hiring engineers to continue searching for what came to be a world-leading brand. Whose money to spend now — and what will happen in not spending this money now — is a top management dilemma and a priority.

10.6. Overall Reflections and Way Forward

Implementing a systematic approach to innovation is not a straightforward process. Any organisation needs to plan for deviations, uncertainty and ambidexterity. The following are a few overall reflections and potential and planned ways forward for Kanthal to increase innovation capability.

10.6.1. *Structure beyond process*

On an abstract level, elements of the IMS at Kanthal provide a structure that is easy to recognise and relates to all the work made in the organisation regarding innovation, not only the processes. The way the elements are interrelated becomes the guiding system for innovation initiatives, most needed in organisations. It represents a structure that provides encouragement and safety among employees involved in the innovation work. Through the lens of the system, it gives an overview of the innovation work and an opportunity to zoom in to explore details. It provides learning for how the elements complement each other, what is expected from each element, and what each element requires of the other. This means that the systemic view makes a difference. Preparing the ground, making the foundation, and building the bridge between the islands is as important as having the bridges in place.

10.6.2. *More function-oriented innovation work and collaboration*

Understanding the interrelationship of the elements will also provide more function-oriented, and less person-oriented, innovation work, which means that informal interactions will have less impact on building bottlenecks in the decision-making process. Also, involving different functions in the decision via the use of the Innovation Board will provide a broader knowledge base and multi-disciplinarity in the decisions. The importance of collaboration between different stakeholders in the organisation and, when needed, externally is also one crucial key takeaway.

On a detailed level, the role of the climate for innovation as part of the culture will make a difference. The main difference in building the capability in innovation is based on making the innovation climate work. By measuring, analysing and exploring the climate for innovation, new knowledge for leaders and insights about the enablers for innovation success at Kanthal were enhanced.

In almost all organisations, there are pieces of IMS elements in place. The approach taken by Kanthal to build from where they were, starting in areas of importance where engagements existed, is also a good lesson learned and maybe a critical factor in making an IMS a reality.

10.6.3. *Innovation campaigns and bridges*

One specific action in the short term is the planned innovation campaign within one narrow area of direction. Based on the strategy, the idea is to define campaigns that can highlight opportunities for future exploration and, where there is a desire, to grow and immerse knowledge development. These campaigns would then go through a lengthy screening process, with deep dives into the need analysis before narrowing down to think about detailed solutions associated with ideas left in the process. This will lead to new knowledge being developed and the gathering of needs in a structured way.

In the long run, more shores around the different islands need to be prepared for the foundation of new bridges and to maintain the bridges that are already built. The process of connecting the elements has just started; much work is still required to make a sustainable innovation capability.

References

Amabile, T. M., Conti, R., Coon, H., Lazenby, J. and Herron, M. (1996). Assessing the work environment for creativity. *Academy of Management Journal, 39*(5), 1154–1184.

Brattström, A., Frishammar, J., Richtnér, A. and Pflueger, D. (2018). Can innovation be measured? A framework of how measurement of innovation engages attention in firms. *Journal of Engineering and Technology Management, 48*, 64–75.

Ekvall, G. (1996). Organisational climate for creativity and innovation. *European Journal of Work and Organisational Psychology, 5*(1), 105–123.

ISO (2019). *ISO 56002:2019 Innovation management — Innovation management system — Guidance*. International Organization for Standardization.

Mintzberg, H. (1987). Five P's for strategy. *California Management Review. Fall* (Reprinted in Henry Mintzberg and James Brian Quinn (eds.), *The Strategy Process: Concepts, Contexts, Cases* (3rd edn.). Upper Saddle River, NJ: Prentice Hall, 1996).

Tidd, J. and Bessant, J. (1997/2009). *Managing Innovation: Integrating Technological, Market And Organisational Change*. West Sussex, England: John Wiley & Sons Ltd.

Wikström, A. (2020). Embedding innovation, the role of clarity, control and self-confidence. *International Product Development Management Conference*, Antwerp.

© 2023 World Scientific Publishing Europe Ltd.
https://doi.org/10.1142/9781800612105_0011

Chapter 11

Karolinska University Hospital: Implementing an Innovation Management System at a University Hospital Providing Highly Specialised Care

Ingrid Kihlander and Åse Lundh Gravenius

Abstract

In 2019, Karolinska University Hospital, Sweden's largest hospital delivering highly specialised care, decided to implement an innovation management system (IMS) in order to enhance the organisation's innovation capabilities through systematic innovation. This chapter focuses on the efforts and effects related to this implementation, from the perspective of the support function Centre for Innovation, which had a key role in the design and implementation of the innovation management system at Karolinska. The guidance standard ISO 56002 Innovation Management System has been used as a reference model in the design of the Karolinska IMS, utilising all elements included in it. This systems approach has provided a useful terminology and a logic for connecting the elements. Further, this case reveals the importance of having a strategy as a basis for action; the need to address an innovative culture in this otherwise risk-averse context; the potential in building internal innovation networks; the key in combined educational and coaching activities; the strength using communication; as well as challenges in designing relevant measurement and evaluation systems for innovation. Finally, building innovation capabilities bottom-up has proved to be essential in a large and multi-faceted organisation such as Karolinska.

11.1. Introduction

11.1.1. *Karolinska University Hospital*

Karolinska University Hospital (Karolinska), in Sweden, is one of Europe's largest University Hospitals. The hospital has over 15,000 employees (whereof 2,600 persons are active in research), 1,100 beds and 1.35 million patient visits/year. Karolinska has received international recognition, being listed in seventh place when Newsweek in 2021 listed World's Best Hospitals (Newsweek, 2021).

The Region Stockholm is responsible for all publicly financed healthcare in the county of Stockholm, hence defining the overall assignment for Karolinska. The assignment can be summarised as "providing highly specialised healthcare together with research and educating the professionals of tomorrow." Recently, the hospital has made an extensive reorganisation whereby a new operational model was implemented. The clinical practice is now organised in Themes and Functions, replacing the old clinic structure. Themes are, for example, defined as Theme Acute and Repair Medicine and Theme Heart, Vessels and Neuro. Functions are, for example, the Karolinska University Laboratory. The thematic care aims to put the patients' collective medical needs into even greater focus but also serves to clarify the requirements for systematic innovation.

11.1.2. *Innovation in healthcare*

In healthcare there is a drive to improve the health of the population and the experience of care (including quality and satisfaction) as well as reducing the costs per capita needed to provide said healthcare, referred to as the Triple Aim (Institute for Healthcare Improvement, 2021). To address this, innovation and hospital innovativeness have been identified as a way forward in contributing to higher clinical performance in healthcare (Salge and Vera, 2009).

Innovation is needed to meet future needs as regards to more efficient treatments, optimised care processes and more cost-effective interventions. When generating innovation from within healthcare organisations, the origin can come from science, technology and specialisation (science-based), as well as daily practice, involving several hierarchical levels and knowledge domains (practice-based) (Salge and Vera, 2009). However, research in innovation in healthcare has to a large extent focused on healthcare organisations as adopters of innovation (e.g., in Greenhalgh *et al.*, 2004) rather than generators of innovation.

Challenges related to innovation in healthcare are often related to the complex network of actors (care providers, procurement, patients, etc.) and the often intricate models for financing and reimbursement, as well as high demands on accountability and potential obstacles originating from policy and regulations (Herzlinger, 2006).

11.1.3. *Developing support for systematic innovation work at Karolinska*

Karolinska University Hospital has a history as a renowned care provider and a research institution. Several activities and initiatives have through the years been initiated to support innovation, corresponding to the diverse set of innovation work that is present in a university hospital (e.g., advanced technology-driven innovation or process innovation regarding care flows and clinical working environment). In 2011, the support function Centre for Innovation (CfI) was established. The primary task of the CfI then was to bring together a number of strategic innovation partnerships and projects performed in collaboration with external, often private industry, partners.

The CfI's scope has, over the years, transformed from primarily working on separate innovation projects and being a hub for leading and coordinating innovation projects into coaching the organisation and being more of a competence centre for innovation, working with the aim of fostering and nurturing internal innovation capabilities. The CfI has always supported innovation as well as promoted an innovation-friendly culture at the hospital, but it was not until 2017 that the more systematic and systemic approach was truly adopted. The number of employees at CfI has varied over the years, but at the time of writing this chapter it employs around 15 persons. The employees at CfI are intentionally recruited with different backgrounds such as healthcare itself, law, communication, engineering and service design.

A process of professionalising of the innovation management support at Karolinska is underway. Education in innovation management has been provided to the employees at CfI, and some of its staff have had the opportunity to enrol in the programme Innovating Health for Tomorrow at INSEAD. Representatives from CfI have also followed, and to some extent been involved in, the national committee for the development of the ISO standards related to Innovation Management. During 2017, a personal certification, following "ISO/IEC 17024:2012 Conformity assessment — General requirements for bodies operating certification of persons" (ISO, 2012), as Innovation Management Professionals was developed in Sweden, and around half of the employees at the CfI have been certified as Innovation Management Professionals.

The assignment for CfI, as defined in 2019, was to be the owner of Karolinska's innovation management support, innovation management infrastructure, innovation management education and innovation measurements. This includes the hospital's overarching innovation methods, financing strategies related to innovation and collaborations, coordinating innovation partnerships, and using innovation methods, terminology and approach in order to speed up implementation of research results and scaling-up the adoption of the same in clinical practice.

Early in 2019, a decision was made to establish a management system for innovation at the hospital with the "ISO 56002:2019 Innovation management system — Guidance" (ISO, 2019) as a reference. The CfI was appointed responsible for developing and implementing the innovation management system at Karolinska. The motivation for implementing an innovation management system was to work systematically with innovation in order to, at least in part, address the overall challenges of providing healthcare according to Karolinska's ambition. The decision drew on positive experiences with having management systems applicable in other areas.

11.2. Designing an Innovation Management System for the Hospital

The ISO 56002 guidance standard has been used as an important source of input in the work of designing a management system for innovation at

Karolinska. Both content and structure have been utilised in different steps such as identifying the state of the organisation prior to implementation as well as forming how the innovation management system could be designed.

11.2.1. *Key system elements*

In designing an innovation management system at Karolinska several perspectives have been addressed in providing a foundation for the implementation and for enabling impact. Undertakings such as this will never be completed but here the first developments in designing and implementing an innovation management system for Karolinska are accounted for. Referring to ISO 56002, the following presentation specifically relates to the elements of innovation strategy (5.1.4), culture (4.4.2), organisational structures (6.3), innovation processes (8.3), competence (7.2), communication (7.4) and evaluation (9.1), respectively.

Giving the work direction: Innovation strategy as a basis for action

The overarching purpose of providing and developing high class healthcare is truly permeated throughout the whole organisation of Karolinska. However, how the organisation relates this mission to its work within the field of innovation has not been as clearly stated.

On a regional level, an innovation strategy is implemented stating that every organisation within Region Stockholm must integrate systematic innovation into its daily management. The regional innovation strategy has not impacted the hospital's innovation management system design as such, but it has nonetheless provided Karolinska with a much-needed emphasis on innovation in general, and systematic innovation in particular.

The CfI has been given an important role in providing expertise regarding innovation and innovation management and to maintain an innovation management system that should address all types of innovation, radical as well as incremental.

Context characteristics and culture that need to be addressed

In designing support for innovation carried out in healthcare, ways of managing characteristics strongly associated with the healthcare context, such as risk aversion and hierarchical structures, must be included.

It is not surprising that the healthcare context is risk aversive due to its foremost mission of saving lives and the high demands on accountability and safety that comes with that. Uncertainty must be minimised, and the daily work relies on evidence-based and well-proven practice. Therefore, it is important to create "safe zones" (in time and space, but also mentally) for testing and experimenting, where it is acceptable to fail. This can be generated through creating projects and initiatives, and using specific methods where this is promoted, creating safe zones for testing but also forcing employees to break away from the "how we've always done" thinking and to enable them to see themselves as innovation generators.

This also calls for a leadership that allows and supports innovation-related work. Of course, leadership which promotes innovation is beneficial, but most critical is to not hinder such ambitions or disrupt important innovative flows. Further, it should also be supported that in a context with clear hierarchies and chains of command for the daily work, higher echelon people should also have the opportunity to enter safe zones in innovation work where the demands on being the ones who know the most is not present.

Responsibilities divided in a dual operating model

Innovation is part of the overall assignment for the Themes and Functions (the organisational divisions) in the hospital. In addition, the CfI is tasked with providing innovation support to the organisation.

From the perspective of the CfI, the offer to the organisation must be well thought through, documented and scalable as it intends to serve a mass of over 15,000 employees with the CfI's mere 15. Therefore, the innovation management support of the CfI aims to build capabilities in the organisation, supporting the organisation in innovating themselves. This is addressed in a systems approach where CfI offers education and coaching of Karolinska's employees, and provides structures, tools, methods, checklists and templates. The CfI is also directly involved in a number of strategically selected innovation initiatives.

An essential inspiration is the dual operating system for change as defined by Kotter (2012), where a more agile network-like structure overlays the existing organisational structure and processes. The two structures should be seamlessly connected, and employees should be active in both. In the Karolinska case, this means that innovation is to be owned by the functional organisation but is strengthened by networks of, for example, people from all parts of the organisation, very knowledgeable in "the innovation way of working," supported (and somewhat orchestrated) by the CfI. The aim is not to have every employee involved in innovation work all the time, but to build critical mass in the networks, and to have the management to facilitate this. Therefore, the educational and coaching activities are identified as core in building innovation capabilities in the hospital.

The distributed responsibility of innovation at Karolinska will ultimately result in Themes and Functions highly influencing their own innovation work. To that end, the CfI has focused on carving out what should be the "minimum common denominator" when conducting work within the field of innovation at Karolinska and has used that when it comes to describing the hospital's overarching innovation processes and support.

Core processes and structures for collaborations

The hospital's innovation process focuses primarily on understanding the need at hand, and thus not rushing into solution mode. The hospital predominantly uses methods and tools from service design and design thinking, promoting prototyping and user involvement. Furthermore, an emphasis on facts and figures, to keep track of the value metrics, is established early on. There is a need to elaborate on business models since reimbursement structures in healthcare are well-known obstacles for further diffusion and scaling of innovation.

Karolinska has great knowledge and experience from collaboration with academia and industry. Examples of support for innovation collaborations with external partners are processes for matching the hospital's needs with the commercial interests of potential external partners, support regarding contracts and intellectual properties, but also knowledge in how to lead and coordinate partnerships and projects.

Building capabilities through competence development

The offering of education and coaching activities to several different target groups has been identified as a core activity in supporting the hospital's innovation work. The reason for this is the decentralised responsibility for innovation, which in essence means that innovation competence has to be spread, not confining it to one unit within the hospital. There is a need to have many people, throughout the entire organisation, with a medium to high innovation competence. To achieve this, education and coaching programmes have been identified as key.

The *Innovation Ambassador* programme is a training course where participants learn methods of working systematically with innovation, based on design thinking. This is offered to a wide range of employees at the hospital. This programme includes coaching where theory is combined with a challenge that the employee brings from their own daily work. The programme *Innovation for Leaders* was initiated in order to take the managerial perspective, and not directly the operational perspective on innovation work. Further, modules addressing innovation have been implemented in the general leadership development, and here is the motivation to also capture clinical leaders in the beginning of their leadership careers and make them aware of their role as leaders in relation to innovation work. In addition, all these programmes are opportunities to build networks related to innovation work further on, which is considered when selecting participants for these programmes. Gaining expertise and cutting-edge knowledge in innovation management is also encouraged. Those who meet the competence requirements as innovation leaders, in accordance with a predefined competence profile, can be registered as such in the HR system.

Communication: Creating awareness and understanding

Communicating around both innovation activities and results have several positive effects such as spreading good examples, providing recognition for the people involved, and raising awareness and interest in what support is available for innovation work. This also creates a foundation for further networking. Communication around results and activities also promotes innovation as something that is a natural part of the organisation, and not just an add-on.

An important issue in the educational programmes, and in the communication in general, is the terminology used. In the educational programmes, a lot of effort has been put into how to address innovation in the healthcare context drawing from both general innovation management and the terminology of the specific healthcare context. This is with hope of employees being able to talk innovation "on a higher level" with different types of stakeholders. While it is beneficial to incorporate a general innovation management terminology, caution has to be taken so as not to use bureaucratic jargon that intimidates clinical staff.

Measuring and evaluating value and performance

The creation of value through providing high-quality healthcare is at the core of everything for Karolinska. However, when identifying relevant indicators, it can be challenging to identify what system limits to relate to. What to include when healthcare is performed in collaboration with several actors? What to include when it is the lifelong effect that is the primary value for the patient, but treatments are time-limited? What values that are created are interesting on several levels: in each innovation initiative, from having an innovation management system, and from the different innovation supporting efforts initiated?

For each innovation initiative, identifying the raised value using facts and figures is encouraged. "Knowing your numbers" will raise possibilities to spread the initiative and implement it in the daily work of others, aided by the ability of being able to communicate the benefit at hand. For the innovation management system, performance indicators can still be considered as immature and will be further developed. In the work of defining future performance indicators, it is carefully taken into account not to determine performance indicators too soon. For example, an interesting strand is to relate the innovation management system performance to both clinical performance and to employee satisfaction in the organisation. It is also relevant to transform, and expand, from just looking at benefits from separate projects into looking at benefits from a systems perspective. Defining value and performance indicators, at both innovation initiative level and the innovation management system level, needs to be very carefully considered, without settling only for measurements easy to perform and measure. In addition, there is a requirement from Region Stockholm to measure innovation and it is expected that this will be done with a refined granularity in the years to come.

11.2.2. *Reflections based on a systems approach*

A challenge in a systems approach is to understand and to easily describe the system since the elements of the system are intertwined. For Karolinska, several of the different system elements defined in the ISO standard for innovation management system were already implemented in the organisation. The system model, as presented in the ISO standard, however, provided a useful terminology and a logic for connecting the elements. For example, it became clear that the support for innovation work needs to be provided from several perspectives such as coaching processes, educating the employees and the promotion of an innovative culture.

Most of the employees do not need to have a detailed knowledge as regards the complete innovation management system, but there should be a general awareness in order to know where to turn to find support for the innovation work. Descriptions of the innovation management system will be available through the intranet and all employees should easily be able to find the entry points into the system so they can find the support they seek or need. Management, however, could be considered as both customer and responsible for the complete innovation management system, including the performance, the evaluation and how it could and should be improved (related to the Plan–Do–Check–Act cycle included in ISO 56002) and should therefore be well acquainted to all parts of the system. The other roles that should be fully knowledgeable of the complete innovation management system are the innovation management professionals at the hospital. The systematic process of evaluation, and improvements of the system, has not yet been fully implemented, due to the newness of the management system.

The plan is not to, at least in the near future, totally integrate the innovation management system with other management systems in the organisation. Focus is on aligning and gaining synergies in the follow-up, evaluation and improvements of the different management systems at Karolinska.

11.3. Implementation Experiences

Karolinska is an organisation with an extensive experience in research and also has a history of developing support for innovation during many years. A professionalisation of innovation management has been developed gradually and several initiatives have been initiated preceding the decision to implement an innovation management system in the hospital.

The decision to implement a management system for innovation at the hospital in 2019 was definitely affected by the fact that the ISO standard for innovation management system was about to be published. An ISO standard in innovation management gave external validity, and this external reference is highly valuable in a context that strives for risk minimising and works based on validated knowledge. Further, in the communication around systematic innovation management it has also been beneficial to refer to this external validity and a globally agreed terminology and thereby be able to communicate around systematic innovation management as a "real" topic.

In 2019, an initial gap analysis between the current state and the ISO 56002 was performed. The gap analysis illustrated that many elements where already available, such as methods supporting the innovation process as well as supporting structures for external collaborations. In the mapping of the current state, a benchmark study was performed targeting innovation work within other university hospitals in Europe, showing that for the time being no direct role model in the implementation of an innovation management system was to be identified. An action plan was created defining what should be developed and who should be responsible. The structure and content of ISO 56002, including the visualisation of the innovation management system, have been used recurrently in the work, both in conducting the gap analysis and as a reference when developing and documenting the new innovation management system at Karolinska.

At the CfI, responsible for developing and implementing the innovation management system, a team focusing on the innovation management system was formed. The team consisted of five people, all working at CfI but with different backgrounds such as law, communication, engineering, chemistry and service design. The development and documentation of the system have been guided by an ambition to provide support and present the system, and the different types of support, in a way that is perceived as inspiring and helpful, and not just as a theoretical model. Great consideration has been put into how to document whole and/or elements of the system in order to make employees want to use the information and the provided methods and tools. At the same time, the innovation management system has been designed based on what can be designed to work for the whole organisation, regardless of in which department an employee works. Even if the innovation management system is not to be integrated with other management systems, effort has been put into aligning the innovation support with existing processes and methods, where possible, in order not to raise the burden for the employees such as adding more demands on documentation or additional decision fora, and to be sustainable over time. This conscious alignment also clarifies where the process should deviate from other existing processes and methods.

11.3.1. *Combination of top-down and bottom-up approaches*

Top management commitment and support has been identified as important in the implementation of Karolinska's innovation management system. The 2019 decision of implementing the innovation management system made by top management was crucial but due to the size of the organisation as well as the autonomy of different management teams for the respective Themes and Functions, this decision has needed to be reconfirmed on a number of occasions in order to enable a true impact of the innovation management system implementation.

Furthermore, the COVID-19 pandemic has affected the possibilities to get the management's attention, since their focus as a healthcare provider, for obvious reasons, has been on handling the pandemic situation. In order not to lose momentum in the implementation of the innovation management system even if the access to top management attention could not be what was planned for, a bottom-up approach has been used, tapping the education of employees as the core activity, building capabilities in the receiving end. This has resulted in the organic growth of the number of employees that are trained in systematic innovation work, building the network supporting the organisations innovation work as intended. The design of the educational and coaching programmes is essential but also how to assign participants. Karolinska has learned that the impact of the education will be much deeper if a Theme or Function enrols more than one person to each programme. During the COVID-19 pandemic, the interest for the educational programmes has been strong, but the drop-out rate has also increased due to exhaustion among the personnel.

Positive effects of the educational programmes have though been acknowledged by Region Stockholm, tasking Karolinska with educating employees from other organisations within the region.

11.3.2. *Communication and documentation*

A management system should be documented. How it is documented can serve as a good base for further communication. As identified in the development work, there are different target groups to consider. There is the management, but also the innovation management professionals, who should have knowledge regarding the whole innovation management system. To the broader set of employees, the key message is not about the innovation management system but instead promoting benefits and importance of systematic innovation and the support available, and also an ambition to build innovation capabilities in the organisation. Employees should know about the process, and how to find support on how innovation work is carried out at Karolinska. An additional target group considered is external actors, who potentially could be an external certification body in the future, if the innovation management system becomes certifiable.

11.3.3. *Measuring performance*

In measuring the performance, and the value created, a transformation was necessary going from computing the value output from separate projects into measuring system output, which also required a new way of thinking. In the development and implementation, there has been a consciousness that the performance indicators will evolve from those during the implementation phase and later when the innovation management system is up and running. Included in this consciousness is an acceptance that the performance indicators in the beginning will be perceived as rather blunt and immature, with the confidence that they will evolve over time.

11.3.4. *Implementation timeline drift*

All in all, the implementation has required more time than originally planned for. In hindsight, the implementation of a true innovation management system takes time. It does not take long to draw up plans for what a management system should look like in an organisation, but to make that system permeate an entire organisation is an entirely different task altogether, varying with the size and culture of that organisation. The implementation would have benefited from being broken down into more phases already from the beginning.

Also, of course the COVID-19 situation has resulted in the whole organisation, both management and clinical staff, being tired. However, the extreme situation also induced that some improvements that had been discussed and prepared for a long time, prior to the pandemic, were tested, iterated and implemented very quickly, such as care using video conferencing as a standard and automation in the laboratory.

11.4. Effects of Systematic Work for Increasing Innovation Capabilities

To identify explicit results and effects from implementing an innovation management system at the hospital is of course rather challenging, both based on the intricate nature of the matter and also on the fact that the work towards implementing an innovation management system according to ISO 56002 has only recently begun.

However, a number of effects from systematic innovation and systemic support for innovation can be illustrated from clinical examples.

These examples elucidate different mechanisms unleashing the value creation, emphasising that value creation through innovation can look different, and therefore motivates a systems approach supporting not only one specific process but building capabilities through the interaction of several elements.

11.4.1. *Innovation as a leadership tool at the Emergency Unit*

The Emergency Unit utilised innovation work and development as a leadership tool, addressing an unwanted situation with, e.g., high staff turnover and low employee satisfaction. Key personnel at the Emergency Unit learned basic innovation methodologies, based on design thinking, and were assigned to systematically drive development work at the Emergency Unit.

The development work was characterised by systematic work, supported prototyping, and involvement of all employees at the Emergency Unit (which might be extra challenging in a 24-7 high-intensity environment as an emergency unit). The systematic work had a clear focus on their own value creation and a utilisation of relevant measurements.

Through creating time and space where the employees felt safe in experimenting, a culture and climate open for testing arose, for example, resulting in "extremely little resistance to testing things, and figuring out problems and daring to change — maybe just for a day to see what the effect was." A culture promoting innovation and development emerged and is now considered as a part of the regular work. Employees are also very generous in contributing proposals on how to improve their own working situation and working methods. This, in turn, has resulted in the Emergency Unit being approached by projects and initiatives from elsewhere, inquiring if the Emergency Unit can be involved in prototyping and experimenting.

The effects have improved performance in several ways, such as both in clinical measurements and the working environment. An emergency unit is very affected by what happens outside of the hospital, and the environment of collaboration and involvement that emerged has helped build a robustness in handling all these rapid influences, and continued work with development, even if the situation is chaotic, with the COVID-19 pandemic being a recent example.

11.4.2. *Supporting structures for an industry collaboration in neuroscience*

There are several collaboration projects between Karolinska and external industrial partners. In a neuroscience project, closely related to ongoing research, the purpose has been to perform interoperative magnetic camera examinations as a part of neurosurgery. By combining possibilities from different domains, fewer invasive surgeries on the patient have been performed, e.g., checks as to whether the tumour was completely removed during the surgery or not. The decreased number of surgeries is beneficial for several stakeholders, such as the patient, who needs to prepare for surgery fewer times, lower risk for nerve damage, shorter rehab time, and quicker return to work. The hospital can perform one operation instead of two, there is no separate process for doing the magnetic camera examination to see how the surgery went, which of course is more resource efficient.

This kind of innovation work, performed in collaboration with different organisations, benefits from having supporting structures. These structures support in connecting relevant competencies, as well as support the communication and navigation between the organisations, covering both legal contracts but also softer networking issues.

11.4.3. *Reducing cancellations of planned surgeries for children*

The head of nursing in the Paediatric Orthopaedics and Neurology unit entered the Innovation Ambassador programme and brought a problem from her own organisation to work with during the programme: It was perceived that there were too many cancellations of planned surgeries for children. Surgeries that the patients (children) and their families had carefully prepared for. Working with this case during the programme a number of key take-aways were identified:

- Methods and tools for identifying the real problem. Solving the right problem means a more effective way of using the resources.
- Methods and tools can help to "break away" from a traditional path of doing things.

- Focus on needs, and not rush into solutions too soon, which is a common pitfall in healthcare when wanting to solve the problems as quickly as possible.
- Involve different stakeholders and understand their different needs, especially the patients.
- Base work on facts and figures (metrics). Get facts and figures straight when investigating needs and problems, but also to use in further communication. Using the metrics was an enabling factor in getting acceptance from management for making experiments.
- Start with creating a small-scale experiment and hypothesis-testing, and if results are positive, expand the experiment.

The solution developed was separated care flows having one emergency flow and one patient flow for planned operations. It was tested on a small scale, in parallel with regular work, and positive results were received. These results generated trust and the management felt safe to expand the testing to additional beds. The initiative resulted in a dramatically reduced number of cancellations of planned surgeries and more patients got their surgery on time, which also contributed to reducing queues.

11.5. Overall Reflections and Way Forward

Sometimes it is desirable to label as many activities as possible with the innovation. For example, it can be somewhat unclear in the interface and overlaps between innovation and research, and innovation and operational development. This lack of clarity does not necessarily equal bad consequences as everything is about creating value. However, such a lack of clarity may inhibit an organisation in using the full potential of systematic innovation and important innovation mechanisms may be counteracted. Therefore, it is important to spread and anchor innovation management as an emerging area of knowledge in its own right, and an understanding of what is meant by innovation, especially in a hospital context.

It has been experienced as beneficial to have an externally validated model, as the ISO 56002, to refer to both when it comes to managerial buy-in and also in general communication. The standard is written in a way that should not exclude any sector, with generic wording and general topics, which was considered to work very well also in the public sector. There were, however, some things that needed to be treated differently pointing to a difference between private and public sector. The most obvious are the metrics, where definitions of created values may not be aligned between public and private sectors, and the types of innovation that are developed in public sector probably differ to some extent, where also the scale-up may not be relevant in the same way as in business-driven organisations.

Other key experiences from the implementation at Karolinska have included, among others: having managerial support; having a dedicated team orchestrating the implementation; using a bottom-up approach in educating employees, building a network of people knowing and doing innovation work; designing an accessible and understandable system; being both careful and accurate in communication; considering the context when it comes to the implementation; enduring in using a systems approach; and having patience.

Finally, when preparing for the implementation of the innovation management system at Karolinska, a lack of general knowledge available in implementing a system such as Karolinska's was identified. Thoughts for the future include continuing the chosen journey, being reflective in going forward, and learning from one's own experiences as well as those of others.

References

Greenhalgh, T., Robert, G., MacFarlande, F., Bate, P. and Kyriakidou, O. (2004). Diffusion of innovations in service organizations: Systematic review and recommendations. *The Milbank Quarterly*, *82*(4), 581–629.

Herzlinger, R. (2006). Why innovation in health care is so hard. *Harvard Business Review*, *84*(5), 58–66.

Institute of Healthcare Improvements (2021). *The IHI Triple Aim initiative*, http://www.ihi.org/engage/initiatives/TripleAim/Pages/default.aspx.

ISO (2012). *ISO/IEC 17024:2012 Conformity assessment — General requirements for bodies operating certification of persons*. International Organization for Standardization.

ISO (2019). *ISO 56002:2019 Innovation management — Innovation management system — Guidance*. International Organization for Standardization.

Kotter, J. P. (2012). Accelerate!, *Harvard Business Review*, November.

Newsweek (2021). *The World's Best Hospitals 2021*, https://www.newsweek.com/best-hospitals-2021.

Salge, T. O. and Vera, A. (2009). Hospital innovativeness and organizational performance: Evidence from the English public acute care. *Health Care Management Review*, *34*(1), 54–67.

© 2023 World Scientific Publishing Europe Ltd.
https://doi.org/10.1142/9781800612105_0012

Chapter 12

KTH Global Development Hub: Developing an Innovation Management System for Global Sustainable Development

Jesper Vasell and Susanne Nilsson

Abstract

KTH Global Development Hub (KTH GDH) was formed in 2017 with the mission to develop and implement new education models and approaches addressing global sustainable development as expressed in the UN 2030 Agenda. KTH GDH is based on the idea that education activities can have a two-fold impact of developing students' innovation competence, while also driving innovation through the solutions being developed by students. A challenge-driven educational concept developed by KTH GDH, CDE^{GDH}, therefore contains a purposely designed innovation management system (IMS). Challenge definitions, stakeholder engagement and leadership endorsement are key aspects of this IMS, which is based on interventions designed to develop consensus around the viability and relevance of challenges, and commitment to participate in the innovation process. KTH GDH works in partnership with four African universities. The IMS has a local component at each university and a global component, which creates a global IMS. The implementation has thus far focused on the capacity to implement the Challenge-Driven Education (CDE) model and IMS. This includes building a capacity to create and sustain innovation processes and developing networks and collaborations in local innovation ecosystems, something that offers specific challenges. We discuss how existing IMS frameworks can be developed to better support global sustainable innovation.

12.1. Introduction

The UN 2030 Agenda for sustainable development describes, through the Sustainable Development Goals (SDGs), the most pressing challenges today. Besides being important challenges, the SDGs can also be seen as a description of a sustainable society to which we need to transform on a global scale.

Universities can, and should, play an important and direct role in that transformation, not just through knowledge production through research. Education also makes important contributions by developing students' competences, not the least their innovation competence, i.e., the competence to drive transformation and societal change through innovation.

One of the most important characteristics of the SDGs is their inherently global nature. It may be true that the challenges expressed by the goals are different in different contexts, but that does not take away the global nature of the challenges. Poverty, for example, cannot be eradicated by just focusing on countries where extreme poverty exists. Solutions must be developed with a global perspective and will likely mean that change and new solutions are needed not just where poverty exists. Similar observations can be made for all the SDGs, which points towards a need for *global* sustainable development.

KTH Global Development Hub (KTH GDH) was created in 2017 by KTH Royal Institute of Technology, Sweden's largest technical university, to develop new models for education and research that can give more direct contributions towards sustainable development in a global perspective. It is based on the idea that education as an activity can contribute not just by training students, but also by education activities making more direct contributions towards solutions for a more sustainable society.

KTH GDH has developed a model for challenge-driven education (CDE), referred to as CDE^{GDH} that aims at having two distinct impacts on society: (i) Increased innovation capacity through developing students' innovation competence for global sustainable development, and (ii) Innovation for a sustainable society, i.e., solutions that are implemented and provide value to identified beneficiaries.

The first impact — Innovation capacity — is achieved through education focusing on innovation competence for sustainable development.

This could be achieved through learning approaches that support students in developing knowledge, skills and attitudes appropriate for addressing broad societal challenges, in direct collaboration with various societal stakeholders in so-called CDE (Högfeldt *et al.*, 2019; Malmqvist, Rådberg and Lundqvist, 2015; Ibwe *et al.*, 2018).

If education along these principles is implemented in such a way that teachers and students at universities located in different parts of the world collaborate on developing solutions to societal challenges, then a global perspective is introduced. The solutions become global and at the same time locally relevant and viable.

The second impact — Innovation — is unusually ambitious in an education setting and means that solutions developed by students should be implemented if possible. This second impact has a direct influence on the learning objectives and how the students are trained. It also requires the development of an innovation process and a shift in values and norms in both students and teachers when it comes to how education is delivered. In addition, it requires the building of a network of stakeholders that are willing to engage in formulating challenges and taking on responsibility for these challenges when student projects are ending to support the realisation of the innovative solutions and create societal impact. The solutions are developed in the intersection between needs expressed as societal challenges, such as energy access, health, access to clean water, economic development, etc., and academic disciplines providing opportunities for solutions.

CDE^{GDH} is typically implemented as a course within which students form teams to work on a specific challenge. Alternatively, it can be a single project implemented as a thesis project, final year project or similar. The learning goals in combination define innovation competence for global sustainable development and are heavily based on the key competencies for sustainable development as defined by United Nations Educational, Scientific and Cultural Organization United Nations Educational, Scientific and Cultural Organization (UNESCO, 2017). By having students from different countries collaborate on solving a societal challenge, the global perspective is introduced. The students have different backgrounds and cultural perspectives and experiences and therefore make different contributions to the development of relevant and viable solutions. Student teams which are multi-perspective and multi-disciplinary offer a broader interpretation of a challenge and a wider range of potential solutions. It also enables the possibility of solutions that can be relevant and meaningful in more than one country.

The education model and a student exchange programme have so far been implemented at partner universities in Kenya, Tanzania, Rwanda and Botswana, i.e., sub-Saharan countries. The reason behind this geographical focus is that we believe that collaboration with developing countries, most of which are found in Africa, is necessary to achieve the goals expressed by the SDGs. Solutions to most of the SDGs must be systemic in nature and cannot be solved by just focusing on where the bulk of those problems, such as poverty, appear. We also believe that developing countries represent a significant opportunity for creating future solutions for a sustainable society in developed countries. People operating in challenging environments need to adapt, often simultaneously, to affordability, resource scarcity and institutional constraints. Working in such a setting can force one to rethink both the process and outcome of innovation and help trigger radically novel resource-efficient and affordable innovations (Pisoni, Michelini and Martignoni, 2018; Zeschky, Winterhalter and Gassman, 2014).

To handle the ambition of creating conditions for global sustainable development through learning and innovation, the implementation of elements in what can be referred to as an IMS has been created. Having global sustainable innovation as an intended outcome means that such a system needs to support not only one organisation but also in and between several organisations that are globally distributed. This places specific demands on the design of the management system in use. The purpose of this chapter is to provide an overview of how the IMS of KTH GDH was developed using key elements in existing IMS frameworks such as ISO 56002 (ISO, 2019) as a lens. In addition, the applicability of these frameworks is critically examined and discussed to enable some new insights on what is required from these frameworks to support global sustainable innovation and societal impact more effectively.

12.2. Managing Innovation for Global Sustainable Development

KTH being the initiator, acts at present as the driver of collaborative development of new tools, methods and processes to support innovation as an integrated part of the CDE^{GDH} concept. What can be referred to as the IMS of KTH GDH has a global and a local level as indicated in Figure 12.1. The local IMS is implemented at each of the partner universities including KTH. The local IMSs are interrelated and form a global IMS.

12.2.1. *The innovation process*

Both the learning and the innovation processes consist of several activities that can be described as training activities in the learning process and intervention activities in the innovation process. From a systems point of view, the learning and the innovation processes are interrelated in that the learning process supports the innovation process and vice versa as Figure 12.1 illustrates. The learning process has innovation competence as its objective, but it also serves as a driver for the innovation process through training. The innovation process is the process where learning takes place, and the theories and methods are applied. The innovation process is also supported by specific interventions through a continuous interaction with stakeholders. Overall, there are four key interventions in the innovation process as shown in Figure 12.1.

- Challenge definition,
- Stakeholder engagement,
- Post-education innovation plan,
- Post-education innovation support.

Challenge definition as the start of the innovation process

The innovation process is initiated by a so-called challenge definition workshop, which is a structured way of developing a description of the challenge in focus. It is a collaborative process involving multiple stakeholders affected.

A challenge is defined as "a desired change for someone," i.e., it describes a change which will be perceived as an improvement (advantage, benefit, etc.) for one or several identified *beneficiaries*. The challenges are identified and defined in collaboration with various societal

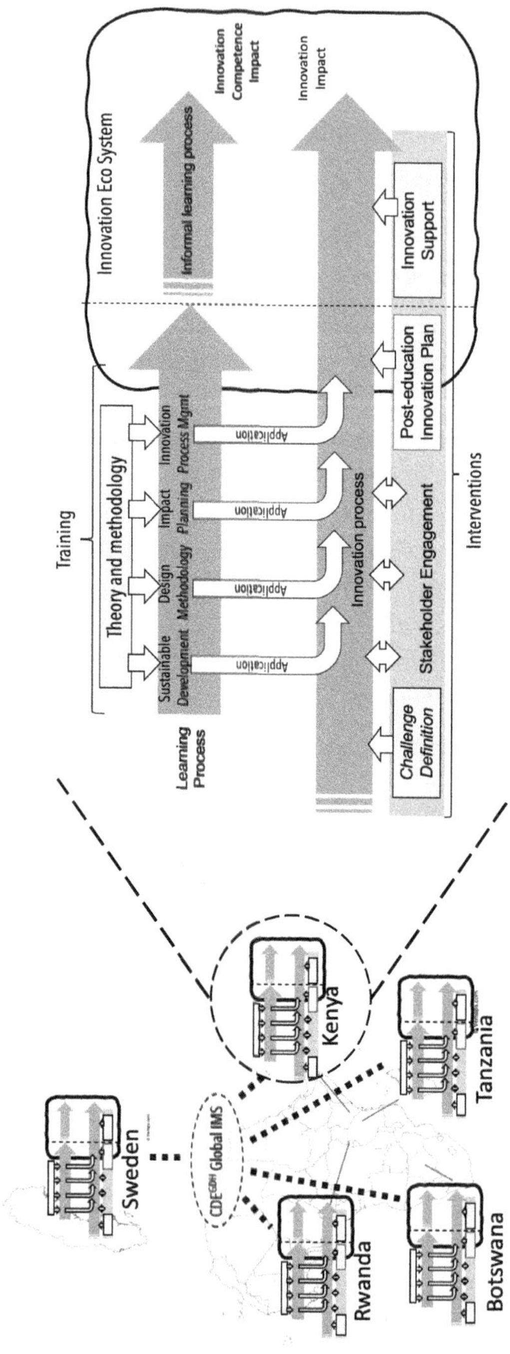

Fig. 12.1. The global (left) and local innovation management system of KTH Global Development Hub (right).

stakeholders: industry, government, civil society, etc. This is to make sure that the challenges are perceived as relevant and important by a broad part of society. The stakeholders participating in the challenge definition also tend to become involved in the innovation process both in the early and later stages.

The challenges are often broadly defined and open-ended, such as: "Improve the livelihood of street vendors in Nairobi" and thereby provide a broad starting point for the innovation process. The challenges frequently are "wicked problems," i.e., problems for which there are no obvious solutions and no obvious path towards a solution. In fact, the challenges are so broadly defined that the students must start out by defining the underlying problems. Typically, there are several potential problems behind a challenge and, consequently, there are many potential solutions and combinations of solutions that address various aspects of a challenge.

All societal challenges are defined and described in terms of the SDGs. This is to create a natural link with the intended overall impact to contribute towards the SDGs.

Stakeholder engagement and post-education planning and support

Stakeholder engagement is a continuous intervention throughout the innovation process, where the students identify and engage with stakeholders. The initial stakeholder engagement is typically initiated by teachers to define relevant challenges. Interaction with stakeholders is initiated by both students and teachers throughout the innovation process. Identifying and interacting with societal stakeholders who have some form of interest in a solution to a challenge — be it a positive interest in the form of a potential gain, or a negative interest in the form of a potential loss from a solution to a specific challenge — plays an important and integrated role in the process. The role of a stakeholder is to represent a particular societal interest in a particular challenge and to be part of the definition, development and implementation of a solution.

Since the $\mathrm{CDE}^{\mathrm{GDH}}$ concept is based on an education activity with a defined start and end point in time, the innovation process will have two phases. The first phase ends when the education activity ends. To make sure that the innovation process may continue, there are two interventions that constitute a hand-over of the innovation process: Post-education innovation plan and innovation support. The post-education innovation plan serves to identify the actors (students and stakeholders) who have an interest in the continued innovation process, and to plan a continued innovation process. The innovation plan is developed by the students through an impact planning methodology which identifies relevant stakeholders and describes a pathway to the desired impact. Post-education innovation support involves engaging local innovation support actors — innovation hubs, business incubators, etc. — in the continued innovation process. This is an integrated part of the process, which is performed by the students in collaboration with local innovation support at the partner university.

Actors in the local innovation ecosystem

The main actors in the innovation process are students and teachers at the universities, and stakeholders related to local challenges. The innovation process is also supported through the local innovation support system at each university. All these actors form what we refer to as the innovation ecosystem. The innovation ecosystem is what sustains the innovation processes created through the education activities, both during and after the learning process.

The students lead the innovation process, whereas the teachers manage the learning process and are also responsible for the connection between the learning and the innovation process and the application of the theory and methods introduced in the learning process. The teachers have an important role as facilitators and support the students throughout the process. Design methodology is selected as the main innovation process model due to its known advantages in situations characterised by high levels of complexity and uncertainty where multi-cultural and multi-disciplinary teams are operating. The design methods are complemented with theories and methods related to the specific course. It may, for instance, include business modelling, entrepreneurship theory or technology management.

The role of the students in the innovation ecosystem is hence to apply the theory and methods when addressing a societal challenge provided by local stakeholders. This is performed through the following steps: (1) analysis of the challenge — definition of underlying problems; (2) impact planning — defining the intended impact of a solution and activities, outputs and outcomes that facilitate the intended impact; (3) actionable problem statement — choose an underlying problem for which it is deemed possible for the students to develop a solution; and (4) development and test of a solution — design a solution and implement a prototype, which can be used to test a solution by presenting it to various stakeholders. These steps hence form the main phases in the innovation process where the students are involved. When the course has ended, the stakeholders involved have the responsibility to further refine and develop the solutions to increase the likelihood for these to lead to a societal impact.

12.2.2. *Leadership and culture*

The IMS is implemented in a globally distributed organisational structure where there is a local innovation ecosystem at each of the four sites. Overall, the leadership of the innovation system is, therefore, based on collaboration between independent entities.

At each of the universities, the CDE^{GDH} education model and its implementation are explicitly endorsed by the university management. It is made part of the overall strategy of the university and implemented in applicable policies for innovation, education, etc. All the current partner universities have made decisions to implement CDE according to CDE^{GDH} broadly, with the goal of covering all academic disciplines in the longer term.

Culturally, the African partner universities are very open to developing the role of the university in society and actively want to seek ways of providing a positive societal impact. This is true at an institutional level, but even more so at the individual level among staff and students. The main reasons for this is that societal challenges are more immediately visible in developing countries, and students and teachers often come from rural communities and low-income backgrounds. Personal experience creates a more direct understanding of societal challenges and the necessity of, and opportunity for, improvements. The innovation and learning processes then provide a framework that can leverage such an impact-driven culture.

At KTH, there is also a strong sense of the importance of the role of a university in addressing societal challenges. Being a university in a western European, developed economy, the drivers are however different and not based on personal experience to the same extent. The drivers are mainly created through education and a systemic understanding of the necessity of a development towards a sustainable society as expressed by the SDGs.

12.2.3. *Additional support and resources*

The implementation of key elements in the local IMS is based on each partner university providing the necessary resources and the support. This is done by integrating CDE^{GDH} in the development and implementation of education activities (courses and programmes).

The local IMS is also supported through the local innovation support system at each university. These systems vary considerably in maturity, competence and resources, and it is a long-term challenge to drive development of the local innovation ecosystems in general. This includes not only direct innovation support, such as incubators and innovation hubs. It also involves the creation of long-term relationships with industry, public authorities, civil society, etc.

The student mobility and training for teachers to build the capacity to implement CDE^{GDH} at all universities is at present funded by KTH while the local implementation in specific courses and the involvement of stakeholders is funded by each university.

12.2.4. *Performance evaluation and improvement*

The IMS is developed with societal impact in mind through improved innovation capacity and innovation. Assessing this impact is complex since it is built up gradually and hence is not easily traced. In addition, the nature of the impact is quite diverse.

For innovation capacity, we intend to do impact assessments over a longer period of time by following up on students with interviews and self-assessments, which aim at revealing what influence the CDE^{GDH} training has had on, for instance, their career choice. A pilot interview round has been conducted giving some preliminary insights. It demonstrates the need for a longer-term study to properly assess the impact on an individual's competence.

For innovation, we intend to follow up on the individual projects and study to what extent and in what ways the innovation processes initiated by the projects have continued and what impacts these have resulted in.

The following indicators are presently in use and serve primarily as a measure of the success of the overall implementation of CDE^{GDH} since the start in 2017 and can also be viewed to indirectly measure the innovation process:

- Number of students in exchange programmes.
- Number of education activities (courses) according to CDE^{GDH} at KTH and partner universities.
- Number of innovation projects performed at KTH and partner universities.

12.3. Implementation of an Innovation Management System for Global Sustainable Development

The development and implementation of the IMS for global sustainable development is an ongoing process. Since its start in 2017, the following main actions have been taken:

(1) *Organisational set up and direction*: Formation of KTH GDH as an organisation, the development of a global sustainable development innovation strategy and helping partner universities with organising for CDE^{GDH}, including identification of relevant stakeholders and societal challenges.

(2) *Building and sustaining commitment to innovation and change*: Development of tools, methods and processes for training and development support for teachers to support innovation and change.

(3) *Developing networks and collaboration in the innovation ecosystems*: Initiating the student mobility programme and developing support for the building of innovation ecosystems at partner universities.

These steps are not strictly sequential and all of them are elements of an ongoing development. The implementation is happening at five universities, including KTH, but the pace of the development differs depending on local conditions.

12.3.1. *Organisational set up and direction*

KTH GDH started in January 2017 based on a private donation. A Director was recruited, and the development of the organisation was started. The strong support from university management at KTH is reflected in the fact that the vice-president for internationalisation is chairman of KTH GDH.

The role of KTH GDH is to drive development of models for education and innovation for global sustainable development and to support the implementation of these models at KTH and the partner universities through partnership and research. This ambition is also reflected through the roles of the five individuals that today are associated with KTH GDH, where education, innovation, partnership and research related to education and to innovation constitute areas of responsibility.

The second step of the implementation was to develop partnerships with 3–5 universities in Africa. Today the active partnerships are with the following:

- Strathmore University in Nairobi, Kenya.
- University of Dar-es-salaam in Tanzania.
- Botho University in Gaborone, Botswana.
- University of Rwanda in Kigali, Rwanda.

These partner universities were approached with an offer to participate in a development of CDE^{GDH} and the IMS. To ensure a sustained commitment, contacts were initially taken at university management level. Typically, at the level of vice-president, Deputy vice-chancellor or equivalent.

At all partner universities, and KTH, the intention is to implement CDE^{GDH} broadly, across all academic disciplines and programmes at each university. The starting point, however, has always been to create a first platform by implementing CDE^{GDH} in a single academic discipline, school or department. In the following steps, this platform is used to create a broader interest and to promote broader implementation within each university.

The partner universities have chosen slightly different ways of organising the implementation of CDE^{GDH}. Some have chosen a more centralised approach, while others have chosen to start in a specific school or department, focusing specially on selected faculty.

12.3.2. *Building and sustaining commitment to innovation and change*

At the partner universities, the strategy has been to seek strong support with university management and to combine that with building and training an initial group of teachers with an interest in developing CDE and making sure that they are given the necessary support from university management. This has been crucial for the success of implementation. However, even with this strategy the implementation has been slow at times, compared to the corresponding development at KTH. The main reasons behind this are a limited capacity to implement change processes with the aim of transforming and developing the university organisation and its activities. This comes out of the fact that the universities operate in a more hierarchical and bureaucratic educational system where a university is comparatively less autonomous than in, for example, most European countries.

The hierarchical culture of the partner universities makes management support important since it validates the effort by individual teachers and permits the use of necessary resources for developing CDE activities — particularly the teachers' time. The permission to do CDE development is thus dependent on a top-down approach. This does not, however, influence the choice of stakeholder interactions and collaborations, which are mostly in the hands of the teachers.

Based on the partnerships formed, the first activity was teacher training for faculty at the partner universities. Initially this was a more general introduction to CDE, but as CDE^{GDH} has been further developed, the teacher training has become more practically oriented to support teachers in implementing the innovation process.

Over time and accelerated by the COVID-19 pandemic, the teacher training has developed into an online form, which makes it possible to train larger numbers of teachers and to enable collaboration also between the teachers at the different partner universities in jointly developing education activities and support for innovation and change.

Teacher training and its development has been the single most important part of the implementation of CDE^{GDH} as it builds the innovation capacity at the universities and forms relations which are necessary for the global level of the IMS. The teachers together with the top management at each university are key actors when it comes to building an innovative culture in their organisations. Through the teacher training, the teachers become not only equipped with tools and methods to support a global sustainable innovation process but are also exposed to new ideas and perspectives. As an example of the latter, one of the key messages in the teacher training is related to the importance of them shifting from a traditional teacher expert role to the role of facilitator for change and innovation.

12.3.3. *Developing networks and collaboration in the innovation ecosystem*

Student mobility and collaboration is a critical component to introduce the global perspective of sustainable development. Student mobility has been implemented as student exchange programmes where the students spend a whole semester at a partner university and participate in a challenge-driven project course. From an innovation perspective, this has occasionally been creating challenges due to the different cultural backgrounds of the students. Those challenges are, however, far outweighed by the advantages of having teams which are truly "multi-perspective" and not just multi-disciplinary. It leads to a broader view on both problem statements and solutions.

The more recent phase in the implementation of the IMS covers the activities related to developing local innovation ecosystems connected to the partner universities. This ecosystem makes up the "back-end" of the IMS as it is the mechanism for sustaining innovation processes beyond the "front-end" in the form of the CDE^{GDH} course.

A general observation is that universities in developing countries typically have a much lower degree of collaboration with the surrounding society compared to universities in developed economies. This highly limits the spread and impact of innovations coming from the universities. For this to change, there needs to be an ecosystem of actors and relationships in place that can sustain the innovation processes that are initiated at the university. This is to a large extent developed in conjunction with the implementation of the CDE^{GDH} course which is highly dependent on stakeholder engagement as described above. In practice this means that the partner universities engage with stakeholders not just in a way that fulfils the needs of a specific project, but also in a way that forms longer-term relationships, particularly with stakeholders who can play an important role in sustaining the innovation processes. These typically represent a broad spectrum of actors, from locally based small firms to representatives of governmental departments.

12.4. Reflections and Future Needs

KTH GDH has lasted for 4 years, and three partner universities have implemented CDE^{GDH} in at least one educational activity. Those who have been involved express positive experiences of the process and a strong dedication to the importance of strengthening the role of universities in global sustainable development. At the partner universities the innovation capacity being developed is also seen as especially important for the development of the countries and their economies.

12.4.1. *Reflections on the innovation management system developed*

There is consensus that the kind of training for global sustainable development provided by CDE^{GDH} needs to be broadened and made accessible for a larger number of students. The African partner universities have all made strategic decisions to have CDE broadly implemented within the universities. This is a critical step towards involving more students and giving them the capacity to contribute to the development of their countries. The global level of the IMS is seen as very positive since it drives and enables collaboration between the partner universities in many areas. As a consequence, a pan-African partnership is now under development with the partner universities as founding members.

However, merely broadening the implementation of CDE within the universities will not provide a global perspective to the students. For that, we need to develop the forms of student collaboration which constitute the global level of the innovation system, i.e., having students collaborate among countries. An important focus in the further development of KTH GDH and CDE^{GDH} is hence to develop new modalities in student collaboration between countries with more elements of online collaboration which can be combined with short-term mobility as a scalable way of providing the global perspective to larger numbers of students. This would strengthen the innovation aspect since the varied perspectives brought into innovation projects by students from multiple countries enables solutions that may not be possible in a local, country-specific context. If the innovation projects bring together multi-country contexts, this will facilitate the development of more broadly relevant and scalable solutions.

In addition, the ongoing work to further strengthen the local innovation ecosystems at the African universities is also crucial as these are the foundation in realising the innovative solutions resulting from the student projects to create societal impact. Understanding what hinders the realisation and how to best identify and support the stakeholders required to make this happen is hence considered an area for further development.

12.4.2. *Towards a self-supporting global sustainable innovation system — Limitations of existing innovation management system frameworks*

The vision for KTH GDH is to create conditions where each university's innovation system can function locally and interact with the other partner universities' systems to form a self-supporting global innovation system.

By this, a global sustainable innovation capacity addressing the SDGs is enabled.

Existing IMS frameworks are however found to be somewhat limited when it comes to supporting organisational systems that aim to create innovations leading to societal impact. The available frameworks for IMSs are implicitly targeted towards less ambitious innovation outcomes, assume an underlying demand and supply-market model and support innovations which occur primarily within a single organisation in relation to organisations in its value chain (Karlsson and Magnusson, 2019). The inherently highly collaborative and globally distributive nature of innovation targeting societal transformation and global sustainable development is hence not naturally captured. For instance, the building of a capacity to manage globally distributed experimentation and learning that is suggested to play an important role when tackling grand challenges (Ferraro, Etzion and Gehman, 2015) is at present not reflected in existing key elements in these frameworks. Furthermore, we argue that the stakeholder dimension needs to be further elaborated on. In CDE^{GDH}, the interaction with stakeholders plays a central and crucial role in the innovation process. Engaging stakeholders directly involved in or affected by an innovation process as suggested in existing IMS frameworks is however not enough. A diverse range of actors such as government, public and private organisations, NGOs and even activists are found to be required to scaling innovation aspiring to create societal impact and change (Westley and Antadze, 2010; George *et al.*, 2016). Since these actors seldom have the same goals and values, the handling of unaligned priorities and worldviews becomes critical. This requires the development of "a structure and rules of engagement that allow diverse and heterogeneous actors to interact constructively over pro-longed timespans" (Ferraro, Etzion and Gehman, 2015). An IMS framework should preferably point to and explain the need to develop such participatory or coordinating architecture rather than merely highlight the need for collaboration if it should become useful also in this context.

In close alignment to the stakeholder dimension, the type of leadership required is yet another dimension that deserves increased attention when it comes to designing IMSs for globally distributed innovation aiming for societal impact. Top management commitment is crucial to support innovation in any organisation. This is reflected in existing management system frameworks as well as in our development of KTH GDH, not the least of which in the more hierarchical African universities. But to create conditions for innovations leading to societal impact, we find that top management commitment is not enough. Also, the teaching staff is found to play a major role in the transformation. Sustaining the engagement towards a complex and uncertain goal in a broad and diverse group of stakeholders requires another form of leadership; a distributed and radical form of shared leadership requiring a focus on the numerous and persisting social interactions within a network (Carson, Tesluk and Marrone, 2007; Uhl-Bien and Marion, 2009).

A framework for IMSs also needs to be able to capture the difference in drivers of innovation that emerges when targeting complex and grand challenges. For societal innovation, innovation processes are driven by an identified need in a societal context rather than an opportunity for organisations to increase their competitiveness or performance as assumed in present innovation management models. This has consequences on the design of the front-end of the innovation process. Not the least there is a need to identify and formulate goals for the innovation process so that these are able to inspire and motive people to engage and contribute effort and resources (George *et al.*, 2016). This is despite the fact that the outcome from such a process may lead to inferior conditions for many stakeholders involved (i.e., require change in individual's consumption behaviours or everyday routines, etc.). In our IMS, the challenge definition itself and the process by which it is defined are of central importance. We have found that the challenge definition needs to be developed using a collaborative approach involving a broad range of stakeholders to create necessary consensus on the viability and relevance of the challenge and the consequences of its solution that may have partly negative consequences for some stakeholders.

In general, the importance of innovation is increasingly recognised, and it is viewed as a key to achieving the necessary transformation of societies on a global scale as expressed in the UN 2030 Agenda. Consequently, IMSs are becoming increasingly important, and the frameworks used for understanding and describing these systems need to be developed to reflect the type of innovation processes and systems needed for societal change.

The need for societal transformation also makes the building of innovation capacity in our societies urgent, particularly individual innovation competence in younger generations. The development of students' global sustainable innovation competence is arguably a key task for universities as this will not only be critical for solving the pressing needs of today but also offer a solution for sustained impact over time.

References

Carson, J. B., Tesluk, P. E. and Marrone, J. A. (2007). Shared leadership in teams: An investigation of antecedent conditions and performance. *Academy of Management Journal*, *50*(5), 1217–1234.

Ferraro, F., Etzion, D. and Gehman, J. (2015). Tackling grand challenges pragmatically: Robust action revisited. *Organization Studies*, *36*(3), 363–390.

George, G., Howard-Grenville, J., Joshi, A. and Tihanyi, L. (2016). Understanding and tackling societal grand challenges through management research. *Academy of Management Journal*, *59*(6), 1880–1895.

Högfeldt, A.-K., Rosén, A., Mwase, C., Lantz, A., Gumaelius, L., Shayo, E., *et al.* (2019). Mutual capacity building through North-South collaboration using challenge-driven education. *Sustainability*, *11*(24), 7236.

Ibwe, K. S., Kalinga, E. A., Mvungi, N. and Tenhunen, H. (2018). The impact of industry participation on challenge based learning. *International Journal of Engineering*, *34*(1), 187–200.

ISO (2019). *ISO 56002:2019 Innovation management — Innovation management system — Guidance*. International Organization for Standardization.

Karlsson, M. and Magnusson, M. (2019). The systems approach to innovation management. In Chen, J., Brem, A., Viardot, E. and Wong, P. K. (eds.), *The Routledge Companion to Innovation Management*. Routledge, London.

Malmqvist, J., Rådberg, K. K. and Lundqvist, U. (2015). Comparative analysis of challenge-based learning experiences. *Proceedings of the 11th International CDIO Conference, 2015.*

Pisoni, A., Michelini, L. and Martignoni, G. (2018). Frugal approach to innovation: State of the art and future perspectives. *Journal of Cleaner Production*, *171*, 107–126.

Uhl-Bien, M. and Marion, R. (2009). Complexity leadership in bureaucratic forms of organizing: A meso model. *The Leadership Quarterly*, *20*(4), 631–650.

UNESCO (2017). *Education for Sustainable Development Goals — Learning Objectives*. UNESCO.

Westley, F. and Antadze, N. (2010). Making a difference: Strategies for scaling social innovation for greater impact. *Innovation Journal*, *15*(2), 1–19.

Zeschky, M. B., Winterhalter, S. and Gassman, O. (2014). From cost to frugal and reverse innovation: Mapping the field and implications for global competitiveness. *Research-Technology Management*, *57*(4), 20–27.

© 2023 World Scientific Publishing Europe Ltd.
https://doi.org/10.1142/9781800612105_0013

Chapter 13

Midea Group: The Systems Approach to Becoming a Global Leader in Household Appliance Sector

Jin Chen, Rongyu Guo*, Ximing Yin and Zhaohui Wang

Abstract

Over the past decades, firms from emerging economies like China have sprung up and reshaped the economic map of the world. This chapter focuses on a miniature of these firms: Midea Group, a global leader in household appliance sector. We give a glimpse of how firms, in a developing China, implement an innovation management system to motivate and integrate the creativity of each innovation element. The story is also an excellent example of the promotion of the ISO 56002. We find that Midea has applied the total innovation management philosophy, developed a future-oriented innovation vision and strategy, leveraged indigenous innovation competence and external resources to support innovation activities, which are followed by the four-level technology roadmap as an action plan. It has also organised the R&D centres as a global collaboration network for the internal and external innovation activities and resources. As a result, Midea established a portfolio of innovation competence that consists of technological and managerial core competencies. Midea's experience in innovation management and development brings important insights to other companies that are on the track of catching-up as well as becoming global innovators.

*Corresponding author.

13.1. Introduction

Midea Group (Midea), established in 1968 in China, is one of the leading companies in the home appliance industry and a global leading robotic and automation technology company. Midea now offers one of the most comprehensive ranges in the home appliance industry and is the world's No. 1 brand of air-treatment products, air-coolers, kettles and rice cookers. Headquartered in Southern China, Midea is a truly global company, ranked 229 in the *2020 Forbes Global 2000 List.* With over 150,000 employees, Midea provides excellent products and creates a better life for more than 400 million customers and strategic partners in more than 200 countries.

The rapid growth of many companies in China in the past decades impressed the world and has changed the world innovation landscape. Among them, Midea is a miniature of those that may not have been born great but has gone a long way to catch up and become one of the world's leading innovators. Midea has adopted and implemented a formal innovation strategy since 2012. With the vision "to bring great innovations to life," Midea is committed to R&D and innovation; this has enhanced its core competitiveness and made impressive breakthroughs. Since 2012, Midea has achieved robust business growth across multiple sectors driven by its innovation in humanising technology. Midea's revenue had increased from 100 billion yuan to about 280 billion yuan by the end of year 2020, and profit from 3.3 billion yuan to 24 billion yuan; its domestic market share has risen 7.6% since 2016 and reached 27% in 2020. What's more, Midea ranks 27th on the list of *Brand Finance Tech 100* in 2019, 16 places up in comparison with the previous year, leading its peers throughout the country.

We are reviewing the development of Midea's innovation to answer the following questions: What's behind Midea's sustainable growth and going beyond catching-up in the past years? How does Midea stimulate the creativity of each innovation element? How does Midea organise and integrate all the innovation elements to realise the maximisation of value creation? To answer these questions, we reviewed public information of Midea Group and interviewed five executives and engineers who oversee different parts of Midea's innovation management, such as strategy, planning, standardisation, digitalisation and user experience.

13.2. Midea's Innovation Journey and Innovation System

It's helpful for understanding Midea's innovation system and why it applies a systems approach of innovation management today if we start with reviewing Midea's development of technology and innovation, which can be divided into two main periods (Figure 13.1).

The first period is from 1968 to 2014, during which Midea focused on technology introduction. To be specific, Midea was structured as a linear functional organisation because its product categories were relatively simple when it was founded in 1968. As its scale and product categories expanded rapidly since 1997, Midea established several business units and further developed gradually. Each unit was relatively independent and focused on its own products and markets, consequently, efficiency and professionalism were greatly improved. As the competition intensified, Midea realised the importance of innovation and attempted to shift from imitation to indigenous innovation in 2001. Since then, it has gradually paid more and more attention to product development and furthered its investments in independent R&D from 2010. The year of 2012 is a milestone in Midea's history when Fang Hongbo took over the management of Midea after He Xiangjian, founder of Midea, stepped down. In 2013, Midea went public.

The second period began in 2014, during which Midea strengthened its indigenous innovation capabilities and became a global leader in the

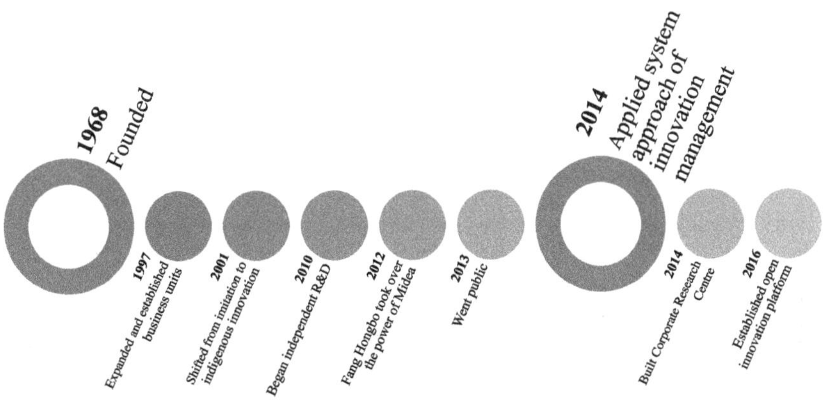

Fig. 13.1. History of Midea's innovation.

Source: Author's design based on interview.

household appliance sector. As the demand for development and innovation soars, it's difficult to develop innovation capability by simply increasing R&D investment and activities. Thanks to the innovation management system improvements in line with the innovation systems approach by ISO 56002 (ISO, 2019), Midea converged all elements of innovation into an innovation ecosystem. Specifically, Midea structured the technology system into four levels, and built the Corporate Research Centre, which focuses on common technology and disruptive innovation, in 2014. At the same time, Midea developed an open innovation platform in 2016 to integrate both internal and external resources and subjects. Today, a well-organised innovation ecosystem has been established.

There are some key elements behind Midea's innovation ecosystem, and they can be concluded as "four strategic objectives (technology leadership, global impact, direct to users, digitisation and intelligence driven), three generations of R&D (first generation is product development, second is platform research and third, core technology development in parallel), 'two-wheel drive' (technological competence and management capacity) and 'one system' (innovation management system)." Figure 13.2 illustrates Midea's innovation ecosystem.

By reviewing the evolution of Midea's innovation system, it's obvious that the structure of a company and its innovation system are determined by its growth and development needs. With the increase of product categories and technical complexity, a systems approach of innovation management is more and more needed for integrating all innovation-related elements as a whole and forming an organic force.

13.2.1. *Future-oriented innovation vision and strategy*

Looking back at the history of the development of a great enterprise, strategic vision and strategy are the keys that distinguish outstanding firms from others. Great enterprises pursue not only profit but also a "higher strategic goal" that goes beyond the economic goal (Collins and Porras, 2002). That is to say, strategic design is a crucial part of overall corporate development, which can empower participants to work together cohesively with a strong and clear purpose in complex processes involved in high-risk and boundary-breaking activities (Fleming and Waguespack,

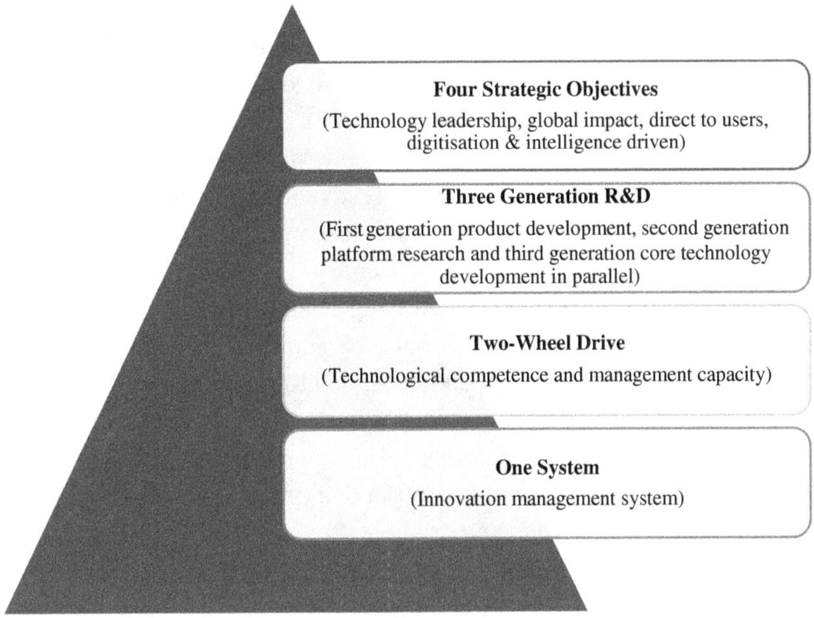

Fig. 13.2. Midea's innovation ecosystem.

Source: Author's design based on interview.

2007). The focus of strategic design is to capture the key factors that affect society, politics, economy, environment, customers and policies in the long run, and identify the general trends and opportunities that affect firms' sustainable growth, as well as clarify firms' own resources endowment and competitive advantages. Therefore, strategic vision can be adjusted and optimised dynamically, so as to lead and empower firms as well as their employees to work together cohesively on disruptive technological breakthroughs and core capability building, so that firms can seize major strategic opportunities and realise exponential growth in the volatile, uncertain, complex and ambiguous (VUCA) development environment, and avoid pitfalls which are known as the "Innovator's Dilemma" (Christensen, 1997) or "the Curse of Success" (O'Reilly and Tushman, 2008).

With the strategy vision as "to bring great innovations to life" and the mission as "to integrate with the world and inspire the future," Midea

Group prepares itself to embrace dynamics and focuses on continuous technological innovation to maintain the company's global leadership position in the consumer appliances market and to catch the next generation of technologies (Chen, Yin and Li, 2020).

"Nothing lasts forever in Midea," said Mr. Fang Hongbo, CEO of Midea since 2012. Midea has constantly, dynamically adjusted and optimised itself in response to the technological and social trends, so having a strategic vision, with innovation as a core value, has played an increasingly important role. In 2012, when Fang Hongbo took over, he realised that global innovation leadership must be achieved through indigenous innovation capability building, and he started to standardise and systematise Midea's innovation management system. "Product leadership, to be efficiency driven, and global operation" were firstly put forward as Midea's three core strategic objectives at that time. "Innovation" has been officially written into Midea's corporate strategy ever since. Especially, the prioritised objective "product leadership" is interpreted as "Our quality products and commitment to innovation make us a leader in our industry." At the beginning of 2021, Midea made a strategic adjustment because it realised that digital, user-driven innovation and globalisation are becoming new innovation frontiers that are more and more important for the firm's long-term development. Consequently, "technology leadership, global impact, direct to users, digitisation and intelligence driven" are identified as four new core strategic objectives, among which "technology leadership" is of top priority.

"Strategy first": Led by the strategic vision, a series of work was done to implement the strategy. To be the leader who brings great innovation to life, Midea can never be content with existing and short-term advantages in technology and business model. This means that Midea needs to focus more on basic and prospective research and cutting-edge technologies. Therefore, it established a corporate-level technology roadmap and organises R&D activities focusing on "three generation R&D" at the same time. This means it can prepare technologies for next-generation or even next-next-generation products while developing the products for existing markets. Moreover, Midea has established a global innovation platform including 28 R&D centres all over the world. Midea locates these R&D centres in places with technical superiorities and tries to stand on highland of technologies as much as possible. Relying on these, Midea can seize opportunities to achieve transition in multiple technological and industrial waves.

13.2.2. *Indigenous innovation competence as the support*

It is widely recognised that differences in terms of technology and innovation are a major source of cross-firm performance variations, in which R&D competence is a driver of core technology building. Although it is more efficient for firms with relatively backward technology to acquire technology from others, the ability to evaluate and utilise outside knowledge is largely a function of the level of prior related knowledge (Cohen and Levinthal, 1990). Therefore, it's almost impossible for firms without prior knowledge to gain cutting-edge technology or build core capability by relying on others' innovation efforts. Indigenous innovation competence is, therefore, a key element of catching-up and building sustainable leading advantages.

The year of 2010 was a watershed for Midea's innovation management. Since then, Midea has transformed from relying on technology import to depending on indigenous R&D. Midea increased the R&D investment rapidly with an average annual growth rate of 20%. As Figure 13.3 shows, during the past 7 years since 2014, Midea has invested over 530 billion yuan in R&D activities and the R&D intensity is now stable above 3.5%, leading the home appliance industry. Midea regards talent as the primary resource, and had launched various programmes to build a diversified R&D talent team. It has over 15,000 R&D personnel, which is about 10% of the total employees. More than 70% of the R&D personnel in Corporate Research Centre have a Master's or doctoral degree, and the company employs more than 300 leading academics and senior experts from all around the world. Aiming at radical innovation, Midea separates research from development, and devotes 20% of the R&D personnel to advanced research that focuses on radical innovation and common technology.

All efforts paid off. Midea has been growing at an impressively rapid speed and has achieved amazing innovation achievements. The company

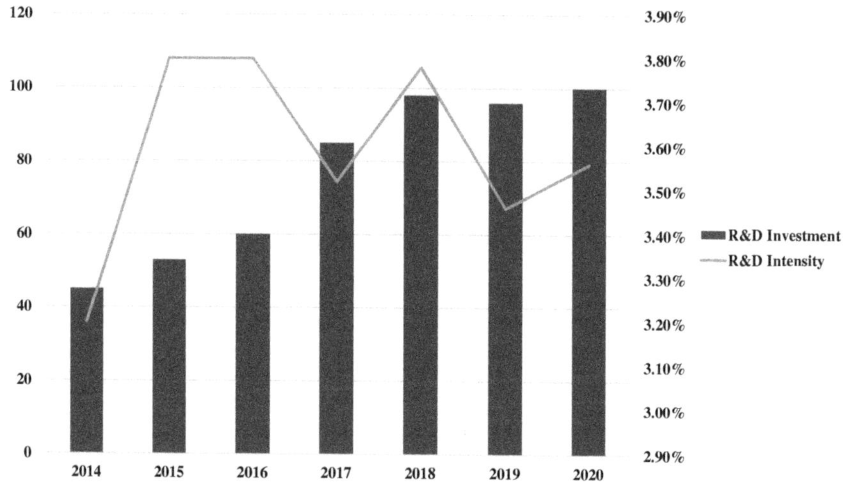

Fig. 13.3. Midea's R&D investment during 2014–2020.

Source: Midea.

has filed 160,000 patent applications and secured more than 62,000 patents by the end of 2020, ranking in the first place in the home appliance industry for four consecutive years.

13.2.3. *External resources as the support for innovation activities*

In order to increase the efficiency of the R&D and meet the market demand better, Midea has established a global open innovation platform. This is because, in the era of knowledge economy and globalisation, open innovation, which refers to the activities by which firms gain external technologies and resources, can make up for the deficiency of internal resources by interacting with external partners (Chesbrough, 2003). These external interactions are helpful for the integration of internal and external technologies. In this way, firms can benefit through the integration of complementary assets and share risks (Teece, 2006). This is because technologies are increasingly complex, and it's hard for firms to develop new technologies for their products internally using relatively "closed" innovation strategies with limited interactions with the outside environment considering the increasing uncertainty and cost (Chen *et al.*, 2020; Fleming and Waguespack, 2007; Wernerfelt, 1984).

Midea's open innovation platform enables multi-subject participants such as non-R&D personnel, users and start-ups in the process of innovation, and, therefore, Midea can integrate the internal and external resources at the same time. Based on this platform, Midea absorbs and turns genius ideas into production, and provides diverse resources for incubation programmes. In addition, users' perceptions and feedback can be taken into account immediately.

13.2.4. *Four-level technology roadmap as innovation action plan*

In conjunction with the increasing investment, Midea established a corporate-level *innovation technology roadmap* and structural technology system in four levels with different focuses and aims (Figures 13.3 and 13.4). First level is corporate-level disruptive, with breakthrough technology innovation and a focus on capturing future 5-or-more-year innovation frontiers. Second level is also corporate level, but with a focus on common technology across categories and foundational technology; R&D programmes at this level aim at future 3-to-5-year technological innovations. Third level is exclusive technology conducted by each business unit or product division, aiming at developing future 2-to-3-year technology. Fourth level is product development, driven by real-time market demand; usually it takes 1 year or less. This system allows Midea to build dynamic core competencies and meet the ever-changing customer demands, with the support of technologies spanning from 1 to over 5 years.

To put the strategy into effect, Midea built the Corporate Research Centre, which focuses on both innovation management and advanced research. For one thing, the Corporate Research Centre is responsible for the management of science and technology, including development and implementation of the Group's technology strategy and product strategy. For the other, the Corporate Research Centre aims at transferring long-term research into common technology, core technology, prospective technological studies and disruptive product platform innovation, and these technologies can be used by several business units and form the

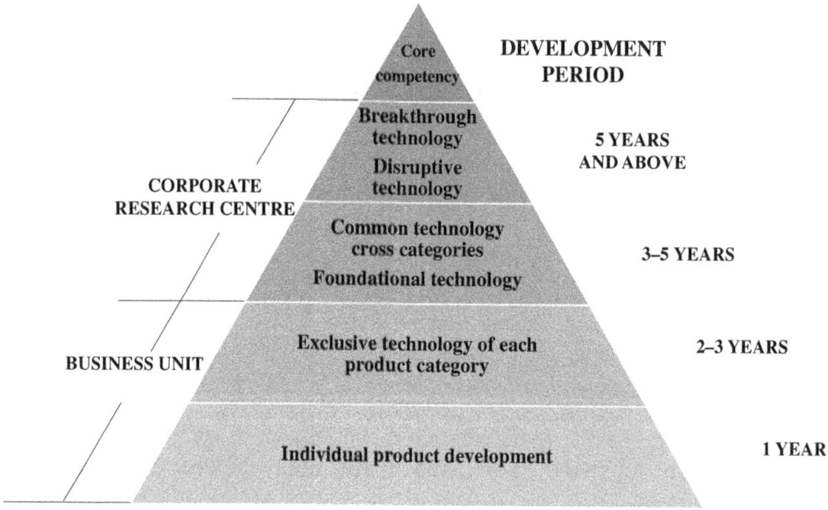

Fig. 13.4. Midea's four-level technology system.

Source: Author's design based on Midea's interview.

foundation of the units' R&D. At the same time, specific business units or product divisions focus on the specific technologies for individual products and devote more to product development. By applying a four-level R&D system with R&D centres, Midea's innovation management covers current product development as well as cutting-edge technology exploration (Figure 13.4).

13.2.5. *Organisational structures for innovation activities*

Led by the strategic vision of "global operation," Midea has established a global R&D network with a "2+4+n" structure, including two global innovation centres in China, and four R&D centres covering technologies of all categories, and *n* (*n* equals to 22 now) R&D centres specialising in individual product development, and there will be more R&D centres across the world (Figure 13.5). As a result, Midea can take advantage of different countries and make use of the resources and market all over the world to conduct globalised research and product design, accelerate technological innovation and strengthen external cooperation.

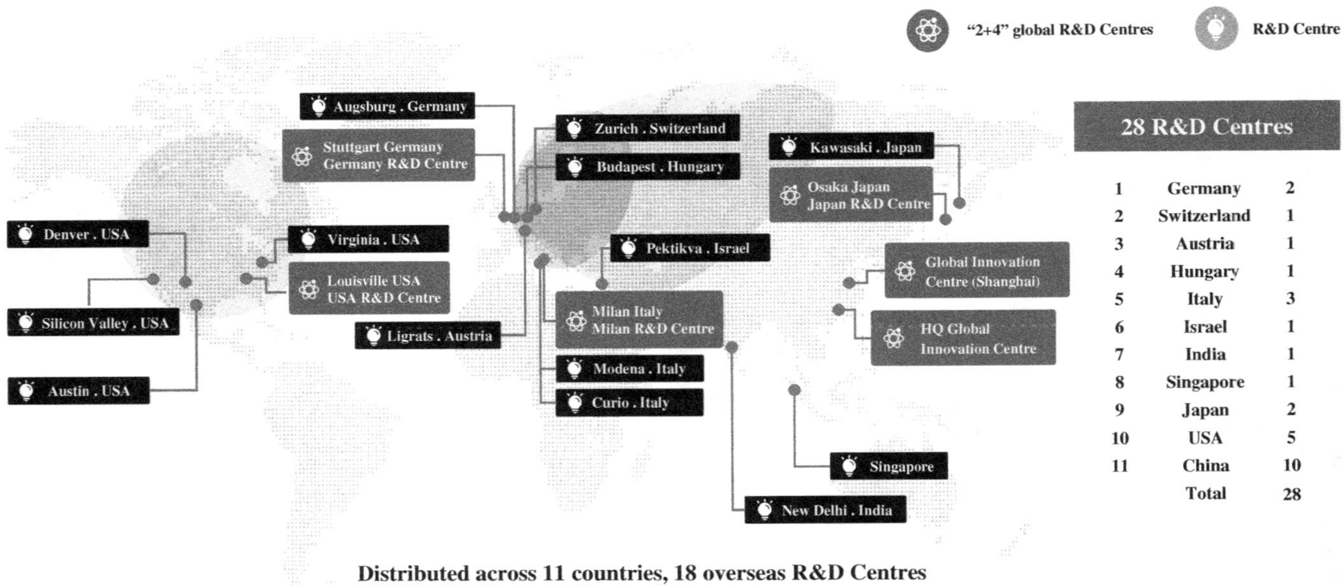

1	Germany	2
2	Switzerland	1
3	Austria	1
4	Hungary	1
5	Italy	3
6	Israel	1
7	India	1
8	Singapore	1
9	Japan	2
10	USA	5
11	China	10
	Total	28

Fig. 13.5. Layout of Midea's global R&D network.

Source: Midea's official document.

Midea's global innovation network enriches its business worldwide. Midea serves 4 billion customers in more than 200 countries and transferred cutting-edge technology into their lives, such as world's first disrotatory AC and the first micro-crystalline refrigerator.

13.2.6. *Internal and external collaboration*

Under the circumstances of iterative and constantly changing innovation, it's necessary to cluster resources, parallelise the process of innovation and collaborate across the subjects of innovation. Apparently, it's simply impossible to make great breakthroughs by adding up all elements of innovation in the open innovation system. This is because different innovation subjects have conflicting goals. Therefore, firms use collaborative innovation strategies to break the barriers between innovation players, and to promote full release and effective allocation of innovation outcomes, and therefore realise collaborative innovation and achieve innovation breakthroughs (Harland, Brenchley and Walker, 2003).

Midea has established a mutually beneficial mechanism to support internal and external collaborative innovation (Figure 13.6). From the perspective of intra-group, Midea, on the one hand, makes clear the technological position of each R&D centre by applying a four-level R&D system and globally distributed network of 28 R&D centres. On the other hand, Midea promotes R&D activities across divisions and emphasises the research of common technologies. Thus, Midea brings each element's superiority into full play and shares the achievements of innovation to the maximum extent at the corporate level.

When it comes to outside of the group, Midea has established extensive connections with diversified innovation players. In this way, Midea has overcome technical challenges and transferred advanced technology into products by cooperating with leading universities and research institutes. By shifting from technology procurement to establishing R&D consortia with leading firms, such as BASF and Honeywell, Midea broke several technological blockades.

Collaborative innovation mechanism empowers Midea's open innovation platform. Consequently, Midea has established a unique, open and

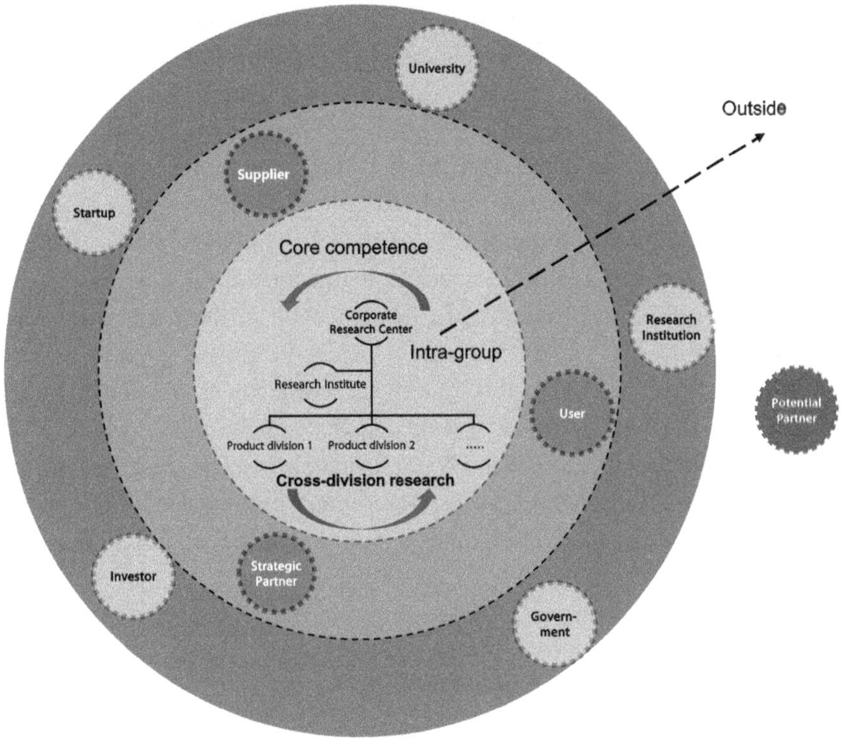

Fig. 13.6. Collaborative mechanism of Midea's innovation system.
Source: Author's design.

holistic innovation system with three dimensions: four-level R&D system, global R&D layout and open innovation platform.

13.2.7. *Midea's lean innovation in digital age*

As competition gets increasingly fierce, it has become a key issue, in the process of enterprise management, to improve the efficiency of R&D, so as to improve the comprehensive benefits of enterprises. In addition, we are coming across a wave of digital technology which is reshaping the competition landscape. A huge number of data resources are pouring in. On the one hand, data resources have become one of the most important factors in production. On the other hand, those who fail in making effective use of digital resources will be banished from the competition. Therefore, accurate allocation and rapid response of innovation resources are becoming more and more important. Midea answered this question perfectly: "How to implement lean innovation in the digital age?"

Midea developed a planning system based on big data named "Midea Big Data Innovation Centre" to realise lean innovation. This system is designed to solve the problems of low efficiency in the process of new product creation since it can integrate data from different sources within one system. With the help of this system, the company obtains insight and comprehensive analysis for analysing the data of the whole process of innovation, including market analysis, user demand, product operation, rapid evaluation, after-sales and installation and new opportunities, so as to support product innovation and operations more comprehensively, accurately and efficiently.

13.2.8. *Midea's innovation management system*

Midea' innovation management system is a typical example of the implementation of ISO 56002. Midea applied the total and holistic innovation management philosophy and strategic vision to motivate multiple-level and diversified innovators to make the most of innovation elements to conduct creative activities at all times and locations so as to create value (Xu *et al.*, 2006).

Led by its strategic vision, "to bring great innovations to life," and the mission "to integrate with the world and inspire the future," Midea has built an innovation management system consisting of technological and managerial core competencies. On the one hand, the open innovation platform enables Midea to gather innovation resources and diversified innovation players. In addition, Midea has built a future-oriented four-level technology roadmap and a global R&D network to make best use of both the internal and external innovation resources and to organise the R&D activities in an efficient and effective way, and therefore, Midea can leverage its future-oriented, technological core capability to develop cutting-edge technologies.

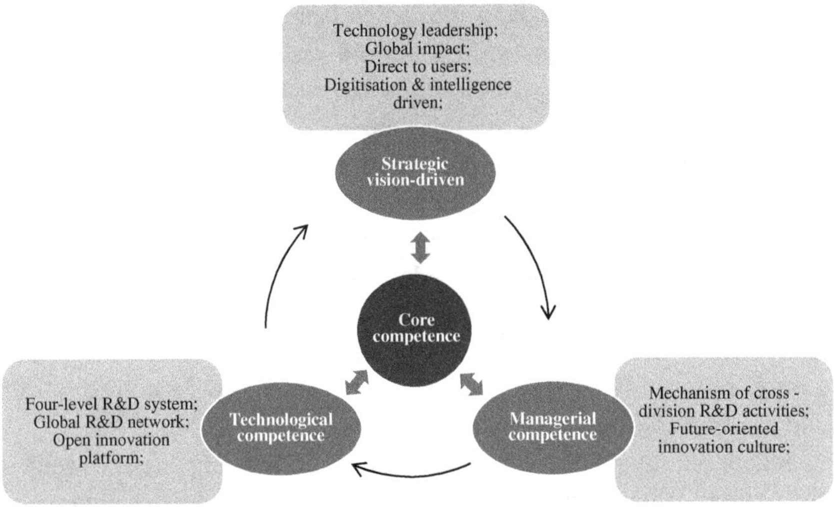

Fig. 13.7. Midea's competence-based holistic innovation management system.

Source: Author's design.

On the other hand, Midea has established the managerial core competence to manage innovation more efficiently. By actively exploring mechanisms of promoting cross-division R&D activities, motivating innovators' creativity, and cultivating the future-oriented and comprehensive culture, Midea can benefit from innovation resources and better operate the innovation ecosystem both inside and outside the group.

To sum up, Midea has developed a strategic core-competence-based holistic innovation management system that is dominated by indigenous innovation competence and empowered by efficient innovation management (Figure 13.7). This innovation management system is driving Midea forward to becoming a world-class company.

13.3. Insights from Midea's Promotion of ISO 56002:2019 Innovation Management System

Based on the innovation systems approach by ISO 56002, Midea has built and constantly improved its innovation management system and established a holistic innovation mode, guided by a future-oriented strategy, and open and constant innovation. And this is exactly a best practice for Chinese companies' focused on catching-up and beyond with the help of ISO 56002 innovation management system. Midea's experience generates at least four meaningful insights for companies that are in search of excellence.

First, a systematic and overall view drives Midea to achieve core capabilities and disruptive innovation consistently. Facing the new industrial revolution, the highly dynamic market demand and increasingly fierce competitions, innovation is no longer limited to research and development. Strategic vision and strategic leadership are more and more important for firms to pursue innovation. By systematically integrating strategy, resources and culture with a long-term view, a company can build a sustainable and dynamic core competence.

Second, a dynamic and future-oriented view has helped Midea achieve meta-innovation capability. This is based on the understanding of external trends and drivers, and it is the base of organisational resilience, which is increasingly important for firms to survive amidst competition (Kantur and İşeri-Say, 2012). According to Midea's customer-oriented, fast-response strategy, the cultivating of core capability and research of disruptive technologies are more important than current revenues. Therefore, Midea implemented a strategic shift from product-following strategy to technology-leading strategy. By developing a standardised, modular R&D process, Midea can integrate, build and reconfigure the resources and competencies to achieve greater innovation flexibility and dynamism (Teece, Pisano, and Shuen, 1997).

Third, it is important to collaborate and balance the internal and external innovation efforts, so as to form the long-term endogenous development on the basis of open innovation ecosystem. We must realise that relying solely on indigenous innovation may not only strengthen the core technology capability, but also improve the path dependence at the same time. While open innovation may be helpful to develop disruptive innovation and avoid falling into the trap of the innovator's dilemma (Christensen and Bower, 1996).

Last, but not least, "two-wheel drive" helped Midea transition into a multi-product global operation group, thereby enriching customers' lives worldwide. Unlike the companies that go beyond the Chinese market by generalising local products overseas, Midea promotes "glocalisation" by mapping R&D activities simultaneously at home and abroad. As a result, Midea adapts products to suit local preference and creates a "glocalised" culture.

13.4. Challenges and Prospects of Midea's Innovation System

Today's world is experiencing a great change that has not been seen in a century and it is obviously impossible to gain profit by maintaining a single competitive advantage (Eisenhardt and Martin, 2000). Only by applying a systems approach, coping with challenges, and gaining temporary advantages constantly can a firm survive in today's "volatile, uncertain, complex, ambiguous" (VUCA) world (Bennett and Lemoine, 2014). Midea also faces many challenges today.

Firstly, Midea needs to strengthen the general-purpose competence of innovation in the dynamic age. Although Midea has made a lot of efforts in promoting innovation capability, such as establishing a corporate-level innovation action plan, increasing investment, stressing foundational innovation and disruptive innovation, and sparking some single cutting-age technologies, there is still a long way to go to form a systematic innovation competence that can secure the stable of amazing innovation achievements and thus provide fast response to the rapid changes of the market.

Secondly, deepening globalisation remains the main task in the near future. On the one hand, as an international brand, it is critical for Midea to deepen globalisation and further promote the globalisation of innovation, talents and standards. On the other hand, the forces against globalisation have risen significantly in the past few years, especially after the COVID-19 pandemic. Therefore, how to take advantage and avoid risks of globalisation is critical for more and more globalised firms like Midea.

The third challenge (it is an opportunity as well) stems from the digital transition. Midea started the digital transformation in 2012, and the application of digitalised management optimises the planning process, improves innovation efficiency, and reduces operation cost. However, with the advent of the digital age, the digitalisation and intelligence capabilities of companies are required to be further improved. How to meet user requirements quickly? How to locate products and make decisions accurately using big data analytics? And how to improve flexible production capacity? These questions and the like are the next major tasks for Midea.

What's more, the most important and everlasting challenge is the continuous update of Midea. "Standing at the turning point of the era, all advantages are dynamic and temporary, and Midea must redefine, refresh and reconstruct itself at an accelerating pace." Mr. Fang said and Midea did so. At the beginning of 2021, Midea renewed its strategy. "Technology leadership, global breakthrough, to be connected with consumer, driven by digital intelligence" are identified as the new four core strategic objectives. "Technology leadership" is on the top of the priority list. It shows that Midea is determined to continue investing in innovation. Constant renewal means embracing challenges and dynamics, and Midea believes that "we will emerge from the storm stronger than ever, able to reach even further ahead."

Acknowledgements

The authors would like to thank the interviewees from Midea, the editors and the anonymous referees of this book for their constructive comments and feedbacks. The authors acknowledge the support from the National Science Foundation of China (Project No. 72104027) and National Postdoctoral Science Foundation of China (Project No. 2021M690388).

References

Bennett, N. and Lemoine, G. J. (2014). What a difference a word makes: Understanding threats to performance in a VUCA world. *Business Horizons*, *57*(3), 311–317.

Chen, J., Yin, X. and Li, J. (2020). Firm innovation system: Paths for enhancing corporate indigenous innovation capability. *Frontiers of Engineering Management*, *7*(3), 404–412.

Chesbrough, H. W. (2006). Open innovation: *The new imperative for creating and profiting from technology*. Boston, MA: Harvard Business School Press.

Christensen, C. M. (1997). *The Innovator's Dilemma: When New Technologies Cause Great Firms to Fail.* Boston, MA: Harvard Business School Press.

Christensen, C. M. and Bower, J. L. (1996). Customer power, strategic investment, and the failure of leading firms. *Strategic Management Journal, 17*(3), 197–218.

Cohen, W. M. and Levinthal, D. A. (1990). Absorptive capacity: A new perspective on learning and innovation. *Administrative Science Quarterly, 35*(1), 128–152.

Collins, J. and Porras, J. (2002). *Built to last: Successful habits of visionary companies*. New York: Harper Business Essentials.

Eisenhardt, K. M. and Martin, J. A. (2000). Dynamic capabilities, what are they? *Strategic Management Journal, 21*(1011), 1105–1121.

Fleming, L. and Waguespack, D. M. (2007). Brokerage, boundary spanning, and leadership in open innovation communities. *Organization Science, 18*(2), 165–180.

Harland, C., Brenchley, R. and Walker, H. (2003). Risk in supply networks. *Journal of Purchasing and Supply Management, 9*(2), 51–62.

ISO (2019). *ISO 56002:2019 Innovation management — Innovation management system — Guidance*. International Organization for Standardization.

Kantur, D. and İşeri-Say, A. (2012). Organizational resilience: A conceptual integrative framework. *Journal of Management & Organization, 18*(6), 762–773.

O'Reilly, C. A. and Tushman, M. L. (2008). Ambidexterity as a dynamic capability: Resolving the innovator's dilemma. *Research in Organizational Behavior, 28*, 185–206.

Teece, D. J. (2006). Reflections on "profiting from innovation". *Research Policy, 35*(8), 1131–1146.

Teece, D. J., Pisano, G. P. and Shuen, A. (1997). Dynamic capabilities and strategic management. *Strategic Management Journal, 18*(7), 509–533.

Wernerfelt, B. (1984). A resource-based view of the firm. *Southern Medical Journal, 5*(2), 171–180.

Xu, Q., Chen, J., Xie, Z., Liu, J., Zheng, G. and Wang, Y. (2006). Total innovation management: A novel paradigm of innovation management in the 21st century. *Journal of Technology Transfer, 32*(1), 9–25.

© 2023 World Scientific Publishing Europe Ltd.
https://doi.org/10.1142/9781800612105_0014

Chapter 14

Moen Incorporated: Initiating and Sustaining Transformational Growth Through a Systems Approach

Joanne Hyland and Mike Pickett

Abstract

This chapter describes and analyses the development of an innovation management system at Moen, between 2007 and 2017. Moen is a consumer products company in the plumbing business, headquartered in the United States. The journey began with asking, "How does a plumbing company chart new paths for growth and sustain an ability to do this over time?" In 2007, an innovation assessment was conducted by breakthrough innovation experts. The conclusions were that Moen lacked an innovation strategy and clarity about how to handle different types of innovation. Further, there was no clear appetite for major (category and breakthrough) innovations that would stretch the company beyond incremental improvements and lead to increasing levels of uncertainty. After much debate, the Executive Team agreed to make the right level of investment in major innovations to successfully pursue Moen's grow ambitions. This is the story of Moen's 10-year journey to build its innovation management system, guided by Rensselaer Polytechnic Institute's (RPI's) pioneering research on breakthrough innovation. While Moen's path to build a sustainable innovation capability predates the release of the ISO 56002 innovation management system standard, RPI's research was a key input to the development of this standard. Therefore, this case parallels closely this standard and is an excellent testament as to its guidance value.

14.1. Introduction to Moen

Moen Inc. is a consumer products company in the plumbing business. By the 2000s, it was facing rapidly changing industry dynamics. While Moen was well-recognised as a first mover in bringing new products to the market, it was in jeopardy of losing this status. Moen was looking to maintain its strong brand recognition and customer loyalty. It had been successful for many years with incremental improvements to its original invention, the single-handed faucet. However, with these changing industry dynamics, this was no longer sufficient to drive growth. Further, the company had not developed a portfolio of breakthrough innovations. With no more breakthroughs in its pipeline, Moen was facing a dilemma of what to do next.

14.1.1. *Growth challenge*

How does a plumbing company chart new paths for growth? Faucets, toilets, showers and drains have only changed incrementally since the advent of indoor plumbing. In 2006, the following questions were facing Mike Pickett, Moen's VP of Global Strategy Development (GSD), and David Lingafelter, who became President of US Business in 2007, about Moen's future. How to:

- Move beyond many incremental offerings for improving existing products each year to achieving significant growth targets and making a difference in the industry?
- Grow and distinguish itself within its parent company of Fortune Brands, which sold everything from padlocks and whiskey to faucets and golf clubs, while at the same time meeting expectations to remain its "cash cow," i.e., providing a steady income stream, AND investing in growth?
- Innovate and keep up with technology, or risk falling behind, despite a strong market position?

14.1.2. *History*

After burning his hand with a two-handle faucet design, Al Moen brought the single-handed faucet to the world during the period of 1937–1939. This invention led to innovations in technical form, like washer-free cartridges, and in fashion plumbing, like the boutique line. It also led to the development of high-quality faucets for home and commercial uses. Moen's history evolved as follows:

- In the 1960s, Moen offered a niche product in an ever-growing industry, with 5% market share.
- By the 1970s, Moen's revenue had tripled to become the number two faucet company. This growth came through its investment in new technologies and a construction boom.
- In 1982, when Al Moen retired, double-digit growth continued.
- In 1990, Fortune Brands acquired Moen, with innovation continuing in the spirit of Al Moen.
- However, by the late 1990s, Moen was no longer producing breakthrough innovations and lost its first mover status. Its product line had become about material improvements and fashion changes per consumer desires.

14.1.3. *Innovation in context of plumbing industry*

From Roman times through to the 1920s, the industry comprised many small designers and manufacturers. Technological innovation was slow. In the early 20th century, technology began to reshape the industry. With it, the cost of manufacturing and installation grew. Several small companies were able to innovate, consolidate positions and capture regional market shares.

Prior to 1990s, most sales in North America were made through large wholesale distribution networks, with professionals doing most plumbing work in homes. In 1990s, Home Depot, Lowes and other large retail stores became a new method of distribution, with Do-It-Yourself (DIY) consumers doing plumbing repairs in homes. Two main forms of product distribution exist today: wholesale and retail. Moen's business units are structured to support these distribution channels and are successful in delivering incremental improvements, not breakthroughs.

14.2. Description and Initiation of Innovation Capability Development

14.2.1. *Innovation assessment — 2007*

Moen was struggling with how to recapture its entrepreneurial roots and return to the business of creating breakthroughs, by looking for new to the world features, significant performance, or feature improvements, and/or substantial cost reductions. While it had a successful pipeline of incremental improvements, it had lost its ability to generate major innovations, critical to Moen's future. This happens to many companies when they move from founder-led breakthroughs to a professional management team. It is typically years, if not decades, in the making. Knowing it could not design its future alone, it reached out to external experts in breakthrough innovation to answer:

- What does growth through innovation mean for Moen and how should we build an innovation capability to be able to sustain growth through major innovations over the long run?

Background on the breakthrough innovation experts and the methodology

Breakthrough innovation experts were hired to conduct an innovation assessment and present their findings and recommendations, as input for Moen's 2008–2010 strategic planning cycle. Three priority areas were defined: (1) establishing appropriate metrics, (2) overcoming cultural barriers, and (3) organising for success.

This assessment was based on research conducted by Rensselaer Polytechnic Institute (RPI) through its breakthrough innovation research programme that started in 1995. In Phase I, from 1995–2000, the key findings were about how to manage breakthrough innovation projects. Seven management challenges and four uncertainties specific to these projects were observed (Leifer *et al.*, 2000). In Phase II, from 2001 to 2008, seven innovation management system elements and three discrete competencies, Discovery, Incubation and Acceleration (D-I-A), were identified. By 2007, Phase II findings were also well documented. Both Phases became the basis of the assessment. In addition, industry practices that had been evolving in parallel since before 1995 also provided invaluable inputs (Arteaga and Hyland, 2013).

Interviews were conducted with innovation stakeholders at all levels within Moen to better understand Moen's level of innovation maturity at strategic, portfolio and project levels. The interviews were conducted individually and probed the areas mentioned in Table 14.1.

Table 14.1. Innovation assessment interview areas and topics.

Interview Areas	Topics
A. Innovation measures of success — Culture, metrics and achievements:	• Values and beliefs are incremental, category and breakthrough innovations • Influences on business opportunity success and failure • Measures of innovation performance • Key innovation achievements and disappointments • Strengths and weaknesses of innovation capabilities
B. Innovation purpose — Mission, role, structure and effectiveness:	• Mission of the innovation team • Structure and history of innovation team • Definition of innovation • Mission support for different types of innovation • Roles and responsibilities
C. Innovation stakeholders — Interfaces and transition management requirements:	• Key interfaces for innovation • Nature of communications • Effectiveness of interface relationships • Resource and organisation issues influencing success • Roles for and effectiveness of project transitions
D. Innovation processes — Project management and evaluation:	• Process followed, stages involved and criteria used • Use of learning-based project management • Pivots/redirects and shutdowns of projects

Source: Dr. Nick Colarelli, adapted by breakthrough innovation experts for interview protocol.

Conclusions

The conclusions from this assessment were that Moen lacked an innovation strategy and clarity about how to handle different types of innovation. The capability did reside on the executive team to develop this strategy, however, the strategic context needed to be defined and a portfolio options mentality adopted. The lack of execution on strategic frontiers was problematic. There was a question if the right opportunities were being pursued for new growth platforms to materialise, and if investments were being made to develop innovation capabilities, necessary to win in the future.

Further, there was no clear appetite for major innovations, defined as category and breakthrough innovations, i.e., those that would stretch the company beyond incremental improvements and result in increasing levels of uncertainty. Emphasis had been on moving Moen to the third generation of leadership, globalisation, process improvement, professional management and expanding the product line. Globalisation and market share capture were sufficient to fuel growth so there had been no apparent need for major innovations in more recent years. Further, there was confusion about Moen's commitment to major innovations and a lack of understanding of how to go about it. Moen also had a history of unsuccessful attempts in moving beyond its fashion plumbing product line, which made it risk averse.

Recommendations

The two breakthrough experts asked the following question for the executive team to reflect upon prior to presenting their recommendations.

As part of fulfilling upon its innovation mission, is the team truly committed to making the right level of investment in major innovations to successfully pursue its growth ambitions? Why start here … because the experts were not convinced of the team's commitment to do what it would take for success.

The recommendations were as follows:

- An innovation management system is required, as described in Figure 14.1. See Table A.1, for a comparison of these system elements with the ISO 56002 innovation management system elements

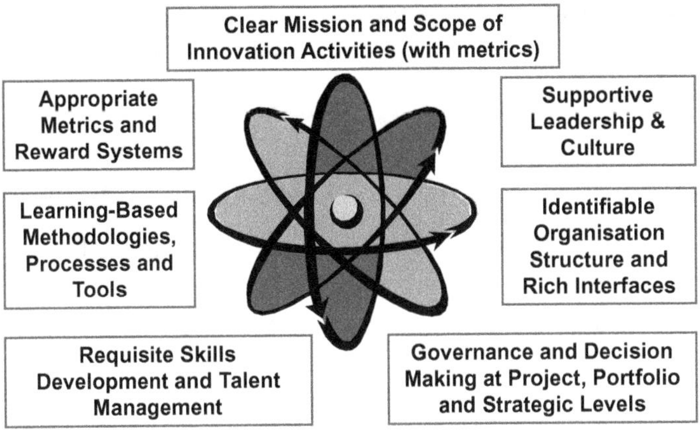

Fig. 14.1. Innovation management system elements.

Source: RPI research.

- Priority one was to define a clear mission and scope of innovation activities (with metrics). The team should:
  - Discuss Moen's appetite or organisational commitment for category and/or breakthrough innovations (major innovations) as part of its growth objectives.
  - Develop and agree upon a mandate for innovation, based on types of innovation and organisational fit.
- Priority two was to establish appropriate metrics to measure progress and results, aligned with the mandate for innovation.

Moen's response

Discussions were initiated by the Chief Financial Officer (CFO) and the Chief Operating Officer (COO) to discuss a way to do this. This surprised the external experts since people in these roles tend to be less favourable to a more strategic innovation agenda. The main topic was how to fund it. The CFO made the case for a portfolio options approach that the President supported. In the end, the executive team did make the commitment to invest in major innovation. It then asked the GSD team, led by Mike Pickett, to commence development of an innovation strategy.

Core to the team's ambition for success of this strategy was to develop an innovation management system that could continually improve over time. The plan was as follows:

- Define Moen's innovation objectives and establish appropriate business metrics (Q3 2007).
- Determine what types of innovation will be led by the business units and the central corporate group (Q3 2007).
- Find the right organisational structure, cultural changes and resource allocation to meet the business objectives (Q4 2007).
- Start to incorporate the Incubation phase to Moen's innovation process (Q3 2007).
- Establish and implement an innovation management system to improve effectiveness and sustainability of Moen's innovation capabilities (Q4 2008)

(Moen 2007).

14.2.2. *Context for innovation within Moen*

For delivering upon its innovation strategy, Moen required a strategic intent to guide its investments. Further, it learned that it had to adapt the continuum of uncertainty (O'Connor and Rice 2013) to fit its capacity and capabilities for implementation.

Creating Moen's strategic intent (see Figure 14.2) was a dynamic process that took place over many months as part of the strategic planning cycle. It was linked with the corporate strategy, with innovation as one of the pillars. The vision was to move from global fashion plumbing to "easy and intuitive controls" to smart plumbing, while at the same time enjoying water wisely. The two other areas, Health and Well-Being and Green, were not the immediate priorities, yet they did become important design and selection criteria for the Intelligent Monitor and Management strategic domain. To act upon this strategic intent, the D-I-A process was followed with opportunities scoped in Discovery (blue), applications tested in Incubation (purple) and products developed in Acceleration (green).

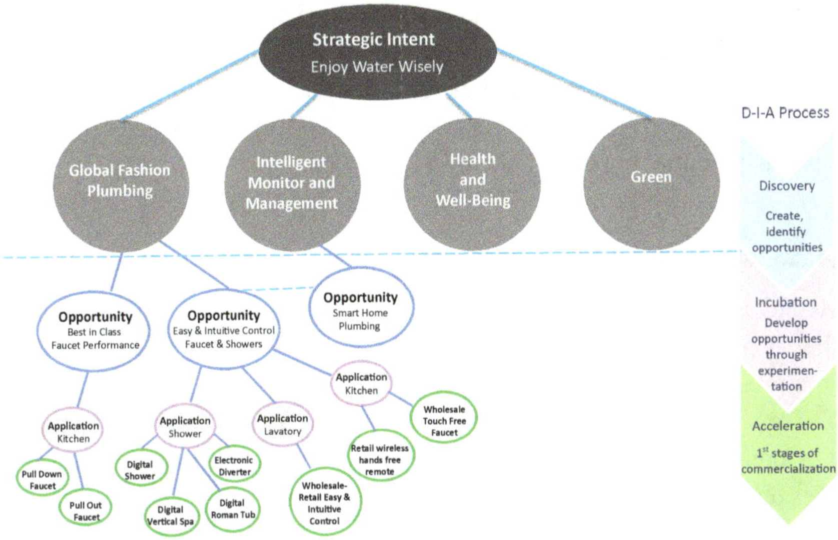

Fig. 14.2. Moen's strategic intent.

Source: Moen (2008–2010).

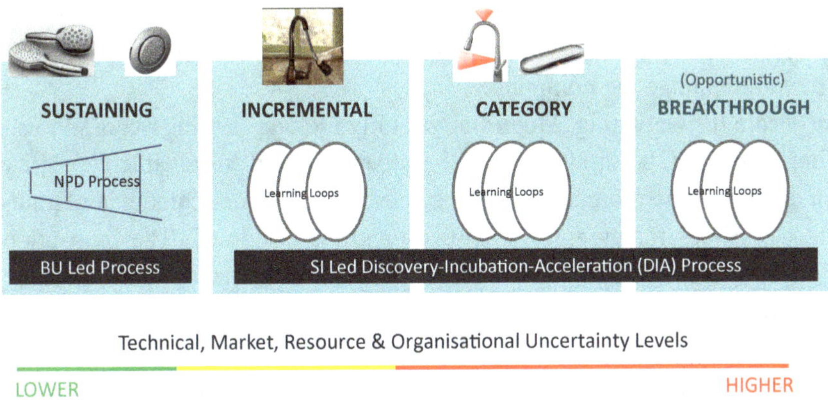

Fig. 14.3. Moen-adapted continuum of uncertainty.

Source: Moen (2009–2011).

As for Moen's continuum of uncertainty (see Figure 14.3), it realised that within its strategic intent, it could not support breakthrough innovations. With its business units' available capacity and limited major innovation capabilities, incremental innovations presented a medium level of uncertainty and category innovations were high. However, if breakthrough innovation opportunities did materialise, they could not be ignored with a dynamic future landscape. The team decided to assess these as potential opportunistic investments only.

14.2.3. *Approach to innovation capability building*

Moen was also working to develop critical innovation capabilities in parallel as part of establishing its innovation management system. It worked on a process by which to develop its Discovery-Incubation-Acceleration (D-I-A) competencies and define its governance operating model (O'Connor *et al.*, 2008). Priority areas were strategic intent definition, roles and responsibilities and measures of success.

14.3. Development of the Innovation Management System at Moen

Getting back to the original question: How does Moen deliver category and breakthrough (major) innovations and build a sustainable capability to grow and change the company?

From the beginning, Moen was not only looking to bring major innovations to market, but it also required a repeatable and sustainable capability for doing so. Therefore, the journey started with D-I-A orientation and training workshops for the innovation team and the design of "The Innovation Hub Playbook" Version 1.0 to develop its innovation management system.

This was guided by RPI's stages of innovation capability development in Figure 14.4 and the "Why, What and How" approach for designing systemic change, as follows:

- Why — Organisation purpose, call to action and initiation and leadership commitment.
- What — Innovation objectives, common language and uncertainty mindset.
- How — Right governance model and incentives, appropriate metrics and learning-based decisions, processes and tools.

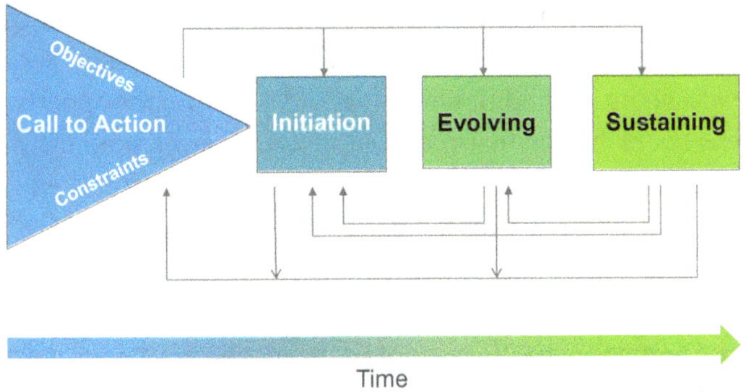

Fig. 14.4. Innovation capability development.

Source: RPI research.

14.3.1. *Call to action and initiation — Starting with Discovery*

The call to action is about clarifying the objectives for a systematic approach and identifying any constraints based on organisational capacity. For initiation, it is about:

- Understanding the mission and innovation agenda, within the context of a strategic intent and the organisational culture.
- Getting the right people on board and developing a structure around D-I-A.
- Communicating an organisational purpose to start or complement the idea-to-opportunity flow (pipeline initially that evolves into a portfolio over time).
- Implementing learning-based processes to build a common language, engage internal and external stakeholders and enable culture change.

Moen started with improving its Discovery area. The New Growth Markets Group (NGMG) was formed in 2007 to discover new areas and opportunities to grow the business. A full-time leader was hired, with others working part-time. The consultants, who conducted the assessment, were hired by the VP of GSD and the NGMG Leader to facilitate the implementation of the D-I-A structure and process as well as develop the governance operating model.

The Moen team priorities were to build a pipeline by scouting for new opportunities, within its strategic intent, and elaborate upon several concepts already being scoped in Discovery. The first major opportunity was the tankless water heater that required a significant amount of technical knowledge and a breadth across many disciplines. Moen lacked engineering expertise and market experience. While it was an attractive technology and market, the tankless water heater failed. The VP of GSD reflected on the reasons why. He concluded that the right people were not on the team, the concept was too far removed from Moen's know-how and too much focus was placed on the technology, to the exclusion of the market.

14.3.2. *Evolving — Moving to Incubation*

Evolving the system is about revisiting the mandate and scope, leadership commitment and governance model. It requires aligning structures across the organisation, ensuring people are in the right roles and adapting processes and tools. As the pipeline becomes more robust, a portfolio emerges that needs to be managed, with appropriate metrics and system resources, linked with organisational capacity.

In moving into Incubation, Moen made significant adjustments as it learned what worked within its environment. It formed a new team of dedicated people with experience in Intellectual Property (IP), Engineering and Marketing. The team's role was to conceive of concepts, conduct in-market experiments during Incubation and adopt a portfolio options mindset. The IP person became the new leader and brought the strategic focus closer to the core of the business, with the objective to grow outwards from there. The priority was to first introduce a single innovation concept, prior to creating a portfolio, and make Moen the best company at everything to do with water in the home.

Discovery was reinvented to feed Incubation by looking for new technologies externally that could fill competency gaps for developing major innovations for Moen's product lines. Its first major success was a smart faucet, with touchless sensor control. This required the successful integration of motion sensing technology into a faucet. This opened a new category for Moen, enabled new relationships and led to new technical competencies in electrical components, sensor development and water technologies to take Moen beyond the core.

The systematic approach to Discovery and Incubation was proving its value.

14.4. Building a Sustainable Capability

A sustainable capability requires moving from a process view of the D-I-A approach to a focus on Discovery, Incubation and Acceleration as discrete competencies. This requires the open sourcing of ideas, technologies, business models, etc.; skills in opportunity generation; experimentation know-how with competent Incubation oversight, coaching and evaluation; and an ability to develop and grow the project into a viable product, solution or business. This is supported by aligning opportunities with strategic intent, rationalising the system and enabling cultures of innovation and operational excellence to co-exist. Ultimately, there needs to be structural flexibility as internal and external business conditions change, a pacing of the portfolio based on organisational capacity, and commitment from leadership across the organisation to be focused on the future health of the company, not any given business unit.

14.4.1. *Sustaining — Transitioning to Acceleration*

By 2012, Moen realised that it required a new direction to build a sustainable capability. Having yet to realise the ambition of developing a major or strategic innovation portfolio, the Marketing person became the leader of the newly named Strategic Innovation Group (SI Group). Additional engineering resources were assigned.

For successful transitions to Acceleration, the SI Group needed to work more closely with a product manager through Moen's phase-gate process. The business units were not mature enough to run with these new projects, yet it was clear that the SI Group alone could not build a sustainable capability. In working more closely with business units, new challenges emerged. How could the SI Group work on new opportunities in Discovery and Incubation, when business units needed help with the projects now in Acceleration? Further, how does the team ensure that critical external Incubation partnerships are successfully transitioned to the business units?

As a first step, business unit involvement was brought in earlier in Incubation to form a stronger internal partnership. The second generation of the smart faucet became the team's next success, which was a significant improvement over the first product launch. Moen had now developed in-house electrical engineering and sensor know-how that it did not have with the first generation.

Through the accomplishments over the last 5 years, the SI Group team learned that relationships, with its external partners and the in-house know-how it had developed, were not easy to transition to the business units. This led to a tighter integration by involving the business units earlier on in Incubation and more directly with external relationships. As the SI Group aimed to build a sustainable model, with it came additional success. The business units wanted strategic innovation projects because consumers were buying them.

14.4.2. *Organisational crossroad*

In 2016 and 2017, Moen was at a crossroad in terms of how to evolve its innovation management system to build a lasting capability. A new opportunity, under consideration in the intelligent monitor and management area, had the potential to return Moen to its first mover status and become the first major smart technology outside of faucets and showers alone. This would open the entire smart home market for Moen and offer integrated systems for water management. Will this project become Moen's third success?

The SI Group's product growth rates were over three times the rest of the industry and its business units. The team, with its internal and external partners, was making a considerable contribution to Moen's revenues and profits. The whole of Moen now believed it had the capabilities, experience and processes required to build depth in Discovery and Incubation. With its limited resources, how does Moen build upon this and sustain it?

True to the initial ambition, a strategic innovation portfolio had emerged, with multiple opportunities in the pipeline. With the strain on SI

Group resources for Acceleration support and limited business unit capacity to absorb these innovation projects, how many strategic innovation opportunities can Moen support and how big can the portfolio be?

As part of evolving the governance model, the Innovation Leadership Committee was formed to steer different types of innovation. Low uncertainty, sustaining innovations would be led by the business units, supported by the SI Group. Medium uncertainty, incremental innovations, and high uncertainty, category innovations, would be led by the SI Group. Breakthrough innovations remained too much of a stretch for Moen and were still considered fraught with high+++ uncertainty. In addition, to set and track metrics and manage budgets, targets of 2–3 sustaining innovations per year were to be delivered by the business units. For the SI Group, its targets were one category innovation every 2 years and one incremental innovation in alternate years.

At this point, Moen had been at it for 10 years and counting! This only reinforces that it is an ongoing journey to evolve and sustain an innovation management system.

14.5. Achievements of the Innovation Management System

In reviewing Moen's journey, the achievements of the innovation management system are as follows:

- **2007:** Innovation assessment led to leadership commitment to develop an innovation strategy and invest in major innovations.
- **2008:** Strategic intent and uncertainty continuum defined.
- **Mid-2008 Ongoing:** New learning-based tools for Discovery and Incubation, supported by evolving governance model.
- **2010:** Refocused to stay closer to the core having gone too far, e.g., tankless water heater, smart water refocused to smart devices. Adjusted its capacity to support incremental and category innovations only. Breakthrough innovations were too much of a stretch, especially for a consumer products company with limited R&D resources.
- **Mid-2012:** Explored beyond the core. Introduced the smart, touchless faucet. It was Moen's most innovative and successful product introduction of all time, with incremental units, net incremental

revenue and contribution margin all beyond the business unit expectations.

- **2013:** Incubated projects beyond the core. Introduced the second generation of the smart, touchless faucet, with similar results.
- **2016–2017:** Product growth rates at three times the industry and the business units. Innovation Leadership Committee formed to steer strategic innovation based on organisational structure and innovation targets for sustaining, incremental and category innovations.

14.6. Overall Reflections and Way Forward

In looking at the RPI innovation management system elements and those that are listed in the ISO 56002 standard (ISO, 2019) (see Table 14.A.1 for a detailed comparison), Moen followed most of the steps in this standard. This is good news because Moen's 10 years of experience, along with over two decades of research and practical industry experiences, provide excellent validation of the merits of this standard. It reinforces that for those who follow the guidance in the standard, they do improve their chances for success in growing and renewing their organisations.

In looking at Moen's innovation management system design and implementation through the lens of the standard, reflections are as follows:

Strengths

- Moen started with understanding its organisational context (4.1, 4.2, 4.3, 4.4) to develop an innovation strategy (5.1.3, 5.1.4), with a concrete plan for moving forward (6.2).
- The executive team was fully committed to setting a direction for major innovations (5.1.2, 5.1.2) and enabling the right culture for success by sponsoring training for the D-I-A process and use of learning-based tools and methods (4.4.2, 7.1, 7.2, 7.6, 8.3).
- A governance operating model was developed and evolved to encourage systems thinking and adapt to changes in external and internal capacity (5.3, 6.3, 6.4, 8.2, 9.3, 10).

Challenges

- Moen did encounter challenges in getting the right people in innovation roles (7.1, 7.2), balancing the level of interaction with its business units based on the maturity of business concepts (4.4.3, 5.3, 7.3, 7.4), and building a robust innovation portfolio due to capacity constraints (6.4).

In 2017, after 10 years of success, Moen was still asking if it had the right system elements in place to sustain its innovation capability. The SI Group had questions about how to create a platform for growth in the smart home market, partner more effectively with the business units, and coordinate Acceleration activities for the business units in addition to its Discovery and Incubation responsibilities. Moen was testing if the Innovation Leadership Committee could help to better align expectations about Moen's future and continuing to ask about how to develop a robust innovation portfolio, with limited time and resources.

A small team working with external experts can accomplish a lot, once the right people with a learning mindset are in place to orchestrate the innovation management system and drive projects forward. Further, an innovation strategy and critical mass are essential for success, which is less about the number of people but rather having funding for external support and a strategic intent to guide investments.

For those interested in embarking on this journey, a few questions to consider are as follows.

- How does an organisation grow and secure industry leadership through a systems approach?
- How does an organisation realise a need for major or strategic innovations?
- Once the need is recognised, how should it be set up? Centralised? Decentralised? Single coordinator?
- What challenges could you face early on? How could you overcome them by establishing and evolving an innovation management system per the ISO guidance standard?

- How can you learn from Moen's ambition to build a sustainable innovation capability, from its call to action and initiating stages to evolving its innovation management system?

14.7. Summary

Was Moen successful in achieving its ambitions for growth and building a sustainable innovation capability? Where is it today?

In 2015, Moen continued to hold the North American market share leadership position in faucets and showers sales. Delta was a close second and narrowing the gap and Kohler was in the number three position. While Moen continued to work on maintaining this leadership position, it was also working aggressively to redefine the industry, with offerings that gave consumers more control over where, when and how they experience water in their homes every day. By transforming the industry to "Smart Plumbing," Moen reversed the trend of commoditisation for faucets and showers and built a new fast-growing segment of products with higher value, higher prices and better margins, in which it held a clear leadership position.

Where Moen is today could not have happened without the work of the SI Group, over a 10-year journey from an ambition set in 2007 to its realisation by 2017. While the focus is about sourcing even more innovation capabilities externally via strategic partnerships and competency-based acquisitions, the fundamentals of an innovation management system to enable this remain very much alive today.

Acknowledgements

Special thanks to insights captured from a first draft of an unpublished case study written by Rensselaer Polytechnic Institute (RPI) MBA graduates Peter Bleday and Dmitri Mata, and Professors Gina Colarelli O'Connor, Lally School of Management, Rensselaer Polytechnic Institute, and Andrew Corbett, Babson College. These insights were edited in subsequent years by Joanne Hyland for teaching corporate entrepreneurship in an executive education MBA module. This case analysis and the rInnovation Group advisory services provided to Moen from 2007 to 2015 served as inspiration for this case study.

References

Arteaga, R. and Hyland, J. (2013). *Pivot: How Top Entrepreneurs Adapt and Change Course to Find Ultimate Success*. Hoboken, New Jersey: Wiley & Sons.

ISO (2019). *ISO 56002:2019 Innovation management — Innovation management system — Guidance*. International Organization for Standardization.

Leifer, R., McDermott, C., O'Connor, G., Peters, L., Rice, M. and Veryzer, R. (2000). *Radical Innovation: How Mature Companies can Outsmart Upstarts*. Boston, MA: Harvard Business School Press.

O'Connor, G. C. and Rice, M. P. (2013). A comprehensive model of uncertainty associated with radical innovation. *Journal of Product Innovation Management*, *30*(1), 2–18.

O'Connor, G. C., Leifer, R., Paulson, A. S. and Peters, L. S. (2008). *Grabbing Lightning: Building a Capability for Breakthrough Innovation*. San Francisco, CA: Wiley & Sons.

Moen company reference materials.

Internet sources. For Moen market share and position from 2015 to 2020.

Appendix

Table 14.A.1. Comparison of RPI innovation management system model with ISO 56002:2019.

RPI Innovation Management System Model	Sections of ISO 56002:2019
Innovation Assessment	Understanding the organisation and its context (4.1) Needs and expectations of interested parties (4.2) Scope of innovation management system (4.3)
1. Clear Purpose, Direction and Scope (with metrics)	Establishing the innovation management system (4.3) Innovation vision and strategy (5.1.3, 5.1.4) Innovation policy (5.2) Innovation objectives and planning (6.2)
2. Supportive Leadership and Culture	Culture (4.4.2) Leadership and commitment, with value realisation (5.1.1, 5.1.2)
3. Identifiable Organisation Structure and Rich Interfaces	Organisational structures (6.3) Collaboration (4.4.3)
4. Governance and Decision Making at Project, Portfolio and Strategic Levels	Organisational roles, responsibilities, and authorities (5.3) Innovation portfolios (6.4) Awareness, Communication, and Documented Information (7.3, 7.4, 7.5) Strategic intelligence management (7.7) Intellectual property management (7.8) Operational planning and control (8.1) Innovation initiatives (8.2) Management review (9.3)
5. Requisite Skills Development and Talent Management	Resources (7.1) Competence (7.2)
6. Learning-Based Methodologies, Processes and Tools	Tools and methods (7.6) Innovation processes (8.3)
7. Appropriate Metrics and Reward Systems	Monitoring, measurement, analysis, and evaluation (9.1)
Strategic Intent and Uncertainty Lens	Innovation vision and strategy (5.1.3, 5.1.4) Managing uncertainty and risk (0.3.3)
Evolving and Sustaining the System	Internal audit (9.2) Improvement (10)

Source: Analysis by Joanne Hyland, ISO and innovation management system expert.

© 2023 World Scientific Publishing Europe Ltd.
https://doi.org/10.1142/9781800612105_0015

Chapter 15

Naturvårdsverket, Swedish Environmental Protection Agency: Innovation Capability in a Government Agency — Key Drivers in a Systemic Innovation Platform

Marie Denward, Oskar Jonsson and Roger Lundegård

Abstract

Naturvårdsverket, the Swedish Environmental Protection Agency, conducts assignments on behalf of the Swedish Government relating to the environment in Sweden, the European Union and internationally. Naturvårdsverket works with complex-system challenges that our society faces, and innovation is designated as a tool for achieving the environmental objectives. In 2016, Naturvårdsverket decided to implement an internal platform for innovation. In 2018, Naturvårdsverket participated in a 1-year knowledge-exchange programme aimed at supporting government authorities in developing systemic and systematic innovation capability. Insights from a Swedish benchmark study of innovation capabilities of 112 government authorities formed the programme's base. The organisational platform for innovation, that comprises building blocks such as innovation strategy, organisation, value networks, innovation projects and results is described. The components capture the key elements of the "ISO 56002:2019 Innovation management — Innovation management system — Guidance." One important outcome from the described design process of the innovation management system is a change in management culture towards innovation and innovative thinking. Both incremental and more transformative innovation work took place, resulting in updated routines, working practices and customer interaction and service.

15.1. Introduction to the Swedish Environmental Protection Agency

Naturvårdsverket, the Swedish Environmental Protection Agency (Swedish EPA), is a central governmental authority with approximately 700 employees (Swedish Environmental Protection Agency, 2021a) that carries out assignments on behalf of the Swedish Government relating to the environment in Sweden, the EU and internationally.

The Swedish EPA's remit is threefold: (1) compiling knowledge and documentation — to develop its own environmental efforts and those of others, (2) developing environmental policy — by providing the government with a sound basis for decisions and by giving an impetus to the European Community (EU) and international efforts, and (3) implementing environmental policy — by acting in such a way as to ensure compliance with the Swedish Environmental Code (Government Offices of Sweden, 2000), and achievement of the national environmental objectives (Swedish Environmental Protection Agency, 2021b).

15.1.1. *Context of organisation and main challenges*

The Swedish EPA is a driving and coordinating force in environmental work. It is responsible for issues relating to climate and air, land, biodiversity, polluted areas, circular economy and waste, environmental monitoring, wildlife management and environmental research.

Every year, the Swedish Government establishes objectives, requirements and a budget for the Agency's efforts in what are known as "appropriation directions." The remit includes the allocation of government appropriations to other actors within fields such as the protection and maintenance of valuable natural environments, remediation of polluted areas, compensation for damage caused by wildlife and support for outdoor recreational organisations.

The Swedish EPA has an important role to play in driving development forward to achieve Sweden's national and international environmental objectives. However, Sweden is not reaching most of the objectives with current or planned measures — indeed, the development is sometimes negative, or in many cases unclear (Naturvårdsverket, 2019a). The European Environment Agency (EEA) states that without urgent action during the next 10 years Europe will not achieve its 2030 goals to address the alarming rate of biodiversity loss, increasing impacts of climate change and the overconsumption of natural resources (European Environment Agency, 2019).

In 2010, Riksdagen, the Swedish Parliament, adopted a new administrative policy objective that highlighted innovation and collaboration. The central government administration should be "an innovative and collaborative central government administration that is legally certain and efficient, has a high degree of quality, service and accessibility, and thereby contributes to Sweden's development and effective EU work" (Swedish Agency for Public Management, 2020).

15.1.2. *Innovation needs and intent*

The Swedish EPA works with complex-system challenges that need to be addressed in a relatively short period of time (Swedish Environmental Protection Agency, 2021c). Innovation is a tool that can contribute to achieving environmental objectives, both nationally and internationally.

In 2016, the Swedish Government inquiry about a Swedish climate and air pollution control strategy suggests "the Swedish ambition to be a front runner in the climate transition should be an overall goal for the enterprise, industry and innovation policy." The Swedish Government points to innovation as a tool for reaching climate and environmental goals in strategies and action plans (Regeringskansliet, 2019, 2020a, 2020b).

The EEA has shown the need for action and transformative solutions to achieve the environmental objectives within the European Union (European Environment Agency, 2015, 2019). "The European environment — state and outlook 2015" showed that incremental development, and neither current nor planned policies, incorporate the required transformative changes (European Environment Agency, 2015).

Furthermore, the UN Agenda 2030 declaration in 2015 calls for "bold and transformative steps which are urgently needed to shift the world onto a sustainable and resilient path" (United Nations, 2015).

15.1.3. *Methodological notes*

Qualitative methods have been used such as the authors' own observations and collaborative insights with colleagues, interviews conducted with stakeholders such as employees and management staff, both past and present. Internal and external documentation such as decisions, plans and reports have been used.

The main author, employed at Swedish EPA, took part in the knowledge exchange programme and was a member of the group that built up the innovation management system in 2016–2019. The second author was recruited in 2019 and has since been part of the innovation management group. In addition, the third author, is a management consultant and one of the initiators and drivers of the exchange programme.

15.2. Description of Innovation Components from a Systems Perspective

15.2.1. *The Swedish benchmark study and the innovation management system*

Innovation Capability is a broad term which in essence refers to how well an organisation can develop new ideas and concepts, implement and apply them in practice, and realise the benefits. However, this overall capability is based on an organisational platform for innovation which comprises a set of building blocks as shown in Figure 15.1.

The model used to describe the Swedish EPA innovation work was developed in the Swedish benchmark study in 2017 where the innovation capabilities of 112 government authorities were mapped and analysed (Lundegård *et al.*, 2017). The study was ordered and funded by Vinnova, the Swedish Agency for Innovation Systems, and executed by consultants at Implement Consulting Group and professors at the KTH Royal Institute of Technology.

The total population of 112 authorities was split into two categories according to how they assessed themselves to be "successful in their innovation work" or "less successful in their innovation work." 62 authorities

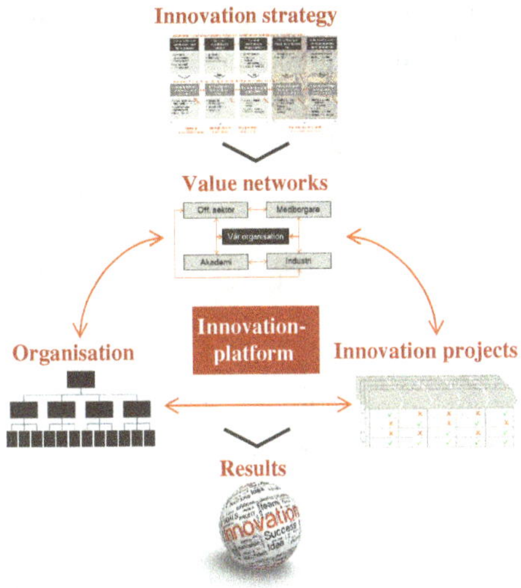

Innovation strategy — Purpose and focus of innovation

Organisation — Internal structure, roles, resources, culture and other conditions in the organisation that drive innovation in an effective manner

Value networks — How the organisation is connected to and interacts with external actors to drive innovation

Innovation projects — How innovation initiatives and projects are conducted from start to finish with innovation process, methods and tools

Results — How innovation results are materialised

Fig. 15.1. The model used for organising innovation work and build innovation capability at the Swedish EPA.

or, 55% answered "successful" and 50 authorities or 45% "less successful." The differences between the two populations were then analysed to identify the drivers of innovation capability. The model for innovation capability was also validated during a 1-year knowledge exchange programme with six authorities, where the Swedish EPA participated together with five other large authorities, which was carried out during 2018 to 2019. The case description of the Swedish EPA, in this chapter, is based on these building components outlined in the different sections later in the chapter.

The pattern was clear in all of the building blocks. The "successful" had to a greater extent a well formulated and communicated strategy outlining the purpose and focus for innovation, which in many cases was stated in the directives from the government. This group also had a clearly defined organisation, e.g., internal structure, roles, resources, competencies and culture, to drive innovation in an effective manner. A pattern also emerged in the context of value networks where the "successful" cooperated with external actors to a greater extent than the "less successful."

Innovation projects were the building blocks that showed the greatest difference and where the "successful" to a much greater extent had approaches, methods and tools in place to work with concrete innovation dilemmas. One hypothesis could be that innovation is all about creativity, and this should not be restricted by approaches, methods and tools. The data indicated the opposite, and this could be explained by the fact that the collective innovation capability and intelligence of a team are enabled by structure. The final building block — results — showed that the authorities that focused on a combination of radical and incremental innovations were more successful than others focusing on only one of them.

The results from the study, and Implement Consulting Group's experience from client assignments, confirm that innovation capability at an organisational level is a result of the maturity in the five different building blocks outlined earlier. The innovation strategy sets the purpose, ambition and guidelines for the Why? and What? of the innovation work and gives direction for how the innovation platform shall be designed, i.e., organisation, value networks and innovation projects. The organisation is the starting point as this sets the platform and context to initiate and drive innovation projects as well as receiving innovation results and putting them into practice in the organisation. Innovation projects without a proper organisational context could be compared to a satellite floating free in space disconnected and out of orbit. The same goes for value networks. Parts of the organisation have to work as interfaces with external actors as well as links into the organisation, internal functions and competencies. Proper structure and maturity for value networks and innovation projects set the proper conditions for external actors and internal resources to work effectively in concrete innovation challenges, to produce the intended innovation results.

In summary, these five building blocks are key components that need to be addressed separately to create favourable conditions for innovation. During the 1-year knowledge exchange programme with the six authorities, a maturity assessment was made using the model. This showed that the Swedish EPA had a higher maturity in managing innovation. To get the five building blocks into place, the interfaces between them need to be handled during the process of managing the "modus operandi" of innovation. This is a systemic approach to managing innovation in a systematic manner.

The building blocks outlined in the model capture the key elements of the ISO 56002:2019 Innovation management system — Guidance, which has been verified by the authors of the standard during the Autumn of 2020. The ISO standard captures 24 key elements grouped in the following clauses: Context & Conditions, Leadership, Planning, Support, Processes, and Evaluation & Improvement (IMCA, 2019). In essence, the building blocks in the organisational platform for innovation used at the Swedish EPA capture the 24 key elements according to the following logic as shown in Table 15.1.

In early Spring 2018, the knowledge exchange programme started with six authorities (Vinnova, 2019). The benefits for the Swedish EPA were to have an arena and opportunity to learn from research, develop the work with innovation "in house," and share practical experiences and good examples. During this period, the Agency developed its innovation strategy and developed an organisation with roles and functions. Systematic work was begun to iteratively explore, design, test and implement

Table 15.1. The elements of the ISO Standard applied in the organisational innovation platform at the Swedish EPA.

Innovation Strategy 1. Understanding of external trends and drivers 7. Innovation vision and strategy 8. Innovation policy	**Value Networks** 4. External and internal innovation collaboration
Organisation 2. Understanding of internal capabilities and assets 3. Culture supporting creativity and deployment 5. Top management commitment 9. Organisational roles, responsibilities 11. Organisational structures for innovation activities 13. Resources supporting innovation activities 14. Competence 15. Communication and awareness 17. Intellectual property management	**Innovation Projects** 10. Innovation objectives and action plans 12. Innovation portfolios 16. Innovation tools and methods 18. Innovation initiatives and projects 19. Configuration of innovation processes 20. Processes to identify opportunities 21. Processes to create and validate concepts 22. Processes to develop and deploy solutions **Results** 6. Focus on value realisation 23. Innovation performance indicators 24. Performance evaluation and improvement

Notes: Numbers on elements refer to IMCA (2019).

components to build an innovation management system. The following sections introduce the entire process of implementing the different components in the organisation.

15.2.2. *Innovation strategy*

The 2017 benchmark study of 112 authorities (Lundegård *et al.*, 2017) showed that the "successful" or "high-performers" have a clearer definition of the purpose, objectives and focus of innovation in the organisation, which can be outlined within the overall business strategy or in a separate innovation strategy.

Most organisations are totally focused on delivering the current services as efficiently as possible, which implies that the innovation agenda can be deprioritised if considered inefficient. In order to manage both agendas in parallel, the purpose and the arena for the innovation agenda need to be clearly defined and clarified on how innovation supports the ordinary business.

The Swedish EPA's innovation strategy was formed in a combined bottom-up and top-down collaboration process — the newly formed innovation management group designed the strategy and held high-level workshops with the top management group.

This resulted in an innovation strategy which was a rather extensive nine-page document approved and decided by the top management team in late 2018. The objective of the strategy was to develop a common understanding of what it was and meant in broad terms and this motivated the length of the document. Apart from describing objectives and strategic areas, the strategy developed the organisational structure, leadership, innovation methods, tools and critical success factors.

Innovation objectives

The innovation strategy (Naturvårdsverket, 2018a) states that the Agency should:

> "(1) be a proactive player that clearly and strategically drives the work to achieve the environmental objectives and the global sustainability goals, by utilising the innovative power of individuals, society at both the national and international level.

(2) continuously develop and strengthen the internal innovation work and in all the Agency's roles — supportive, driving and unifying — always considering how innovation can contribute to faster and more efficiently achieving the environmental goals" (p. 3).

Furthermore, the strategy's objective was to strengthen the innovation capability and promote a focus on innovation among the leadership, staff members and collaborators. All areas (Naturvårdsverket, 2018a) that "have a need to take bigger leaps to reach environmental goals are to be selected and focused on annually" (p. 3). Five strategic areas would be selected as a frame for concrete activities, aiming at increasing innovation capability.

Critical success factors

The following prerequisites for success were identified (Naturvårdsverket, 2018a) and "must be in place for the strategy to be implemented":

- The management team and managers are involved in the innovation development work.
- The established innovation management group continuously sets aside time and resources to drive the innovation work. Employees who want to work with their or others' innovation ideas must have the necessary time set aside to realise them.
- The innovation work and its associated activities are integral parts of the organisational planning process and are made visible in the annual operational plan.
- Key functions such as communication, law and finance have time set aside for the development and implementation of innovation work.
- The Agency captures and directs the involvement and driving forces of external actors in the innovation work to reach the (national) environmental objectives and the global sustainability goals.
- The innovation work means that employees and managers dare to try new working methods, projects and activities. Failures are part of the innovation process and lessons learned are important for future work (p. 8).

The second bullet point — setting time aside for employees that would work with realising and developing innovative ideas — was discussed enthusiastically. During a defined time period, a certain percentage of an employee's working time should be dedicated to innovation and supported by management — 10–20% for minor projects and more than 50% for larger ones.

15.2.3. *Organisation*

The 2017 benchmark study of 112 authorities (Lundegård *et al.*, 2017) showed that innovative "high-performers" in general had better conditions in place within the organisation than the "low-performers" in terms of:

- Understanding of innovation among managers and employees,
- A critical mass of resources working with innovation,
- A specialised group focusing on innovation, and
- Clear governance of the innovation agenda.

The Swedish EPA assigned an innovation coordinator in 2016 to develop a systematic way of working within the organisation and with external actors. The innovation coordinator collaborated with two other staff members to drive the innovation agenda. The work was influenced by the UN Agenda 2030 declaration in 2015 calling for bold and transformative steps. A strategic decision was made to form an innovation management group in the Environmental Objectives Unit at the Sustainable Development Department, one of the subdivisions of the organisation. The Environmental Objectives Unit coordinates national assessment, analysis and recommendations to the Government regarding the Swedish environmental objectives and Agenda 2030 work. This stresses a challenge-driven approach to offer support to innovation initiatives targeting the objectives.

The innovation management group (Naturvårdsverket, 2018a) supports the organisation from "both top-down and bottom-up" perspectives and employs a methodology that "forms all overall innovation development to create anchoring, feasibility, mandate, engagement and participation in the organisation's innovation work" (p. 2). The Agency's innovation strategy states that innovation must be integrated in relevant governing documents, in the organisation, in processes and management. The management should know the basics of innovation management and stimulate and support innovation development among the employees.

In 2018, the Swedish EPA decided on having a system in the organisation with an internal innovation community, innovation ambassadors and so-called pilot units, units that would dedicate time to innovation work. Several communication measures were taken internally to promote the community and its work. By subscribing to the community's internal emailing-list, staff members would get news, inspiration and seminar and study visit invitations. An informative intranet webpage was also launched. The Agency's innovation activities, both government commissions and the results of the internal work, were also published on the external web. Moreover, an introduction to the innovation management system was part of the material presented to newly employed agency staff.

During the knowledge exchange programme, the innovation management group grew to include around 5–8 innovation ambassadors. The innovation ambassadors were staff members who had an interest in innovation or who had worked with innovation as part of their ordinary assignments. They contributed actively to the formation of the innovation management system. This group worked as a support team for those who wished to employ innovation methods to develop their core processes or needs, and organised internal seminars, workshops and experience exchange.

The launching of several pilot units was a way to implement and develop the innovation management system more widely. The pilot units' activities aimed to instil consciousness and courage in working with innovation as a tool, trying out innovation processes, and thus creating organisation-specific experiences of innovation. The initial intention was that the innovation ambassadors would support the units, but as the initiative grew to 20 pilot units and several staff members changed jobs and positions, the ambition for a small group to support 20 pilot units became too high. The initiative with ambassadors, pilot units and the internal innovation network was therefore paused in the middle of 2019. The innovation management group changed focus to offer support to individual units in their work in prioritised areas such as climate and air, biodiversity, plastics and digitalisation, instead of directing innovation activities and educational activities more broadly.

The innovation management group also struggled for quite some time to develop a functional innovation process, trying out different process concepts and tools such as service design. In 2020, an activity plan and a simplified process for creating and validating concepts were presented that would work for idea generation at unit level, using the Agency's working practices with projects, assignments and tasks, and the decision-making through decision briefings.

Competence development intensified in 2018 with promotion of introductory courses, seminars and advanced courses that were regularly updated. Experience-sharing took place internally and externally. The aim was to create a structure, systems and support that could strengthen, encourage and reward the work with innovation and that would support innovative employees.

The innovation management group restarted the internal innovation interest network during 2021 and the team has the ambition of relaunching the innovation ambassador system. There is no plan to restart the system with pilot units.

As described previously, the Swedish EPA and other authorities received government assignments that included or focused on innovation. These activities were carried out at different units and departments, both as previously planned (technical) development and as current government commissions.

15.2.4. *Value networks*

The term open innovation is well established in some authorities which engage external innovation partners in the innovation process, in addition to the organisation's own resources. The term value network is defined as a sub-set of all actors in the total innovation ecosystem who actively cooperate with an authority to drive a common innovation agenda. The benchmark study of the 112 authorities showed that the innovative "high-performers" engage external innovation partners to a greater extent than the "low-performers" who have a more internal focus.

The Swedish EPA has the role to drive and coordinate Sweden's environmental work, both nationally and internationally. The Agency has a mandate to work with actors on an international level as well as within the European union, with Sweden as a member state. Nationally the Agency collaborates with 187 appointed government agencies, the 21 counties, and the 290 municipalities (Naturvårdsverket, 2021). They are all potential network partners for innovation collaboration. For example, Vinnova as an "expert agency" is an important network partner with which recurrent collaborations occur. Other potential innovation partners are members in agency-wide networks like the network for service design, for artificial intelligence and for systemic innovation where experience exchange is the focus.

Other partners in the value network are universities, research institutes and research funders with whom the Swedish EPA collaborates in different ways such as partners in the Agency's research programme and in externally financed innovation projects, e.g., a Vinnova funded artificial intelligence knowledge building project using language technology and neuro linguistic programming.

According to Swedish laws, public organisations cannot work directly with one or a few business enterprise sector partners. But the Swedish EPA takes part in dialogues with branch representatives and may invite companies to public procurement initiatives. However, different tools and methods can be used to collaborate within legal frames such as open innovation. Examples are the innovation competitions Zero Microplastics Challenge 2020 (RISE, 2021) and Circular and Digital Construction 2020 (Smart Built Environment, 2021). Together with a handful of agencies, the Swedish EPA engaged civil society and different companies and initiated the country-wide hackathon "Hack for Sweden 2015," which has been run annually since then (Agency for Digital Government, 2021).

The Swedish EPA has several internal networks that are important for the organisation's collaboration with external actors. There are more than 10 internal cross-disciplinary networks at the Agency — horizontally organised around interests, themes or actual assignments — that must be considered when addressing value networks. Many employees are experts in their field such as climate, biology, biodiversity, sustainability, clean tech, circular economy, wildlife management, avalanche and snow movements, and environmental law. This horizontal organisation allows employees to exchange knowledge and experience, carry out external monitoring, conduct analyses, formulate common challenges and needs, as well as keep each other updated on interesting seminars, monitor latest news in respective areas and share external contacts and collaborations — and they have a potential of forming innovation teams. The Agency's staff members possess a broad and deep expertise in many areas and their knowledge is an important prerequisite in their collaboration with the innovation management group that has the skills about methods and tools for the innovation process.

15.2.5. *Innovation projects*

One belief could be that innovation is a creative process which should not be constrained by using structures, methods and tools. However, the 2017 benchmark study (Lundegård *et al.*, 2017) showed that innovative "high-performers" have specific structures, methods and tools in place to drive the innovation process and projects end-to-end. The use of structured approaches supports the innovation process and enables persons and teams to be more creative and innovative.

Previously to adopting the innovation strategy there were no consciously selected methods and tools for how to drive innovation projects. Although, service design had been tested and found applicable. Hackathons were also organised, and a data-driven lab concept tested. Different methods and tools were tried out and experience exchange-sharing carried out with other government agencies. However, the input from the knowledge exchange programme made it obvious that there were advantages with selecting a few methods and tools and to use a consciously pre-designed innovation process. The innovation management group worked intensely to create an innovation process that could fit into the project–assignment–task system for internal work processes at the Agency.

At the Swedish EPA, innovation initiatives are initiated top-down as with regulation letters, or bottom-up as in the case where an internal network or a group of experts suggests and conducts innovation projects. In the bottom-up case, project ideas are based in units' challenges, needs and priorities and can be supported and developed together with the innovation management group. The innovation management group plays an important role when several units are involved and when a higher degree of innovation is needed. Innovation projects are to follow the beforementioned project–assignment–task system, where decisions on running them, or not, are taken at unit and department levels. Some of these initiatives are incremental, but others grow to become more transformative in form. For incremental innovation that takes place in internal line work or external work processes with counties and municipalities, open innovation, service design, policy labs and a method called "customer groups" work well. In customer groups, methods and work processes are used for several users with common needs, like municipalities, to conduct common innovation procurements. When it comes to societal challenges that would need radical transformative steps to solve, other innovation process models are employed.

Business enterprise innovation is mostly conducted with the aim to creating business value for the company. For public authorities, the main innovation purpose is to create societal value and effect. An innovation process consists, simply speaking, of three phases: (1) identifying challenges and opportunities, (2) experimenting, testing and the development of different solutions, and (3) deployment and creation of value and effect. Public sector innovation work can be undertaken in one, two or completing all three phases together. For example:

- Phase one — Identifying an environmental challenge and launching calls for studies and research within the area.
- Phase two — Conducting innovation competitions and projects with external actors from enterprise, public sector, academia, civil society and citizens about the challenge. Working on a municipality, regional, national, EU and international level in order to get the multi-level policy-practice system to work with the intended purpose.
- Phase three — Implementing regulations, measures, guidance, services and developing further improvements of the Agency and State management.

Examples from the phases are initiating calls for research funding (Swedish Environmental Protection Agency, 2022), innovation competitions (Naturvårdsverket, 2020a), innovation projects (Naturvårdsverket, 2022a) and pre-procurement networks for deployment of new methods (Naturvårdsverket, 2022b).

The Swedish EPA initiates innovation projects with external partners such as the UNDP, the United Nations Development Programme (Environmental Governance Programme, 2021), other national agencies, organisations and Governmental collaborative platforms (Naturvårdsverket, 2022c).

15.2.6. *Results*

The 2017 benchmark study (Lundegård *et al.*, 2017) investigated to which extent innovation results occur in an incremental fashion or in a more radical fashion. One assumption could be that organisations choose one of these alternatives, incremental or radical. However, the study showed that the innovative "high-performers" did both, i.e., they generated innovation results both in an incremental and radical fashion. It also revealed that the innovation results occur in terms as external (services to customers) as well as internal (e.g., routines and working practices).

The systematic innovation management work, with support from top management, a strategy and a dedicated innovation management team, has enabled the organisation to be bold and set necessary transformative goals for innovation. The Swedish EPA's innovation strategy points out the urgent need for radical transformative innovation over step-by-step incremental innovation to enable reaching the environmental challenges and needs.

One example is the 1-year innovation competition "Transformative Infrastructure — Ground-breaking Innovation for Zero Emissions" whereby 29 companies and organisations participated to develop zero emission solutions for large-scale infrastructure projects, using the bridge between Denmark and Sweden, Öresundsbron, as an illustrative case (Naturvårdsverket, 2018b). Much value creation was reached during the project workshops where multi-disciplinary participants from different, and in some cases competing, branches and sectors collaborated. Participants got an opportunity to get deeper insights into challenges and new change potential in a sector that has substantial climate and environmental footprint. The competition led to a dialogue with the Swedish Government (the Minister for Environment and the Climate and Minister for Infrastructure), several Government agencies, the business sector, and research institutes. Four new competitions were launched and conducted based on the method developed from the Zero Emissions competition.

A second example is the 3-day hackathon in 2019 about biodiversity and agriculture where three international teams worked with the challenge of creating a new international and European financial support system for farmers that could steer both EU policy decision-makers' and farmers' actions towards increasing agricultural landscape biodiversity (Openhack, 2021). The three winning solutions were presented in dialogue seminars with international experts of the UN Convention on Biological Diversity, the EU Commission, the European Environmental Agency, Swedish Government agencies, research institutes, and civil society organisations. The results gave new insights into possible leverage points, project suggestions and regulatory work to be carried out in the near future. The project suggestions are included in the Swedish EPA's 2021 operational plan.

Examples of accomplishing both internal and external value from idea to finished product is the digitalisation of the hunter's theory test (Naturvårdsverket, 2020b) and the electric bike application allowance system for citizens (Naturvårdsverket, 2019b). Both digitalisation projects are examples of external innovation — customer interaction and service — as well as internal, e.g., routines and working practices.

These four examples of innovation projects show the mix of radical and incremental innovation projects that appear both as a result of having launched an innovation management system and as line-organisation development work and innovation activities. It also shows how the Swedish EPA uses its broad value network.

15.3. Summary and Conclusions

All in all, the Swedish EPA has succeeded in getting some important key fundamentals in place in the pursuit of establishing a solid platform for innovation. However, even if the components have been designed and implemented, it is very hard to determine if the target has been met. What does the optimal solution look like for the Agency and is it good enough?

An innovation platform is an organisational construct within another organisational construct — the line organisation — where the two are meant to live and evolve in symbiosis. Being innovative is not a state, it is a journey, a way of being where the dynamics and progress are key. The bottom-up and top-down organisational dynamics have worked well, although with hardships on the way. The size of the innovation team was small and the ambitions too high coupled with a fast growth, which created an uneven spread of the innovation ambitions and activities throughout the organisation. Although, the last years' innovation work has changed the organisational culture at the Agency, according to Martin Eriksson the former head of the Policy Development Department responsible for the unit where the innovation management team is situated. It has formed a culture that "sees innovation as part of change management, and this has made change work less dramatic. Although the shift is not evenly distributed throughout the organisation, the management's support to build the innovation management system has been of utmost important during the process" (Eriksson, 2021).

15.4. Reflections

The key questions all (public) organisations need to ask themselves are: How can we improve our work, the results of our assignment? How can we improve our service to the citizens, to the nation, to the globe?

"The solution is to change the entire approach; ways of doing things, find new solutions, new policy instruments. This is what makes a good public agency that is in pace with our age," says the former department manager who continues, "The entire enterprise to develop an innovation management system was one employee's initiative that had ideas of creating change through innovation, how to faster reach the environmental goals. Every wise top management understands that creative and fruitful ideas often come from beneath" (Eriksson, 2021).

The hierarchy of a line organisation can be extremely powerful where different organisational units focus on different areas with their own bosses, employees, cultures, responsibilities, working practices, budgets and key performance indicators. The division of labour and compartment-based view of the organisation often results in silo thinking, makes the hierarchy very resilient and able to resist and handle anything which comes in its way, like innovation. However, this was not the case with the Swedish EPA. The innovation management system was built up in an agile, iterative manner between the top management and the bottom-up initiatives from engaged employees.

An innovation platform needs to be designed and implemented as an integral and natural part of the line organisation with sufficient mandate and resources to make a difference. But most importantly, the line organisation must be open and ready to embrace the platform and engage in the innovation agenda. The design and implementation of the Agency's innovation platform was done in an incremental and agile manner. It was not about building the perfect and complete version before starting to innovate. We recommend starting with an initial beta version. Test, learn, adopt, adapt and evolve. Innovate how to innovate. It is a continuous long-term activity that must contain an engaged top management, professional innovation managers, engaged employees and open minds, risk-taking and trust.

Acknowledgements

We, the authors of the chapter, could not have written this without our colleagues. We would like to mention all the colleagues without whom we could not describe the Swedish EPA's journey towards a more systemic approach of innovation. These colleagues — who have taken leaps into the unknown, taken risks, delivering fruitful innovation results — are not mentioned by names, although some of the projects are mentioned. But they know who they are. In different ways they have all taken part.

We would like to mention Martin Eriksson, Eva Dalenstam and Rickard Nätjehall, at the Swedish EPA, as well as Jonas Winqvist, at Implement Consulting Group, with whom we have discussed the text, anchored crucial parts, and got important feedback. We also would like to thank Vinnova for initiating the knowledge exchange programme, which gave us an important context to grow in! Thank you all!

References

Agency for Digital Government (2021). *Hack for Sweden*, https://www.digg.se/utveckling-av-digital-forvaltning/hack-for-sweden.

Environmental Governance Programme (2021). *About the Programme*, https://www.environmentalgovernanceprogramme.org/about-the-programme.

Eriksson, Martin (2021). Former department manager of the Policy Development Department at the Swedish Environmental Protection Agency (Personal interview, March 8, 2021).

European Environment Agency (2015). *The European Environment — State and Outlook 2015: Knowledge for Transition to a Sustainable Europe*, https://www.eea.europa.eu/soer/2015.

European Environment Agency (2019). *The European Environment — State and Outlook 2020: Knowledge for Transition to A Sustainable Europe*, https://www.eea.europa.eu/soer/2020.

Government Offices of Sweden (2000). *Ds 2000:61 The Swedish Environmental Code*, https://www.government.se/legal-documents/2000/08/ds-200061/.

IMCA (2019). *Innovation Management Capabilities Assessment.* SIS Swedish Institute for Standards.

ISO (2019). *ISO 56002:2019 Innovation management — Innovation management system — Guidance*. International Organization for Standardization.

Lundegård, R., Ritzén. S., Nilsson. S., Winqvist. J. and Wallenholm. H. (2017). *Innovation och förnyelse inom 112 svenska myndigheter*, https://www.vinnova.se/publikationer/innovation-och-fornyelse-inom-112-svenska-myndigheter/.

Naturvårdsverket (2018a). *NV-07573-16 Strategi för Naturvårdsverkets innovationsarbete, Strategi verksövergripande.*

Naturvårdsverket (2018b). *Innovationstävlingen Transformativ infrastruktur — banbrytande innovation för nollutsläpp: erfarenheter, resultat och process — mer än en tävling, mer än nollutsläpp: Slutrapport.* Naturvårdsverket, ISBN 9789162068554.

Naturvårdsverket (2019a). *Fördjupad utvärdering av miljömålen 2019 — Med förslag till regeringen från myndigheter i samverkan*, https://www.naturvardsverket.se/978-91-620-6865-3.

Naturvårdsverket (2019b). *Rapport 6894 Elcykling — vem, hur och varför? — En utvärdering med elfordonspremien som utgångspunkt*, https://www.

naturvardsverket.se/globalassets/media/publikationer-pdf/6800/978-91-620-6894-3.pdf.

Naturvårdsverket (2020a). *Innovationstävling för hållbar plastanvändning*. Report 6939, Naturvårdsverket, ISBN 978-91-620-6939-1.

Naturvårdsverket (2020b). *Digitalt teoriprov för jägarexamen lanseras i mars 2021*, https://www.naturvardsverket.se/om-oss/aktuellt/nyheter-och-pressmeddelanden/det-digitala-teoriprovet-for-jagarexamen-foljs-upp-och-utvecklas.

Naturvårdsverket (2021). *Om miljöledning i statliga myndigheter*, https://www.naturvardsverket.se/vagledning-och-stod/miljomal-och-miljoledning/miljoledning-i-staten/.

Naturvårdsverket (2022a). *Pågående projekt*, https://www.naturvardsverket.se/amnesomraden/plast/pagaende-projekt.

Naturvårdsverket (2022b). *Teknikutveckling och innovation inom efterbehandling*, https://www.naturvardsverket.se/amnesomraden/fororenade-omraden/teknikutveckling-och-innovation-inom-efterbehandling/.

Naturvårdsverket (2022c). *Demonstrationsplattformen Smart City Sweden*, https://www.naturvardsverket.se/om-oss/regeringsuppdrag/pagaende-regeringsuppdrag/demonstrationsplattformen-smart-city-sweden/.

Openhack (2021). *Case challenges*, https://www.openhack.io/challenges.

Regeringskansliet (2019). *Prop. 2019/20:65 En samlad politik för klimatet — klimatpolitisk handlingsplan*, https://www.regeringen.se/rattsliga-dokument/proposition/2019/12/prop.-20192065/.

Regeringskansliet (2020a). *Cirkulär ekonomi — strategi för omställningen i Sverige*, https://www.regeringen.se/informationsmaterial/2020/07/cirkular-ekonomi---strategi-for-omstallningen-i-sverige/.

Regeringskansliet (2020b). *Prop. 2019/20:188 Sveriges genomförande av Agenda 2030*, https://www.regeringen.se/rattsliga-dokument/proposition/2020/06/prop.-201920188/.

RISE (2021). *Zero Microplastics Challenge 2020*, https://www.ri.se/en/what-we-do/projects/zero-microplastics-challenge-2020.

Smart Built Environment (2021). *Cirkulärt digitalt anläggningsbyggande — Innovationstävling*, https://smartbuilt.se/projekt/innovationer-och-nya-tillaempningar/innovationstavling-cirkdigg/.

Swedish Agency for Public Management (2020). *An Innovative and Collaborative Central Government Administration*, https://www.statskontoret.se/in-english/publications/2020/an-innovative-and-collaborative-central-government-administration/.

Swedish Environmental Protection Agency (2021a). *About us*, https://www.naturvardsverket.se/en/about-us/.

Swedish Environmental Protection Agency (2021b). *The National Environmental Quality Objectives*, https://www.naturvardsverket.se/en/environmental-work/environmental-objectives/?msclkid=3ccadfc0cf4a11ecac4efab5c9fab8b2.

Swedish Environmental Protection Agency (2021c). *Mission and Vision*, https://www.naturvardsverket.se/en/about-us/about-the-swedish-environmental-protection-agency/.

Swedish Environmental Protection Agency (2022). *The Environmental Research Fund*, https://www.naturvardsverket.se/en/environmental-work/research/the-environmental-research-fund.

United Nations (2015). *Transforming our World: The 2030 Agenda for Sustainable Development*, https://www.un.org/development/desa/dspd/2015/08/transforming-our-world-the-2030-agenda-for-sustainable-development/.

Vinnova (2019). *VR 2019:14 Offentlig verksamhets innovationskraft*, https://www.vinnova.se/contentassets/9fab4046146e48379590a157481d3d7d/vr19-14-uppdaterad1.pdf.

© 2023 World Scientific Publishing Europe Ltd.
https://doi.org/10.1142/9781800612105_0016

Chapter 16

Norconsult AS: Management by Definition — The Role of Terminology and Shared Understandings in Implementing an Innovation Management System

Markus Søbstad Bensnes

Abstract

Norconsult takes a shot at implementing ISO 56002 Innovation Management System in their complex engineering consulting business corporation. Initial work reveals that fundamental understandings of innovation differ enough that questions of systems management cannot be addressed before a more precise and shared understanding of the fundamental concepts can be reached. Working in parallel to reimagine the internal story about innovation while developing definitions to capture the essence of concepts relating to innovation management, the profession slowly but surely finds a new place in the company. The effects of rebranding innovation and innovation management lay the foundations for a future broader system implementation. This chapter outlines the context and the company, the planning and implementation, and offers reflections on how to adapt the ISO 56002 to a complex consulting corporation. One important insight proves to be the importance of shared definitions and a common understanding of innovation for deciding on how to manage innovation systemically. In planning for the way forward, experimentation to maintain momentum when complexity exceeds capacity is proposed as a feasible approach for Norconsult.

16.1. Background and Introduction

16.1.1. *About Norconsult as an innovating company*

Norconsult is a consulting engineering company based out of Norway, specialising in infrastructure projects, planning processes and construction, with branches and projects in more than 50 countries across the world. Counting thousands of engineers, architects and other building specialists distributed across well over 100 offices, it is a complex corporation.

In addition, the Norconsult corporation includes a portfolio of companies under the corporation's direct ownership, including domain specialists, support functions and an IT-company specialising in systems development and software services. Acquiring new companies to be integrated as part of this portfolio has been a main source of growth and development for Norconsult. Many companies have been acquired in the last decade and the trend is expected to continue.

The company's great diversity of geography, structure and competency brings with it great complexity. Adding to that complexity is the fact that the company has chosen to adapt an organisational structure where most units enjoy a high degree of freedom and autonomy regarding operational variables such as key markets, strategies and more importantly for the purpose of this chapter: Innovation.

The high levels of autonomy and diversity has given rise to a plethora of approaches to innovation, varying from a dedicated department for innovation management, specialised innovation projects, a general 80/20 principle for budgeting time between core and development practices, and acquisition as a cornerstone of growth and innovation strategies. The innovation initiatives and projects across the corporation are numerous, to a satisfactory degree successful, and largely not known to top management, save for a few of strategic imperative.

16.1.2. *About engineering consulting as an industry for innovation*

The market for engineering consulting services in infrastructure and construction is under strain. Margins are for the most part relatively low, as services demand a high level of proficiency and education on the part of the consultants, which drives up the cost of goods sold (COGS), while many of the services offered vary little in terms of jobs to be done, making price the key differentiator. Because of this it is key to secure projects and assignments with high volume.

From the outlook of Norconsult, engineering consulting thus is a *high volume–low margin industry*, where small variances in rates and COGS can make significant impact on the bottom line and the value creation of the company. The natural focus of innovation and business development is therefore increasing rates and limiting COGS for services offered.

Another effect of this market situation is that most employees in Norconsult are evaluated on billing rate, leaving little incentive for middle management and front-line engineers to invest valuable hours in risky innovation initiatives or creative processes. At least outside of their client projects.

Conversely, many assignments, especially the more interesting ones, do indeed demand a high level of creativity, if not innovation. Engineering is at its core about problem solving. And solving problems well can be immensely valuable. In fact, when taking an outsider perspective, the most valuable innovations Norconsult produces is arguably great engineering in the context of client projects. When they reduce cost by replacing an expensive type of steel in a construction or calculate a new and more efficient route for a railroad, savings and gains can be tremendous for both Norconsult's clients and members of society relying on the solutions designed.

This is a significant thing to understand in order to effectively analyse Norconsult from an innovation management system (IMS) perspective. The processes that lead to great engineering in client projects are not very easily influenced in a complex and diverse organisational system. They are challenging to manage with high demands on productivity, high barriers of domain knowledge, and limited will from the client side to invest in innovation in assignments. This limits the applicability of process models derived from software and production companies and brings into question the idea of a centralised approach to innovation management.

It is also important to realise that not all Norconsult projects fall in the category of creative problem solving and great engineering. In fact, a large portion of Norconsult's services is based on *client needs of compliance*. Construction is a heavily regulated work process, and throughout the process there are targets that need to be met in order for clients to meet requirements in regulation and law. Nearly all these services are considered commodities, as the variation of quality is very limited. Thus, price is the dominant variable in competition for these services, along with convenience and trust.

A third and smaller category of Norconsult's services are pressed to be innovative as it is a *premise to remain competitive*. This is to varying degrees true of Norconsult's digital services, information systems, data analysis, urban planning, renewable energy and some of Norconsult's complex long-term infrastructure projects. This is a natural area to focus Norconsult's innovation management efforts on a systems level.

When considering the variance in types of services and how they differ in regard to innovation as a factor of competitive advantage, it is clear that Norconsult as a company needs to be very strategic about where to invest in innovation. An organisational structure that limits the reach of central management and systems governance only makes these prioritisations more important. Considering these points, IMSs are especially interesting as guides to help refine discussions about strategy; to help identify approaches that can bolster *specific* innovation initiatives as well as increase output from innovation across the corporation; and to do so with a minimal investment in additional management.

In the next section, we will look at how the systems structure of Norconsult compares to the elements described in ISO 56002 (ISO, 2019), and dive into how implementing an innovation management system with the above lessons in mind has played out so far.

16.2. Main Challenges and Purpose of Implementation

16.2.1. *Situation and status of IMS*

From the outside one could come to think of Norconsult as a materialisation of a distributed approach to an innovation management system. It is an argument that could at least in part be plausibly made as many of the processes relating to innovation are functionally adequate. But that would imply intentionality: That a management system for distributed innovation was purposefully implemented. This does not appear to be the case. Rather it would seem that a loosely connected system of largely independent processes and subsystems has evolved over time and adapted to address the most pressing needs at hand, as per the respective parts of the corporation.

In terms of an IMS as defined and detailed in the ISO 56000 series, Norconsult must be seen as having only a very limited setup as assessed through the lens of ISO 56002. Norconsult's strategic context analysis has little emphasis on innovation; there is no explicit innovation strategy (although there are certainly parts of the strategy that is geared towards inspiring and facilitating innovation); there is no mainstreamed set of innovation processes; and there are no established KPIs for innovation performance generally, or for IMS performance specifically.

Now, this may seem a bit outdated and possibly unreasonable. However, when taking into consideration the previously discussed characteristics of the industry context and of the company it does make some sense. Managing innovation is demanding, and often costly. Actively managing innovation across the entirety of the Norconsult corporation — even for the mere purposes of assessing and adjusting the entirety of the organisation as a systems unit — would be an overwhelming task.

Obviously then, for Norconsult to consider engaging in additional cost-driving management efforts there must be a rationale that is tied to their ambitions and concerns: To Norconsult's goals. However, at the moment, Norconsult — by most objective measures — is succeeding. The company is thriving financially (Norconsult, 2021) and has repeatedly been among the top three most attractive places to work for engineers in Norway (Universum, 2020). To be sure, these indicators of success are not proof that there is no need for innovation management. Perhaps, it rather masks the more *specific* needs for innovation management in distinct areas of the company.

When considering the applicability of the elements in the IMS as described in ISO 56002, the question becomes what parts of the organisation and which innovation processes and initiatives would benefit the most from the level of management that a system approach and an IMS can deliver? Where can one argue that investing in management system components would give valuable returns for the company in short, medium and long-term perspectives? A key question is understanding what parts of the organisation would likely see an increase in value returns from systems level management, or otherwise benefit from implementing the principles and system elements outlined in ISO 56002.

An implementation of an IMS would thus have to make an informed assessment of what to prioritise and provide a sufficient rationale as to why, complete with expected outcomes and effects.

This assessment has been at the heart of the efforts undertaken to implement an IMS in Norconsult, and these efforts are outlined in the following sections.

16.3. Implementation of the IMS

16.3.1. *Background and rationale*

In the first quarter of 2020, Norconsult expanded their innovation management department with three new employees in Norway at the very same moment that the COVID-19 pandemic led to a soft lockdown of the country. Due to the new situation and related volatility and unprecedented changes in Norconsult's markets, a clear focus on digitalisation of key processes and business development was adopted for the new roles.

The author, as one of the innovation managers hired, led the work on implementing an innovation management system, in part as a response to the volatilities mentioned, and to build a better resilience to change over time. Norconsult wanted to shift towards a more innovative mindset, better manage the flow of innovative initiative and ideas, as well as act on the sense of urgency coming from the pandemic to bring about a more systematic approach to growth and development. This, together with the fact that the author had relevant experience with setting up IMSs, provided the rationale to commence an implementation project for an IMS in accordance with ISO 56002.

16.3.2. *Setting up the implementation project*

To maximise flexibility to pursue the most promising aspects of an innovation management system and make timely changes to the direction and design of the implementation project, a modest start focusing on three activities was suggested:

- Preliminary compatibility analysis.
- Mapping of innovation management competencies.
- Updated and documented terminology and definitions.

The preliminary compatibility analysis set out to map the management structure and systems relating to innovation against the elements described in ISO 56002. The intended outcome was a conformity matrix, reporting on the degree to which described elements were in place in Norconsult.

The mapping of innovation management competencies was designed as a fundamental mapping of key competencies relating to innovation management as a profession in the Norconsult system. The intended outcome was a competency matrix with proficiency levels, qualification criteria, and plans for a competency network.

The activity on terminology and definitions was meant to simply develop and establish key definitions relating to innovation management, building on ISO 56000 and supplemented with examples from Norconsult to increase relevance.

Together the three activities were intended to inform a second phase of the project, selecting possible next steps among proposed items such as mainstreaming innovation processes, setting up portfolios, developing innovation strategies, and more.

Arriving at these three activities was both a product of compromise, limited resources and strategic priorities.

Assessing the situation in Norconsult it quickly became apparent that establishing clear definitions of innovation was the most pressing concern in the implementation of an IMS, as most if not all the other initiatives suggested depended on a solid and shared understanding of key concepts of innovation.

Over the first 6 months in Norconsult, the author observed a worrying inconsistency in the way the term innovation was being used to describe outcomes and processes in the organisation. The understanding of innovation as a result and a competency was both inconsistent and inaccurate, for example, equating technology and innovation, and process facilitation and innovation management. The lack of a shared understanding of what innovation is and why it is important led to an incoherent and misinformed discussion about innovation as an outcome and about innovation management as a function.

Answering questions together is impossible if you cannot make sure that you are having the same discussion. Thus, to assess the IMS, evaluate how to implement it, decide what to focus on, and so on, it is absolutely necessary to have a common understanding of what we are talking about when we talk about innovation.

Next, in order to mobilise innovation management as a strategic resource, it would be necessary to document the prevalence and proficiency levels of relevant innovation management competencies. This would have to be based on the preceding work on terminology, and to a larger extent build on examples from the collective Norconsult experience.

The compatibility analysis was of less immediate importance and would primarily serve as a guide and help inform a discussion about strategically feasible options for continued work on setting up an IMS in Norconsult.

Balancing active experimentation and testing with a continuous focus on fit to purpose and accurate evaluation of strategic opportunities was established as a fundamental principle for the implementation project.

16.3.3. *Narrative recollection-the implementation project*

In suit with the adopted principle of experimentation and readjustment, the three activities were quickly amended and reorganised in order of priority and perceived value.

The compatibility analysis relatively quickly came to a preliminary conclusion. Having realised that even though a fundamental level assessment was completed in due time, and could speak to compatibility with ISO 56002, the information derived from the exercise was in itself not very useful. Getting a deeper understanding of the intricacies of systems and processes in the company and analysing their relative comparability to the elements described in the standard would be a demanding project requiring a solid time and resource investment. In the context of Norconsult, some of the questions would be tough to provide meaningful answers to — or assessments of — with the large variety of approaches and processes in the organisation. Furthermore, it was not clear at that point how it would come to inform decisions that would lead to direct benefits for the company. What changes could likely be deemed feasible with the insight such an investigation would provide? What new decisions would plausibly be taken?

Mapping Innovation Management Competencies equally swiftly reached a first milestone in concluding that the ideas circulating about innovation management as a profession and a field of competency were, if not incompatible with each other, at least far apart, inconsistent, and having limited basis in the professional and academic discourses on the topic. Thus, it became clear that defining innovation as an outcome, and innovation management as a practice would both be necessary prerequisites for a meaningful discussion around competencies and their prevalence in the Norconsult system. That leaves terminology and definitions.

Being in a practical sense the easiest of the three tasks, the work started early and got through a first iteration relatively quickly. The process of gathering feedback from stakeholders revealed, however, that the road ahead was both wider and longer than anticipated. Two main areas of contention formed — both relating to the very purpose of the work. Firstly, we identified a need to clarify the difference between agreeing upon definitions to be used in a management system and a general discussion about words and terminology. Second, possibly as an effect of the diversity of opinion, there was difficulty in separating innovation from other development processes. More specifically innovation as an integral part of all Norconsult's processes as opposed to a much more specific idea about what innovation fundamentally is and is not, and what it means for the Norconsult organisation.

The two problems are interesting for at least one reason: They highlight the relationship between definitions and management. One of the most important reasons for an organisation as Norconsult to define innovation as different from core processes, business development, organisational development, and what have you, is that *innovation requires different management*. This is also the main rationale for having a management system for innovation. To determine what activities to manage as innovation, it becomes paramount that you can accurately identify and differentiate those activities.

These observations and insights led to several anticipated conclusions. First, without agreed upon terminology and definitions, progress on implementing any other part of the system would likely be temporary, unnecessarily difficult, and provide diminished returns. Second, most of the other proposed activities relating to the IMS (mainstreaming of processes, innovation strategy, competency platforms, etc.) would have to be directly informed by definitions. And thirdly, establishing clearer definitions alone could over time have massive impact, considering the incongruence between existing understandings and the negative implications of that.

The focus therefore became to establish definitions and terminology that were accurate, rooted in ISO 56000, reflective of innovation as a practice in Norconsult, and that could inspire ownership among key stakeholders.

16.3.4. *More change and complexity — Definitions remain paramount*

Only a couple of months into the IMS-project, a wave of new changes came flushing in with the transition to a new CEO. Over the course of a relatively short time frame a great many processes directly or indirectly relating to innovation were set in motion: a new corporate strategy; an Innovation strategy; a new strategy for the innovation management department; a new competency network (internal) for innovation managers; a new corporate structure; and a renewed desire in top management to move forward with the IMS-project.

As one would expect, all these new initiatives and changes impacted in various ways on the focus and tempo of the IMS-project. Mind you, all these changes come on top of an ongoing pandemic and strict government regulation having unprecedented and unpredictable effects on Norconsult's markets and operations.

The first effect on the work on terminology and definitions was that it was put on hold. Figuring out how the definitions would relate to and affect key items for innovation management, such as the innovation strategy and Norconsult's competency matrix, was considered imperative to determine *before* proceeding with the work. In addition, the discussion about what parts to prioritise in the IMS resurfaced and discussions about Norconsult's focus and strategic priority came back on the menu.

Fundamentally, these discussions all circled around the same question that had led to a near singular focus on definitions and terminology to begin with: Where should we start?

After a short intermission, this led to once again taking on the work on terminology and definitions, with added gusto and higher ambitions. Specifically, the team had noted the need not only to develop a shared terminology but also to implement and strengthen the use of these definitions in Norconsult's processes and practice. This led to the formulation of a three-part strategy for establishing a clear and shared understanding of innovation fundamentals.

Firstly, it was decided to focus on establishing normative definitions in their first version rapidly, keeping the door open for later adjustments based on new insights at a later point. Also, it was elected to use a structure for terminology where examples and nuances for each term could be included to further specify and delineate each term, as well as connect it to the experienced world of Norconsult.

Second, the innovation management department decided to prioritise assignments with clear association to innovation management with the aim to *rebrand* innovation and innovation management in the organisation. This materialised in a clearer set of criteria for accepting assignments, norms for conducting qualifying dialogues with internal and external stakeholders prior to accepting assignments, and perhaps most importantly a continued effort to tell stories about innovation management successes in the department's interactions with other parts of the organisation. Building on these conversations a new discussion about the role of innovation and how it could be reimagined began emerging.

Third, the innovation management department took lead on developing the innovation strategy work item to help answer where innovation management as a practice and the IMS as a management tool can have the most meaningful impact in the context of strategic priorities. Innovation strategy is one way to actualise how innovation can matter as a component in critical business processes, and a way to show what innovation means: How a better understanding of innovation translates into better business.

The last point illustrates how in Norconsult's case finding the right order of implementation activities facilitated momentum and hopefully better results from implementing the IMS over time. Having a common understanding of innovation helps guide the work on innovation strategy, and ISO 56002 provides a framework for thinking about how to build a system for pursuing that strategy.

16.4. Achievements, Results and Impact of the IMS

At the time of writing, several initiatives relevant to the IMS implementation project are in the process of forming or in the first stages of implementation. An innovation strategy, innovation management organised as its own competency area internally, and talks about rethinking where innovation management is situated in the organisation, to name some.

Building on these developments, rethinking the relevance of a compatibility analysis is in order, as the main point of interest is back on top: The interrelation and interaction of elements. Now that Norconsult is developing an innovation strategy, it is natural to consider how innovation management interacts with other core processes, roles and professions. The innovation management department will also likely be playing a broader role in facilitating those interactions and designing processes and systems for managing them.

Most clearly, the work on IMS generally and definitions especially has inspired changes in perceptions of what innovation is. Greater emphasis on business development, value creation, evidence-based strategic decision-making, service innovation and client focus has in sum changed the conversation about innovation management and about innovation as a component of Norconsult's business model. Innovation is already being talked about differently; innovation is associated with more relevant business processes; requests to the innovation management department are beginning to shift towards core competencies of innovation management; and innovation is at the heart of corporate level discussions.

This movement is getting traction, and informal networks of people, who are committed to an updated idea of what innovation management is, are beginning to form and starting to affect how decisions about the role of innovation in assignments as well as in internal processes are being made.

Cases demonstrating that innovative business development can lead to profitable service innovation and provide competitive advantage have inspired a small surge in requests for service innovation processes. Especially as a response to demands of higher competitiveness and correcting for diminishing returns in an increasingly challenging market. At the same time, there is a growing consciousness about the factors determining feasibility when deciding whether to invest in innovation, leading to more qualified requests and a more efficient route to *NO* when that is the right answer.

Overall, the implementation of the IMS thus far has helped create momentum through providing a framework for thinking about innovation that makes ambitions to professionalise Norconsult's approach to innovation management possible. Understanding and agreeing upon what innovation is has been a necessary step in the process of answering how to prioritise the application of innovation management for Norconsult.

16.5. Overall Reflection and Way Forward

In implementing an innovation management system in a highly complex organisation that is undergoing deep changes, challenges of making the right strategic priorities, on the best possible basis, while not losing momentum, require the right balance between experimentation and exploration — curiosity and resolve. But even more, they require the assurance that we are having the right discussion, and the same discussion, about what is most important, right now. The best way to achieve that was in this case to establish normative terminology and demonstrate what the words mean in action.

Drawing on this experience the author proposes that the successful implementation of an IMS requires first the establishment of definitions, starting with the fundamentals of innovation, innovation management, innovation strategy and innovation process.

Next, the recurring question has been what needs to be managed: Where should Norconsult prioritise to apply the principles and guidance of ISO 56002 in order to get the maximum return? What are the critical innovation initiatives and activities that would benefit (critically) from being managed in a systemic way?

The process of answering these questions would benefit greatly from documented experience and a better developed business case for ISO 56002. However, it is likely that concluding information about this question will continue to be elusive. A more credible approach would be to start experimenting with designing and implementing system elements based on urgency and experience across the corporation. As mentioned, the need and readiness for innovation varies greatly, but some areas of business must innovate to reach growth targets. A sensible approach would be to establish *ad hoc* system structures such as innovation processes, strategies, portfolios, support systems and preliminary evaluation systems to begin building both system structures and documented empirical data about what works in the specific context(s) of Norconsult.

Sharing our results will be Norconsult's contribution to answering the question of not only how innovation needs to be managed but what is best managed in an IMS.

References

ISO (2019). *ISO 56002:2019 Innovation management — Innovation management system — Guidance*. International Organization for Standardization.

Norconsult (2021). *Norconsult Financial Information*, https://www.norconsult.com/about-us/about-norconsult/#Financial+Information.

Universum (2020). *The Universum Professional Survey 2020*, https://universumglobal.com/no/professionals-2020/.

© 2023 World Scientific Publishing Europe Ltd.
https://doi.org/10.1142/9781800612105_0017

Chapter 17

Oki Electric Industry Company: Implementation of Yume Pro, an Innovation Management System

Ingrid Kihlander, Mats Magnusson and Hiro Nishiguchi

Abstract

Oki Electric Industry Company, OKI, a Japanese company with more than 140 years' history and proud traditions, decided to introduce Yume Pro, an innovation management system (IMS) directly corresponding to ISO 56002. Motives for this effort were both radical changes in the business context, and an identified need to enhance the entrepreneurial orientation of the employees. OKI works with all elements identified in the IMS. OKI has developed an innovation strategy with a strong emphasis on addressing the Sustainable Developments Goals, as defined by the United Nations, which supports in creating related value propositions. Key activities for building an innovation culture include awareness building, training and support. OKI has also embarked upon an ambitious plan to train many employees within a few years. Further, a strong management commitment is expressed in several ways, such as a clear strategic direction for innovation, reviews of innovation activities, as well as an involvement of the president in innovation promotion activities. OKI has implemented key performance indicators to capture the elements in the system as well as the system itself. The introduction of Yume Pro is led by the company's Chief Innovation Officer (CINO) and the Innovation Promotion Centre (IPC).

17.1. Introduction

17.1.1. *OKI — Background*

OKI Electric Industry Co., Ltd. (OKI) is a Japanese information and technology company, which manufactures products, technologies and solutions for telecommunications and information systems, as well as related ICT services, with infrastructure grade reliabilities — thereby supporting realisation of the information society. The company founder Kibataro Oki started the company in 1881 (manufacturing Japan's first telephone), and in 1889 the company's name was changed into OKI Electric Works. OKI has over the years developed technologies and products and, in 2018, OKI was selected to the list of Top 100 Global Tech Leaders (Thomson Reuters, 2018). Today it has about 17,000 employees worldwide.

17.1.2. *Needs for innovation and change*

Both external and internal drivers can be identified as motivating the ongoing changes at OKI. Externally, both opportunities and threats are present. For example, the development of enabling technologies and services is opening up new opportunities. However, a transition into a cashless and paperless society (Arvidsson *et al.*, 2017; Dahlberg *et al.*, 2008) has strong implications for OKI since the ATM and printer business areas have served as a part of the foundation of current earnings. Further, the company's customers are also experiencing changes that affect current business structures. This, in turn, also influences relations between OKI and its main customers, where long-term customers may now ask for new value offerings, instead of traditional ordering of products and services from the current portfolio.

In parallel to these external drivers for change, internal motivation can also be found. From the very top of the company, a need was recognised, not only to adapt to external changes in the business environment but to "transform the corporate culture from a passive product-out stance based on the receipt of orders to an active stance based on proposing effective value propositions and solutions with a well-validated business model."

17.1.3. *Decision to introduce an innovation management system*

In August 2017, the president of OKI decided to start preparing for a more systematic organisation management system, including implementation of an Innovation Management System (IMS). This decision was based on the identified needs for transformation and change, and on an awareness of the development of a global standard for IMSs. In the past, innovation activities were regarded more as bootlegging by small number of employees, and the president wanted to change such a perception as well as to start a new culture and practices within OKI.

In October 2017, an Innovation Promotion Project team was initiated. An active transformation effort was launched, supported by a close collaboration with Japan Innovation Network (JIN), and their innovation management support expertise.

17.2. Yume Pro — OKI's Innovation Management System

The IMS at OKI is named Yume Pro. "Yume" stands for Dream (which is related to the company slogan "Open up your dreams") and "Pro" is taken from the company's three main objectives — Programme, Project and Professional.

Yume Pro has been developed in parallel with the development of ISO 56002 (ISO, 2019). OKI originally followed JIN's Innovation Compass, which is JIN's IMS framework based on several success cases in Japan. OKI conducted internal interviews according to the Innovation Compass framework. The interviews revealed several internal challenges to innovate continuously, and it was decided to design an IMS to overcome these challenges. Key concepts of Innovation Compass were later blended into ISO 56002, since JIN is a national representative of Japan for ISO 56002. Thus, transition from the Innovation Compass to ISO 56002 after publication of ISO 56002 was very smooth. Yume Pro is guided by the corporate mission and the values in the Sustainable Development Goals (SDGs) to: (1) find opportunities where the company can create and deliver new value, (2) collaborate with partners to address these targets, and (3) provide fruitful processes and methods to support this development. The

Fig. 17.1. The logo of Yume Pro.
Source: OKI, © Copyright 2021 Oki Electrical Industry Co., Ltd.

Yume Pro was launched in April 2018 and a groupwide deployment began in December 2020. The logo of Yume Pro uses 17 colours of SDGs to express the image of OKI spiralling up while solving social issues together with co-creation partners (Figure 17.1).

17.2.1. *IMS overview*

The ambitions with the IMS are to: (1) generate a culture where innovation is a part of the daily activities, (2) have a strategy where the SDGs are explicitly focused on (for instance, aiming to resolve social issues), (3) have an innovation process deployed in the whole company group, (4) offer full support for innovation activities, (5) have plans targeting challenging objectives, and (6) enable continuous effective evaluation and improvements of the complete system.

When ISO 56002 was published, its content and structure were incorporated in Yume Pro, using this standard as a model for improving ongoing systemic change. Key elements in Yume Pro, and how they are related, can be summarised as follows (with references to corresponding clauses in ISO 56002 in brackets):

- The foundation is an Understanding of the organisation and its context (4.1), as well as its Culture (4.4.2).

- The identified need for culture change is a driving force for a more active stance towards innovation, as reflected in the present Leadership and commitment for innovation (5.1).
- It is important that the Organisational structures (6.3) enable proactive activities supported by leadership and commitment (5.1) and Innovation Policy (5.2), but also leading to an increased Awareness (7.3).
- Increased Awareness should result in an understanding of the need to invest Resources into innovation activities (7.1).
- In addition, Leadership and commitment (5.1) make it possible to allocate Resources (7.1), and Organisational structures (6.3) play a central role in promoting the Innovation process (8.3). Value created from the Innovation process (8.3) increases Awareness of the IMS (7.3); and leads to changes in the Organisational culture (4.4.2). This leads to further investment of Resources (7.1), and strengthens Competence (7.2), which can be seen as a key to stimulating innovation activities.

In Figure 17.2, the numerous interdependencies between the system key elements can be seen, clearly reflecting circular relationships and potential positive reinforcement of these relationships.

17.2.2. *Key elements of Yume Pro*

Related to the key elements of the IMS used by OKI, important points can be made about the organisation of the innovation work, process, culture, competence development, management support and measurement.

Organising innovation at the group level

OKI is organised in different business areas and a number of corporate functions. The president has overall responsibility for the innovation in OKI. A corporate support function, the Innovation Promotion Centre (IPC), has been established, led by a Chief Innovation Officer (CINO).

The IPC's primary tasks are to lead specific innovation initiatives in their early phases, as well as a broader set of activities aiming to build innovation capabilities in the whole organisation, while the Business

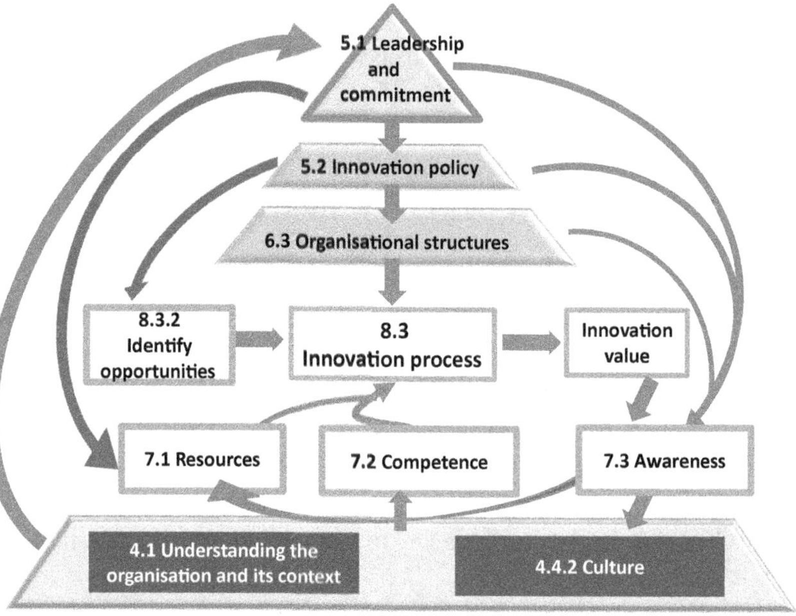

Fig. 17.2. Visualisation of OKI Yume Pro: Key elements and complete system.
Source: OKI, © Copyright 2021 Oki Electrical Industry Co., Ltd.

Divisions focus on further development and commercialisation. The specific innovation initiatives include carrying out research and development (R&D) based on the OKI innovation strategy, and piloting new business creation initiatives in accordance with the overall innovation process. The IPC also plays a key role in fostering company-wide innovation capabilities by being responsible for establishment, implementation, assessment and continual improvements of the IMS; as well as facilitating education (e.g., innovation training) and awareness activities (increasing recognition both inside and outside OKI) based on Yume Pro. The CINO is responsible for the activities of the IPC, which means that it is under the direct supervision of the president who receives reports on activities and reviews the current efforts monthly.

The Business Divisions all have established internal organisations to oversee innovation work within their areas. Every second month, the CINO and the IPC review and exchange information about innovation activities with the individuals appointed being responsible for the different divisions' innovation efforts. This lays a foundation for a close cooperation between the IPC and the divisions regarding their respective responsibilities in the innovation work. In addition, innovation activities are reviewed recurrently by the president and top management for each business division.

Process for value creation

The process part of the system starts by identifying opportunities from the SDGs and analysis of related end user needs. A draft business model is an integrated part of the concept/hypothesis developed and is validated later in the process. In parallel, the technology side of the process includes addressing identification of opportunities, intellectual property issues, technology development and validation, and co-creation with partners. The resources needed, including budgeting and staffing, are provided in accordance with the progress of the process. OKI has developed the Yume Pro business process and Yume Pro technology process based on the innovation process defined in the Chapter 8 of ISO 56002. A goal for OKI is that all parts of OKI deploy this defined process.

The IPC oversees the earlier steps of the process being responsible for identifying opportunities, formulating business model hypotheses, and validating business model hypotheses, whereas the Business Divisions oversee the later phases developing and adopting solutions, and business plan confirmation. Hence, the responsibility of the process is clearly divided for the early and the later process steps.

In general, the process aims to be more "pull" from the demand side than "push" from the technology side. All development personnel are encouraged to rethink business models and to meet and listen to customers and their needs "more than a hundred times," in order to connect the business needs and the technological capabilities. For example, Key Performance Indicators (KPIs), related to employees meeting customers, have been incorporated in the process.

Challenges are identified in the transfer of innovation initiatives from the early development into the work of the Business Divisions. This may be related to the difference in logics and planning horizons between the

Business Divisions, which deploy a planning logic, based on fiscal year, and the more emergent logic in innovation initiatives. Therefore, the organisational set-up of the ICP aims to improve the coordination and collaboration between the two logics.

Building culture, and developing competences through education, awareness and support

Transforming the corporate culture has been explicitly addressed in the preparations for introducing an IMS, and OKI has a clear ambition to build a culture in which innovation is a part of everyday activities. A specific roadmap towards achieving this within 5 years has been formed. The aim is to transform the corporate culture from what OKI expresses as a "passive stance, waiting for customer orders" (based on stable relations to long-term customers) into working actively with innovation and creating new businesses. This would be for new and current customers, where the customers also face changes in their respective value networks.

A change from "push to pull" relates both to culture and attitude as well as to processes and skills. Process-wise the employees involved in development are encouraged to explore social issues, to meet the customers and to focus on the value created for the customers. To enable such an approach, and to foster an entrepreneurial orientation, employees need to develop skills to see opportunities, and be able to design proposals and relevant business models. For this reason, substantial training efforts are made towards raising employees' skills and knowledge related to what is covered in the concept of Business Model Canvas (Osterwalder and Pigneur, 2010), in order to allow them to purposefully develop business models and validate hypotheses based on interviews with customers and end users.

A significant aspect of an innovation culture is how to deal with opportunities, risks and failures. Arguably, there needs to be a significant acceptance of failure, and a capacity to learn from such failures. This change of attitude is easier said than done in a corporate setting. An invaluable factor in addressing this has been the president's engagement, where he has been sharing personal experiences from a long career and shown an openness regarding learning from failures. Related to the inherent uncertainty in innovation processes, making it challenging to guarantee specific outcomes, OKI has implemented an updated evaluation system for employees, assessing processes and activities rather than direct results.

Key activities within OKI for building a fruitful innovation culture are the awareness building, training and support activities. Awareness building is done with an internal as well as an external focus. Internally, there are forums and events where top management meet and communicate with employees. For example, the Innovation Dialogues are biweekly direct dialogues between the president and about 10 employees. In addition, the CINO and IPC head convene internal seminars (called Yume Pro forum) addressing why OKI is adopting the IMS and the targets of these efforts. These events are also reported within OKI through posting articles on the intranet. Externally focused awareness-raising activities around Yume Pro have several purposes. First, it promotes OKI as an innovation partner. Second, it aims to create effects internally from having external positive evaluations, and thereby serve as external motivators for employees in the internal cultural change.

The training of employees is designed to focus *understanding of innovation, fostering a spirit of pursuing challenges*, and *skills* related to developing business models. A number of training programmes have been designed for different target groups:

- Basic training for all employees (meaning of innovation, methods for developing business hypotheses based on the problems that customers face).
- Training on the SDGs for sales and product planning staff (to understand the SDGs and experience hands-on business development methods from an SDG perspective).
- Advanced training for staff in charge of new business planning (experience hands-on hypothesis validation methods).
- Practical business support for divisions in charge of new business planning (practical ways to identify new themes in each division and to validate hypotheses in line with innovation processes).

To enhance the understanding of innovation, the training has been designed to make the participants reflect on the transformations and technology shifts they have experienced themselves. Further, to understand fundamental value propositions, the participants get to reflect on well-known cases for creating a new value proposition that profoundly impacts a market. The content of the training was designed by JIN specially for OKI to reflect on their specific challenges. JIN originally conducted training sessions, but simultaneously trained internal trainers in order for OKI to be able to deliver the training internally. OKI executives and managers have been highly engaged in performing this training, underlining its importance, and fostering shared views and values across hierarchical levels in the company.

OKI also launched supporting activities intended to further contribute to building innovation capabilities. One example is the offering of consultation meetings, where serial entrepreneurs are engaged as senior advisors. Another example is the Yume Pro Challenge, an internal idea contest for participation from the entire OKI company. The winners receive an investment (up to 100 million yen) to cover the costs of hypothesis validation and demonstration. The president and top management serve as judges.

Management attention and support

The attention for and support of innovation from the very top management is signalled in several ways. For example, a clear direction is given, including an explicitly expressed ambition for OKI to be an innovation partner, to implement an IMS, and to address the SDGs. In addition to this, reoccurring follow-ups (biweekly, monthly or bi-monthly) on managerial levels regarding the status of activities (based on KPIs in accordance with the Yume Pro process) signal management's clear and consistent commitment. Finally, top management has engaged in communicating, with the president's engagement and visibility in the Innovation Dialogue format as interesting examples. Executives, department heads and managers in the organisation who provide employee training are other examples of showing management attention for innovation.

Measurement

The structure of the Yume Pro is based on ISO 56002, and on a systems level, the Plan–Do–Check–Act (PDCA) cycle is used to improve the IMS itself. KPIs related to input, output as well as throughput are used, encompassing both quantitative and qualitative indicators. Along with the preparations and implementation of the IMS, a development of KPIs to be used throughout the OKI organisation is under way. In addition, OKI has a process for reviewing the IMS through annual interviews with all executives. Each IMS element is dealt with, and issues, statuses and enhancement measures are identified correspondingly.

17.3. Implementation Experiences

The implementation of an IMS at OKI is characterised by a structured approach, clear management attention and support, and an aim to reach the individuals in the organisation for transforming the corporate culture.

17.3.1. *Internal assessment and planning for implementation*

As presented in the introduction of this chapter, the preparations for implementing an IMS started based on insights regarding a need to respond to ongoing changes in the business context and to address internal renewal, combined with an awareness of the development of international standards for innovation management.

The current IPC was preceded by the initiation of the Innovation Promotion Project (with around seven people) in 2017, leading to the establishment of an Innovation Promotion Department in 2018. In the same year, a CINO was also appointed. In 2020, the IPC was formed, with approximately 140 employees.

An initial activity was for OKI to enter into a partnership agreement with JIN in order to utilise JIN's innovation management expertise. OKI originally utilised the Innovation Compass, which is JIN's IMS framework based on success cases in Japan. As a first step, it was decided to identify the current reality in the organisation regarding innovation capabilities according to the Innovation Compass. Based on structured interviews with about 50 internal key people, challenges were identified related to areas such as corporate culture, skills, and process for innovation. The most important findings were as follows:

- Innovation activities were regarded as a non-core individual activity.
- Intrapreneurs often had to fight against the existing system.
- Little respect was paid to such efforts, especially when efforts did not produce results.
- Despite the president's desire, his message was not clearly understood by the employees.

The report was discussed by the president and the internal Innovation team almost every week. Obviously, the findings were not pleasant ones, and there were several heated and emotional discussions between the president and the team. However, based on continuous discussions, a shared understanding was reached. The ability to achieve a common understanding about the current state and issues was a key step in the IMS adoption. In addition, JIN has been representing Japan in the development of the global standard for IMS. Thus, JIN's Innovation Compass concept was used as input in the ISO working group discussions when developing ISO 56002. In fact, the Innovation Compass articulated the needs for Vision, Leadership, Nonlinear Innovation Process, Education and External Collaboration, which are also found in the ISO framework. The president and the Innovation team also reached agreement on the most important KPIs for the 5-year period through FY2022, which were to: (1) realise a culture in which innovation is a matter of course in everyday activities, and (2) establish OKI's innovation brand. Further, a suitable organisation and plans for achieving these goals were also agreed upon.

17.3.2. *Training and communication*

The awareness raising, training and supporting activities have followed an ambitious path, covering several different types of activities, reaching out both internally and externally:

- Frequent promotion activities using both internal and external sources (posting a total of 296 articles to date on the website, 450 intranet postings and 121 published articles in newspapers and magazines).

- The training activities have had a clear cascading approach, starting at the very top. Workshops are held by members of the Top Management Conference, including the president. This is followed by training for managers at the division general manager level, then by training for managers at the department manager level.
- They originally had an ambition to train 1,000 employees through the Basic training every year. The four training programmes have at the time of writing this chapter had over 3,000 employees participating, where most have followed the Basic training. OKI has a plan that 6,000 individuals (half of all domestic employees) should have taken the Basic training by the end of year 2022.
- In total, 660 employees have participated in the Innovation Dialogues (between the president and 10 employees each time) during 2018–2020.
- Over 2,000 employees have participated in the Yume Pro forum: Innovation seminars (Chairman/CINO/IPC head).
- Consultation meetings have to date been held 22 times, and included consultations on 52 projects.
- Yume Pro Challenge (the idea contest) has had 37 (2018), 45 (2019) and 147 (2020) proposals.

In a December 2020 press release, OKI officially announced a group-wide IMS establishment, underlining the company's clear commitment to innovation. This positioning had several purposes to:

- Signal OKI's ambition to be an innovation partner to existing and potential customers,
- Further encourage and motivate OKI employees to take an active role in the company's innovation efforts, and
- Contribute to the widespread adoption and use of ISO 56002 in Japanese companies, as this will further facilitate external innovation collaborations and in the end support the competitiveness of the Japanese industry.

17.3.3. *Critical factors and challenges during the implementation*

During the work of building innovation capabilities and preparing an introduction of an IMS, several critical factors and challenges have been identified and addressed.

Further to the commitment of top management, it is critical that the president and those promoting innovation, including the CINO and the IPC, share the same understanding of the current state of the organisation, its vision, a sense of urgency, a desire to solve the problems, and implementation priorities. In addition, it has been beneficial to collaborate with external innovation management experts. The value of the collaboration with JIN is explicitly communicated by stating that "... the internal Innovation team alone could not have launched Yume Pro."

In addition, OKI had a history where earlier experiences with innovation initiatives had been less fruitful, such as an internal venture business model that was considered unsuccessful and eventually disappeared. This contributed to a somewhat sceptical and cynical attitude for yet another innovation initiative, and Yume Pro "started from a negative position rather than a clean slate." This was addressed by comprehensive communication and awareness building both internally and externally. Since the timing of these efforts coincided with the start of activities promoting innovation, before any real direct innovation results had come about, the communication was a particularly delicate balancing act.

A substantial challenge has been to change the corporate culture from a more passive stance to one characterised by a proactive approach to innovation. The fight against scepticism also needs to be included in their planning. This has been addressed through efforts in designing the innovation process, as well as in communication and training, ultimately, to enhance both innovation skills and attitudes.

OKI is a large organisation. This likely contributed to the challenges of reaching a common understanding and shared vision. It is critical to achieve a comprehensive, shared understanding between the IPC and Business Divisions of intentions regarding opportunities so that any promising new concepts can be handed over smoothly to the Business Divisions. Therefore, work is ongoing at a detailed level and with formulating innovation strategies. Further, differences in enthusiasm among facilities and divisions are evident. While innovation activities are gathering steam at facilities in the greater Tokyo area, they are proceeding with less energy at facilities in rural regions, mostly consisting of OKI's factories. Therefore, OKI, has plans to use innovation evangelists also in factories with the purpose of promoting the IMS approach, working with manufacturing to innovate their business models in order to create value for their (internal) customers.

17.4. Effects of Implementing an Innovation Management System

Since the adoption of Yume Pro was initiated quite recently, it is still too early to claim specific benefits from implementing the IMS Yume Pro in terms of its commercialised project results and their final contributions to the economic value of OKI.

In any large organisation, such as OKI, changes take time but there are certain positive effects that can be seen both externally and internally regarding the impression of OKI as an innovative company. For example, in the yearly review of Yume Pro (interviews with executives), progress regarding the corporate culture has been identified "despite differences in degree among facilities and divisions, emerging signs point to a shift towards a corporate culture of pursuing challenges" (from the review of 2020). In addition, utilising activity-based measures, the ambitious training and awareness building may serve as indications for further progress.

Finally, by implementing an IMS, a common language regarding innovation is emerging internally. By relating to the ISO standard, this language will also be common with other organisations, which will be beneficial for global collaboration.

17.5. Overall Reflections and Way Forward

Yume Pro will continuously be evaluated and improved. OKI has a long-term ambition to identify and address gaps between the current state of the IMS and its vision of the system. This means continuous work according to the overall direction, including a humble respect for the efforts needed to build a shared understanding of innovation, and how to orient the organisation at large towards identifying and creating new opportunities. However, it seems clear that the original scepticism has evaporated as a result of continuous improvement over the past 3 years.

Training and awareness will remain as keys in the further work and the collaboration with Japan Innovation Network will continue. Among many topics, developing advanced training addressing the different needs of innovation competence development of the organisation will be critical.

OKI also has an ambition to align with the IMS certification standard ISO 56001 that is to be developed, and to be certified accordingly. In relation to this, it is worth noting that the Ministry of Economy, Trade and Industry encourages Japanese companies to introduce IMSs. At the time of writing this chapter, the IS0 56002 is a top selling standard in Japan.

Acknowledgements

OKI has shown great dedication to the topic by openly sharing information and spending time participating in several valuable interviews. Moreover, the chapter draws upon the rich knowledge and insights of the OKI case provided through the close collaboration with JIN.

References

Arvidsson, N., Hedman, J. and Segendorf, B. (2017). Cashless Society: When will merchants stop accepting cash in Sweden. A research model. In Feuerriegel, S. and Neumann, D. (eds.), *Enterprise Applications, Markets and Services in the Finance Industry: Revised Papers of the 8th International Workshop, FinanceCom 2016* (pp. 105–113). Heidelberg: Springer. Lecture Notes in Business Information Processing, Vol. 276.

Dahlberg, T., Mallat, N., Ondrus, J. and Zmijewska, A. (2008). Past, present and future of mobile payments research: A literature review. *Electronic Commerce Research and Applications*, 7(2), 165–181.

ISO (2019). *ISO 56002:2019 Innovation management — Innovation management system — Guidance*. International Organization for Standardization.

Osterwalder, A. and Pigneur, Y. (2010). *Business Model Generation — A Handbook for Visionaries, Game Changers, and Challengers*. Hoboken, New Jersey: John Wiley & Sons Inc.

Thomson Reuters (2018). *Thomson Reuters 2018 Top 100 Tech Leaders*, https://www.thomsonreuters.com/en/products-services/technology/top-100.html.

© 2023 World Scientific Publishing Europe Ltd.
https://doi.org/10.1142/9781800612105_0018

Chapter 18

Oregon State University: Impact Studio — Advancing a University's Institutional Innovation Capability

Richard Duncombe and Edward Feser

Abstract

Public research universities in the United States (US) and many around the world face rising challenges associated with escalating costs, shifting demographics, changing public perceptions of the value of college degrees, growing student loan debt and eroding public sector support, among other things. Arguably, the scale and pace of change universities must execute to address those challenges are rising. Yet, as highly decentralised organisations with strong traditions of shared governance, advancing institutional innovation within universities can be difficult. Many universities need to increase their rate of institutional innovation in order to protect and strengthen delivery of their research, teaching and engagement missions. Moreover, universities need to innovate faster and more effectively to capitalise on opportunities that emerge and are pursued rapidly by others in an increasingly competitive higher education sector. In 2018, Oregon State University established a function and set of associated practices — called Impact Studio — that are designed to expand the institution's internal innovation system and capability. The aim is to strengthen Oregon State's ability to identify or create new value and respond creatively and nimbly to fast-changing trends in higher education, while still respecting shared governance norms and the locus of expertise naturally resident at different levels of the organisation (departments, schools, colleges, and administrative divisions and units). Since its genesis, Impact Studio has stewarded the development and launch of eight adjacent growth initiatives. In the process, Oregon State has learned a number of lessons about institutional innovation that may inform other universities' efforts.

18.1. Background/Introduction

18.1.1. *Challenges in US higher education*

Higher education challenges in the US were well documented even before the unprecedented disruption from the COVID-19 pandemic. Competitive pressure to maintain enrolment has increased as the number of high school students in the US has flattened and has started to fall in some states. The cost of higher education has continued to grow faster than inflation, increasing the burden on students and families. Reaching historically underserved students who seek a post-secondary education depends on expanded programmes for student success and access starting in primary education to bridge cultural and socioeconomic divides. Adult learners seeking a career change or advancement have driven the need for part-time, asynchronous and remote course delivery that has rapidly transitioned to a mainstream offering at many universities. State funding for higher education has dropped precipitously over the last 20 years and is at an all-time low in many states, putting some public universities at serious risk. Public opinion of higher education in the US reflects deep divides leading some to question the value of higher education, research and science.

Under these conditions, the organisational instinct is often to retrench and focus on preserving core activities, as any investment in new initiatives could be perceived as diverting funding from the essential to the non-essential, especially by faculty facing what they perceive as demands to do more with less in terms of resources and support. For example, it would be natural for universities to focus their limited resources on cutting costs, maintaining enrolment and supporting core services for students. For some research universities, the tendency may be to shift the focus to those disciplines most capable of attracting external research funding while also making wide use of non-tenure stream faculty to control teaching costs and expand online enrolment.

18.1.2. *Challenges in university institutional innovation*

Yet, a strategy of retrenchment is misguided. What the trends summarised in the previous section imply is that the business model that built US public research universities — and that created the institutional norms, culture and practices within them — is not the same business model that will ensure they thrive going forward. The financial and operational conditions facing universities are changing along with the substance of what they must do differently in research, teaching and public engagement.

In research, scientific convergence and interdisciplinary approaches are essential to making gains in society's understanding of climate change, energy, environmental sustainability, health, inequality and economic development. Universities need stronger partnerships with foundations and industry, in addition to government, to finance research, and thus they need to translate more of their research into use and application. In teaching, learners are becoming more diverse in background and life experience; there are fewer traditional first-year students and more students transferring from other higher education institutions; and reskilling and lifelong learning are becoming increasingly important to advanced economies. New ways of delivering instruction are proliferating, with new modalities, better tools and technology for online learning, and better practices for blending synchronous and asynchronous learning. And, in the domain of engagement, universities must find ways to get their research more readily into usable forms.

Undertaking institutional change to capture new opportunities and counter threats is not a strength of many universities, especially research universities. Some of the reasons are common to any organisation, such as the tendency to overstate the downside of taking risks. But a dynamic that is especially characteristic of research universities is the heavy premium faculty place on stasis and stability within the institution itself. This makes sense from the standpoint of the individual scholar, who naturally values maximum opportunity to focus on the problems he or she is studying. The highest quality research — that which has the highest impact in generating new knowledge or innovating in application — takes tremendous mental energy. Dealing with disruption in one's working environment and arrangements, much less contributing actively to introducing it and advancing it — is a significant negative for many scholars. And, given that most consequential decisions in US universities are made jointly by faculty and administrators, consistent with deeply held shared governance norms, there is a general tendency to favour low risk, marginal changes executed over extended periods and informed by much collective debate.

Therefore, the challenge in realising institutional innovation in research universities is to create support structures and practices that can facilitate positive change and associated sound investments without undercutting either shared governance or the stability and predictability that are essential to the successful delivery of the core research mission.

18.1.3. *Oregon State University's experiment*

As the State of Oregon's land grant university, Oregon State has defined its mission as one of promoting economic, social, cultural and environmental progress for the people of Oregon, the nation and the world. In fall 2020, the university's total enrolment exceeded 32K, making it the largest university in Oregon. Its operating budget was over $1.4B for fiscal year 2020, including over $340M in funded research. The university employs about 5.5K people, with a traditional organisational structure comprising 11 academic colleges. Oregon State is ranked in the top 1% of global universities and is known internationally for its research in ocean sciences, forestry, agricultural sciences and robotics. The university's online unit — Ecampus — is ranked #5 in the nation by *US News* and *World Report* and has maintained a Top 10 ranking for the sixth straight year as of this writing. Last year, Oregon State was ranked the 33rd most innovative university in the nation and 1st in the Pacific Northwest.

Since 2003, the university has prioritised regular and consistent strategic planning and outcomes tracking (see Table 18.1). This approach was aided by the long tenure of President Ed Ray, who served from 2003 to 2020 and oversaw the development of four strategic plans, each building on the last. The current strategic plan — *SP4.0: Transforming Excellence* — was informed by a university-wide exercise to envision what Oregon State strives to achieve by 2030. A key finding of the *Vision 2030* effort and subsequent strategic plan was that Oregon State needs to prioritise surfacing opportunities to generate net revenue growth in ways that remain consistent with its land grant research mission and academic goals. The university recognised that traditional funding streams were not going to be

Table 18.1. Oregon State's legacy of planning and transformation.

2003: Oregon State begins preparing its first modern-day strategic plan with the appointment of Ed Ray, the university's 14th president since the university's founding in 1868. Enrolment totals 18,974 students

2004: Strategic Plan 1.0 released

2007: The Campaign for Oregon State University, the university's first-ever capital campaign, launches with a goal to raise $625 million. New research grants and contracts total $185 million

2009: Strategic Plan 2.0 released

2013: The National Science Foundation (NSF) selects Oregon State University to lead the design of as many as three new academic research vessels. In 2017, the NSF awarded Oregon State $121.88 million to launch construction of the first vessel, to be based at Oregon State's Hatfield Marine Science Center

2014: Strategic Plan 3.0 released

2014: The Campaign for Oregon State University concludes, raising $1.14 billion that helped construct or renovate 28 buildings; endow 79 faculty positions; provide $189 million for scholarships and fellowships, and increase support for Oregon State's teaching and research initiatives. Construction projects included new homes for four of Oregon State's nine cultural resource centres

2016: The university launches its Student Success Initiative, which by 2020 commits the university to raise first-year retention rates and 6-year graduation rates for all students. The Oregon State University Foundation commits to raising $150 million to support the initiative. OSU-Cascades opens its new campus in Bend, OR, with the capacity to serve 3,000 to 5,000 students in Central Oregon

2017: Oregon State University launches OSU150, a 15-month, state-wide celebration of the university's 150th anniversary, its unique mission and ongoing impact

2018: In fiscal years 2016–2018, Oregon State faculty attract $1.13 billion in external research funding — marking the three highest years in the university's history. Oregon State programmes in forestry, oceanography, agricultural sciences, robotics and online degrees earn top-tier rankings. Impact Studio is founded to develop a portfolio of adjacent growth opportunities

2019: Oregon State launches Strategic Plan 4.0 to guide the university over the next 5 years. Enrolment stands at a record 32,011, making Oregon State the largest university in the state for the 5th year in a row

Source: Oregon State strategic planning and outcomes tracking.

adequate to sustain the progress established over the previous two decades. A second finding was that the university would need to become nimbler and more capable of change.

To deliver on these ideas, in 2018, Oregon State established a new central function — based in the Office of the Provost but serving units across the institution — with a specific charge: To lead and support teams of faculty, students and staff in the development and launch of bold initiatives that advance Oregon State's strategic goals. Eventually settling on the name Impact Studio, the unit's objective is to strengthen capabilities in Oregon State's internal innovation system. Impact Studio is responsible for stewarding the creation and management of a portfolio of adjacent innovation initiatives that create significant external impact, drive culture change, advance the teaching mission and improve the university's financial strength.

18.2. Description of the Innovation System and Components

18.2.1. *Oregon State's innovation system overview and assessment*

The development of the university's *Vision 2030* and SP4.0 is an opportunity to reflect on the maturity of the overall innovation system. Table 18.2 provides a snapshot of the Oregon State innovation system's maturity level based on the innovation management maturity model for assisted or self-assessment based on ISO 56002 (ISO, 2019) developed by the Swedish Institute for Standards (IMCA, 2019). The table also indicates which topics are included in the following detailed sections.

The Swedish Standards Institute also provided a recommended maturity level assessment rubric. Table 18.3 describes the scoring criteria used by Oregon State.

18.2.2. *Context and conditions*

Innovation occurs in every unit across the university. Figure 18.1 shows the spectrum of innovation from incremental to radical innovation. Core

Table 18.2. Oregon State innovation system components and maturity.

Capabilities	Assessment Criteria	Maturity	Included
Context and Conditions	1. Understanding of external trends and drivers	3	
	2. Understanding of internal capabilities and assets	3	
	3. Culture supporting creativity and deployment	4	Y
	4. External and internal innovation collaboration	3	Y
Leadership	5. Top management commitment	4	Y
	6. Focus on value realisation	4	Y
	7. Innovation vision and strategy	3	
	8. Innovation policy	3	
	9. Organisational roles, responsibilities	3	
Planning	10. Innovation objectives and action plans	4	
	11. Organisational structures for innovation activities	4	Y
	12. Innovation portfolios	4	Y
Support	13. Resources supporting innovation activities	3	Y
	14. Competence	3	Y
	15. Communication and awareness	4	Y
	16. Innovation tools and methods	5	Y
	17. Intellectual property management	4	
Processes	18. Innovation initiatives and projects	5	Y
	19. Configuration of innovation processes	5	Y
	20. Processes to identify opportunities	4	Y
	21. Processes to create and validate concepts	5	Y
	22. Processes to develop and deploy solutions	4	Y
Evaluation and Improvement	23. Innovation performance indicators	4	Y
	24. Performance evaluation and improvement	3	

Source: The Swedish Institute for Standards (IMCA, 2019).

or incremental innovation focuses on the continuous improvement of offerings for Oregon State's current audiences. In Oregon State's context, core innovation includes improving courses, adding new degrees, improving student services and so forth. Innovation in the core is essential but often does not grow the number of new learners served.

Impact Studio primarily engages in *adjacent innovation.* Adjacent innovation is developing new offerings and reaching new audiences resulting in net new growth. On the positive side, adjacent innovation

Table 18.3. Overview of Oregon State maturity levels.

Level	Description
1: Nothing, Informal or *ad hoc*	The capability is not established or established in an informal or *ad hoc* manner
2: Managed at a Basic Level	The capability is established at a basic level and is not managed or measured across the organisation
3: Defined and Managed	The capability is defined and established. It is managed proactively across the organisation
4: Systematically Managed	The capability is defined, established and aligned across the organisation. It is systematically reviewed centrally with coordinated improvement plans
5: Optimised	The capability is continuously improved and optimised centrally. It is managed based on active monitoring, feedback and learning

Source: The Swedish Institute for Standards (IMCA, 2019).

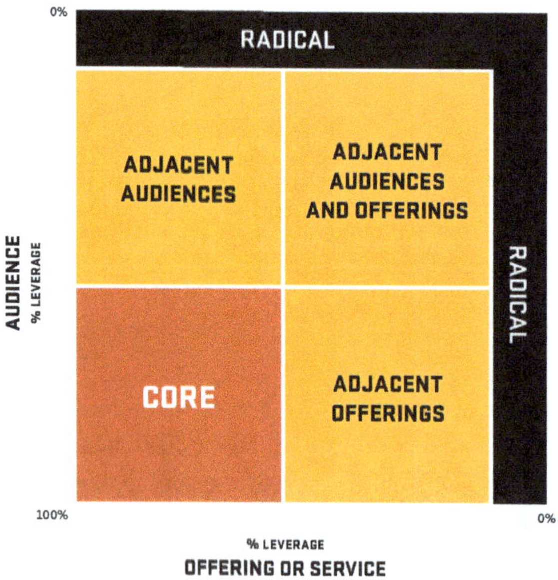

Fig. 18.1. Innovation spectrum.

Source: Oregon State, adapted Nagli and Tuff (2012).

leverages an organisation's current capabilities and assets. However, developing new offerings and serving new audiences creates higher uncertainty, and execution is complex because cross-university capabilities are required.

Impact Studio is a carefully designed vehicle for Oregon State to recognise and leverage its world-leading capabilities to create new value and respond creatively and nimbly to fast-changing trends in higher education. Impact Studio has developed and launched eight adjacent growth initiatives in 3 years, including supporting transfer student onboarding and success, expansion into international online markets, new tuition pricing models, workforce development solutions for one of the state's largest economic sectors and new transdisciplinary educational programmes.

18.2.3. *Leadership*

Top management commitment

As shared previously, Oregon State has a long history of collaboratively developing strategic plans to focus the institution on the most important priorities to achieve its mission. Well-designed strategies and plans are not enough. The organisation predictably looks for leadership to demonstrate its commitment consistently and systematically, including the thoughtful allocation of resources to move the mission forward. At Oregon State, the Board of Trustees is engaged in monitoring progress towards the plan. The university's Provost manages a detailed metrics dashboard that tracks progress for each of the SP4.0 actions and asks the action owners to report progress at university leadership meetings.

The Provost founded Impact Studio to provide central expertise and funding to accelerate initiatives that intersect multiple strategies and actions in SP4.0. For example, an initiative on transfer enrolment and student expansion supports two of four SP4.0 goals and four of 20 actions. All initiatives developed through the portfolio show a similar pattern of driving innovation across SP4.0.

Focus on value realisation

Oregon State has a robust performance evaluation process for leadership and their units. That starts with a comprehensive review of the performance metrics, conducted annually with quarterly updates. The annual planning process establishes the shared goals for leaders and organisations with specific financial and non-financial metrics. Those key metrics include student-focused metrics such as retention rate, graduation rate and the amount of debt students take to complete their degrees. Oregon State uses this disciplined approach to deliver the value that students and families desire, which goes well beyond a degree to include experiential learning, job readiness and job placement.

A specific advancement in value realisation was the university's decision in 2017 to implement a new Responsibility Centre Management (RCM) budget model to incentivise and empower university leaders to make financially sound long-term investments required for success. The RCM model — which is aligned with the state's funding formula for public universities — directs funding streams to colleges based on performance factors that directly relate to the university's strategic plan, with special emphasis on student outcomes and research activities. The model influences colleges to prioritise solid enrolments, graduation rates, the diversity of their students, and the expansion of their programmes to serve learners worldwide. Following a long tradition of historical and incremental budgeting, adopting and using the RCM budget model has been difficult. Still, it has accelerated progress on the mission and increased the incentives for taking risks to create new value.

18.2.4. *Planning*

Impact Studio is a direct outcome of Oregon State's response to serving the state, nation and world for the next 150 years. It added or strengthened Oregon State's capability in the following IMS Planning elements:

(1) Defined and developed the objectives and governance of adjacent innovation activities to stretch the organisation beyond incremental innovation.
(2) Created an organisational structure that readily partners and supports the established academic and administrative units.
(3) Led the organisation to utilise proven methodologies to pursue initiatives with a high level of uncertainty.
(4) Established a communication and engagement plan to inform and partner with individuals inside and outside of the organisation.

(5) Developed an organisation to manage, evaluate and communicate the portfolio of innovation initiatives in terms of their strategic and financial contributions.

Impact Studio's mission is to develop and manage a portfolio of initiatives through a deliberate process to surface new innovative ideas, vet those ideas and allocate resources to those most promising. Ideas are solicited from across the university and partners outside of Oregon State.

To accomplish this objective, the organisation needs to allocate resources to support adjacent innovation capabilities consistently. Research shows that consistently allocating even 5% of an organisation's new development funding for adjacent innovation will significantly improve growth over no or an inconsistent investment (Nagli and Tuff, 2012). It is ill-advised to depend on the return of individual initiatives given their high uncertainty. However, achieving a level of predictability at the portfolio level is possible through a properly constructed portfolio with opportunities that depend on diverse sources of upside and uncertainty.

18.2.5. *Processes*

Impact Studio methodology

Impact Studio developed a comprehensive operational capability for adjacent innovation. Figure 18.2 shows the methodology and lifecycle for initiatives from idea identification, opportunity development, concept validation, solution pilot and acceleration. The Impact Studio methodology to create, develop, test and launch new adjacent initiatives has been applied and refined over two decades. Each initiative flows through these phases with tailored time and emphasis.

Impact Studio's approach depends on the following foundational capabilities:

- The system depends on discovering many diverse ideas and criteria to select high potential ideas aligned with the portfolio objectives for development. Oregon State started by engaging over 100 leaders across the university to introduce them to Impact Studio and solicit ideas. Ideas now flow organically from people across the institution serving in many roles. Future ideation will include calls for ideas to

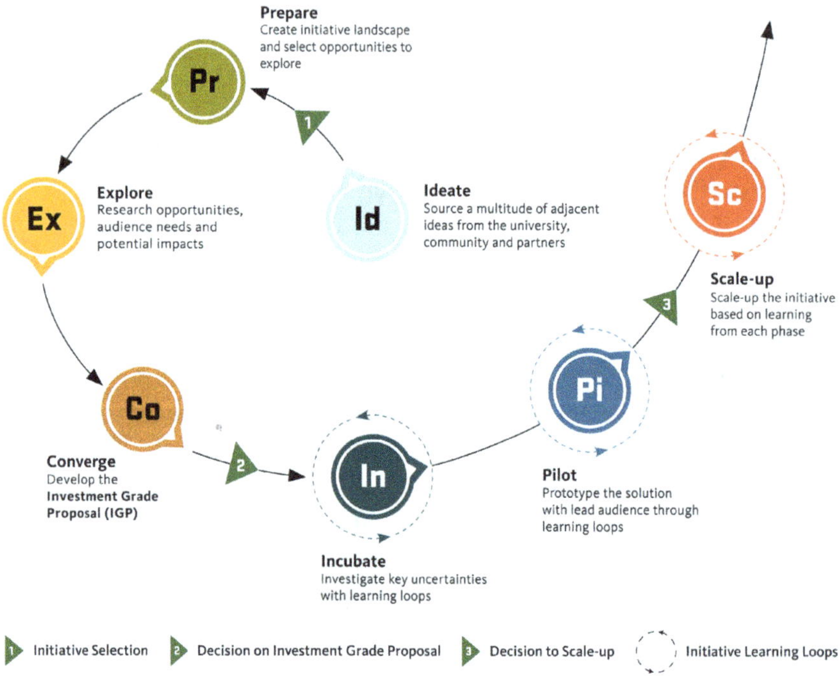

Fig. 18.2. Methodology and initiative lifecycle.

Source: Impact Studio.

address specific needs and issues. Idea selection considers the following selection criteria: external impact, net revenue, culture change, teaching mission, building capability, Oregon State reputation and internal collaboration.

- The system's power comes from talented and motivated faculty, staff, students and external partners. Sponsors represent senior leaders who support the initiative with in-kind resources and agree to take the initiative after it is ready for scale-up. Core team members are the heart and soul of the initiatives and generally come from the sponsoring organisations. They commit to over 100 hours of work over 5 months to develop the fledgling idea to a solid concept, prototype and eventual scalable solution. Over 120 people have served in these roles to bring forward eight initiatives in the first 3 years.

- Great ideas and a motivated team are essential but not sufficient to create and launch a compelling initiative. Impact Studio's methodology uses proven tools and approaches to discover the possibilities and uncertainties inherent in early-stage ideas. The core team is led through two diverge and converge cycles during the *Prepare* and *Explore* phases to look at the opportunity from many perspectives. One idea is selected before entering the *Converge* phase, where due diligence guides the development of an Investment Grade Proposal. If approved, the team investigates key uncertainties and prototypes the solution before scale-up.

Impact Studio governance

Lastly, the governance and investment processes are foundational for the system to produce its desired outputs. Figure 18.2 shows the decision points to enter the process, receive an investment for incubation, pilot and approve scale-up. An Impact Studio Advisory Committee is charged with the following responsibilities:

(1) Provide general oversight of Impact Studio's progress on meeting its mission and advise the Provost accordingly.
(2) Conduct quarterly performance reviews of Impact Studio's portfolio of projects.
(3) Provide an equitable and independent perspective to the Provost on Impact Studio's recommendations for investments in particular projects.
(4) Assist Impact Studio in partnering with colleges, schools, departments, divisions, programmes, institutes and centres to identify promising ideas.
(5) Assist with initiatives and programmes as requested by Impact Studio.
(6) Advocate for Impact Studio.

The Provost is responsible for making the investment decisions based on the Investment Grade Proposal and consultation with sponsors and other relevant stakeholders. Most investments include new seed funding from the Office of the Provost, combined with funding and in-kind resources from the sponsoring organisations. The goal is to bring three investment opportunities forward for consideration each year.

18.2.6. *Evaluation and improvement*

Adding Impact Studio to create an adjacent portfolio of initiatives was a new capability and needed careful evaluation as a pilot. Oregon State selected a 3-year evaluation period as a suitable time frame based on case examples from industry. Based on the early success, the evaluation period was shortened to 2 years using the following evaluation methods:

- At that time, five initiatives were funded, four initiatives were preparing their proposals and two were not funded. Seven performance metrics were used to evaluate the five initiatives with launch funding. The evaluation results clearly showed the forecasted financial benefit and the contribution to external impact, culture change, teaching mission, building capacity, reputation and internal collaboration.
- A survey of people with direct engagement with Impact Studio, either as idea submitters, partners, initiative sponsors or initiative core team members, demonstrated overwhelming support, with 96% recommending that Oregon State maintain or expand the current capacity to develop three new initiatives per year, with two, on average, receiving incubation funding.
- *US News & World Report's* Most Innovative Schools in 2019 ranked Oregon State University #33 among national universities. An evaluation of the top 37 national universities, ranked #33 or higher, was conducted to understand their strategy and approach to developing a portfolio of adjacent initiatives. Only 3 (8%) of the universities evaluated featured this capability as part of their top-level university strategy.
- Finally, the Provost conducted a confidential leadership assessment of the Impact Studio Director. The favourable results were another critical outcome from the university leaders, the partners and sponsors for Impact Studio's work.

18.3. System Implementation

18.3.1. *Impact Studio actions and timeline*

We chose to focus the system implementation section on Impact Studio as Oregon State's newest university-wide innovation capability. The Provost hosts Impact Studio and the growth portfolio to support and fund initiatives with colleges and divisions beyond what they would generally undertake. The evaluation of Impact Studio demonstrated the effectiveness of this approach. This section highlights the plan to create a sustainable capability, a well-known issue for organisations described in the literature as innovation hubs.

In *Beyond the Champion*, the authors bring together 25 years of longitudinal research to make strategic innovation (or adjacent innovation) more sustainable in established organisations (O'Connor *et al.*, 2018). They wrote, "Strategic innovation is not a process, a program, or the result of a long-shot, once-in-a-while opportunity that occurs thanks to a strong-willed intrapreneur. Rather, it is an organisational mainstay with specific responsibilities. The innovation function has a clear purpose and a management system designed to reinforce its aims."

Table 18.4 highlights the innovation system components as they relate to Impact Studio. The status describes the current capabilities with the (+) items describing the planned steps to improve and sustain Impact Studio.

18.3.2. *New barriers in the innovation system*

The ever-accelerating rate of change in the private sector is now the reality in public higher education. Without deliberate attention, this rate of change will erode the mission-based, long-term commitment that has contributed significantly to people and society. The question then is how to create a new level of fluidity in leading and delivering results over the next 150 years. An underpinning of the Innovation Management Standard is that we must not leave such a fundamental decision to individual leaders. The institutional pattern to start and stop innovation activities every 4 or 5 years based on the whims of the economic cycle is ineffective at best and likely damaging.

Oregon State is committed to institutionalising a robust system that defines, incentivises and delivers results representing real progress towards its mission. The Innovation Management System provides a valuable assessment rubric to look at the broader system regarding its current capabilities. The system's application will help identify capability and process gaps that must be elevated as actions to achieve Oregon State's strategic plan.

Impact Studio provides a dynamic capability that can be applied to drive innovation where the needs and urgency are the greatest. For

Table 18.4. Impact Studio innovation system design.

System Components	Definition	Impact Studio Status and Recommendations
Mandate and Scope	Define the focus for adjacent innovation and what capabilities to leverage	The mission is to launch bold initiatives that advance Oregon State's strategic goals and improve the university's financial strength + Work with key stakeholders to target specific domains and needs from the university's strategic plan to feed into structured ideation sessions for the annual opportunity selection process
Leadership and Culture	Leadership and culture to learn rapidly by discovering, building and testing solutions	Impact Studio reports at the Provost level to serve all colleges and administrative units and uses mature and proven methodologies + Selecting opportunities for Impact Studio to support innovation in the core expands support and contribution to culture change
Skill/Talent Development	Identifying, developing and retaining talent	Over 120 faculty, staff and students have engaged with Impact Studio, in some cases spanning multiple years + The goal is to integrate this experience into Oregon State's talent development programme
System Resources	Consistent and predictable funding for the strategic innovation function	The funding has been consistent and purposefully lean, contributing to a total portfolio break-even time of 4 years + The goal is to include funding targets for portfolio management and secure an endowment through philanthropic support
Organisational Structure and Interfaces	Consistent reporting structures and internal roles	The Impact Studio reporting structure to the Provost has provided the needed visibility and partnerships to achieve the mission + The Oregon State Board of Trustees, Foundation and other critical external partners are actively supporting Impact Studio

Table 18.4. (*Continued*)

System Components	Definition	Impact Studio Status and Recommendations
Governance and Decision-Making	High ambiguity decisions improve with diverse perspectives	Formed the Impact Studio Advisory Committee (ISAC) to advise the Provost and initiatives + An improvement is forming an external advisory board to expand engagement and investment
Process and Tools	The process and tools accelerate learning to reduce uncertainty	The process and tools represent several decades of research and application experience + Promote Oregon State as a thought leader in higher education innovation through conferences and publications
Portfolio Metrics	Specific metrics needed for a portfolio	Portfolio metrics are updated twice per year. + Integration of the portfolio into Oregon State's 10-year financial plan

Source: Impact Studio.

example, ideas for new initiatives have primarily come from academic and administrative units and leaders. Future ideation cycles will likely select a few target areas and broadly tap internal and external thought leaders in the ideation process.

18.4. Achievements of the Innovation Management System

18.4.1. *Performance versus goals for Impact Studio portfolio*

Over the first 3 years, Impact Studio has funded eight high-impact initiatives that deliver wide-ranging benefits for Oregon State and those served. Three of the eight initiatives target improvements in Oregon State's core activities. These are examples of using the Impact Studio methodology to accelerate incremental innovation. Table 18.5 summarises the results for the initiatives against Oregon State's portfolio criteria. The Impact Studio Advisory Committee applies the criteria during the initial selection process and then as the initiative moves through incubation, pilot and launch phases. After taking

Table 18.5. Impact Studio portfolio results.

Initiative	Phase & NRPV	External Impact	Culture Change	Teaching Mission	Building Capacity
Transfer Student Experience	Scale-up Core	1,000 students engaged to improve their experience	Used empathy-based approach with many units	Identified non-academic barriers for student success	Enhanced reputation and service for transfer students
Transfer Enrolment and Success Expansion	Scale-up Adjacent $41M	2,000+ students engaged, 234 matriculated, 6 community college partners	Brings together student success, community dev. and engagement	Achieves goal to expand student success and access	The partnerships open many new opportunities
Outdoor Recreation Economy	Scale-up Adjacent $44M	Leading the charge to address the workforce needs for a $430B sector	Building deep partnerships with industry and agencies	Achieves goal to expand student success and access	Building national partnerships in this sector
Capacity-Based Pricing	Scale-up Adjacent $28M	Non-resident students can access unique and highly ranked degrees	New approach to micro-target unique/ranked degree programmes	Identify/serve purpose-driven non-resident students	Leadership for highly targeted programmes

International Online	Pilot 2 Adjacent $30M	Significantly increases access for international students	Leverages three highly successful partners to build a new market	Expands the pedagogical approach for online students	All partners will develop their capacity to build a new market
Design for Societal Impact	Pilot 1 Adjacent $34M	Develops cross-disciplinary designers to address society's challenges	Cross-discipline client-based experiential learning programme	Serve students seeking technical education with design breadth	Expanded client and alumni engagement
University Financial Management	Pilot 1 Core	Colleges can optimise their impact within their budgets	Creating the tools and process for transparent decisions	Creates visibility for faculty to optimise their programmes	Develops financial acumen for strategic decisions
Pathways to OSU	Pilot 1 Core	Culturally responsive pre-college pathways for Black, Native and Latinx students	Broad partnership model with K-12, communities and families from 6th grade to alumni	Working directly with educators and communities on barriers to success and access	Developing a backbone to provide individualised resource access

Source: Impact Studio.

in the recommendation from the advisory committee, sponsors, core team and important initiative partners, the Provost makes the final decision.

External Impact evaluates whether the initiative will create a significant and broad impact in society that would not otherwise occur. *Culture Change* looks at whether the initiative provides broad and deep exposure to new methods and new ways of working with partners. The criteria for *Teaching Mission* evaluate how the initiative expands Oregon State's teaching offering in unique and impactful disciplines, modalities or audiences. Finally, *Building Capability* looks for how the initiative significantly expands capabilities and reputation that can be broadly leveraged for long-term growth and leadership.

The financial metric used for initiatives and the portfolio is Net Revenue Present Value (NRPV). NRPV represents the discounted net revenue over 10 years from each initiative. It is difficult, if not impossible, to forecast the financial impact for individual initiatives accurately. This is why building a diverse portfolio is so important. The portfolio goal is to select initiatives where the upside and uncertainties are uncorrelated. The Impact Studio portfolio has achieved a reasonable level of diversity. The plan is to grow the portfolio to 20 initiatives over the next 5 years to reach the portfolio level's desired predictability.

18.4.2. *Achieved capabilities*

Impact Studio deployed proven methodologies within a highly successful organisation. The most important capability is engaging faculty and staff with new ideas and nurturing them through a structured process. Oregon State is no longer dependent on the relatively rare champion that not only has a great idea but also has the wherewithal to move the idea forward through a complex organisational structure. Now, the idea champion only needs to find Impact Studio to provide an honest and realistic assessment. If promising, the process to move from an idea into the market is well understood. The specific capabilities offered by Impact Studio include ideation, human-centred design, opportunity divergence/convergence to open the design space, market landscape development, due diligence, solution co-design, financial analysis, investment proposal model and a structure to launch it through incubation, pilot and scale-up.

18.4.3. *Impacts on the innovation system beyond Impact Studio*

Impact Studio added new capabilities to Oregon State's innovation system. First, managing projects with high uncertainty is outside the norm for organisational leaders. The Impact Studio methodology helps communicate how to transparently manage high uncertainty and make the right decision to discontinue if the assumptions do not prove out. Working across multiple academic and administrative units is generally viewed as challenging from a political perspective. With Impact Studio as a neutral party, organisations come together around a shared opportunity. Developing Oregon State's talent is the most significant long-term contribution. Over 120 people have contributed to initiatives, including senior leaders, directors, department heads, faculty, administrative staff and student design interns. Working on an initiative is an immersive learning experience, and individuals share that they can apply these concepts more broadly.

18.5. Overall Reflections and Way Forward

18.5.1. *Fundamental parts — What makes a difference?*

Culture change underpins systemic innovation at the organisational level. Within the first month of forming Impact Studio, the Director met with over 100 university leaders to understand their top criteria for selecting adjacent initiatives. They identified that driving culture change is the second-highest priority for this work. The awareness from those leaders most embedded in the organisation turned out to be an excellent harbinger of the success to come. The ideas put forward for selection and the resulting initiatives and launched programmes reflect many advancements in breaking down cultural norms. For example, every one of the initiatives that have advanced involves multiple colleges and administrative units. It is normal for people to avoid leading an effort across this level of internal organisational complexity. Sponsoring Impact Studio in the Office of the Provost has reduced this barrier to internal collaboration.

Oregon State serves diverse audiences, and this trend is accelerating. Long gone are the days when most incoming students and their families walked through campus in celebration at convocation. Although the university still cherishes this tradition, it now has students, researchers and faculty located worldwide. Oregon State's students come from a vast array of cultural and socioeconomic backgrounds with a wealth of lived experiences. They are lifelong learners, taking ownership of their personal and professional growth via many online programmes while raising a family and holding down a job. They include learners who did not see themselves as college graduates, professionals changing careers, and traditional students who graduated high school and look forward to a campus experience. This diversity is core to Oregon State's mission and purpose. Moreover, it requires a higher level of expertise and capacity to understand and respond to their needs. Impact Studio is an important internal capacity to apply human-centred design methodologies to give the institution new tools to design for changing audiences' needs.

A subtle but fundamental aspect of this work within Oregon State is re-thinking and owning how to leverage its leading capabilities. It is easy to view the entire institution, its people and expertise through the broad and generalised ranking lens. The merits of institutional rankings aside, adjacent innovation operates at a much more granular level. The opportunities arise when we understand Oregon State's unique capabilities, and more importantly, how new combinations of those capabilities come together to lead the way in serving the needs of Oregon and beyond.

18.5.2. *Critical factors*

Impact Studio's focus is shifting to building a sustainable capability to serve Oregon State for the coming decades. Actions include:

- The majority of the investment must go towards launching initiatives. Some additional hiring is needed to provide sufficient initiative support as the portfolio grows to 20 initiatives.
- The Director serves on the Provost's senior leadership team and is responsible for the Impact Studio's portfolio performance, including setting metrics, tracking investments, and forecasting the net revenue

for Oregon State's budget. This includes engaging with the Oregon State Board of Trustees, the university's fundraising foundation and other external advisory groups to identify opportunities to create a venture fund to match Oregon State's investment.

- The cohort of student design interns is a critical resource for Impact Studio's success. The staffing will grow with the number of initiatives as well as positions for administrative support.
- The Impact Studio Advisory Committee is an essential function. The time required to serve on this Committee will grow as the portfolio grows, leading to changes in membership and position expectations.
- A best practice to achieve a sustainable growth portfolio is to engage committed external stakeholders. The Director will seek representation from Oregon State alumni, thought leaders and public sector stakeholders. Contributions include guiding Oregon State's strategic investigation areas, providing networking and mentorship for initiatives, advocating for the Oregon State portfolio approach, and supporting efforts to create a stable financial base and investment pool.
- Every employee that engages in an Impact Studio initiative is developing key leadership skills. A structured talent development plan will identify, develop and promote current Oregon State employees with the interest and capacity to lead this work.

References

IMCA (2019). *Innovation Management Capabilities Assessment.* SIS Swedish Institute for Standards.

ISO (2019). *ISO 56002:2019 Innovation management — Innovation management system — Guidance*. International Organization for Standardization.

Nagli, B. and Tuff, G. (2012). Managing Your Innovation Portfolio. *Harvard Business Review*, *90*(5), 66–74.

O'Connor, G., Corbett, A. and Peters, L. (2018). *Beyond the Champion.* Stanford, CA: Stanford Business Books.

© 2023 World Scientific Publishing Europe Ltd.
https://doi.org/10.1142/9781800612105_0019

Chapter 19

Sime Darby Plantation: A Top-Down Approach to Innovation Management in a State-Owned, Globally Integrated Plantation Company

Suraya Sulaiman, Azim Pawanchik, Law Zhi Xiong and Syakiratul Ezwana Shahrul Niza

Abstract

Based in Malaysia and operating in 16 countries, Sime Darby Plantation (SDP) is the world's largest oil palm plantation company. Its drivers to innovate include the sustainability focus and reducing dependency on foreign labour. As a 100-year-old large company, SDP operates in a hierarchical manner, relying on top-down decisions in their day-to-day operations. The study explores the challenges it faced in implementing a systematic innovation management process while drawing parallels to the ISO 56002 components to highlight how these were vital in ensuring the company's success in innovation. SDP's innovation journey begins from the inception of its Group Innovation Strategy Department in 2016, followed by new initiatives after its de-merger from the Sime Darby Group and its new innovation efforts in response to the recent COVID-19 pandemic. Several successful top-down initiatives are highlighted in this study, including the Innovation and Productivity Charter to create the urgency of achieving its goals, the Review Panel to oversee all innovation activities and the Value Creation process aimed at commercialising new ideas.

19.1. Introduction

Sime Darby Plantation (SDP) is the world's largest oil palm plantation company, producing about 3.3% of the global crude palm oil (CPO)

output. It is also the world's largest producer of Certified Sustainable Palm Oil (CSPO), accounting for around 20% market share of the world production by capacity (Sime Darby Plantation, 2018). As a globally integrated plantation company with operations across 16 countries (Sime Darby Plantation, 2020), SDP's business spans the full palm oil value chain, with offerings ranging from Upstream and Downstream activities to R&D, renewables and agribusiness.

The inception of the company can be traced back to Malaysia's British Colonial days in 1910, where it was founded as a rubber plantation by British businessmen William Sime, Henry Darby and Herbert Darby. Over the years, through many mergers, acquisitions and diversification, Sime Darby Berhad was incorporated in 1979 (Sime Darby Berhad, no date). This journey through two World Wars cemented its diversification into oil palm due to the threat from synthetic rubber. Along the way the company also secured sole dealerships within Asia for many global brands. In 2007, following the mergers of three plantation companies, Sime Darby, Guthrie and Golden Hope, SDP became the largest oil palm plantation in the world. After the merger, the plantation division was one of the major contributors to revenue and contributed 34% of Sime Darby Group's profit. Sime Darby Group was also one of the largest listed entities on the KL Stock Exchange. In 2017, following a major restructuring, SDP de-merged from the Sime Darby Group to become an independent listed entity.

SDP is considered a state-owned enterprise, through a majority controlling stake via Permodalan Nasional Berhad (PNB), a government backed sovereign fund and the Employees Provident Fund (EPF), the statutory body that manages saving and retirement plans of private workers in the country. As such, in addition to conventional business decisions, SDP is committed to national development activities, such as job creation, economic development and environmental issues. This means that decisions on large-scale innovation investments may not be made independently, as political and societal issues also need to be taken into consideration.

Operating with a strong Asian culture also means that employees are more tightly organised, and hierarchies are revered and well-respected. Valuing harmony and cohesiveness, challenging ideas of superiors are often frowned upon. This invites cognitive biases that may hinder innovation. Strong hierarchies also limit collaboration and make it challenging for ideas to surface from the employee level.

This case study was conducted by innovation management consultants in the region, based on insights gathered from direct experience from working with SDP and interviews with key employees and management within the company. Research was also conducted based on public domain information.

19.2. SDP's Innovation Management System

This chapter explores the creation of SDP's innovation system and its development over the years, up to 2020.

19.2.1. *Innovation before the de-merger*

Being part of a behemoth with five large divisions, SDP's journey into innovation was initiated in a big way by a structural change at the Group level to signal the intent for innovation to permeate more extensively throughout the organisation. This led to the inception of the Group Strategy and Innovation (GSI) Department in 2016.

External and internal challenges towards innovation

As with many other companies, SDP was no stranger to business challenges. At this stage, there were four main themes that concerned SDP: volatile CPO prices, climate change, pressure from NGOs on deforestation and regulations were impacting SDP, such as the ban on the use of palm oil in production of biofuels by the European Union. Alongside these were the long-standing rise of operational costs and heavy dependency on foreign labour, which made up 63% of their ground workers in Malaysia.

Adding to the external challenges mentioned above was the absence of a common understanding of what innovation meant within the company. Previously, innovation was predominantly associated with R&D, hence the language of "innovation" was not widespread in other departments. Secondly, there were no clear channels for employees to share their ideas, nor the culture to drive innovation within the company.

Taking the bull by the horns, the entire organisation was rallied to be involved when SDP kick-started innovation through three core actions. First was the creation of a clear process to evaluate innovation projects by employing a phase-gate methodology. Secondly, the launch of the Sime Darby Ideas Portal and the thirdly, the launch of a performance-driven cultural transformation initiative called RISE. Underlying these strategies was a clear target project portfolio, where the majority of projects planned were related to SDP's core business, with a smaller focus on adjacent and new projects. Clear financial targets were also set for the group revenue and group profit after tax and minority interest (PATAMI).

Phase-gate methodology to manage innovation

The phase-gate methodology was useful as it provided clear and uniform guidelines for project teams to execute their ideas. Given the high failure rates of ideas in the innovation process, it was important to review each project in phases, such that ideas that do not work can be shut down effectively at each gate. This allowed resources to be diverted to more promising alternatives. The Group's Strategy and Innovation Leadership Council (SiLC) was formed to assist in decision-making at each gate of the innovation process.

Ideas portal and innovation events

The launch of the Sime Darby Ideas Portal in late 2015 served as a formal channel for its then 135,000 employees to submit and rate each other's innovative ideas. The portal, which was launched at the company townhall by the President and Group CEO, proved to be a success, with 1,000 active users within the first 2 months of launching. The ability to comment on others' ideas on the portal also provided a key avenue of interaction between the top and senior management, with other staff.

In an effort to further drive adoption of the digital platform, internal hackathons were hosted. Some were open hackathons brandishing business challenges sponsored by the various departments. Others were more intense and focused on addressing specific issues. The latter brought in specifically selected employees and addressed issues such as customer-centricity and “plantations of the future.” One of the outcomes was the Sime Darby Connect app, which consolidated customer profiles and provided a unified experience across Sime Darby, unearthing cross-selling opportunities. Many actionable ideas relating to plantations of the future were also unearthed, catalysing SDP’s digital, mechanisation and automation endeavours.

Developing culture through RISE

To drive the enculturation and innovation mindset within the company, the third initiative that was launched was Results, Innovation, Sustainability and Energy (RISE), a performance-driven transformation initiative aimed to bolster innovation through a culture of accountability. There were six winning mindsets defined as part of RISE: Deliver Results, Customer First, Value Talent, Build Trust, Continuous Improvement and Empowered Decisions. Employees were able to provide each other instant recognition and feedback when they displayed any of these values. The instant positive feedback on the displayed behaviours and actions went a long way in terms of reinforcing the culture change.

Achievements and challenges

The initiatives implemented were successful in creating awareness among employees on innovation. However, the buy-in at a Group level was fragmented and innovation was not yet ingrained into the company’s day-to-day activities. The organisation also faced challenges in gaining sustainable traction to the Ideas Portal, due to the lack of insistence from supervisors to contribute, in addition to employees’ unfamiliarity with the process. The rate of new projects being implemented was also low. While SDP found great success in innovating within its core business and where direct engagements were done, they had to adopt a very judicious approach to develop and scale more disruptive ideas. The focus of the company at this point was to ensure that there were sufficient projects in the pipeline, while prioritising high-impact projects in its core business.

19.2.2. *Innovation after the de-merger*

After the de-merger in 2017, SDP's innovation which had previously been managed at a Group level was now executed at the company level. This allowed a more intense focus in communication and execution, as well as greater independence in decision-making. The Ideas Portal was relaunched as Innovation Portal in March 2018 as a channel for employees to share new ideas related to the business, suggest process or operational improvements, or even propose new business models. In addition to this, SDP added the following initiatives to take its innovation activities up a notch.

Innovation and Productivity Charter

This document highlighted the company's commitment to innovation as a means of reducing environmental footprint, using more renewable resources and recyclable materials, while optimising its ability to meet increasing global demand for palm oil. Led by the Plantation Leadership Board, the Innovation and Productivity Charter was crucial in bolstering the urgency to innovate within the company (Sime Darby Plantation, no date).

As part of the charter, the Transformation Office (TO) and the Operational Excellence and Innovation Business Management Strategy (OEIBMS) 2.0 were set up, where OEIBMS 2.0 focused on strategic stewardship, tactical development of capacity and competency, as well as cultural transformation to achieve the Charter's objectives. Clear and quantifiable targets were also set, for the company to achieve MYR 550 million (US$136 million) in cumulative operational excellence benefits by FY2022, via measures including cost savings, improved revenue generation and sustainability performance. The TO was created to drive, track and monitor the Charter's initiatives.

Some of the efforts in this direction have already borne fruit, paving the way for SDP to achieve its targets. One of the outcomes was an open access online platform that traces the company's supply to the mill level, increasing accountability of mills such that they do not participate in illegal deforestation. Bolstering this effort, the GenomeSelect initiative was launched, which created a new palm breed that enabled a yield improvement of at least 15%, allowing an increase of production without increasing land clearance.

RISE to APEX

In December 2018, the RISE initiative was combined with SDP's value creation programme, APEX (Accelerating Performance Excellence). While RISE focused on the cultural transformations, APEX aimed at accelerating the performance of core businesses through results-driven initiatives. APEX monitored and fast-tracked high value, quick turnaround initiatives through a structured and vigorous execution process. These activities were overseen by the TO, who was the custodian of APEX to ensure effective planning, development and timely delivery of the projects (Sime Darby Plantation, 2019).

Among the activities rolled out were the Idea Generation Workshops, which saw a total of 1,603 ideas generated within the seven work streams across the global operations. From these, a total of 522 initiatives were validated. Subsequently, 91 initiatives successfully reached the implementation stage, while 14 initiatives were commercialised. Complementing these were roadshows and innovation forums to recognise employees' outstanding performances in relation to the projects. A monthly internal publication called *MindQuest* was also created to keep employees up to date on the trending innovation news both within and outside the company.

Plantation Innovation Committee and Value Creation process

Recognising the value that committees offered to the oversight process, SDP continued with the measure by setting up the Plantation Innovation Committee (PIC). Its members consisted of cross-functional leaders that served as the first gatekeepers of SDP's idea incubation and development pipeline. With committee members which included, among others, the Chief Financial Officer (CFO), Chief R&D Officer (CRDO) and Chief Strategy & Innovation Officer (CSIO), it was responsible for evaluating any new ideas that came through the Innovation Portal. Employees were required to pitch their ideas to the PIC, and viable ideas were subsequently moved forward to the Value Creation (VC) process.

The VC process was a six phase (L0-L5), tailored phase-gate process utilised to monitor the implementation of ideas from ideation (L0) to profit creation (L5). At L1 a trial is conducted, followed by creation and impact analysis, project roll out, project completion and finally the profit creation at L5. Any project fed into the VC process is overseen by the TO.

In an effort to create a safe environment for innovation, the PIC was less stringent on the evaluation of ideas pitched. The Innovation Team, which was driving the innovation activities, would also offer guidance on aspects of idea development, such as financial modelling prior to the actual pitch. This not only ensured ideas were not killed off too early in the process, but also encouraged employees to come up with more disruptive solutions.

In the scaling stage, the PIC assisted the project owner in convincing business units to adopt their ideas. The credibility of the committee was crucial in this case to remove any friction which sometimes arose during implementation.

19.2.3. *Achievements and challenges through innovation*

SDP's innovation efforts thus far were successful due to extremely strong support from the Board and top management, evidenced by the numerous initiatives developed over the years. Their innovation efforts also yielded them global recognition.

In January 2019, the company's internal "War on Waste" programme was awarded the "Most Innovative Approach to Driving Culture Change" at the OPEX Business Transformation World Summit in the USA. Meanwhile, its Renewables team won the PNB Group Innovation Challenge (PGIC) with an idea involving the usage of Multistage Turbines to generate higher power output at mills. SDP's Process Rationalisation Labs, which were focused on operational efficiency, were also successful in implementing 18 initiatives to improve efficiencies via tender processes, reports and HQ visits, reducing time spent on these activities by 66%.

During this period, some of the disruptive ideas that emerged include a beverage product made from the palm fruit, which challenged the notion that the fruit was only useful for oil production. Others include a game created in partnership with university students to boost awareness on sustainable palm oils, which was a novel approach towards public education.

While evidence of success was abundant, innovation activities were still sporadic in nature, with higher activity seen in departments such as R&D, Operations and Digital. Ideas which were not central to the company's competencies were also more challenging to be accepted and commercialised.

A PIC committee member noted that there were not many organic innovation activities outside the organised events and only employees who were working on innovation projects had innovation as part of their KPI. The main challenges faced by employees were time constraints for idea development, support from their respective direct supervisors, as well as difficulties in building the right team to execute their ideas. Teams also recognised that they faced many gaps in terms of knowledge around product development, such as packaging, business models and marketing strategies.

19.3. Evolution in Response to the COVID-19 Pandemic

In March 2020, Malaysia went into total lockdown in response to the pandemic. With the new norm being that most of the office-based employees were working from home, SDP had to devise new approaches to ensure success in the increasingly volatile business environment.

The new circumstances further accelerated the need for SDP to switch its innovation focus to address rising costs and dependency on foreign labour. With support from the Board, there is now greater emphasis on addressing issues relating to cost reduction, digitalisation and automation of its operations.

19.3.1. *Renewed focus of the Innovation Portal*

As part of the reinvigoration, the Innovation Portal was relaunched to highlight the larger scope of the digital platform. New functionalities were added to enable a more comprehensive management of ideas and projects. Features such as the dashboard monitoring interface and push notifications from the portal will enable a more profound engagement of employees. In order to remove redundancies and increase traction, all pitching processes are now done on the portal.

Taking cue from previous experience, SDP is also embarking on a more collaborative and decentralised approach towards driving participation on the portal. SDP created the role of "Innovation INfluencer" whose responsibilities include promoting innovation activities, conducting engagement workshops and acting as the communication liaison between their respective departments and regional areas with the centrally located Innovation Team.

Investing in the development of the INfluencers was an important agenda for SDP. As part of their onboarding, INfluencers attended an innovation management training certification to build proficiency in the innovation techniques and processes, such as ideation and prototyping. Recognising the importance of culture in enabling innovation, the INfluencers are also responsible for spreading the innovation culture and driving collaboration via the Portal.

19.3.2. *Renewed role of leaders*

Coupling the augmentations in the Innovation Portal was a shift in the committee that oversees the innovation projects. The PIC was renamed as the Innovation Technical and Review Panel (ITRP), and now works closely with Group Digital. Members of the panel still include the CRDO, CSIO, with new additions being the Group Managing Director, Managing Director for Sime Darby Oils and the CEO of Upstream Indonesia. Their responsibilities remain unchanged, where they evaluate ideas on the Innovation Portal, approve funding for proof of concepts, and endorse new technologies and innovations. Recognising their strengths in overseeing projects core to their business, they are exploring more projects in adjacent and new realms. The ITRP meets quarterly to review and stay updated on innovation activities within the company. The TO was also renamed as the Results Delivery Office (RDO), where they continue to oversee the VC process.

The Company's CSIO expressed a desire to drive innovation through "pull factors" as opposed to hard KPIs. This was translated to using intrinsic motivation to encourage participation. As such, innovation will be encouraged as a means of gaining exposure to top decision-makers in the company, as well as an opportunity to network and collaborate with colleagues. In addition, the CSIO will craft a compelling raison d'être for why everyone should gravitate towards the portal to contribute their ideas, especially those revolving around cost reduction, digitalisation and automation of its operations.

Adding to this will be a series of innovation training sessions for leaders and innovators within the company to reinforce the knowledge and competencies on innovation. A checkpoint assessment on where the company as a whole is in terms of innovation leadership, strategy, capability, culture and process is also planned for later in the year.

19.3.3. *Integrating open innovation*

While ideas were readily accepted by the Innovation Team, the employees found that it was challenging to find support to flesh out ideas that are not of the company's core competencies. In the case of the palm fruit-based beverage, employees required additional expertise with regards to marketing, packaging and branding to fully develop and commercialise their ideas. While the team was successful in securing a grant from external parties to fund some of these efforts, it was very challenging as they did not have much experience in the area.

In light of this, SDP is adopting new approaches to tap into open innovation via external parties such as government agencies, start-ups and universities. This is achieved by the setting up of an open innovation platform to foster collaboration. This effort will prove to be extremely useful as the company approaches its collaborators on adopting new technologies, or in complementing the gaps in expertise.

19.4. Achievements of the Innovation Management System

It is important to note how SDP's initial innovation process evolved into a more comprehensive innovation management system. While early efforts revolved heavily around building the culture, context and leadership, subsequent efforts gave more emphasis to the process and support required.

19.4.1. *Mapping the system components to those of ISO 56002*

While not deliberate, SDP's strategy towards implementing innovation within the organisations highlighted many parallels with ISO 56002 (ISO, 2019) components. These have particularly surfaced well in the following three areas.

Context and conditions

SDP demonstrated a strong understanding of external trends and drivers that serve as the company's innovation purpose. In addition to managing ongoing challenges in sustainability and price volatility, the company was quick to identify new focus areas necessary to remain competitive in the business. In response to the pandemic, SDP acknowledged the urgency to embrace digitalisation and automation as key innovation efforts while experimenting on new technologies such as drones, robotics and AI.

Enabling the innovation effort was a strong top-down culture which encouraged creativity and empowered the staff while supporting deployment of initiatives, evidenced by RISE to APEX. This was also somewhat evident at the middle management level, where hackathon winners revealed that their managers encouraged their efforts, giving them time and additional resources to further their ideas.

The presence of the online digital platform for idea submission was equally a game changer towards overcoming the bureaucracy and hierarchical challenges as it flattened the company structure, while providing the level of transparency and recognition that are always crucial to innovation. This was supplemented by pitching to a cross-functional committee for decision-making, ensuring that ideas are evaluated without cognitive bias.

Cognisant of the internal capabilities of employees, management had also prioritised advancing employee knowledge around innovation through various training, certification programmes and relevant exposure.

Leadership

The company's success in innovation could be largely attributed to its strong top-down visionary leadership. SDP's vision and strategy manifested through its Innovation and Productivity Charter, which was combined with the company's resolve to push forward on the innovation agenda and align the entire organisation towards a common innovation direction.

This was evidenced by the presence of key top management in the PIC, TO and more recently the RDO and ITRP. Overcoming stumbling points along the way, leaders in the company were relentless in championing innovation. The fruits of their labour were evident in the form of SDP's strong innovation capabilities and recognitions. Leaders in SDP continue to enhance its strategy towards embedding innovation within the company to improve VC.

In the execution phase, oversight of the selected projects under the supervision and support of the RTO and ITRP via the VC process, up to commercialisation or deployment, was vital as it signalled the endorsement from the highest level for these projects. The involvement of top leaders in the process also paved the way for a heightened level of acceptance of radical ideas within the company.

Processes

The Innovation Portal adopted by SDP served well to provide structure towards the realisation of ideas conceived. With each of the steps, from identifying opportunities, to generating concepts and plans, validating the ideas and concepts, to enabling them to be developed and deployed as valuable solutions, they are all evident on the portal. This was crucial to remove any confusion among employees regarding the process, especially in a large organisation such as SDP. The consolidation also avoided any duplicated projects within the company.

Allowing employees to collaborate and interact on the same platform was also beneficial at the opportunity identification and concept creation phase. A common platform where employees could view, comment and build on each other's ideas meant that SDP could rely on its collective intelligence to bring forward high value ideas. Promising ideas were methodologically funnelled through the pitching and VC process. This disciplined approach, combined with the clear criteria for idea selection, was vital in ensuring innovation flourished without breaking the bank.

In addition to R&D activities, SDP organised Hackathons, Idea Labs and other activities that served as additional prompts for collaboration and idea development.

19.4.2. *Development opportunities for a total innovation management system*

While SDP has had success in the aforementioned aspects of the ISO standard, there are some strategies which could strengthen its existing innovation management system.

Support

In an effort to fully harness the innovation capabilities of the larger pool of employees, guidance in developing more compelling solutions, which are aligned with the overall company strategy or have direct impact on the current operations, are essential. These should also explore the realm of more radical innovation to push SDP ahead of competitors. As such, a more intense, consistent and concerted communication and advocacy from all leaders within the various departments of SDP on the paramountcy for all employees to contribute would be helpful in permeating the message throughout the company.

The impact from shifting towards a decentralised approach, appointing INfluencers to trigger more participation from the various departments and to provide more comprehensive guidance for contributors, is good. Ideally, there should also be involvement from "experienced" innovators to provide additional assistance. An option here is to have an avenue to tap on an external network of "specialists" as mentors for selected projects to assist with aspects of business models, product positioning, pitching, etc.

Performance evaluation, improvement and planning

SDP had already begun measuring impact and value generated from the projects that were initiated. Adopting a "carrot" rather than "stick" approach, SDP has plans set to intensify the rewards garnered from participation on the innovation platform, incorporating gamification strategies, where each action on the platform is tied to a reward. For this strategy to blossom into a sustained effort, it needs to be communicated strategically throughout the organisation. Tactfully highlighting successful achievements, and contributions from various employees. A misstep could mean that employees may instead shun the platform.

Taking into consideration the level of analytics that are possible on the innovation platform, it may bode well for the ITRP to analyse performance by departments to learn which are doing well and why so. Successful elements could then be replicated in other departments, and the communication process of onboarding more employees to the platform could also be tweaked.

The ITRP currently looks into aspects of planning, evaluation and improvement during their quarterly meetings, which are already inundated with other agendas such as following up on ongoing projects (which would be increasing over time), and endorsement of new technologies. For changes to be more dynamic, a more robust and short-term feedback loop may prove beneficial to develop a more refined and proactive approach to innovation. These can leverage the real-time data analytics. Remote decision-making will hasten judgements, facilitating more dynamic pivot points where required. Additionally, there should be an active attempt to ensure that emerging trends are always in the line of vision of the company leaders, so that opportunities would not be missed.

19.5. Reflections and Way Forward

SDP demonstrated that a combination of strong commitment from the top management, coupled with a clear innovation vision and a methodological review process at the various stages within the innovation cycle, can serve as effective innovation management strategies.

Organisations that are more traditional and hierarchical in nature will find these methods applicable. In cases where the number of employees is large, these top-down initiatives will be effective in ensuring the call to innovation is well communicated through all levels of the organisation. Involvement and visibility of top managers is crucial and cannot be understated, in boosting morale and ensuring radical ideas are championed.

Building on these initiatives, organisations should also develop clear innovation policies that document the idea selection criteria, the necessary steps to pitch, as well as methods to seek support and drive projects to completion. This is crucial to ensure that there is alignment on the innovation process, especially when employees are expected to work in a cross-collaborative manner in a large organisation such as SDP. Clear allocation of budgets and criteria to secure these are similarly essential for facilitating a swift decision, while maintaining transparency in the process.

In an effort to ensure a constant stream of fresh ideas, organisations should also seek to spark innovation beyond *ad-hoc* hackathons and other one-off events. Leaders should look to incorporate innovation into the employee's daily activities, via KPIs or otherwise, while providing the required support and resources. This would ensure that innovation is embedded as part of the organisation culture over time.

Another item to consider is the ability to convert disruptive ideas into value. As a company's innovation maturity grows, its challenges shift from the idea generation stage to the VC stage, especially for the commercialisation and scaling of ideas that go beyond its core competencies. The right processes and infrastructure, including clear guidelines on open innovation, will need to be set up for these disruptive ideas to bloom, strengthening the company's innovation capabilities. Having a clear portfolio of projects — what is core to the business, and what is new — is equally essential so that management can have a pulse on the organisation project pipeline, ensuring that it keeps up with shifting ecosystem trends and market needs.

References

ISO (2019). *ISO 56002:2019 Innovation management — Innovation management system — Guidance*. International Organization for Standardization.

Sime Darby Berhad (n.d.). *History: Sime Darby Berhad*, https://www.simedarby.com/company/history.

Sime Darby Plantation (n.d.). *Sime Darby Plantation Innovation and Productivity Charter*. Sime Darby Plantation, https://simedarbyplantation.com/wp-content/uploads/2021/12/SD-Plantation-2018-Sustainability-Report.pdf.

Sime Darby Plantation (2018). *Sime Darby Plantation Becomes The Largest MSPO Producer To-Date*, https://simedarbyplantation.com/sime-darby-plantation-becomes-the-largest-mspo-producer-to-date/.

Sime Darby Plantation (2019). *Annual Report: 6-Month Financial Period Ended 31st December 2018*. Sime Darby Plantation, https://www.insage.com.my/Upload/Docs/SIMEPLT/SIMEPLT%20FP2018.PDF#view=Full&pagemode=bookmarks.

Sime Darby Plantation (2020). *Annual Report 2019*. Sime Darby Plantation, https://www.insage.com.my/Upload/Docs/SIMEPLT/SIMEPLT%20FY2019.pdf#view=Full&pagemode=bookmarks.

© 2023 World Scientific Publishing Europe Ltd.
https://doi.org/10.1142/9781800612105_0020

Chapter 20

Södra Skogsägarna: The Sustainable Innovator

Catrin Gustavsson, Dan Oscarson and Magnus Karlsson*

Abstract

This chapter describes and analyses the development of innovation management capabilities at Södra, a large forestry group based in the southern part of Sweden, between 2014 and 2020. Applying the framework of "ISO 56002:2019 Innovation management — Innovation management system — Guidance," on the different aspects of innovation management at Södra reveals that most of the critical elements of the system have been addressed to various degrees. Driven by both necessity and opportunity, the new innovation strategy and process from 2014 paved the way for focused strategic innovation arenas and roadmaps that were instrumental for the innovation achievements during the period of this case study. With even more significant innovation challenges ahead, foremost related to the transition to a circular and bio-based economy, Södra has identified the next iteration of improvements to its innovation management system that can include an even more focused strategic direction for innovation, stronger top management commitment, clarified roles and responsibilities and improved communication efforts.

20.1. Introducing Södra Skogsägarna

Södra Skogsägarna, or just Södra, is a large forest industry group based in the southern part of Sweden. It is also the largest economic forestry

*Corresponding author.

association in Sweden, with more than 53,000 independent forest owners as members.

Södra was founded in 1938 and started to invest in its own pulp mills in the late 1950s since the needs of the sawmills did not provide a sufficiently big market for the increasing growth of the more and more professionally run forests. The three pulp mills at Mönsterås, Mörrum and Värö led the expansion in international markets and are still part of the core business.

Today, Södra has about 3,100 employees in Sweden and internationally, with sales amounting to €2.3 billion in 2019. The group was then organised in three business areas: Södra Cell — paper pulp, bioproducts; Södra Wood — wood products and building systems and Södra Skog — forestry management. In this way, Södra has control over the entire value chain from "seed" to customer. Södra is also a producer of energy since the group produces more electricity than it uses.

Södra has invested in research and development (R&D) to various degrees since the mid-1980s. This has resulted in increased technical know-how, process optimisations, environmental efficiency, product improvements and the development of new product and process innovations. Several projects were linked to Södra's sustainability targets for fossil-free production and transportation. It also included new and sustainable products based on renewable raw materials. Building systems, biomethanol and textile pulp are some examples of successful innovations.

Södra also funds external research and innovation projects through the Södra Foundation for Research, Development and Education. The foundation has received €30 million in contributions since its establishment in 1995 and funded more than 200 projects.

The most recent group strategy from 2020 puts a focus on sustainability, profitability, resource efficiency, digitalisation, as well as on new products and innovations. Södra's product portfolio mainly comprises high-volume products, such as pulp and sawn timber. Innovations in existing product areas and increased processing are an essential part of the strategy.

At the same time, Södra will continue to invest considerable resources in bringing new and innovative products to market. The commitment to efficient commercialisation of new offerings with clear commercial potential will increase. Södra's ambition is to strengthen its position in the bioeconomy by using every part of the tree to create value (Södra, 2020; Rushton, 2020).

The purpose of this chapter is to describe and analyse the development of innovation management capabilities at Södra between 2014 and 2020 using the management system framework of ISO 56002 (ISO, 2019) and to relate those capabilities to its innovation performance.

This chapter has been authored based on selected external references and publicly available information but even more importantly on internal documents and memos from Södra and the knowledge and experience of the authors of this chapter from Södra Innovation and New Business.

20.2. Towards an Innovation Management System

During the period between 2014 and 2020, Södra established several key capabilities taking the shape of an innovation management system. The core element was the innovation strategy that was developed during 2014 and implemented in early 2015.

20.2.1. *Innovation vision, strategy and governance*

As part of the strategy work, an innovation vision for Södra was established: Södra is an innovative company that launches new and sustainable offerings on the market and creates new businesses.

Several strategic innovation areas of opportunities were identified, and a number of scenarios for new products, services and businesses were developed in each area. A significant contribution to the overall business was predicted, conditioned by a specific investment level and an updated financing model. The new model stipulated that external research and the development of new products and services should be centrally financed. Each business area should fund the development and improvement of existing products and processes. Cross-functional coordination was secured by two new decision-making fora.

20.2.2. *Strategic roadmaps and planning*

The strategic innovation areas, or innovation arenas, were: (1) Forest, (2) Sawn Timber, (3) Paper Pulp, (4) Textiles, (5) Chemicals, and (6) Energy. Each innovation arena was developed over time, in an iterative manner, into a strategic roadmap by a dedicated team of technology and innovation experts. The purpose of the strategic roadmaps was to guide the daily work and specific actions needed to implement the overall innovation strategy. They should also contribute to awareness, understanding, and engagement internally to ensure a joint mission and alignment across different parts of the organisation. Finally, the roadmaps fulfilled the important purpose of guiding the allocation of resources to maximise benefits for the company.

Each strategic roadmap included a clearly defined scope of the arena, an analysis of the external context, including technologies, markets, customers, competitors and sustainability impact, an analysis of the internal conditions of Södra, including current activities, processes, business models, partners, patents and other assets and resources, a description of the vision for the arena, including a set of detailed focus areas with innovation objectives, an analysis of possible long-term future scenarios, an analysis of the relationship between the arena and the overall group business and sustainability strategy of Södra, and finally, a detailed action plan with roles, responsibilities and key performance indicators for each of the detailed focus areas within the innovation arena.

The different detailed focus areas of each arena were categorised according to the decided strategic approach: Offensive — Södra should be a proactive leader, Opportunistic — Södra should look for the right opportunity or timing to invest, Imitating — Södra should source developed solutions externally, or Monitoring — Södra should follow developments reactively.

The innovation arenas have continuously been updated based on strategic intelligence, customer insights and extended external collaboration.

The innovation arenas were mainly driven by Södra Innovation and New Business together with the business areas, but also in partnerships with customers and in external networks with universities, research institutes and companies further upstream in various value chains.

20.2.3. *Innovation process, projects, planning and context*

The development of the new innovation process was guided by some requirements. The process should increase the commercial focus in the early stages, establish a common and unified view of the different innovation projects, and clarify the responsibilities for the different stages of the process. The overall purpose was to increase the innovation capability of Södra.

The new process had four main phases:

(1) **Strategy** — The starting point for the innovation process was the innovation strategy that in turn supported the group business strategy.
(2) **Arena development** — Roadmaps were developed for each innovation arena with a situation analysis, desired outcomes and key activities as outlined above. Insights and ideas were captured from employees and customers.
(3) **Selection process** — Ideas and concepts developed related to the innovation arenas were evaluated based on the current situation, business potential and critical factors for implementation. Specific tools were developed to support evaluation and prioritisation.
(4) **Project phase** — Projects with an appointed sponsor and allocated resources were established following the selection process. Two different process methods were used depending on the type of project: the process for the development of new businesses or the process for developing existing businesses.

A strategic intelligence process was also established with a focus on market trends and other external issues. With the new processes, the governance of innovation projects was also simplified.

20.2.4. *Innovation indicators and follow-up*

The project portfolio was followed up in a systematic way by Södra Innovation and New Business to ensure a balance between different arenas, phases and risk levels.

A set of key performance indicators were established to monitor, analyse and evaluate the performance of the innovation process: total investments in research, development and innovation in relation to overall business revenues, number of ongoing projects per focus area and process stage, the total amount of expected commercial value, portfolio balance between research, development and innovation projects, the share of sales from new products and services, and the number of new ideas handed over from external research and strategic intelligence.

20.2.5. *Collaboration*

Attracting new talent was one reason for Södra to establish partnerships on various issues with several universities and other partners. One example was the cooperation between Södra and Chalmers University of Technology within the research cluster group AvanCell established in 2005. Several new technologies and innovations have emerged through external collaboration, including kraft pulping kinetics and cellulose dissolution and regeneration.

Working closely with customers has been another vital collaboration approach. Södra Innovation and New Business has been working with individual customers on their specific improvement and innovation issues. Customers are also a source of insights into future needs. Close collaboration between the innovation team and technical product managers has been one way to capture insights and ideas.

20.2.6. *Leadership and innovation culture*

The new strategic direction had to be supported by the right organisational culture. With a broad innovation mission covering the range from incremental to radical innovation across the three business areas, all parts of the organisation and its employees had to do their part. In the words of Catrin Gustavsson, Head of Södra Innovation and New Business: "I want to ensure a culture that allows mistakes, where employees take responsibility and know they are trusted. I encourage people to dare to test." A secure and supportive environment was important to dare to try and to learn from mistakes.

To better understand the relationship between culture and leadership at Södra, a values survey was conducted in 2020 supplemented with selected in-depth interviews. The assessment included several leaders and managers across the Södra group. The analysis from the study found several strong values, including curiosity, exploration, flexibility and change, that were part of the organisational culture. It was also noted that productivity, rationality and growth were rated high values that are beneficial to support operational activities but might be a challenge for encouraging innovation activities.

20.2.7. *Summary of key elements*

Applying the framework of ISO 56002 Innovation Management System — Guidance (ISO, 2019) on the different aspects of innovation management at Södra reveals that most of the key elements of the system have been addressed to various degrees.

An understanding of the external and internal context was instrumental for establishing the innovation vision and strategy as well as for the different innovation arenas and the planning of the detailed focus areas of each arena. Collaboration and organisational culture were proactively addressed as part of the innovation strategy.

A degree of top management commitment was established as the new innovation strategy took shape with dedicated funding, organisational structures and roles and responsibilities. Furthermore, innovation activities were planned by means of strategic innovation arenas that provided strategic focus and clear objectives with a portfolio approach. Innovation projects were executed using a defined process with shared methods and tools and commonly agreed on performance indicators.

20.3. Implementing Innovation Management Capabilities

20.3.1. *Investments in R&D and innovation activities*

Södra has built innovation management capabilities in a systematic and step-by-step manner. A central R&D unit with a focus on paper pulp was created in 2005 at the Värö plant, and at the same time, collaboration activities were initiated with Chalmers University of Technology. Södra invested about 0.6% of its revenues in R&D at the time, equal to the level of some competitors.

The R&D unit was reorganised in 2010 and formed a new group function, reporting to the CEO. The scope of the new function was extended beyond paper pulp to cover all business areas of Södra. The name of the function eventually became Södra Innovation and New Business to emphasise its broader mandate.

This development was part of a more extensive industry transformation, driven by both opportunity and necessity, to go beyond papermaking and diversify into new areas. The transformation was triggered by technology shifts as well as profoundly new market conditions. Decreasing demand for traditional paper products and increased interest in alternatives to fossil fuels opened up an innovation space for industry players, including Södra (see, for example, Novotny, 2016).

20.3.2. *Developing the innovation strategy*

Södra developed its first group innovation strategy in 2014. This work was triggered by challenges that were identified during the overall strategy work the year before when it was decided to make innovation and new products a strategic focus area. Södra had been investing considerable resources in R&D but experienced difficulties in commercialising the results from these activities. For example, some innovation projects with low potential had been kept alive for too long, using valuable resources, before closing them down.

Two reasons were identified behind these challenges: the lack of a common innovation strategy for the group and the lack of an efficient innovation process to guide development all the way to market launch. A clear and well-aligned innovation strategy should ensure that resources were used more strategically and efficiently. The innovation process should involve the whole of Södra, where the different parts of the organisation could contribute to different phases. Finally, the structure, governance and funding of the project portfolio should be clarified and established.

20.3.3. *Implementing the new innovation setup*

The new innovation setup was implemented during 2014 and 2015. To reach the strategic goals, it was decided at an early stage to focus on a few selected projects and take them through the innovation process. Two things were achieved with this approach. First, the process was developed and improved based on practical innovation work. And second, the selected projects contributed to the strategic goals related to new products and value creation from innovation efforts.

Several important investments were made during 2017 to boost the innovation agenda, for example, related to cross-laminated timber (CLT) and biomethanol. Both these product areas were handed over to the line organisation at Södra Wood in 2019 and Södra Cell in 2020, respectively.

The overall results of the new innovation setup are a higher degree of commercialisation of ideas and research results, improved and more efficient innovation processes, and more detailed and insightful strategic roadmaps as part of the defined innovation arenas.

The goal of more commercially oriented innovation activities was achieved. At the same time, the innovation projects have contributed to the objectives of the sustainability agenda. Two examples are fossil-free solutions and increased resource efficiency.

20.3.4. *Sustainability as an innovation driver*

Forests are essential for the global transition to a circular economy and can deliver sustainable products and solutions. These include, for example, clothing, new packaging materials, various types of filters and vehicle fuels.

According to Magnus Björkman, president of Södra Cell, "Not only does our industry absorb huge amounts of CO_2 growing our forests, we also have the product "substitution effect," where we are replacing products that are much higher in CO_2, for instance, steel or concrete for construction" (Rushton, 2020).

Södra aimed to commercialise at least three products with better sustainability performance than currently available alternatives until 2020. Product areas included next-generation biofuels, replacing oil-based chemicals with bio-based chemicals, and identifying new material concepts. In 2019, the goal was reached as Södra had in the past few years commercialised five new products with improved sustainability performance. Another five products were launched during 2020.

20.4. Innovation Achievements

The systematic build-up of innovation management capabilities at Södra between 2014 and 2020 has resulted in several commercially viable innovations. Three examples are textiles, biomethanol and building systems.

20.4.1. *Textiles from forest fibres*

Södra Cell has been producing dissolving pulp since 2012. The pulp is used to make cellulose-based textile fibres, such as viscose and lyocell. Using this technology, forest-based fabrics can replace synthetic fibres and cotton.

Only a very small proportion of the global production of clothing and textiles is recycled. The vast majority is either incinerated or sent to landfills. Södra was the first in the world to introduce industrial-scale recycling of textile fibres from blended fabrics. Södra has specifically developed the "OnceMore" technique for recycling textiles. It was launched in 2019 and produced at the Mörrum mill.

The recycled textiles are used to make new dissolving pulp, which can then become new viscose and lyocell. The solution enables circular flows in the fashion and textile industry. Södra is building a network of partners and other stakeholders to provide transparency and traceability throughout the value chain.

In 2019, Södra received their Recycled Claim Standard (RCS) certificate, and in 2020 Södra won the Encouragement for Action sustainability award in the "Closing the Loop" category for a more circular fashion industry based on the OnceMore innovation.

The process technology used was developed by Södra Innovation and New Business in collaboration with external partners as part of the strategic innovation arena textiles. Several Södra-owned patents have been the result of this work. Currently, the Södra Research Foundation is funding external projects with RISE Research Institutes of Sweden and Chalmers University to further develop textile recycling (Södra, 2020).

20.4.2. *Energy from biomethanol*

Energy accounts for a considerable share of Södra's operations, with products such as district heating, electricity, pellets, tall oil and bark. In 2020, Södra Cell inaugurated the world's first fossil-free biomethanol production plant at the pulp mill in Mönsterås.

Methanol is a liquid biofuel that can replace fossil fuels, providing further use for forest products. Biomethanol can be used as a stand-alone fuel, as a raw material for the production of biodiesel, or as a fuel additive. The production of biomethanol is a resource-efficient way to extract more products from the raw materials used in the paper pulp process. Biomethanol processing has been developed as part of the strategic innovation arena energy (Södra, 2020; Rushton, 2020).

20.4.3. *Multi-storeyed constructions from wood*

Building systems is a growing business within Södra Wood. The main product is cross-laminated timber (CLT), and it allows for large solid wood constructions with up to 18–19 floors.

Compared with concrete, using CLT for construction has many benefits, including lower CO_2 emissions, lighter transportation and shorter construction times. Södra opened its first CLT facility at Värö in 2019.

Apart from the wood products, Södra Building Systems also includes services related to design, construction and logistics, covering the entire value chain. The strategy is to deliver turn-key solutions together with partners. This business was developed from the strategic innovation arena sawn timber.

20.5. Way Forward

With the purpose to further strengthen the innovation efforts of Södra, a strategic initiative was launched during 2020. The goal was to update the innovation strategy with regard to ambition level and prioritised innovation areas. The initiative also included a management review to identify challenges and opportunities to be able to increase innovation management capabilities, including innovation culture and external collaboration activities.

The management review was conducted using the framework of the Innovation Management Capabilities Assessment (IMCA, 2019). It is a maturity model published by SIS Swedish Institute for Standards based on "ISO 56002 Innovation management — Innovation management system — Guidance" (ISO, 2019). The model comprises 24 capabilities related to the different key elements of the innovation management system rated on a maturity scale from one to five.

Södra Innovation and New Business led the initiative involving representatives from Södra Cell, Wood and Skog. Workshops and interviews were held with top management and other key managers. One part of the initiative had a specific focus on culture and leadership, relating to two of the eight innovation management principles of "ISO 56000:2020 Innovation management — Fundamentals and vocabulary" (ISO, 2020).

The assessment identified several strong capabilities, including innovation collaboration, culture, strategy, portfolio and project management, as well as innovation processes and related tools and methods. Some areas were prioritised as important for further improvement, for example, clarifying roles and responsibilities, including the role of top management, and communicating innovation activities and achievements to further boost engagement, culture and collaboration. In March 2021, the new business area Södra Innovation was established to reflect the increased importance of innovation efforts and the new innovation strategy.

20.6. Conclusions and Reflections

Södra is an innovation leader and demonstrates several innovation management capabilities that were established between 2014 and 2020. Driven by both necessity and opportunity, the new innovation strategy and process from 2014 paved the way for focused strategic innovation arenas and roadmaps that were instrumental for the innovation achievements during the period of this case study.

According to Catrin Gustavsson, "Södra has dared to invest in and been driving several areas, which has created very good conditions for the future, including well-invested industrial facilities, high competence, a first-class laboratory, established partnerships with institutes and colleges, good customer relations, and ambitious sustainability goals."

Looking forward, the demand for innovations will only accelerate. Södra and the forest industry will face even more significant innovation challenges related to the transition to a circular economy. There will always be weak elements of an innovation management system that must be addressed and improved. With the proactive review, Södra has identified the next iteration of improvements that can include an even more focused innovation strategy, stronger top management commitment, clarified roles and responsibilities and improved communication efforts.

Taken together, the innovation management review of 2020 revealed that Södra had implemented a robust innovation management system during the last couple of years. It provides a solid foundation for further strengthening the performance of future new business development and innovation efforts.

References

IMCA (2019). *Innovation Management Capabilities Assessment*. SIS Swedish Institute for Standards.

ISO (2019). *ISO 56002:2019 Innovation management — Innovation management system — Guidance*. International Organization for Standardization.

ISO (2020). *ISO 56000:2020 Innovation management — Fundamentals and vocabulary*. International Organization for Standardization.

Novotny, M. (2016). *Breaking the chains — A Technological and Industrial Transformation beyond Papermaking: Technology Management of Incumbents*. Doctoral Thesis, KTH Royal Institute of Technology, Stockholm, Sweden.

Rushton, M. (2020). We must grow — in all areas. *Paper360*, May/June 2020.

Södra (2020), www.sodra.com.

Part III

Reflections

© 2023 World Scientific Publishing Europe Ltd.
https://doi.org/10.1142/9781800612105_0021

Chapter 21

Common Themes and Success Factors

Joanne Hyland, Magnus Karlsson and Jimmi Normann Kristiansen

Abstract

In this chapter, the editorial team reflects upon common themes from the cases, how the standard was used, prerequisites for success and practical guidance it can offer for a successful journey. Organisations embarked on their innovation management system (IMS) journeys for different reasons. For some, it was about external triggers, e.g., positioning with the UN Sustainable Development Goals (SDGs) or responding to industry shifts and technology disruptions. For others, it was about internal triggers, e.g., as an enabler for organisational restructuring or building innovation capabilities. Three cases (INTI, Karolinska, OKI) explicitly used the ISO 56002 guidance standard to fully implement their innovation management systems. Three cases used it to implement selected elements of the standard (Airbus, Norconsult, Södra). Four cases (CIMC, Evonik, Midea, Moen) implemented a systems approach before the standard was published. Others (HIF, Kanthal, KTH GDH, Naturvårdsverket, Oregon State, SDP) used ISO 56002 as a lens to reflect on their innovation capabilities and to reinforce and validate steps already taken. Regardless of the standard's use, organisations have been able to move from *ad hoc* or process-driven activities to a systems orientation, create a common language to collaborate, clarify their innovation ambitions and start their journeys via a bottom-up, top-down or combination of both approaches.

21.1. Why an Innovation Management System Journey?

21.1.1. *Reasons for IMS journeys*

Organisations embarked on their innovation management system (IMS) journeys for different reasons. All recognised the need for change and viewed innovation as a key enabler. They also understood that systematic and systemic models were critical for success that required a systems approach. The ISO 56002 innovation management system standard provided guidance for these journeys to design, implement, reinforce and validate how to professionalise innovation management within the contexts of their organisations. Triggers were externally driven, internally motivated or a combination of both, across diverse sectors.

This section sets the context for the themes that follow in Sections 21.2–21.4. Concrete highlights are described as follows as to what triggered these 16 organisations to begin their IMS journeys. For ease of reference, the cases are organised consistent with the order in which they appeared in Part II. Refer to Chapter 4 for an overview of the organisations.

21.1.2. *External triggers*

External triggers came from changing conditions outside the organisation. Organisations concluded that these new challenges could only be addressed by using a systems approach to innovation management. These triggers included new customer and user needs, technology disruptions, industry commoditisation, changes in government policies, industrial development objectives, national environmental objectives, UN Sustainable Development Goals (SDGs), global crises response, etc.

An overview of external triggers that drove organisations to change are as follows:

- **Airbus** — Reduction of EU funding in defence changed the industry dynamics from a technology push, policy-driven focus to a need-seeking, customer-centric one.
  - "To do better with less and speed up the time to market."
- **CIMC and Midea** — Ability of senior management to recognise external waves of change and dynamically adapt to technology and societal trends.

- CIMC: Rode the wave of globalised, "glocalised," digitalised, pandemic, etc. trends to transform itself from a commoditised container company to a logistics and energy equipment provider.
- Midea: Positioned itself in the digital age to become an innovation leader in the household appliance industry.

- **HIF** — Need for urgent problem solving for humanitarian crises response.
  - "Humanitarian crises require urgent problem-solving, often when conventional solution avenues are blocked. They represent a key arena in which innovation is required and in recent years there has been growing interest in viewing the process not as an isolated event but as something which could be organised and managed."
- **INTI** — Promoting industrial development via fostering innovation throughout the ecosystem.
- **Karolinska** — Focusing on the triple aim in healthcare of improved care, improved health and reduced costs.
  - "Innovation is needed to meet future needs as regards to more efficient treatments, optimised care processes and more cost-effective interventions."
- **KTH GDH and OKI** — Addressing the UN SDGs via challenge-driven innovation approaches (KTH GDH) and integration of SDGs in corporate strategy (OKI).
- **Naturvårdsverket** — Moving beyond sector incremental development focus to meet national environmental objectives.
  - "In-depth evaluations of the national environmental objectives, carried out every parliamentary term, have shown that the objectives are not met. The UN and the European Environmental Agency EEA have pointed out the need for urgent transformative steps rather than incremental development."
- **OKI** — Changing business environment, emerging technologies and services, transition to cashless/paperless society and customers looking for new value-added offerings.
- **Oregon State** — Rising challenges in education in terms of demographics, funding models and public expectations.
  - "Public research universities in the U.S. and many around the world face rising challenges associated with escalating costs, shifting demographics, changing public perceptions of the value

of college degrees, growing student loan debt, and eroding public sector support, among other things."

- **SDP** — Embracing a sustainability agenda, mitigating market volatility and reducing dependence on foreign labour.
    - "At this stage, there were four main themes that concerned SDP: volatile CPO (crude palm oil) prices, climate change, pressure from NGOs on deforestation and regulations..."
- **Södra** — Responding to technology shifts and new market conditions in the emerging bioeconomy.
    - "...to strengthen its position in the bioeconomy by using every part of the tree to create value."
    - "The transformation was triggered by technology shifts as well as profoundly new market conditions. An increased interest in alternatives to fossil fuels opened up an innovation space for industry players, including Södra."

21.1.3. *Internal triggers*

On the other hand, internal triggers came from changing conditions within the organisation that required a more holistic, systems approach. These triggers included ambitions to build sustainable innovation capabilities, become more systematic in approaches to innovation, capitalise on organisational restructuring activities, bring about culture change, deliver upon corporate vision and innovation strategy goals, maintain or achieve market competitiveness and innovation leadership, grow through strategic innovation, change role from only adopting to generating technologies, capture more value from R&D investments, etc.

An overview of the internal triggers that motivated organisations to change are as follows:

- **Airbus** — Restructuring the organisation to be more responsive to change, how to create a company culture for sustainable and breakthrough innovation and finding ways to safely disrupt the company.
    - "The systemic approach for innovation started in 2014...During the creation of Airbus Defence and Space, employees needed a new perspective to become engaged through a strong company culture."

- "…disrupt the company in the core business in a safe manner? A first innovation unit was then created and called 'Innovation Cell' sparking innovation as an organisation and supported by methodologies creating a new context to support innovators across the company."

- **Evonik** — Increasing capabilities related to radical innovation through defined strategic growth fields and becoming more efficient at managing strategic innovation opportunities.
  - "...process for incremental innovation was well-developed within the organisation" yet "management system for uncertainty-driven, strategic innovation had to be rethought."
- **HIF** — Adopting more systematic approaches to innovation for more effective operations in a world of perpetual crisis.
- **INTI** — Becoming an innovative organisation via awareness and training programmes to develop an innovation culture that would successfully foster innovation across a wide range of internal and external stakeholders.
  - "In parallel to the awareness and training programme, several workshops were carried out with top management to enable discussion of the importance of INTI as an innovative organisation, and how to develop an innovation culture within INTI and at the same time developing the Innovation Vision and the Innovation Strategy."
- **Kanthal** — Securing future innovativeness by leveraging historical leadership position and becoming more systematic and systemic regarding innovation capability building.
  - "The legacy of innovation from Kanthal is profound. The company is world-leading within high temperature and resistance material… The journey began with late-night thoughts and discussions by the coffee maker on leveraging the organisation's potential regarding innovation capability. There was a feeling that an improvement could be made."
  - "The assessment revealed a focus on incremental innovation, barriers in the climate for innovation, and an inability to take advantage of the expertise and competencies available in the organisation."

- **Karolinska** — Becoming generators of innovation rather than only being adopters.
    - "When generating innovation from within healthcare organisations, the origin can come from both science, technology, and specialisation (science-based), as well as daily practice... However, research in innovation in healthcare has to a large extent focused on healthcare organisations as adopters of innovation rather than generators of innovation."
- **KTH GDH** — Assuming an active role for the university to address the SDGs, not just by training students, but also by undertaking education activities for society.
    - "Universities can, and should, play an important and direct role in that transformation, not just through knowledge production through research."
    - "It is based on the idea that education as an activity can contribute not just by training students, but also by education activities making more direct contributions towards solutions for a more sustainable society."
- **Midea** — Driving change through a formal innovation strategy with a commitment to R&D and innovation.
    - "Midea has adopted and implemented a formal innovation strategy since 2012. With the vision 'to bring great innovations to life', Midea is committed to R&D and innovation; this has enhanced its core competitiveness and made impressive breakthroughs. Since 2012, Midea has achieved robust business growth across multiple sectors driven by its innovation in humanising technology."
- **Moen** — Finding new paths for growth via strategic innovation and building a capability to sustain it.
    - The journey began with the question: "How does a plumbing company chart new paths for growth and sustain an ability to do this over time?"
    - Conclusions from a 2007 assessment: "Moen lacked an innovation strategy and clarity about how to handle different types of innovation."
- **Naturvårdsverket** — Acknowledging and supporting staff initiatives by the agency's top management about the needs of increasing the

organisation's innovation capability and creating a systematic innovation platform.

- **Norconsult** — Building resilience for change and coordinating within the organisation to gain synergies across many local approaches to innovation.
    - "…innovation management system, in part as a response to the volatilities mentioned, and to build a better resilience to change over time. Norconsult wanted to shift towards a more innovative mindset, better manage the flow of innovative initiative and ideas, as well as act on the sense of urgency coming from the pandemic to bring about a more systematic approach to growth and development."
- **OKI** — Transforming culture from passive to active stance.
    - "Transform the corporate culture from a passive product-out stance based on the receipt of orders to an active stance based on proposing effective value propositions and solutions with a well-validated business model."
- **Oregon State** — Building an internal system and capability to respond to fast-changing trends in higher education.
    - "In 2018, Oregon State University established a function and set of associated practices — called Impact Studio — that are designed to expand the institution's internal innovation system and capability. The aim is to strengthen Oregon State's ability to identify or create new value and respond creatively and nimbly to fast-changing trends in higher education…"
- **SDP** — Making innovation work in a top-down, hierarchical decision model in the absence of understanding what innovation is.
    - "Strong hierarchies also limit collaboration and make it challenging for ideas to surface from the employee level."
    - "Adding to the external challenges above was the absence of a common understanding of what innovation meant within the company."
- **Södra** — Creating value through an innovation strategy and systematic approach that goes beyond R&D for more efficient commercialisation of new offerings.
    - "Södra had been investing considerable resources in R&D but experienced difficulties in commercialising the results from these activities… A clear and well-aligned innovation strategy should ensure that resources were used more strategically and efficiently."

Having reflected upon the reasons for why and what triggered organisations to embark on their IMS journeys, the next section describes how relevant the international standard was for guiding or reinforcing these decisions and captures the themes that emerged.

21.2. How Has the International Standard Been Used?

21.2.1. *Overview*

The international standard for IMS ISO 56002 (ISO, 2019) has been used as the guiding framework for all the case studies presented in this book. The key elements of the standard were identified as starting points and formed a common approach (see Chapter 4) that authors used when outlining the cases. The purpose was to enable comparisons among the cases on how the systems approach and the international standard have been interpreted and used by the organisations. Depending on the nature of the different cases, the authors decided to follow the common approach to varying degrees.

All organisations represented in the cases have implemented systematic innovation practices and built innovation management capabilities in different ways and degrees. Some have been working more pro-actively over a longer period than others. This diversity is intentional in order for us to study how the international standard is, or can be, used related to different maturity levels of organisations.

Over half of the cases refer to situations where the international standard has been explicitly used by the organisations to understand, assess and drive actions to improve innovation capabilities. Some of these organisations (INTI, Karolinska and OKI) have had the ambition to implement an IMS, according to ISO, in its broader sense. For other organisations, the standard has been used to develop selected innovation management capabilities, such as an innovation culture through training programmes (Airbus), as a starting point for a more adapted systems approach (Norconsult) and to support in identifying innovation capability gaps and creating awareness (KTH GDH, Naturvårdsverket, Kanthal, Södra).

In the rest of the cases, the international standard has been compared to existing system models or specific innovation capabilities. These capabilities have typically been developed before the standard was published or without the explicit mentioning of it. The standard has been used by the case authors to interpret, assess and map the innovation capabilities of the organisation to gain insights into its applicability in different contexts. In the cases of Moen, Evonik, CIMC and Midea, an explicit IMS had already been implemented based on models that were developed before the ISO standard was available. For HIF, Oregon State and SDP, they had most or several IMS components in place and used the standard to reinforce and validate steps already taken.

21.2.2. *Cases that explicitly used the international standard*

OKI, INTI and Karolinska took active decisions to fully implement an IMS based on ISO 56002. As a first step, the standard was used as a guide for assessing innovation capabilities and identifying gaps. Several capabilities were already in place in the organisations, and the standard helped to provide a structure for designing actions for improving and extending them.

OKI implemented their version of the IMS named OKI Yume Pro in partnership with Japan Innovation Network, an external innovation management expert and innovation accelerator. The elements of Yume Pro correspond to a large extent to the content of ISO 56002. Their implementation was guided by their corporate mission and the values in the UN SDGs.

The IMS at INTI was also developed with the support of external consultants. ISO 56002 was taken as a model even though it was under development when implementation started. A handbook, including a process map and a model for categorising innovation projects, was developed based on the standard.

Even if Karolinska used the standard explicitly, it was necessary to interpret its content to be relevant for the healthcare and hospital context. The fundamentals of the standard were supportive for this work, even if some terms and definitions had to be adapted to be understood in the organisation.

Ensuring credibility and legitimacy

For all three organisations, it was essential that innovation capability building was based on an internationally agreed standard. It gave credibility and legitimacy to the work to be done.

In the healthcare sector, standards and certifications are important and, in this case, facilitated the top management decision at Karolinska. It also created additional visibility and increased the status of the hospital-internal group of innovation management professionals.

Also, for OKI, it has been important to establish internal visibility of the standard to boost internal motivation and engagement, strengthen the brand and signal interest in partnering externally. OKI officially announced in a press release their decision to establish a group-wide IMS, underlining the company's clear commitment to innovation activities.

Even if ISO 56002 is not a certifiable standard, INTI was certified according to the national requirement standard IRAM 50501, which is very similar to ISO 56002. OKI has stated its ambition to be certified according to the forthcoming standard ISO 56001.

Developing innovation capabilities

Airbus, Södra and Norconsult are examples of organisations that have explicitly used the international standard to assess and develop innovation capabilities. However, they have not formally decided to implement the entire IMS according to ISO 56002.

Airbus used the standard to foster an innovation culture and to manage innovation projects. After an assessment of the existing innovation culture, the innovation strategy was established with a focus on influencing that culture to involve more decentralised engagement, ecosystem interaction and tolerance of failure. In addition, different innovation management roles, support for monitoring projects, as well as tools and methods for innovation practitioners were established.

The main instruments to build these capabilities were training programmes for competence development explicitly based on the framework of ISO 56002. The purpose of these programmes was to create awareness of the systematic approach to innovation management, particularly among innovation project managers at Airbus. The standard also provided innovation coaches with a common methodology for engaging with project managers.

Södra had been developing innovation capabilities in a systematic and systemic manner for several years before introducing the framework of ISO 56002. The standard was then used explicitly to assess capability gaps at the group level and to create top management awareness. It was concluded that most elements of the standard had been implemented to varying degrees, including an understanding of the external and internal context, an innovation vision, strategy and roadmap, with detailed focus areas and a portfolio approach. Organisational structures, innovation processes, tools and methods had also been defined and established. The standard also helped to identify areas for improvement, including further clarifying roles and responsibilities and enhanced communication efforts to boost engagement and collaboration.

Norconsult explicitly used the standard as a trigger and starting point for developing innovation capabilities. However, because of the different needs and levels of readiness, as well as the complexity and diversity of the consulting organisation, it was concluded that one single solution for an IMS could not be established. Norconsult took a more pragmatic approach and created room for local adaptation resulting in a more limited implementation of the IMS.

In the case of KTH GDH, Kanthal and Naturvårdsverket, the ISO standard was used as a lens to reflect and help identify relevant factors and elements for innovation capability building, even if they did not use it to guide implementation as such. In the case of KTH GDH, it helped to identify innovation capabilities and gaps related to the chosen model for challenge-driven education, even if applying the complete IMS framework was considered difficult. The focus was on developing the innovation competence of students related to global sustainable development using the international standard as a backdrop.

Two additional observations can be made from the cases that have explicitly used the international standard in their organisations.

Establishing a common language

First, the importance of the standard for providing a common language has been highlighted in several cases. For example, in OKI, a common language was critical to achieving a shared understanding of key innovation concepts across the different units and business divisions in order to facilitate collaboration and the smooth handover of promising opportunities. In Södra, it was recognised that some degree of a common language was necessary to make a case for strategic innovation in the organisation.

Promoting a deeper understanding of what innovation really is can also boost the innovation culture. At Norconsult, it was discovered early that inconsistencies in terminology, for example, equating innovation with technology, led to misinformed conversations about innovation capabilities and performance. Also, at Karolinska, the group of innovation management professionals identified that the common language provided by the standard was an essential success factor. The importance of a common language is also highlighted by several cases that did not explicitly use the international standard, such as HIF and SDP.

Driving training programmes

Second, Airbus (described above), OKI, INTI and Karolinska in particular, had a clear focus on communicating and creating awareness by deploying training programmes reaching broad groups of employees internally. For example, INTI completed training programmes for its technical and managerial staff with a focus on the contents and benefits of an IMS and encouraged reflection on the role of innovation at INTI. A strong emphasis on the realisation of value was part of the employee training conducted at OKI. Finally, the Innovation Ambassador programme was provided to a wide range of employees at the Karolinska University Hospital. The programme included tools and methods for practical, systematic innovation work, such as design thinking. Another programme, called Innovation for Leaders, had a more managerial perspective.

In summary, the ISO 56002 standard has been used in different ways by organisations to assess and drive activities to enhance innovation capabilities and performance. The standard has provided guidance, legitimacy, a common language and the basis for competence development.

21.2.3. *Cases that did not explicitly use the international standard*

Several cases described in this book developed innovation capabilities without explicitly using the ISO 56002 framework. We can still gain insights into the validity of the framework by applying the common approach to the analysis of the cases.

Taking a systems approach to innovation management

Moen and Evonik had developed an IMS in their respective organisations before the publication of the international standard. The systems approach used was based on the findings of the RPI research projects (see discussion in Chapter 2) with an explicit purpose of building a sustainable capability for strategic innovation. It should be noted that the findings from the RPI research were inputs for the development of the ISO standard.

In the Moen case, it was concluded that the implemented model showed a high degree of alignment with the ISO guidance standard that came later. Among the success factors mentioned were an established innovation strategy to guide investments and a group of people with the right mindset to orchestrate the IMS. Other key elements that were implemented included top management commitment for strategic innovation, the right culture promoted through training programmes and a governance operating model encouraging adaptability and systems thinking.

For Evonik, the main challenge was to build capabilities to deliver radical innovations. Similar to the Moen case, the description of the implemented IMS highlighted innovation strategy, organisational structures and a strategic innovation process as essential elements. The Evonik case also discusses the challenge of building capabilities for both incremental innovation and strategic innovation in the same management system.

In addition, both companies focused on the importance of a common language, understanding how to handle different types of innovation, and developing multi-year training programmes.

CMIC and Midea are also examples of organisations that took a systems approach to building innovation management capabilities. Some key elements of their systems are highlighted in what follows.

Emphasising selected innovation capabilities

Several other cases report that most of the innovation capabilities outlined in the international standard had been implemented by the organisation when ISO 56002 was used as a lens. In the cases of SDP, Oregon State and HIF, the standard reinforced and verified the steps taken by the organisations.

Even though Kanthal and Naturvårdsverket did use the standard to explicitly reflect on their innovation capabilities, they did not use it to guide their implementation. Some of their implementation activities are also included in what follows.

Across the cases, several key elements described in the standard are highlighted as important for the organisations when building innovation capabilities. For example, related to the understanding of the context of the organisation, the ability to respond to waves of external changes was essential in the cases of Midea and CIMC. Capturing insights from the market was an essential capability for Kanthal and SDP, while the humanitarian innovation (HIF) community is entirely focused on urgent problem solving triggered by external events.

Promoting a culture supporting innovation initiatives, including encouraging employees to contribute insights and ideas, was observed as essential in the cases of Kanthal, Naturvårdsverket, SDP, CIMC and Oregon State.

Related to leadership and planning, the vital role of senior leadership in, for example, SDP, Oregon State, Midea and CIMC was described as a success factor. An articulated innovation vision (e.g., SDP and Midea), a clear innovation strategy (e.g., Naturvårdsverket and Midea) and adaptable organisational structures (e.g., Midea, Naturvårdsverket, and Oregon State) were seen as a result of top management commitment.

In support, the availability of several elements has been observed in the cases, including nurturing and training talent for developing, coaching and managing innovations (e.g., CIMC, HIF, SDP, Naturvårdsverket) as well as measures for communication and awareness creation.

Finally, in terms of operations, SDP, HIF and Kanthal are examples of organisations with visible and reproducible innovation processes, and in the case of Midea and Naturvårdsverket, complemented with an explicit approach to open innovation.

Using ISO 56002 as a lens when outlining the cases in this book, elements that were missing in the organisations were also identified. Examples of the most frequent gaps are the lack of top management commitment, the absence of a clear innovation strategy and the lack of performance evaluation and improvement of the IMS.

21.2.4. *Selected issues identified when explicitly or implicitly using the standard*

From all the cases in this book that used ISO 56002, either explicitly or implicitly, as discussed above, concerns or issues emerged related to the scope and applicability of the standard.

Scope

The first set of issues are related to the scope of the management system. In the case of Norconsult, it was discussed whether one general IMS could handle all the different variations and complexities of the organisation and to what degree adaptations were necessary for the system to be relevant. At Södra, the issue was the relationship between a group-wide IMS and such systems at business area levels. To what extent are they, and should they be, interrelated? Another question raised in the Evonik case was whether one IMS would be flexible enough to handle both incremental and radical innovations, or if these differences are better handled by two separate systems that can be more distinct and precise in their recommendations.

Sector relevance

The second set of issues are related to the applicability of the management system. In the cases of HIF and Karolinska, it was discussed whether a general IMS would be flexible enough to be relevant for all sectors, or to what extent sector adaptations would be necessary, in these cases, the humanitarian aid and healthcare sectors. A related issue raised by the KTH GDH and HIF cases was the applicability of the IMS for initiatives aiming for broader societal impact and social development. When addressing social challenges or missions involving and requiring contributions from many different organisations, the general question is whether the IMS is also applicable at the multi-organisational level across the innovation ecosystem.

Organisational agility

A final issue discussed in several cases is the relationship between the system for managing innovation and the system for managing operations in an organisation. This is sometimes referred to as an ambidextrous organisation. For example, in the cases of INTI and Naturvårdsverket, there was a challenge of finding the right balance between a focus on efficiency and a focus on renewal. Innovation activities run the risk of being down-prioritised for the benefit of more urgent operational matters. How do organisations become sufficiently agile to support both?

21.3. What Emerged as Prerequisites for Success and Why?

In looking across the cases, prerequisites for success also emerged. The most important ones were:

- Definition of a clear innovation strategy.
- Innovation culture (people and leadership), networking and training of people.
- Top management involvement and commitment.
- A systematic process for managing different types of innovation.

In the following, examples of the above themes are highlighted in relation to select cases, and subsequently a summary of prerequisites for success in IMS implementation is provided.

21.3.1. *Definition of a clear innovation strategy*

Karolinska and Naturvårdsverket identified innovation strategy as a driver for innovation in the organisation in general, which enabled a more systematic approach towards innovation. Concurrently, a centrepiece of the development of an IMS in Södra was an innovation strategy that was implemented in early 2015.

The development of a gradually maturing innovation strategy was at the heart of CIMC's development journey. CIMC had developed from an internal-external, market-driven strategy, a transition to a resource-based strategy, to a championing strategy (all incorporated). The latter had enabled CIMC to have a global footprint both in depth and width of their container R&D, enabling them to be a world leading company within the field. Moreover, in the strategy periods of the 21st century, CIMC has gradually expanded into new fields of vehicles, energy and chemicals, as well as airports.

INTI also developed a new innovation strategy at the same time of standard implementation, which was a centrepiece for the innovation journey in the years to come. Midea, moreover, had a principle of "strategy first," which was then followed up by a strong emphasis on leadership. In the case of OKI, an innovation strategy, with a strong emphasis on the UN SDGs, was a priority.

21.3.2. *Innovation culture, networking and training of people*

The strategic emphasis put forward in CIMC on where the company needed to be in the future markets were coupled with a deep focus on talent development, learning routines, systemised guidance for portfolio management, requirements for new innovation opportunities, as well as employee incentives. In sum, the work with the innovation strategy later on enabled an internal governance system in CIMC that would support innovation portfolios, processes and people in the organisation. Kanthal started its journey via a strategic path by conducting a "climate assessment" to understand the context of the organisation, especially with respect to its culture and people. This analysis contributed to the innovation success at Kanthal by clarifying innovation roles for its teams.

Airbus launched training initiatives with the aim of affecting the innovation culture in the company. A strong linkage was identified between the innovation strategy and how to use culture (i.e., the set of behaviours, routines and symbols of innovation) in the organisation to foster change. It was found that behaviours and routines enable a reinforcement of values identified in the innovation strategy. Furthermore, this was enhanced by physical labs, e.g., the PlayLab in Toulouse, offering ample space to try out new ideas and, more importantly, making everyone in the company know about the lab.

Airbus accentuated that sharing of culture was particularly accelerated through a network of catalysts, consisting of events that are designed to cross-fertilise and prevent silos from building up in the organisation. Innovation activities in Airbus have helped it build an Innovation ecosystem, which, once formalised; has fostered an array of initiatives, such as an Airnovator programme (an innovation programme within Airbus), specific training of innovation coaches, an overview of innovation opportunity management phases and other concrete initiatives. To Airbus, these initiatives had the possibility to thrive due to a strong emphasis on innovation culture, networking of people and focusing intensively on upskilling employees.

Evonik also looked for ways to change its culture and upskill its employees. It first initiated a pilot in 2013, then a comprehensive training programme for its employees from 2017 to 2019. The KTH GDH implemented a challenge-driven approach — linked to the UN SDGs. This had an emphasis on training of individuals, but also the linkage to the IMS in the organisation.

21.3.3. *Top management involvement and commitment*

SDP, as well as Oregon State, accentuated the need for setting vision and also enabling and providing structure in the organisation to deploy the strategy. The HIF found that senior management responsibility was important yet challenging. One key topic was to discuss the variability in how senior management sometimes address innovation in organisations, depending on the nature of projects. In a similar vein, a key priority for INTI was senior stakeholder involvement and alignment for success. This enabled clear support for developing a process for innovation based on the standard. Additionally, the senior stakeholder involvement enabled extensive collaboration (and awareness hereof) with partners for innovation. This emphasis was coupled with a balanced approach to the innovation portfolio; continuously checking for alignment with strategy to omit potential opportunities that were out of scope, whitespace opportunities. The case from Moen indicated a clear strategic imperative through the commitment of upper management. This was emphasised by an endorsed strategic intent, as well as supporting the initiation and evolution of an innovation governance system in the organisation. This strong direction from upper management, along with multi-year training programmes, was used to professionalise innovation in the organisation. It also contributed to building an organisational capability for innovation that could be sustained across the company in the future, and not relying on champions or any given business unit.

21.3.4. *A systematic process for managing different types of innovation*

Any system generated should allow for both incremental and strategic innovation. As shown in the cases of Evonik and Moen, the required tools, methods and processes, as well as governance, was different for incremental and strategic innovation. In effect, organisations should consider whether they create a dual system, or if an integrated system can be expedient. Even with an integrated system, careful consideration of the governance setup is required to avoid inexpedient governance and processes for strategic innovation. This underscores the importance of considering, and carefully developing, the organisational structure for innovation. The journey at Norconsult started with a preliminary compatibility analysis, which found that a "single IMS" was too complex, yet it needed to be adapted locally to fit the projects that needed development.

21.3.5. *Towards practical guidance*

OKI had developed an overview of the IMS as they saw it, and understood the relationships between leadership, their innovation policy, innovation structures, the innovation processes as well as culture and context. Even with a fully envisioned IMS, OKI realised that the implementation of such a system comes in gradual steps. Consequently, the case demonstrates well the need for both an envisioned IMS, as well as a "roll-out" approach for where, when and how organisations will start maturing the system in the organisation.

Depending on the IMS maturity, as well as the size of the organisation and strategic priorities, this is a development that will take some time. The organisation should decide whether such a journey would start bottom-up, with people and projects, or top-down, via leadership and strategy, or perhaps even a combination of both.

Implied by the cases analysed, a good start for any organisation would be to sketch a potential IMS, and then, based on resources and a gap analysis on current maturity (e.g., Karolinska), devise a plan for how to implement and improve the IMS, as appropriate. In reflecting upon the cases, it has become clear that for a given innovation journey starting points can be as follows:

- Bottom-up: Identifying opportunities and training employees to work with concrete methods, processes and tools, within the appropriate employee culture.
- Top-down: Looking at innovation strategy, governance, top-management involvement and strategic intent.
- Combined: An approach starting both bottom-up and top-down, balanced in different ways by the organisation.

The paths taken in the organisations (from the onset) varied, yet the conclusion for a sustained innovation capability is that organisations must actively work on strategic, portfolio, project and people level approaches. Further, organisations recognised the importance of dedicating people and providing them space and time to be truly successful with innovation. As a result, the final approach sometimes became a combination of complementary and mutually supporting initiatives of both a top-down and a bottom-up nature.

21.4. What Practical Guidance Directs a Successful Journey?

This section covers a summary of the practical guidance for success in the innovation journey, derived from the 16 cases featured in this book.

Starting from a systemic perspective, making an overview of the necessary elements needed in the IMS is truly valuable, as it can help guide any subsequent step. For instance, organisations such as Norconsult, INTI and Kanthal began with getting an overview of the innovation maturity/requirement status of the organisation. This potentially includes all the elements as described in Chapter 2, from understanding the context of the organisation, including its culture and innovation ambitions, through to the support and implementation priorities, in terms of portfolios, people, tools/methods, processes and performance. As aforementioned, the innovation journey can either start bottom-up or top-down or some combination of both; where a crucial element for many organisations, retrospectively, is how to roll out different innovation initiatives in the organisation step by step.

Regardless of the approach, visibility and commitment from top management are common themes across the cases; hence — top management involvement and concrete commitment to an innovation journey are crucial.

21.4.1. *Bottom-up*

From a cultural perspective, the case of Airbus showed us that a network of catalysts from across the organisation helps build the IMS. This was coupled with careful considerations on which key competencies were needed, which people do we want as part of the programme, how do we make a checklist/portfolio overview of ongoing projects, etc.

For the KTH GDH, it had a key emphasis on the interplay between learning and innovation processes, enabling training activities and intervention activities to be interrelated. This prevented a "locked system" — and allowed for iterations and adaptation along the way.

As shown in the case of INTI, the continuous onboarding of people and training to provide qualification has been a main driver for success. Over time, maturing this system with both technical and management expertise helped grow the IMS. This should be done through a common language and mindset, built over time (Moen).

21.4.2. *Top-down*

The case of Evonik demonstrated the establishment of a strategic innovation centre (i.e., formalising the organisation for strategic innovation, getting visibility and identity to the innovation activities taking place here).

Similarly, the Evonik case showed an early identification of the organisation, via the pilot in 2013 and the follow-on programme in 2017, on important points that the organisation wanted to work on. Hence, this led to an identification of the priority areas to improve in the IMS and a continued focus on improving these areas.

In the Kanthal case, an analysis of the organisational context as well as the climate for innovation was the starting point. Any strategic "readiness assessment" or organisational assessment of the innovation capability can help guide the direction and set the necessary requirements for appropriate training, qualification, governance, etc., to match the innovation initiatives with current priorities of the organisation. Similarly, Södra, SDP, Oregon State as well as OKI showed strong visibility and dedication of top management in enabling and deploying their innovation journey. This implementation was also guided by a key strategic and visionary driver set forward by these organisations.

As shown in the Midea case, innovation strategy was pivotal in the development journey and competitiveness of the organisation over time. This was coupled with a clear and systemic approach to managing different types of innovation in the organisation. This also included executive onboarding and orientation over time, to calibrate the activities conducted in the organisation, and align language (Norconsult), and mindsets, related to both strategic innovation as well as incremental innovation and operations (Moen).

21.4.3. *A combination*

In the SDP case, the focus was on how to overcome the challenges of a hierarchical top-down decision model. This required senior management direction to encourage employees to innovate as part of a clear corporate strategy in a risk-averse culture. It also involved creating employee programmes to clarify what innovation meant within the company and support employees in generating ideas. Per above, Moen also focused on a common language for innovation and encouraging an uncertainty mindset with its employees, supported by a clear strategic direction from leadership. Naturvårdsverket and Karolinska worked on the innovation development in the organisation with a combination of top-down and bottom-up approaches.

In the end, while there are common themes and systematic steps that have emerged, designing, implementing and evolving IMSs do vary considerably from one organisation to the next based on changing external and internal conditions. From the cases, those organisations that have followed the complete standard explicitly or implicitly, such as, OKI, INTI, Karolinska, Moen, and CIMC, have been successful in anticipating and responding to their changing environments.

References

ISO (2019). *ISO 56002:2019 Innovation management — Innovation management system — Guidance*. International Organization for Standardization.

O'Connor, G. C., Leifer, R., Paulson, A. S. and Peters, L. S. (2008). *Grabbing Lightning: Building a Capability for Breakthrough Innovation*. San Francisco, CA: Wiley & Sons.

© 2023 World Scientific Publishing Europe Ltd.
https://doi.org/10.1142/9781800612105_0022

Chapter 22

Conclusions and Path Forward

Joanne Hyland, Magnus Karlsson, John Bessant, Ingrid Kihlander, Jimmi Normann Kristiansen and Mats Magnusson

Abstract

In this chapter, the editorial team looks across the cases and the emerging themes to offer insights about the standard and its implications for the innovation management community and the future of the innovation management discipline. For practitioners, the case is made for a call to action to rally around the benefits of the standard as a foundation for dynamic innovation capability and innovation community building that will stand the test of time. For academic educators and researchers, it is teaching about open, connected innovation models that go beyond internally focused ones and understanding through research the system element interdependencies and how these elements can be adapted in different organisational contexts. For standard developers, a key issue is to ensure that a core innovation management system can handle the variations and complexities of different organisations and types of innovations. For professional associations, it is about continuing to build the identity of the profession and supporting professionals to strengthen the innovation management discipline in organisations. For policymakers, it starts with understanding where the standard could have policy relevance and broadening the range of innovation policy instruments available. Finally, it is about imagining a future where in 10 years innovation management is a well-recognised discipline and profession, with systemic and systematic approaches that accelerate learning to realise value more quickly for a better world.

22.1. Implications for the Innovation Management Community

22.1.1. *Overview*

In looking across the common themes and success factors in Chapter 21, one key take away is that organisations should decide whether their innovation management systems journeys start bottom-up, with people and projects, or top-down, via leadership and strategy, or perhaps even a combination of both. Regardless of the path chosen, the visibility and commitment from top management is critical for success.

With these findings from analysing the case studies as a starting point, the following offers insights about the implications for the innovation management community. These implications are viewed from the perspectives of practitioners, academic researchers and educators, standard developers, professional associations and policymakers.

22.1.2. *Practitioners*

From the cases, we saw that an innovation management system standard helps to move forward innovation agendas, create the right culture for innovation, secure the support of senior management and build capabilities that can be sustained over the long term. A guidance standard is an invaluable roadmap for innovation management practitioners, regardless of the level of innovation maturity of their organisations. A standard also provides a fruitful foundation to pursue innovation in a systematic and systemic manner. Systematic underscores the need for a repeatable capability so that innovation activities are not viewed as one-time serendipitous events. Systemic acknowledges the interdependencies of the various elements of the system that need to be considered together, thereby ensuring that innovation is not hampered by a lack of critical capabilities or by missing links between critical interdependent activities.

As we have seen in the cases, not all organisations will decide to implement complete innovation management systems. However, as practitioners, it is important to understand which elements are most critical to move your organisation forward. Considering that innovation is about a "new or changed entity realising or redistributing value," innovation management is also about change management that requires a system to enable it.

With common definitions and a language for innovation, it makes it easier for internal and external stakeholders to agree upon what innovation is and is not within the contexts of their organisations. Through a credible and consistent framework, organisations are in a better position to assess their level of innovation maturity. By knowing which strengths to leverage and gaps to fill, organisations can then implement and evolve their innovation capabilities to repeatedly deliver value. Ultimately, a management system standard raises the importance of innovation management as a profession and viable career path, within a well-connected community of supporters.

Potential benefits

Within the ISO 56002 standards team, a communications taskforce was formed to help with positioning the value of the standard (ISO, 2019a). Benefits that the standard could offer were captured based on the experiences of its members. They are summarised as follows:

Within the organisation — innovation capability building:

- Improved common understanding and language for innovation.
- Engaged and empowered people in the organisation.
- Increased ability to manage uncertainty.
- Improved sustainability and resilience.
- Sustained renewal of the portfolio of offerings.
- Enhanced reputation and valuation of the organisation.

Within the innovation ecosystem — innovation community building:

- Increased satisfaction of users, customers, citizens and other interested parties.
- Increased growth, revenues, profitability and competitiveness.
- Reduced costs and waste, and increased productivity and resource efficiency.

- Increased ability to attract partners, collaborators and funding.
- Improved ability to understand another organisation's ability to innovate.
- Facilitated compliance with regulations and other relevant requirements.

In considering the experiences of the communications taskforce members, with those cases featured in this book, many of the benefits are the same, especially on the innovation capability side, e.g., understanding innovation, empowering people, managing uncertainty, enhancing reputation, etc. However, in looking to innovation community building, while a few of these benefits emerged, e.g., increasing satisfaction and growth, there is more work to be done in connecting with the innovation ecosystem through a systemic model for change.

Is a standard right for my organisation?

As a practitioner in any organisation whether for profit or non-profit, small to large, public or private, etc., questions to consider are as follows:

- Is the pace of technological and societal change and the emergence of new entrants challenging your core focus and purpose?
- Are you seeing increasing competition and changing user demand that require you to innovate regularly?
- Are you looking for how to establish collaborative innovation ecosystems within your region, country or globally yet lacking a common language and consistent framework to do so?
- Are you missing competencies that are critical to innovate in a rapidly changing world, such as, systems thinking, strategic skills, new business development know-how, etc.?
- Are your existing approaches to innovation not delivering sufficient value in terms of organisational transformation, growth, competitiveness, sustainability, benefit to society, etc.?

If any of these questions resonate with your challenges, then an innovation management system guidance standard that offers a systematic and systemic way to innovate could be the right solution for your organisation.

Words of caution

A guidance standard is not intended to be prescriptive or provide a one-size-fits-all recipe. It does not provide a solution. It offers a framework for organisations to assess their capacity and appetite to innovate and what to consider should they choose to build innovation capabilities. Following a guidance standard does not guarantee that an organisation will become innovative. This depends on the actions that one takes.

The standard aims for a model of innovation excellence, not operational excellence. Innovation management is different from other areas of standardisation, such as quality and project management. It is less about having answers than about knowing the right questions to ask. A management system can look very similar in structure across the disciplines; however, the areas of emphasis and implementation flexibility can be very different. It is important to understand that organisational agility is required to manage for today in an operationally driven world yet also be able to dream about tomorrow in an entrepreneurially driven one.

22.1.3. *Academic educators and researchers*

In many ways the perspectives and cases in this book offer a confirmation of a long-term trend towards "systemification." Innovation management emerged as a discipline from three core directions: engineering schools, business schools and a number of departments beyond these which also focused on the smaller business/start-up question.

Despite their different starting points, research and teaching around these themes has converged to what is now widely recognised as "innovation management" (Tidd and Bessant, 2020). Much of this has involved the assimilation of different "partial" models of how the process operates, from simplistic linear models of the 1960s, through more sophisticated "coupling" models of the 1980s, which still put the enterprise at the centre, to today's network and ecosystem approaches, which emphasise on the importance of managing external relationships via an "open innovation" model. In parallel has come a sophistication in terms of the diverse elements within the system, which need to be incorporated on human, economic, technological and strategic dimensions.

The emerging picture, which the book highlights, is that both the public and private sectors are now engaged with this systemic and systematic challenge. Teaching and research in the academic world need to reflect this. On the "supply side," in terms of teaching new generations of innovation managers, there is a need to continue developing integrated systems models for how ideas will create value. This includes doing so to support diverse contexts, from the small start-up organisation through to large established organisations and across all sectors. The role of guidance frameworks like the ISO 56002 and its templates for skills and capability development among individuals provides a valuable platform for delivering value across this diversity.

On the research side, there is much "colouring in" of the map to be done. In its present form, it is a generic framework model. We need to understand how it plays out in different circumstances and what the challenges are. A few of the cases did cover how not-for-profit organisations might benefit from taking a systematic and systemic view and how they might adapt current models. Or how small enterprises can absorb and embed the core principles of the model without creating unwieldy bureaucratic procedures and structures to enable innovation.

In particular, there is a need to maintain the shift in emphasis to the inter-organisational level, taking into account how collaborative and networked structures support innovation and what this means for the locus of decision-making in the innovation process. Research needs to provide clearer tools and templates for effective strategic operation in multi-player systems. It also should look across the elements of the innovation management system, rather than taking on specific topics. It is essential as a research community to understand the interdependencies of these elements to build more effective and efficient innovation capabilities.

22.1.4. *Standard developers*

From the cases, we saw that the guidance standard for innovation management system (ISO, 2019b) has been used in different ways by the organisations. It has been used to assess and develop innovation capabilities, ensure credibility and legitimacy, establish a common language, and provide the basis for competence development. It has also been used as a lens to reflect upon as well as validate and study the innovation capabilities that are in place in the organisation in order to create awareness of strengths and weaknesses. The management system standard has been both applicable and practically useful for the organisations studied, whether explicitly, implicitly or as a retrospective lens.

These findings suggest that further standardisation in the area of innovation management should build upon and further strengthen these benefits. At the same time, several issues and concerns are raised related to the standard across the cases (see previous chapter) and by scholars in other contexts (Tidd, 2021). These discussions provide valuable input to be considered when updating existing standards and developing new ones (Hyland and Karlsson, 2021).

Issues to be considered

Issues related to the scope and applicability of the standard raise the question if one general innovation management system can handle the variations and complexities of different types of organisations. These variations can be found within larger organisations with different units and levels, in organisations from different sectors, or across collaborating organisations.

Another question is whether one system for managing innovation can or should cover both incremental and radical innovations, and how to deal with its relationship to systems for managing operations in an organisation.

Addressing the issues

To address these issues, further standards development may consider the flexibility and adaptability of the management system to ensure its relevance in different settings and use cases. More specifically, it is suggested that the following topics should be considered:

- Focus standardisation on the generic core innovation capabilities that are relevant to a broad range of organisations regardless of size, sector or maturity. This is especially important when developing the certifiable standard ISO 56001. The experience so far is that different organisations have more in common related to innovation management than what might be the first impression.

- Provide additional guidance on how the innovation management system can be adapted and configured to be relevant for different organisations and constellations of organisations. For example, based on the cases, public organisations and SMEs would likely require adaptations. Consider if sector specific guidance or supplementary standards are necessary to support any adaptations.
- Clarify how the standard can be relevant for different types of innovations, for example incremental and radical innovations, or product, service, process, as well as social innovations. The focus on value realisation of the innovation management system can be used to demonstrate that value can be realised by different types of innovations within a portfolio approach. And that these innovations require different approaches related to processes, structures, tools and methods, depending on the situation, degree of uncertainty, etc.
- Consider how the innovation management system standard can be applied by a group of organisations that are seeking to innovate together. The purpose can be to achieve a common goal or mission when collaboration is necessary to combine resources and capabilities. Furthermore, aligning and integrating ISO 56002 and the guidance standard for innovation partnership ISO 56003:2019 (ISO, 2019c) can provide a way forward.
- Maintain the universal and inclusive language to ensure that the system standard is applicable to all organisations. The cases in this book demonstrate that the framework can be useful for private, public and not-for-profit organisations alike. This means avoiding expressions, such as growth, profit, and competitiveness, that might be relevant in the private but not in other sectors. Consider the use of non-commercial terms, such as mission over market, value over profit, etc.

Continuous validation

The cases in this book are the first comprehensive collection of diverse organisations that have used a systems approach to build innovation capabilities. The guidance standard for innovation management system is still new and the awareness is low among organisations, in general. As the standard gains traction and organisations start to use it, continued study and research is necessary. This includes the experiences of, for example, SMEs that are not covered by the present case studies.

We have just started the journey to better understand how organisations can benefit from implementing an innovation management system. Continuous validation of its use and usefulness will provide valuable input to further standardisation efforts.

22.1.5. *Professional associations*

The development and adoption of international standards can contribute to strengthening the innovation management discipline and profession. Key roles for professional associations are to continue building the identity of the profession and support professionals to strengthen the innovation management discipline in organisations. Innovation management professionals in various forms and roles have been working in different organisations for at least the past 20 years. They have been instrumental for implementing the systems approach to innovation management in several of the cases featured in this book.

With the emergence of standards for innovation management, the profession can further mature and develop its identity. Standards can serve as a reference framework and be part of a common body of knowledge for innovation management professionals. This can further clarify what the profession is, what core competencies are required, and in what roles professionals can be effective. It can also help build a community of professionals that share a common knowledge foundation that facilitates training, job mobility and mentoring.

The professional model for innovation management can include a job description, competence framework, body of knowledge and personal certification. One example is the personal certification programme for innovation management professionals developed and provided by the certification arm of RISE Research Institutes of Sweden (RISE, 2021). This development is similar to the maturation of other disciplines, such as project management and quality management professionals. Professionalisation is, in turn, paving the way for more effective implementation of innovation management practices in all kinds of organisations.

Professional associations at national and international levels are promoting this development. Examples are the Association for Innovation Management Professionals in Sweden (Innovationsledarna) and Innovate Island in Ireland. Internationally we have, for example, ISPIM (International Society for Professional Innovation Management) and IAOIP (International Association of Innovation Professionals).

The associations provide community building services to members and are referencing international standards in their activities. One example is the ISPIM Special Interest Group for an innovation management body of knowledge. Other member services include conferences, research networks, publications, funded projects, diverse special interest groups, community building, news, future insights, mentoring, training and innovation paper awards.

The existing and new professional associations will play an important role in shaping the discipline and profession going forward. New members, including students of innovation management at universities, can more easily find guidance, a career path and a professional identify. Moreover, experienced members can provide valuable input to further standards development.

22.1.6. *Policymakers*

Types of policies

International standards for innovation management will open up new possibilities for developing more effective innovation policies. During the last 20–30 years, such policies have focused on the role of innovation activities for economic performance. More recently, the scope has broadened to include the solution of social challenges, such as climate change or humanitarian aid. Some examples are provided by the cases in this book.

Edler and Fagerberg (2017) make the distinction of three types of policies affecting innovation activities: (1) mission-oriented policies seek solutions to specific challenges that have been identified on the political agenda, (2) invention-oriented policies focus on the R&D or invention phase and are often related to advances in science and technology, and (3) system-oriented policies with a focus on the supporting system and its related parts and stakeholders provide the conditions for innovation activities, typically at the national level.

Policymakers are uniquely positioned to help further innovation activities that now extend well beyond economic performance. To do this, it is important to understand how the international standard could help define areas of policy relevance and make available policy instruments to further evolving innovation objectives.

Areas of policy relevance

The importance of effective innovation within economies is clear; organisations that succeed in delivering a steady stream of new products and services and who improve their processes to become more productive are a vital part of raising living standards through employment, economic growth and, increasingly, meeting the bigger Sustainable Development Goals (SDGs) required by the planet. So, innovation policy is, not surprisingly, high on any political agenda at both regional and national levels.

However, policy involves more than simply throwing money at the challenge. The insights from the book and cases point to some important policy implications. There are three areas where standards for innovation management could have policy relevance.

- *How innovation works*: The first is in underpinning understanding of how innovation works at the enterprise level and targeting policy to align with this. Policy is still often predicated on simplistic linear models or assumes a "one size fits all" enterprise. But extensive research evidence challenges this; organisations differ widely in their ability to innovate. Such capability can be enhanced through reflective management action and the framework outlined in the book provides a useful way of guiding this.

One policy option is then to use policy instruments like loans and grants for innovation but link them to a commitment to build management capacity (and to demonstrate this via assessment against a normative framework). Such an approach was a powerful change lever in the earlier moves towards both quality and environmental management improvement over the past 30 years and could also work in the innovation context.

- *Designing and implementing innovation policy*: A second direction is, of course, inside policy agencies and specifically to the development of understanding among the civil servants responsible for designing and implementing innovation policy. Improving the ways in which they understand how the process works and particularly its systemic nature could help shape the design of better policies and enabling instruments in the future.
- *Adopting normative frameworks*: A third policy direction is via procurement mechanisms. States represent major purchasing power. As was shown in the earlier implementation of quality and environmental standards, their use of this leverage can help accelerate widespread adoption of relevant normative frameworks.

Innovation policy instruments

The guidance standard for the innovation management system (ISO 56002) can serve as the foundation for broadening the range of innovation policy instruments available to policymakers. Examples of common policy instruments, in addition to loans and grants referenced above, are R&D subsidies, promotion of public procurement, support for universities and science parks, and regulations related to, e.g., technology investments, intellectual property rights and technical standards.

The standard can help to get data, set goals and implement actions to make these policy instruments more relevant in an innovation context.

- *Get data*: ISO 56002 can be used to assess the aggregated innovation maturity in a set of organisations, for example, in a specific sector. The purpose can be to understand critical capability gaps as input to policy design. The maturity level can be measured using a survey for assisted or self-assessment. Examples of such surveys based on ISO 56002 are the Innovation Management Capability Assessment (IMCA, 2019) published by SIS Swedish Institute for Standards and the Innovation Scorecard developed by Enterprise Ireland (Enterprise Ireland, 2021).

Related to the development of the innovation management profession, it is possible to survey the number of trained or certified professionals based on a common body of knowledge, for example, in a specific sector. The data can be used to understand the competence levels as input to policy design, for example, supporting and providing training programmes.

When the certifiable standard ISO 56001 is published, a survey of the number of certified organisations can be used to understand the overall innovation readiness in a sector, for example.

- *Set goals*: With data related to innovation maturity of organisations and professionals, it is possible to set measurable goals at policy level. Goals can be established to reach a specific maturity level of organisations, number of trained and certified professionals, and number of organisations certified according to ISO 56001 when it is available.

  Innovation maturity goals can be established for specific sectors, types of organisations and for organisations contributing to specific missions or challenges.
- *Implement actions*: Policy measures can include providing or subsidising innovation management support services, based on international standards, to selected sectors or types of organisations, for example, SMEs. The purpose can be to build innovation capabilities to increase the level of maturity. Services can include support for understanding the context, establish an innovation strategy and setting up effective and efficient innovation processes and structures.

  Training and personal certification programmes can also be provided or subsidised to build the competence of innovation management professionals. They can be employed in organisations or act as consultants or advisors to organisations. Support can be provided to establish a pool of trained and certified consultants and advisors who are able to deliver the innovation management support services discussed above.

With a guidance, and in the future a certifiable, innovation management system standard in place, it is possible to set requirements for organisations to be eligible to apply for government funding or other benefits. For example, an organisation must be able to demonstrate that it has reached a certain innovation maturity level to qualify.

Next generation innovation policies

The next generation of innovation policies can be better informed regarding the innovation maturity level inside organisations and provide more targeted measures to improve. In summary, international standards for innovation management can provide a credible and legitimate framework to assess capabilities and implement actions targeting both organisations and professionals. It can strengthen mission-, invention-, and system-oriented innovation policies as well as the innovation ecosystem. This is very much needed as a supplement to traditional innovation policies, if we should be able to address pressing innovation needs in organisations and societies.

22.2. Changing the Dynamics and Impact of Innovation Management

Imagine a future where in 10 years innovation management is a well-recognised discipline and profession. Imagine a systemic and systematic approach to innovation management that accelerates learning to realise value more quickly and successfully. This is what an innovation management system standard can offer the world.

So how do we get there? To predict the future is always challenging. However, in looking to the cases, common themes have emerged that can help make this a reality. By adopting a proactive systems approach to innovation management, organisations will be able to create the right environment for them to succeed. By acknowledging and legitimising the discipline of innovation management, it then has the power to enable transformational change. By measuring the value of innovation and communicating what it is, and how it can be led and organised, in a convincing way, organisational resistance to change can be overcome. Finally, by promulgating that by being systematic and systemic about innovation activities, we are better equipped to capture opportunities and tackle challenges that we face as individuals, organisations and societies.

22.2.1. *Proactive systems approach*

A *proactive systems approach* to innovation management would be beneficial for several reasons. It can help us understand how different elements may be, or should be, related, but also in actively preparing for transformation. The systems view on innovation management is useful when planning what to do, since it can demonstrate how elements can reinforce each other, creating positive spirals. It also can be used as guidance for training by providing an overview or roadmap and the flexibility for organisations to focus on their most important elements. Further, the systems view of innovation management provides an opportunity for those driving transformation to not lose track of the overarching system, by being able to focus on certain systems elements at different points in time.

22.2.2. *Discipline of innovation management*

An *acknowledgement of the discipline of innovation management*, including that innovation management systems are effective enablers of change, provides a baseline from where improvement can be made and serves as a centre for accumulated learnings and experiences. An awareness and commitment among top management and recognising innovation roles in society will ensure that even if it is impossible to guarantee that all prerequisites for successful innovation work are fulfilled, at least the major obstacles can be overcome. Related to balancing operational excellence and entrepreneurial behaviour, it is important to aim for mitigating risks and embracing uncertainty in order to develop flexible, adaptable organisations that can handle plural futures. Additionally, adopting a common framework for managing and supporting innovation activities does not mean a standardisation of the output, i.e., the innovations. It is about enabling a more effective and efficient system for realising these outputs.

As with other disciplines, advancements in technology will have a significant impact on what and how we learn. In innovation management, we have already moved beyond "the art" alone to a combination of art and science. New areas, such as, "neuroinnovation" are emerging to bring together research, innovation and neuroscience that could develop our next generation of system thinkers. Artificial intelligence algorithms could be used to spot patterns, trends and system element interdependencies across complex ecosystems to design adaptable innovation management systems. Immersive environments could help to make immediately real innovation concepts that are only understood through experience and the accumulation of tactic knowledge. These are merely examples of what could come to accelerate our pace of learning. The innovation management discipline has been decades in the making. It is our view that progress in the next decade will bring transformational changes that we cannot even imagine today. Using the standard for innovation management system will be the foundation for unlocking the code.

22.2.3. *Impact of innovation*

Related to a growing acknowledgement of the discipline of innovation management, we see that both *terminology* and *what and how to measure innovation* will evolve. A common terminology becomes an enabler for a shared understanding, which in turn is an enabler for action and true impact. We saw from the cases that enhanced understanding within the same organisation decreased inherent hindrances, and could, therefore, be an enabler also for wider collaboration around larger missions when interested parties from several sectors need to co-create. Moreover, understanding the value and impact of innovation work, and thus *measuring* it, is relevant for all sectors. In the case studies, we saw several examples where preliminary models for measuring were tested. There was also a clear understanding that measuring innovation is something to be handled delicately and needs to be further developed as knowledge and experiences grow around managing innovation systematically and systemically.

Finally, supporting systemic approaches to innovation are critical to success, especially in highly collaborative, complex and distributed innovation ecosystems that target grand challenges in societal transformation and global sustainable development.

22.2.4. *Future role of innovation*

If delivering upon the UN SDGs (UN, 2021) becomes a measure of future success to protect the planet and its citizens, then a game changing approach to innovation work is required to deliver upon these ambitious goals. Innovation as an enabler likely plays a role in most, if not all, of the 17 goals. As we look across the case studies, their focus on innovation capability building is already making a difference in a number of the SDG areas. Addressing these challenges through an innovation management systems approach is already happening in isolation. Now is the time to consider which ones as a community can we take on together to change the dynamics and impact of innovation management.

Finally, our planet is in crisis. This is the most important call to action of them all. Innovation, in how we pursue emerging technologies and uncover new ways of working, is critical to meet this challenge. Systematic and systemic approaches for innovation management are required to accelerate the pace of change by exploring new possibilities, experimenting with options, and exploiting these new discoveries quickly, within a connected, collaborative innovation ecosystem. They also require people and organisations with the right mindsets to make this call to action become a reality. The challenge is not about why we need innovation any more, it is being clear on what it is and how to make it work. To make innovation work is not only an option, but a responsibility.

References

Edler, J. and Fagerberg, J. (2017). Innovation policy: What, why, and how. *Oxford Review of Economic Policy*, *33*(1), 2–23.

Enterprise Ireland (2021). *Innovation Scorecard*, https://www.irishtimes.com/sponsored/innovation-partner-profiles/scorecard-strategy-moving-the-dialon-innovation-capability-1.4582037?msclkid=b27eab49cef511ec8c02d2251657090b.

Hyland, J. and Karlsson, M. (2021). Towards a management system standard for innovation — Letter from standardization. *Journal of Innovation Management*, *9*(1), XI–XIX.

IMCA (2019). *Innovation Management Capabilities Assessment*. SIS Swedish Institute for Standards.

ISO (2019a). *ISO TC 279 Innovation management — Innovation management system — Enhance innovation management capabilities*. WG1 Communications Taskforce.

ISO (2019b). *ISO 56002:2019 Innovation management — Innovation management system — Guidance.*

ISO (2019c). *ISO 56003:2019 Innovation management — Tools and methods for innovation partnership — Guidance*. International Organization for Standardization.

ISO (forthcoming). *ISO 56001 Innovation management system — Requirements*. International Organization for Standardization.

RISE (2021). *Certified Innovation Management Professionals*, https://www.ri.se/en/what-we-do/services/certified-innovation-management-professional.

Tidd, J. and Bessant, J. (2020). *Managing innovation* (7th edn.). John Wiley and Sons.

Tidd, J. (2021). A review and critical assessment of the ISO 56002 innovation management systems standard: Evidence and limitations. *International Journal of Innovation Management*, *25*(1), 2150049.

UN, United Nations (2021). *Sustainable Development Goals*, https://sdgs.un.org/goals.

© 2023 World Scientific Publishing Europe Ltd.
https://doi.org/10.1142/9781800612105_bmatter

Index

A
academia, 21, 177, 251, 289
academic educators, 6, 375
achievements, 133, 151, 231, 270, 305, 317, 320, 340
Action Learning Network for Accountability and Performance (ALNAP), 105
activity-based measures, 287
adjacent innovation initiatives, 294, 299
adoption of innovation, 23
agile methods and tools, 22, 53, 58
Airbus, 39, 45, 356
ambidexterity, 68, 98
areas of opportunity, 333
Argentina, 121
Association for Innovation Management Professionals in Sweden (Innovationsledarna), 380

B
benefits, 373
body of knowledge, 9, 379
Botswana, 180
boundary-breaking activities, 200
breakthrough innovations, 11, 198, 208, 218, 225
breakthrough technology, 205
building blocks, 242
business areas, 334
business development, 270
business expansion, 74
business management tools, 70
business model canvas, 60
business model innovation, 22
business model options, 92
business models, 13, 85, 163, 279–280, 290
business support, 281

C
call to action, 6, 387
Cambridge Dictionary, 29
capabilities, 299, 337, 357
case selection, 37
- geography, 38
- relation to ISO 56002, 42
- type of organisation, 42

case studies
- Airbus, 45
- CIMC, 65

Evonik, 85
HIF, 103
INTI, 121
Kanthal, 139
Karolinska, 157
KTH GDH, 177
Midea, 197
Moen, 217
Naturvårdsverket, 237
Norconsult, 259
OKI, 273
Oregon State, 289
SDP, 313
Södra, 331
Centre for Innovation (CfI), 159
certification, 18, 133, 288
challenge-driven education (CDE), 178–179, 192
change management, 61, 254, 291
Chief Innovation Officer (CINO), 107, 277
China, 65, 197
China International Marine Containers Group (CIMC), 39, 65, 360
chemicals industry, 85
circular economy, 343
collaboration, 54, 130, 163, 172, 194, 208, 249, 309, 326, 336, 342, 378
commercialisation, 332, 340
common approach, 38, 354
common language, 117, 287, 376, 378
common themes, 6, 347, 369
common understanding, 286
communication, 164, 169, 284, 286, 298, 326
competence development, 248, 376
competency matrix, 269
competitiveness, 17, 213
corporate innovation, 94
Colarelli, O'Connor, Gina, 234
Corporate Research Centre, 203, 205
corporate strategy, 224, 268
cost-driving management, 263
cost-saving innovation, 70, 321
COVID-19 pandemic, 168, 170, 190, 213, 321
culture change, 14, 135, 162, 171, 185, 274, 300, 308–309

D

Darby, Henry, 314
Darby, Herbert, 314
definitions and terminology, 12, 265, 268, 271
defence and space industry, 45
design thinking, 25, 58, 59, 163
diffusion of innovation, 23
digitalisation, 210, 253, 262, 321
digital technology, 209
digital transformation, 213
Discovery-Incubation-Acceleration (D-I-A), 221, 224, 226
disruptive innovation, 13, 81, 212, 321
diversification, 74, 210
dual operating system, 163
dynamic capability, 303

E

early-stage ideas, 301
educational and coaching activities, 5, 163
Elrha, 108
engineering consulting industry, 259
environmental issues, 13, 82

Environmental Objectives Unit, 239, 246
European Environment Agency (EEA), 239
European Union (EU), 237, 239
Evonik industries, 39, 85, 359
experimentation and exploration, 28, 193, 266, 271
external factors, 204, 206, 242, 253, 274, 308, 311

F

Field Ready, 114
Forbes Global 2000, 198
forestry industry, 331
framework, 375
France, 45
Frascati Manual, 129
front-end innovation process, 23, 114, 194
fundamental level assessment, 266
future scenarios, 334

G

gender diversity, 135
Germany, 85
globalisation, 213
global R&D network, 210
global sustainable development, 180, 187, 191, 239
Global System for Mobile Communications Association (GSMA), 108
governance, 22, 90, 131, 226, 289, 298
government authorities, 237
group strategy, 332
growth fields, 87
growth platforms, 222
guidance standard, 374
guiding framework, 354

H

hackathon, 249, 253, 316
healthcare industry, 159
hidden champion, 67, 73, 75–76, 81
higher education, 178, 290
home appliance industry, 198
Hongbo, Fang, 199
hospital, 157
household appliance industry, 198
human-centred design, 310
humanitarian innovation sector, 5, 111, 354
Humanitarian Innovation Fund (HIF), 39, 103, 361
Humanitarian Innovation Guide, 108
human resource management, 75

I

idea champion, 308
idea selection, 300
ideation process, 124, 299, 305
identifying opportunities, 126
impact, 386
Impact Studio, 289, 294, 297–299, 301–302, 304, 306
implementation project, 57, 134, 167, 170, 174, 186–187, 242, 250, 264, 283, 285, 337
implications, 371
  academic educators and researcher, 375
  policymakers, 380
  practitioners, 372
  professional associations, 379
  standard developers, 376

ISO 56002 Innovation management system, 5–6, 354, 373, 382
  benefits and challenges, 16–17
  case comparison, 46, 66, 97, 117, 125, 146, 161, 180, 211, 236, 242, 262, 276, 294, 324, 337
  common language and approach, 5, 31
  elements, 5, 15
  explicitly used, 355
  issues identified, 361
  not explicitly used, 359
  principles, 14, 268
incremental innovation, 13, 79, 89, 93, 226, 252
incubation programmes, 56, 205, 228, 319
indigenous innovation competence, 197, 199, 203
industrial heating resistance materials industry, 139
industry transformation, 338
information and technology industry, 274
Innovate Island in Ireland, 380
innovation
  activities, 184, 205, 284, 320, 337
  Ambassador, 164, 247
  ambition matrix, 28, 132
  capability building, 55–57, 212, 213, 220–222, 226–231, 240, 300, 302, 308, 325, 335, 373, 387
  capacity, 117, 191, 375
  culture, 23, 53, 186, 280, 336
  ecosystems, 48, 56, 184, 190–200, 248, 373, 387
  initiatives, 250, 260, 299
  indicators, 130, 335
  intent, 12
  performance, 21, 23, 193, 333
  platform, 254–255, 327
  portal, 318, 325
  portfolio, 16, 28, 132
  practice, 24, 30
  process, 23, 129, 148, 163, 181, 251, 263, 334, 342
  roles, 62, 107, 126, 164, 226, 250, 284, 286
  strategy, 161, 198, 222–223, 226, 231, 242, 244, 252, 263, 268–270, 272, 338
  vision and strategy, 124, 333, 337, 200
Innovation Compass, 275, 283
Innovation Cell, 50
Innovation Labs, 115
innovation management, 4, 118, 265–266, 342
  assessment, 142, 220, 283, 342
  capabilities, 4, 170, 282, 354, 376–377
  discipline, 4, 385, 379
  impact and dynamics, 4, 384
  maturity, 221, 294, 384
  principles, 5, 11, 14
  profession, 4, 160, 379
  research, 5
  structure, 57, 246, 269, 303, 338
innovation management journey, 348
  external triggers, 348
  internal triggers, 350
innovation management system, 85, 95, 97, 180, 188, 192–194, 197, 200, 210–211, 217, 222, 224, 236,

253, 261–262, 315, 324, 326–327, 348
innovation process model for the humanitarian sector, 109
Innovation Promotion Department, 283
Innovation Promotion Project, 275, 283
innovator's dilemma, 53, 201
Instituto Nacional de Tecnologìa Industrial (INTI), 39, 121, 355
intellectual property, 16, 27, 51, 204
International Association of Innovation Professionals (IAOIP), 380
International Collaboration Platform for Innovation Management System (ICP4IMS), 7
International Federation of Red Cross and Red Crescent Societies, 104
International Organization for Standardization (ISO), 7, 116
International Society for Professional Innovation Management (ISPIM), 7, 380

J

Japan, 273
Japan Innovation Network (JIN), 275, 282–283, 286, 288

K

Kanthal, 40, 139, 357
Kanthal innovation climate assessment, 142, 147
Karolinska University Hospital, 40, 157, 355
Kenya, 180
Key Performance Indicators (KPIs), 27, 90, 99, 148, 152, 165, 255, 263, 279, 282–284, 335
KTH Global Development Hub (KTH GDH), 40, 177, 351
KTH Royal Institute of Technology, 178, 186

L

language of innovation, 97
leadership, 185, 193, 322, 336
leading capabilities, 310
lean innovation, 210
Leanovation, 65, 67, 72
Lean Start-up, 58
Learning Plans, 92–93, 193
Lingafelter, David, 218
logistics and energy equipment industry, 65

M

Malaysia, 313
management information systems, 69
market-pull, 27
measuring innovation, 169, 226, 231, 243, 282, 386
Médecins Sans Frontières (MSF), 107
mentoring, 126
mergers and acquisitions, 71
methods and tools, 160, 172, 250
metrics, 220, 223, 297–298
Midea Group, 40, 197, 360
mindset, 7, 58, 264
mission, 223, 292, 310
Moen Incorporated, 40, 217, 359

Moen Innovation Leadership Committee, 232
Most Innovative Schools, 302

N

national environmental objectives, 238
national strategy, 126, 314
Naturvårdsverket, 40, 237, 357
NESTA (UK National Endowment for Science, Technology, and the Arts), 108
net present value, 22, 93, 308
new business development, 343
new capabilities, 309
new opportunities, 287
new product development, 24
nonlinear process, 129
Norconsult, 41, 259, 356
Norway, 259
North, Douglass C., 66

O

Office of the Provost, 309
oil palm industry, 313
Oki Electric Industry Company, 41, 273, 355
Oki, Kibataro, 274
open innovation ecosystem, 22, 58, 200, 204, 208, 212, 323
operations, 210
Oregon State University, 41, 289, 361
Organization for Economic Co-operation and Development (OECD) Oslo Manual, 13, 129
organisational agility, 375
organisational structure, 23, 94, 96, 188, 206, 298
organisational system, 261
organisations, 5, 241, 373, 387
organising innovation, 277
outcomes, 4, 262

P

partnerships, 192, 336
path dependence, 66
people, 7, 387
perception thermometer, 134
performance evaluation, 4, 88, 94, 165, 186, 305, 327
performance reviews, 301, 341
personal certification as Innovation Management Professional, 160, 379
phase gate, 26, 316, 320
Pickett, Mike, 218
Plan–Do–Check–Act (PDCA), 72, 166, 282
PlayLab, 54
plumbing industry, 217
policy considerations, 5, 7, 254, 380–381
portfolio management, 27, 63, 118, 223, 308
post-education innovation plan, 184
practitioners, 6, 372
prerequisites for success, 6, 245, 347, 362–368
process facilitation, 195, 266
process innovation, 30, 111, 159, 332
procurement, 49, 249
product core technology, 77
product development, 24, 200, 321
product innovation, 30, 111, 210
product leadership, 202
profession, 18, 265, 384
professional associations, 5–6, 379
project evaluation systems, 85
project management, 9, 342

prototype, 54, 114
public sector, 158, 251

Q

quality management, 9, 29

R

radical innovations, 11, 28, 52, 79, 98, 117, 203, 252, 326
Ray, Ed, 292
reflections and way forward, 153, 173, 191, 232–234, 271, 287, 309, 328
regulations, 251
Rensselaer Polytechnic Institute (RPI), 18, 220, 359
RPI innovation management system elements, 232
research and development (R&D), 48, 124, 126, 142, 199, 206, 332, 337, 376
researchers, 5–6, 375
resources, 69, 184, 186, 267, 210, 301
Responsibility Centre Management, 298
roadmaps, 331
roles and responsibilities, 117, 162, 322, 337, 342
Rwanda, 180

S

SAPPHO studies, 23
science-push, 27
senior leadership team, 300, 310
service innovation, 163, 270–271
shared vision, 286
Sime Darby Plantation (SDP), 41, 313, 361
SDP Group Strategy and Innovation Department, 315
SDP Plantation Innovation Committee, 319
Sime, William, 314
Sistema de Gestion de la Innovation (SGInn), 124
small and medium size enterprises, 54
social innovation, 13
societal impact, 61, 186, 192, 195
societal innovation, 194
Södra Skogsägarna, 41, 331, 356
Södra Innovation and New Business, 334, 338, 342
Södra Research Foundation, 332, 340
specialised innovation projects, 260
spectrum of innovation, 294, 296, 336
stakeholder management, 92, 128, 173, 183, 193
standard developers, 5, 6, 376
start-ups, 58
steering committees, 26
strategic approach, 89, 118, 127
strategic innovation, 87–88, 94, 99, 229–230, 303, 333, 341–342
strategic innovation arena energy, 341
strategic intelligence, 125, 335
strategic intent, 224, 226
strategic objectives, 214, 269
strategic partners, 198
strategic roadmaps, 334
strategy, 12, 337
sustainability, 17, 239, 332, 339
sustainable innovation system, 192, 229, 310

Sweden, 139, 157, 237, 331
Swedish Environmental Protection Agency (EPA), 237–238
Swedish Standards Institute (SIS), 294
systematic innovation, 159, 213, 354
systems approach, 4, 6, 166, 199, 259, 262, 272, 300, 348, 354, 385, 387
  benefits, 4
systems thinking, 588

T

talent development, 311, 336
Tanzania, 180
teaching mission, 308, 376
technical institute sector, 121
technological innovation, 67, 69–70, 202, 206, 212
technology push, 47
technology roadmap, 205, 210
terminology and definitions, 265, 269, 271, 386
three generation R&D, 202
top-down and bottom-up approaches, 168, 313
top management commitment, 16, 72, 168, 189, 223, 245, 286, 297, 337
top management support, 254, 280, 282–283
training programme, 125, 134, 164, 280–281, 284, 288
transformational innovation, 96, 237
Translators Without Borders (TWB), 114–115
types of innovation, 218, 220, 222, 225–226, 231, 378

U

UK Department for International Development (DFID), 105
UN 2030 Agenda, 194
UN Sustainable Development Goals (SDGs), 178, 180, 183, 186, 348
uncertainty and risk, 12, 26, 88, 90, 127, 131, 134, 220, 224, 298
United Kingdom (UK), 105
United Nations Development Program (UNDP), 252
United Nations Educational, Scientific and Cultural Organization (UNESCO), 179
United Nations World Humanitarian Summit, 106
United States (US), 217, 289
University of Oxford's Humanitarian Innovation Project (OxHIP), 107, 336
UN Office for the Coordination of Humanitarian Affairs (OCHA), 105
universities, 177, 188, 289

V

value chain, 165, 332
value creation process, 252, 270, 279, 319
value networks, 237, 241, 248
value propositions, 281
value realisation, 297
values survey, 336
Vinnova, Swedish Agency for Innovation Systems, 7, 240, 249
Vision 2030, 292
vision for innovation, 124
von Kantzow, Hans, 140, 151
Volatility, Uncertainty, Complexity, Ambiguity (VUCA), 82, 123, 201

W
Water, Sanitation and Hygiene (WASH), 105
Words of Relief project, 114

X
Xiangjian, He, 199

Y
Yume Pro, 275–276, 281, 287

Series on Technology Management

(Continuation of series card page)

Vol. 34 *Managing Innovation: Internationalization of Innovation*
edited by Alexander Brem (Friedrich-Alexander-Universität Erlangen-Nürnberg, Germany & University of Southern Denmark, Denmark), Joe Tidd (University of Sussex, UK) & Tugrul Daim (Portland State University, USA)

Vol. 33 *Managing Innovation: What Do We Know About Innovation Success Factors?*
edited by Alexander Brem (Friedrich-Alexander-Universität Erlangen-Nürnberg, Germany & University of Southern Denmark, Denmark), Joe Tidd (University of Sussex, UK) & Tugrul Daim (Portland State University, USA)

Vol. 32 *Managing Innovation: Understanding and Motivating Crowds*
edited by Alexander Brem (Friedrich-Alexander-Universität Erlangen-Nürnberg, Germany & University of Southern Denmark, Denmark), Joe Tidd (University of Sussex, UK) & Tugrul Daim (Portland State University, USA)

Vol. 31 *Innovation Heroes: Understanding Customers as a Valuable Innovation Resource*
by Fiona Schweitzer (Grenoble École de Management, France & University of Applied Sciences Upper Austria, Austria) & Joe Tidd (University of Sussex, UK)

Vol. 30 *Innovation Discovery: Network Analysis of Research and Invention Activity for Technology Management*
edited by Tugrul Daim (Portland State University, USA) & Alan Pilkington (University of Westminster, UK)

Vol. 29 *Exploiting Intellectual Property to Promote Innovation and Create Value*
edited by Joe Tidd (University of Sussex, UK)

Vol. 28 *Promoting Innovation in New Ventures and Small- and Medium-Sized Enterprises*
edited by Joe Tidd (University of Sussex, UK)

Vol. 27 *The Role of Creativity in the Management of Innovation:State of the Art and Future Research Outlook*
edited by Alexander Brem (University of Southern Denmark, Denmark), Rogelio Puente-Diaz (University Anáhuac, Mexico) & Marine Agogué (HEC Montréal, Canada)

Vol. 26 *Total Value Development: How to Drive Service Innovation*
by Frank M Hull (Cass Business School, UK & Fordham University, USA) & Chris Storey (University of Sussex, UK)

Vol. 25 *Small Firms as Innovators: From Innovation to Sustainable Growth*
by Helena Forsman (University of Tampere, Finland)

Vol. 24 *The Knowledge Enterprise: Innovation Lessons from Industry Leaders (Second Edition)*
by Edward Huizenga (University of Amsterdam, The Netherlands & Benthurst & Co, The Netherlands)

Vol. 23 *Open Innovation Research, Management and Practice*
edited by Joe Tidd (SPRU, University of Sussex, UK)

Vol. 22 *Discontinuous Innovation: Learning to Manage the Unexpected*
by Peter Augsdörfer (Technische Hochschule Ingolstadt, Germany),
John Bessant (University of Exeter, UK),
Kathrin Möslein (Universität Erlangen-Nürnberg, Germany),
Bettina von Stamm (Innovation Leadership Forum, UK) &
Frank Piller (RWTH Aachen University, Germany)

Vol. 21 *Workbook for Opening Innovation: Bridging Networked Business, Intellectual Property and Contracting*
by Jaakko Paasi (VTT Technical Research Centre of Finland, Finland),
Katri Valkokari (VTT Technical Research Centre of Finland, Finland),
Henri Hytönen (VTT Technical Research Centre of Finland, Finland),
Laura Huhtilainen (University of Eastern Finland, Finland) &
Soili Nystén-Haarala (University of Eastern Finland, Finland)

Vol. 20 *Bazaar of Opportunities for New Business Development: Bridging Networked Innovation, Intellectual Property and Business*
by Jaakko Paasi (VTT Technical Research Centre of Finland, Finland),
Katri Valkokari (VTT Technical Research Centre of Finland, Finland),
Tuija Rantala (VTT Technical Research Centre of Finland, Finland),
Soili Nystén-Haarala (University of Eastern Finland, Finland),
Nari Lee (University of Eastern Finland, Finland) &
Laura Huhtilainen (University of Eastern Finland, Finland)

Vol. 19 *From Knowledge Management to Strategic Competence: Assessing Technological, Market and Organisational Innovation (Third Edition)*
edited by Joe Tidd (University of Sussex, UK)

Vol. 18 *Perspectives on Supplier Innovation: Theories, Concepts and Empirical Insights on Open Innovation and the Integration of Suppliers*
edited by Alexander Brem (University of Erlangen-Nuremberg, Germany) &
Joe Tidd (University of Sussex, UK)

Vol. 17 *Managing Process Innovation: From Idea Generation to Implementation*
by Thomas Lager (Grenoble Ecole de Management, France)

Vol. 16 *Perspectives on User Innovation*
edited by Stephen Flowers (University of Brighton, UK) &
Flis Henwood (University of Brighton, UK)

Vol. 15 *Gaining Momentum: Managing the Diffusion of Innovations*
edited by Joe Tidd (SPRU, University of Sussex, UK)

Vol. 14 *Innovation and Strategy of Online Games*
by Jong H Wi (Chung-Ang University, South Korea)

Vol. 13 *Building Innovation Capability in Organizations: An International Cross-Case Perspective*
by Milé Terziovski (University of Melbourne, Australia)

Vol. 12 *Project-Based Organization in the Knowledge-Based Society*
by Mitsuru Kodama (Nihon University, Japan)

Vol. 11 *Involving Customers in New Service Development*
edited by Bo Edvardsson (Karlstad University, Sweden),
Anders Gustafsson (Karlstad University, Sweden),
Per Kristensson (Karlstad University, Sweden),
Peter Magnusson (Karlstad University, Sweden) &
Jonas Matthing (Karlstad University, Sweden)

Vol. 10 *Open Source: A Multidisciplinary Approach*
by Moreno Muffatto (University of Padua, Italy)

Vol. 9 *Service Innovation: Organizational Responses to Technological Opportunities & Market Imperatives*
edited by Joe Tidd (University of Sussex, UK) &
Frank M Hull (Fordham University, USA)

Vol. 8 *Digital Innovation: Innovation Processes in Virtual Clusters and Digital Regions*
edited by Giuseppina Passiante (University of Lecce, Italy),
Valerio Elia (University of Lecce, Italy) &
Tommaso Massari (University of Lecce, Italy)

Vol. 7 *Innovation Management in the Knowledge Economy*
edited by Ben Dankbaar (University of Nijmegen, The Netherlands)

Vol. 6 *Social Interaction and Organisational Change: Aston Perspectives on Innovation Networks*
edited by Oswald Jones (Aston University, UK),
Steve Conway (Aston University, UK) & Fred Steward (Aston University, UK)

Vol. 5 *R&D Strategy and Organisation: Managing Technical Change in Dynamic Contexts*
by Vittorio Chiesa (Università degli Studi di Milano-Bicocca, Milan, Italy)

Vol. 4 *Japanese Cost Management*
by Yasuhiro Monden (University of Tsukuba, Japan)

Vol. 3 *From Knowledge Management to Strategic Competence: Measuring Technological, Market and Organizational Innovation (Second Edition)*
edited by Joe Tidd (SPRU, University of Sussex, UK)

Vol. 3 *From Knowledge Management to Strategic Competence: Measuring Technological, Market and Organizational Innovation*
edited by Joe Tidd (SPRU, University of Sussex, UK)

Vol. 2 *The Knowledge Enterprise: Implementation of Intelligent Business Strategies*
by J Friso den Hertog (MERIT, Maastricht University & Altuïtion bv, 's Hertogenbosch, The Netherlands) &
Edward Huizenga (Altuïtion bv, 's Hertogenbosch, The Netherlands)

Vol. 1 *Engines of Prosperity: Templates for the Information Age*
by Gerardo R Ungson (University of Oregon, USA) &
John D Trudel (The Trudel Group, USA)

www.ingramcontent.com/pod-product-compliance
Lightning Source LLC
LaVergne TN
LVHW010329220926
848484LV00004BB/862
9781800612099